MW00442504

**Praise for** *Security Information and Event Management (SIEM) Implementation*

"The first ever book on SIEM breaks new ground by teaching readers how to implement and operate today's SIEM tools."

*—Dr. Anton Chuvakin*
Security Warrior Consulting

"This book provides a meticulous roadmap of the various attacks one may experience on their organizational assets. Additionally, it clearly and concisely demonstrates methods and best practices for configuring one's enterprise resources to provide quicker analysis and mitigation of threats."

*—Hank Ritzert*, CISSP, ERP
Security Analyst

"The authors have teamed up for a readable and understandable book on one of today's important security system elements, SIEM. They have provided a good cross-section view of the power and potential of such devices when properly deployed in your environment. It is my opinion that if your organization is considering a SIEM or overwhelmed by manual log review processes, *Security Information and Event Management (SIEM) Implementation* is an easy-to-read guide that provides a solid foundation to better understand deployment and tuning within your environment."

*—Jeff Comstock*
Manager for IT Security and Compliance for BSRO,
a large auto and tire services provider

"*Security Information and Event Management (SIEM) Implementation* defines threats, practices, and methodologies with real-world perspective. The authors' understanding of secure information systems is conveyed in a practical and well-structured manner. This is *THE* book to read if you are planning to implement a SIEM system in your infrastructure."

*—Andrew Creech*
Director of Information Technology, Creeco Systems
Hollywood, Florida

# Security Information and Event Management (SIEM) Implementation

DAVID R. **MILLER**
SHON **HARRIS**
ALLEN A. **HARPER**
STEPHEN **VANDYKE**
CHRIS **BLASK**

New York   Chicago   San Francisco
Lisbon   London   Madrid   Mexico City   Milan
New Delhi   San Juan   Seoul   Singapore   Sydney   Toronto

The McGraw-Hill Companies

**Cataloging-in-Publication Data is on file with the Library of Congress**

McGraw-Hill books are available at special quantity discounts to use as premiums and sales promotions, or for use in corporate training programs. To contact a representative, please e-mail us at bulksales@mcgraw-hill.com.

**Security Information and Event Management (SIEM) Implementation**

1234567890   DOC DOC   109876543210

ISBN    978-0-07-170109-9
MHID     0-07-170109-5

| | | |
|---|---|---|
| **Sponsoring Editor**<br>Megg Morin | **Copy Editor**<br>LeeAnn Pickrell | **Illustration**<br>Apollo Publishing, Lyssa Wald |
| **Editorial Supervisor**<br>Patty Mon | **Proofreader**<br>Martin Benes | **Art Director, Cover**<br>Jeff Weeks |
| **Project Editor**<br>LeeAnn Pickrell | **Indexer**<br>James Minkin | **Cover Designer**<br>Jeff Weeks |
| **Acquisitions Coordinator**<br>Joya Anthony | **Production Supervisor**<br>James Kussow | |
| **Technical Editor**<br>Brock Pearson | **Composition**<br>Apollo Publishing | |

# About the Authors

## David R. Miller

David R. Miller is a consultant specializing in information systems security, compliance, and network engineering. He is a lecturer, an author, and a technical editor of books, curriculum, certification exams, and computer-based training videos. He is regularly invited to perform as a Microsoft Subject Matter Expert (SME) on product lines, including Microsoft Server 2008, Microsoft Exchange Server 2007, and Microsoft Windows Vista and Windows 7. He holds the following certifications: PCI QSA, SME, MCT, MCITPro Windows Server 2008 Enterprise Administrator, MCSE Windows NT 4.0, MCSE Windows Server 2000, and MCSE Windows Server 2003: Security, CISSP, LPT, ECSA, CEH, CWNA, CCNA, CNE, Security+, A+, N+, and more...

David is the principal author of several information systems security books, including *Security Administrator Street Smarts*, First and Second Editions, for Sybex. He also co-authored two books on Microsoft Windows Server 2008 and Microsoft Exchange Server 2007 for Microsoft Press and two books on Microsoft Windows Vista for QUE Publishing.

David has written curriculum and performed instruction in live boot-camp-style classrooms and for computer-based training videos on Microsoft Windows Server 2008 and IT security courses on topics such as CISSP, SSCP, Security+, and CWSP for the Career Academy, Logical Security, and TestOut Corporation, among others. He has lectured on network engineering and information systems security to many prestigious groups, including The Smithsonian Institute, the U.S. Military Academy at West Point, the U.S. Army Advanced Battle Command at Fort Huachuca, the U.S. Department of the Interior, Oracle Corporation, and JP Morgan Chase & Co. Global Financial Services.

## Shon Harris

Shon Harris, CISSP, is the founder and CEO of Logical Security, a computer security consultant, a former engineer in the Air Force's Information Warfare unit, an instructor, and an author. She has authored three best-selling CISSP books, been a contributing author on previous editions of *Gray Hat Hacking: The Ethical Hacker's Handbook* (McGraw-Hill Professional), and is currently working on a Certified Ethical Hacker (CEH) book. Shon has developed a full digital information product series for Pearson publishing.

Shon has taught computer and information security to a wide range of clients, including Microsoft, the Department of Defense, Department of Energy, National Security Agency, Bank of America, Defense Information Systems Agency, RSA, U.S. Military Academy at West Point, and many more.

She has consulted for several Fortune 500 companies in the United States, including Cisco, American Express, Warner Brothers, Bridgestone\Firestone, CitiBank, CitiFinancial, and many more. Her competencies range from setting up risk-management programs and developing enterprise network security architectures to constructing enterprise-wide security programs that connect computer security and business needs in a synergistic manner.

Shon was recognized as one of the top 25 women in the Information Security field by *Information Security Magazine*.

## Allen A. Harper

In 2007, Allen Harper retired from the military as a Marine Corps Major after a tour in Iraq. He has more than 20 years of IT/security experience. He holds an M.S. in Computer Science from the Naval Post Graduate School and a B.S. in Computer Engineering from North Carolina State University. Allen led the development of the GEN III honeywall CDROM, called roo, for the Honeynet Project. Allen was a co-author of *Gray Hat Hacking: The Ethical Hacker's Handbook,* First and Second Editions, and is currently working on the Third Edition. He was a member of the 2004 winning team (sk3wl of r00t) in the DEFCON Capture the Flag contest. He is a faculty member for the Institute for Applied Network Security and has worked as a security consultant for the Internal Revenue Service (IRS) and for Logical Security, LLC. His interests include reverse engineering, vulnerability discovery, and all forms of ethical hacking. Allen is now the President and Founder of N2NetSecurity, Inc.

## Stephen VanDyke

Stephen VanDyke is a consultant focusing on intrusion detection, incident handling, vulnerability assessments, network architecture, and network engineering. He has been working in the IT field for over 10 years in a wide variety of environments. He has primarily worked with the U.S. government as a consultant for such organizations as the U.S. Army Reserve Command, the U.S. Army, and Multi-National Forces Iraq (MNF-I) on several projects. He holds the following certifications: CISSP, SnortCP, MCSA, BCCPA, BCCPP, A+, Network+, and Security+.

## Chris Blask

Chris Blask is a seasoned security technology professional with more than 20 years of experience in engineering and marketing information technologies. In 1993, he invented the BorderWare Firewall Server with Clyde Stevens and Paul Hunt, a leading product in the early firewall market. In 1998, Chris assumed responsibility for Cisco's struggling PIX firewall product line and led it to a multibillion dollar position of global leadership. Protego Networks—a SIEM vendor later sold to Cisco—was founded by Chris and three others in 2002. Lofty Perch—a critical infrastructure cybersecurity services company— was founded by Chris in 2005. He has also spent time helping NSS Labs develop PCI testing regimes, was VP Operations at N2NetSecurity, and is currently on faculty at the Institute for Applied Network Security and is Vice President of Marketing at AlienVault.

## About the Technical Editor

### Brock Pearson

Brock Pearson works as a senior consultant with a major global consulting firm in the United States, assisting many enterprise organizations with their security needs. He builds monitoring capabilities using various SIEM products including ArcSight ESM. He has also worked at ArcSight, Inc., as an instructional designer creating all Event Security Manager (ESM) instructor-led workshops, including performance objectives, content, and related materials. He has written and taught curriculum, not only for ArcSight Inc., but also for G.E. Security's physical security software platforms, as well as G.E. Security's hardware panels, contacts, CCTV, and perimeter monitoring systems to various levels of users. Students he has taught include employees and contractors of large corporations and government agencies worldwide.

Brock has been involved in many ArcSight ESM installations using his security experience and product knowledge to aid large-scale implementations and provide successful outcomes. Within many of these engagements, Brock has provided solid product training, customized use-case training, and advanced product customizations within the security infrastructure. These contributions to implementation projects have enabled ArcSight's customers to realize the many benefits of all of the ArcSight product lines.

Brock has been in the information technology industry for over 13 years in varying capacities, including network administrator and MIS manager for a manufacturing firm in the south Florida area. He holds the following certifications: MCP +I, MCSE Windows NT 4.0, MCP Windows 2000, CISSP, A+, and N+. He has a B.A. in Information Systems and is currently pursuing a master's in Instructional Technology.

I dedicate this, and each of my books, to my brilliant daughter, Veronica, and my equally brilliant son, Ross. With all my love, appreciation, and admiration...

—*David R. Miller*

I would like to dedicate my portion of this book to my Grandmother, Marge Fairbarin. Thanks for all your love and support Grandma!

—*Shon Harris*

This book is dedicated to all those who serve in distant lands for our freedom at home. All gave some, some gave all. Semper Fi.

—*Allen A. Harper*

I would like to thank my mother Myra, my significant other Donna, and our boys Tyler and Andrew for being with me during this process. I would also like to thank William Sartin and Dan Halstead for their guidance when I needed it most.

—*Stephen VanDyke*

To Donna, without whom none of this would be possible.

—*Chris Blask*

# At a Glance

| Part III | SIEM Tools |
| --- | --- |

# Contents

## Part I

### Introduction to SIEM: Threat Intelligence for IT Systems

**Part II**

**IT Threat Intelligence Using SIEM Systems**

**Part III**

**SIEM Tools**

# Foreword
## by Shon Harris

While today's information security threats are only increasing in numbers and severity, the diversity of our networked environments is increasing exponentially. Most of us know that practically no homogenous environment exists anymore, and the complexity of the various technologies in our networks can get overwhelming, to say the least. On top of that we are expected to understand how the different types of events within the environments can affect devices, user workstations, and—most important—business processes.

Let's look at an analogy. If there is political unrest in Russia, a thwarted terrorist attack in Iraq, a suicide bomb attack in Palestine, and a newly elected leader in Iran, how do these events directly and indirectly affect the United States today? Who knows? All of these events are discrete and distributed, just like the events that take place on our networks today. What if one day a potential worm is downloaded on a user's workstation, your firewall detects a suspicious number of ICMP packets, something bounces one of your routers, someone plugs in a device that is not allowed by your security policies, and your database experiences a SQL injection attack—all before your lunch break? How would you have a holistic view and understanding of all the events and potential abuses that are taking place within your organization? This possibility did not exist before Security Information and Event Management (SIEM) technology and products.

Now more than ever, it is important to collect and correlate the different activities happening on critical networks. This type of information is critical to being able to identify, prioritize, and respond to cyber attacks, policy breaches, and compliance violations. We no longer have the luxury of just scanning logs, responding to individual event alarms from different operating systems, or waiting for SNMP agents to tell us when something has changed on our workstations. We are expected to react to today's threats in real-time, but we can't do this without having the necessary information in real-time. SIEM products centralize the storage and interpretation of event data collected from software and devices throughout an enterprise network. SIEM helps you not only collect the pieces of the puzzle, but also put the pieces of the puzzle together so you can see the whole picture.

While SIEM technology and products have been around for several years, solid material for understanding, implementing, and maintaining this type of technology has not. Until now.

Here it is! *Security Information and Event Management (SIEM) Implementation* examines from different angles how to truly understand the convergence of data from various sources. After dissecting the full anatomy of the SIEM technology, this book analyzes specific commercial and open source products, illustrates how to integrate a SIEM into any incident response program, and explains how to use these tools properly for business intelligence. This is truly a book that is overdue in our profession.

David Miller is the real hero behind this book. While a great team has been assembled to build and publish this work, my hat must go out to David Miller for his tremendous efforts. I have known David for over ten years now and have had the esteemed pleasure and opportunity to work with him on several different consulting, teaching, and publishing projects. If you appreciate this book as much as I do, your real thanks should go to David for driving this project home.

# Acknowledgments

I wish to thank my fellow authors on this book who have been, or have become, my friends: Allen, Shon, Steve, and Chris. Thanks goes out to the many talented and dedicated people at McGraw-Hill for their support and guidance, including Joya Anthony, Jane Brownlow, Megg Morin, and our technical editor Brock Pearson. The various vendors of the SIEM systems written about in the book have each provided a level of support during the research phase of our work. Thank you all very much for that support. Finally, I wish to thank Zackary Payton, who helped develop the outline for the book, but then had to withdraw from co-authoring the project due to unforeseen circumstances. I hope we get the chance to work together again…. but next time, I hope we actually get to complete the project together.

—*David R. Miller*

I would like to thank David Miller for having the patience and perseverance to put this whole book together. Without David, there would be no SIEM book.

—*Shon Harris*

Allen would like to thank, first, his Savior, Jesus Christ, who strengthens him and sustains him. Next, he would like to thank his beautiful wife Corann and daughters Haley and Madison, who continue to support him, even when his projects take time from them. Finally, Allen would like to thank his friends, family, church members, and coworkers, who provide encouragement and guidance. To the N2NetSecurity, Inc., team, our best days are still ahead—press on.

—*Allen A. Harper*

I would like to thank Brock Pearson for his technical support.

—*Stephen VanDyke*

I would like to thank McGraw-Hill and my fellow authors for the opportunity and the tenacity to complete this project. Thanks also to Tobias Mayer at Cisco Systems for his inimitable reliability, expertise, and assistance.

—*Chris Blask*

# Introduction

The Security Information and Event Management system (SIEM) is relatively new to the information technology (IT) mainstream. Early components of SIEM systems began emerging in various forms between 10 and 20 years ago, but have only just begun to become well integrated, finding their foothold within organizations. The *SIEM system* is a complex collection of technologies designed to provide vision and clarity on the corporate IT system as a whole, benefitting security analysts and IT administrators as well. As you will see in the following chapters, you can do all of that with a SIEM system—and more. It is a powerful addition to the IT infrastructure of virtually every small, medium, or large business, department, or government entity.

 **NOTE** Security Information and Event Management (SIEM) systems are also known as *Security Information Management (SIM)* systems, *Security Event Management (SEM)* systems, and *Security Event and Information Management (SEIM)* systems.

Security professionals and analysts use the SIEM system to monitor, identify, document, and sometimes respond to security affronts. Some of these security events are obvious, like willful and malicious denial-of-service (DoS) attacks and virus outbreaks. The SIEM system can also identify more elusive security events. Many events are so subtle or so obscured by thousands of events per second that without the aid of a powerful and finely tuned SIEM system, they would go completely unnoticed. These more elusive security events include violations of policy, unauthorized access attempts, and those of the highly skilled and focused attacker, methodically and stealthily working his way into your IT environment.

A major objective for the security analyst using a SIEM system is to reduce the number of false-positive alerts, these being the haystack in the proverbial concept of the "needle-in-the-haystack." Less sophisticated security systems, such as the intrusion detection system (IDS), are famous (or more appropriately, infamous) for alerting on many false-positive events. These numerous false-positive alerts waste the security analyst's time and energy, and often dull the analyst's focused attention, making it much easier to overlook and disregard the rarer and more significant true-positive alert.

Many devices, like IDSs, accommodate the reduction of false-positive alerts by applying a blanket "ignore" on certain events, or by marking the source or the traffic as "friendly." These blessings of events and traffic are far from *fine* tuning; these are all-too-often too broad a stroke and will provide conduits that may allow the bad guys free and unnoticed passage into your IT systems. With the more sophisticated SIEM system, the reduction of false-positive alerts is accomplished by careful creation of filters and correlated event rules, often referred to as *SIEM content,* to identify and alert on only those highly qualified security events while properly scrutinizing and accurately disregarding the bulk of the false-positive events. The development of these filters and correlated event rules is the focus of much of this book.

While the SIEM is designed and targeted toward the security aspects of an IT system, network operations personnel and IT administrators can use the SIEM in their more routine and hopefully less eventful "operations" role. IT operations can use the SIEM to identify various types of operational problems within a network, like downed servers and malfunctioning or misconfigured systems, applications, and appliances. The SIEM can be used to identify routine IT system needs, for instance, additional capacity requirements, user training issues, and buggy applications that may need patching, upgrading, or replacing.

In addition to these internal IT security and network operations benefits and uses, there are aspects of the powerful SIEM system that have only recently begun to be explored. By thinking outside your own IT infrastructure, and turning the sights of the SIEM in a different direction, marketing divisions, business owners, and even governments can monitor and be alerted, in near real-time, to important external activity that could indicate significant changes in their competition and marketplace. SIEM systems can be focused externally on news feeds, search engines, and libraries of content and alert on changes in trends and increases in market-specific or topic-specific types of inquiries, research, and news events. Using the SIEM to gather market, business, or political intelligence, you can identify and quantify external forces that include both subtle and significant changes to your market, external markets, the global economy, and even political forces in action. Using a SIEM system, you can gain insights into otherwise unseen activities of the competition, or of foreign governments. Ah, but too much is being said too early in the book. Read on, and you will come to realize just how powerful this tool can be in the hands of the IT security staff, the IT operations staff, and even creative and outward-thinking marketing professionals, business owners, and government entities.

# What the Heck Is a SIEM Tool?

The Security Information and Event Management (SIEM) system is generally thought of as providing the following collection of services:

- Log management
- IT regulatory compliance
- Event correlation
- Active response
- Endpoint security

This book will address discrete software tools or appliances that may perform one or more of these functions for those small- to medium-size businesses and departments that require these services, but may not need, or be able to justify or afford, the full-blown, fully integrated SIEM systems. The book will also demonstrate how full-featured SIEM systems perform these discrete functions and integrate them to produce the powerful and more complete collection of security and compliance services needed by those organizations that can justify and afford the SIEM.

## Log Management

Log management, in a SIEM system, starts with configuring the nodes in an IT system, particularly the more important or critical nodes, to send relevant system and application events (*logs*) to a centralized database that is managed by the SIEM application. This SIEM database application first parses and normalizes the data sent by the numerous and very different types of nodes on an IT system. Then the SIEM typically provides log storage, organization, retrieval, and archival services to satisfy the log management requirements that businesses may have. These services are often required by businesses for compliance purposes. This data feed into the log management component of the SIEM system lends itself to the additional use of near real-time analysis and data mining on the health and security status of all the IT systems feeding their data into the SIEM system. The more nodes that feed into your SIEM system, the more complete and accurate your vision is of the IT system as a whole.

The nodes whose logs get fed into the SIEM system are typically quite diverse in nature. These nodes include computer systems running various operating systems, primarily Linux, UNIX, and Windows. Other nodes that would feed into the SIEM include network infrastructure systems and appliances, like routers, managed switches, firewalls, proxy servers, intrusion detection systems (IDS), remote access systems, and all sorts of other network devices. These diverse systems come from many different vendors, that often put their own proprietary twist on how logs are structured and how event reporting to upstream logging servers functions on the system.

Systems may have built-in syslog-type client services installed to satisfy this hierarchical logging objective, such as those on routers and other network appliances, or you may need to install third-party syslog client software on network nodes to export logs, like Winlogd or Snare. The SIEM vendor may also provide a collection of custom agents to be installed on certain types of nodes to perform this export function.

## IT Regulatory Compliance

Now that all the events from important and critical systems are being logged, you can build filters or rules and timers to *audit* (monitor against a standard) and validate compliance, or to identify violations of compliance requirements imposed upon the organization. The rules that get checked against the logs that are fed into the system might include monitoring the frequency of password changes, identifying operating system (OS) or application patches that fail to install, and the auditing frequency of antivirus, antispyware, and IDS updates for compliance purposes. While you might build your own collection of filters or rules to aid in compliance, many SIEM vendors include prepackaged collections of rules specifically designed to satisfy requirements for the different laws and regulations that businesses need to comply with. These are typically packaged add-ons that are provided by the vendors or even after-market value-added resellers to the SIEM customers for a fee.

Virtually all SIEM systems include full-featured reporting systems, many with precanned and customizable reports. These reports are often needed by businesses to provide evidence of self-auditing and to validate their level of compliance.

## Event Correlation

Event correlation brings a higher level of intelligence into the equation. You don't just see a single event and then choose to react or not react. With event correlation, you teach the system to consider various conditions before you trigger the alarm. For example, a server running at 100 percent CPU utilization could be caused by many different things. It might indicate a problem is occurring that needs to be corrected, or maybe not. It could be a failed application that has locked up the server. It could also be an indication that the system is overloaded with legitimate activity, and indicate that one or more services or applications should be distributed across additional servers, as in a cluster. The server might be reaching full capacity due to a worm executing a denial-of-service (DoS) attack on the system. Or it might just be momentary and natural server activity.

The correlation engine on a SIEM can investigate and consider (correlate) other events that are not necessarily related to CPU utilization, but can provide a more complete picture of the health status of the server to rule out specific theories on the cause of the problem. For example, in the case of 100 percent CPU utilization, the SIEM could be configured to consider the following:

- Has the antivirus (AV) application identified malware on this server?
- Have the AV applications on other systems recently reported malware?
- Are any other servers running at 100 percent CPU utilization? Have they reported virus activity?
- Has one application, or have multiple applications or services, stopped responding?
- Is there a peak of similar, normal network traffic to this server, possibly implying a legitimate but high demand for an application?
- Is there a peak of similar, atypical network traffic to this server, possibly implying a DoS attack? From different sources? Possibly a distributed denial of service (DDoS) attack?

This is correlation. The SIEM's alert, and your response, will be vary considerably, depending on which of these conditions are true.

## Active Response

Now that you have all the right systems feeding events into the SIEM, your rules and filters defined, and your correlation rules in place; do *you* want to take action and perform the incident response for all verified security events, or should you configure the SIEM to respond automatically and actively to specific types of correlated events? Having the SIEM automatically take corrective action to perceived threats or misconfigurations would, of course, take many tasks off the plate of the security analyst, and even perhaps the IT department. Many SIEM systems can perform active response, for instance, adding IP and port filters on the access control list (ACL) on a router or firewall. The SIEM's triggered, automated, and active response to the perceived threat would probably occur much faster than if humans were simply alerted and then required to perform these reactive tasks. That would be a good thing, right?

Although there are some obvious benefits to the SIEM providing automated responses, only on a mature installation and finely tuned SIEM should automated, active response be implemented. If this process isn't carefully thought-out and precisely implemented, your SIEM system might be responding to a collection of false-positive events, and you might be performing a DoS attack on your own network. Active response could easily become a double-edged sword.

## Endpoint Security

Most SIEM systems can monitor endpoint security to centrally validate the security "health" of a system. Many SIEM systems can monitor whether the firewall on a PC or server is running, and can identify when the AV definitions were last updated and when a node becomes infected with spyware. Some SIEM systems can even manage endpoint security, actually making adjustments and improvements to the node's security on the remote system, like configuring firewalls and updating and monitoring AV, antispyware, and antispam products on the nodes within the system. Furthermore, some SIEM systems can push down and install the updates, or in Active Response mode, adjust the ACL on a misconfigured personal firewall.

# The Growing Momentum Behind SIEM

The SIEM marketplace is growing rapidly, even in spite of the recent economic downturn. If you work in the IT industry, you may find yourself faced with being responsible for the specification, selection, implementation, monitoring, and maintenance of a SIEM system. Because of the technology's relatively new emergence in the marketplace, there are few publications that address more than a single product. This book will address the discrete components of a SIEM system and then describe products and applications that satisfy one or more of the objectives of a SIEM system, as well as several complete and full-featured SIEM systems.

The following chapters will discuss the how's and why's of SIEM components and systems. They will describe many of their strengths and weaknesses, the challenges of implementation, and offer up some guidance to aid in implementation. The chapters will finish with advice on techniques to perform advanced tuning and improve the accuracy and clarity of analysis of these various component applications and full-featured SIEM systems.

A SIEM system can be a beast to understand and configure, but it is one of the up-and-coming technologies that IT and security professionals should be paying attention to. Many companies and government departments are choosing to implement these tools to help with the administration and security of their IT systems. Many companies are basically forced into implementing a SIEM system to satisfy legal or regulatory compliance requirements so they can avoid government- or market-imposed fines and penalties and hopefully stay in business.

Many companies need the services that a SIEM system provides, but cannot afford the full-blown SIEM system, or the skilled staff it takes to implement, maintain, and monitor the system adequately. The good news, in this case, is that there are smaller, more affordable, individual tools that can be pieced together to satisfy many of the functional requirements of a SIEM system.

It can be a daunting challenge to get a SIEM tool properly specified to meet a business' needs. The challenge increases as you move to vendor and product selection, and on to implementation and management over time. This book was written to provide SIEM-related guidance and solutions to

- Small and medium-size businesses, divisions, and departments
- Large businesses and departments
- Government departments

Furthermore, the book will show you how to use the SIEM tool to develop business intelligence—beyond the realm of being just a fancy IT security or operations tool. Properly deployed, the SIEM can provide comprehensive IT system vision—aggregation and correlation beyond human capabilities, and identification and qualification more quickly and accurately than human recognition.

## Return on Investment

Of course, these integrated and sophisticated SIEM systems are not inexpensive. As you approach management with the proposal of adding a SIEM to the environment, management will probably challenge you for a calculated "return on investment" (ROI). Unfortunately, the SIEM is more geared to "cost avoidance" than on generating a ROI. By providing a more complete vision of IT operations and on the security and protection of the valuable information assets within an organization, it is expected that, with the SIEM in place, the company will experience fewer losses. When faced with the challenge of cost justification for a SIEM system, you must identify these avoidable costs (losses) and show that eliminating some or all of them with the SIEM can often outweigh and compensate for the price of the SIEM:

- First, with a SIEM, many monitoring, alerting, analysis, correlation, and reporting functions are automated. These processes are typically performed substantially more efficiently by the SIEM than by the homegrown systems.

Without the SIEM system, these processes are performed manually. With a SIEM in place, you'll get more essential, often compliance-mandated, security-related work done in a fewer number of hours.

■ Second, if your organization must comply with regulations or laws regarding IT and security, the SIEM system will help you identify and correct noncompliant systems and processes and can help you to avoid compliance-related fines and penalties.

■ Finally, and perhaps most significantly, having and using the SIEM system can dramatically reduce an organization's attack surface. This, combined with the faster recognition, alerting, and response capabilities provided by the SIEM will benefit the organization by reducing the likelihood of a security breach and by minimizing the potential losses that could occur during a security breach or other type of loss event.

# So What's Up with This Book, Anyhow?

The book is divided into three major parts. These three parts are followed by an appendix.

## Part I – Introduction to SIEM: Threat Intelligence for IT Systems

The first part of this book will introduce you to the various types of business models, each with a slightly different collection of needs and security concerns, and how these different sets of needs can be addressed by the components within a SIEM system. You will examine different IT threat models, their mechanisms of attack, and how information asset losses are incurred, either willfully or unintentionally, within the IT system. Next, you will walk through the different phases of a classic attack, and recognize the telltale signs of an attack in progress. This will tell you where and how your SIEM system should be tuned to identify the attack quickly. Part I also covers security-related legal and regularity compliance requirements and focuses on the nature of the security needs within an IT system and the various threats that could negatively affect the system.

## Part II – IT Threat Intelligence Using SIEM Systems

In Part II, you will examine the various functions that a SIEM system performs, and you will learn about several products and applications that can help you perform many of those discrete functions. These solutions are geared toward small to medium-size businesses and departments. A full-featured SIEM system is too expensive for many organizations to afford, and too complex for many organizations to maintain, so these companies must settle for the smaller components that satisfy their most critical security functions.

A security event, identified and brought to the attention of the security analyst by the SIEM system, requires a response. With this in mind, Part II continues by examining the details of incident response and how the SIEM can be utilized in this response. You will also consider the benefits, and the potential risks, of using the SIEM in an automated response to an incident.

Finally, in Part II you will explore the possibilities of turning the SIEM system outward into the public domain to uncover professional, business, and even political information, trends, and eventually intelligence that may lead you to conclusions hours, days, or even months ahead of your competition, whoever they may be.

## Part III – SIEM Tools

In Part III, you will learn about implementation processes, as well as advanced configuration and analysis techniques, for four of the leading products in the SIEM industry:

- Open Systems Security Information Management (OSSIM), recently reorganized as AlienVault LLC, US and AlienVault Europe
- Cisco Security – Monitoring, Analysis, and Response System, aka CS-MARS, by Cisco Systems
- QRadar, by Q1 Labs, Inc.
- ArcSight Enterprise Security Management (ESM), by ArcSight, Inc.

Each of these products has risen to the top of the market for a reason, with specific strengths and fulfilling similar implementation niches, yet each has notable technical differences. These areas of technical uniqueness, and variations in terms of concepts and even the terminology used, will be explored in Part III.

Even if you aren't using these specific products, you are encouraged to read and digest these sections. While the techniques presented to accomplish a specific goal for one product may be different on your product, the concept and the objective itself may be relevant to your environment, and once the correct procedures for your SIEM system are defined, you may find that you can improve the efficiency and utility of your system.

## The Ways and Means of the Security Analyst

This appendix begins with a guide to developing your mindset and your skills toward the goal of becoming a security analyst. This appendix includes descriptions of the typical background required to be a security analyst, fields of specialized study, personality traits, a description of the role of the security analyst within an organization, and some common technical certifications often pursued as a component of the security analyst's resume.

This is followed by several case studies demonstrating the use of the SIEM system by a security analyst while working various security events that escalate into security incidents, and how the analyst then uses the SIEM system to aid the incident response process.

## What You Can Expect to Get from This Book

Understanding this complex and powerful security system will make you a more valuable asset within IT operations and within IT security. The properly deployed, tuned, and monitored SIEM system will help you and your organization develop a better vision of your IT systems, understand the organization's security status, help with log management, monitoring, auditing, and reporting for compliance purposes, prudently reduce risks to the IT systems, and minimize losses if and when a security breach may occur.

Whether you are planning to use a SIEM system, or are already using a SIEM system, in a small, medium-size, or large business, department, or within a government organization, or whether you are studying to expand your professional horizons and open new career paths, this book can provide valuable insights and skills to benefit you and your organization.

# PART I | Introduction to SIEM: Threat Intelligence for IT Systems

# CHAPTER 1 | Business Models

As the number of cybercrime events, incidents of identity theft and theft of intellectual property, and cyber attacks continue to rise, the need to provide adequate network security to defend against these types of threats to organizations will increase. Defense against these types of threats is very difficult for an organization, and the attacker will always have the advantage. While you, as a security professional, are looking at all the possible threats to your environment, an attacker only needs to concentrate on what it is he or she is looking to accomplish. This will always put you at a disadvantage. In order to best secure your environment, you need to use all the information at your disposal to determine how to deploy the limited resources at hand. When approaching a new environment or reevaluating an environment that you are currently a part of, determining the best security strategy will rely heavily on your organization's business model.

# What Are IT Business Models?

As a security professional, you have to learn to adapt to a wide variety of environments, each with its own specific threats and concerns. You may go into a type of environment that you have worked in before and feel comfortable, or you may be in a totally new environment. When entering a new environment, the first thing you want to focus on is gaining a clear understanding of the organization's goals and management. The easiest way to understand the direction of your company and how it operates is to understand your company's business model.

The subject of business models is a very big concept. A company's business model is a conglomeration of the company's values, what products or services the company is producing, how the company produces its products or services, the company's strategies, the company's goals, and what the company is looking to accomplish. These factors are just a few of the various factors that come together to form a company's business model. Based on the corporation's business model, your IT department will develop an overall IT business model outlining the management of your IT department.

Why do you, the security professional, need to know this about your business? A common misconception is that IT departments are the same no matter the type of business. However, some business models require stricter security policies and adherence to those policies in order to ensure compliance with regulatory agencies. Your organization may be processing customer or employee medical information, which requires compliance with the Health Insurance Portability and Accountability Act (HIPAA). If your company processes credit card information, the Payment Card Industry (PCI) standards need to be followed. Your company's overall security program should start with a high-level view of the organization's goals and then drill down into the actual operations. You will work closely with your management team to assess these organizational goals and with the operations team to determine how to implement solutions to meet those goals.

Unfortunately, the operations and security teams in many IT shops view each other as competitors. The operations team thinks the security team is hamstringing its effort to run the network, whereas the security team thinks that operations wants to bypass all security protocols to get the network working. A balance between the needs of the operations team and the concerns of the security team can be found. The easiest way to accomplish this balance is to understand, from a business perspective, what is most important to your organization. On occasion, management will accept the risks of not implementing your recommended security measures in order to ensure continued operations and continued revenue streams or other business-related operations. This is management's right. Many security professionals may find this upsetting, but sometimes security will take a back seat to operations. When this does happen, reevaluate the situation and provide security solutions that are in keeping within your organization's business model.

There are many different types of business models, but you will most likely come across a few typical ones during your career. As an overview, this chapter has broken the models down into three basic classifications, some with their own specific subsections. The three higher-level business model classifications are

- Government
- Commercial
- Universities

You should be able to apply one of these models to the vast majority of business environments you may find yourself in.

# What You Have to Worry About

If you monitor security news feeds, you are constantly reading about new vulnerabilities being identified and organizations that are being compromised because of those vulnerabilities. You might think that most of the security breaches occur within large corporations with important and valuable secrets that other people want. While these targets are of great interest to the bad guys, that does not mean that a smaller business will not be the victim of similar security incident. A smaller environment makes a nice, easy target for an attacker because the small company may not be as security conscience or as well defended as the larger organization.

Even though the threats to an organization's valuable information assets, such as financial information or trade secrets, are the main focus of security professionals, *personally identifiable information (PII)* for employees and perhaps customers or others may also be on the network. PII is any information that can be used to impersonate another person. This information includes social security numbers, drivers license numbers, email addresses, mailing addresses, and anything else that is unique to an individual. Each of these is valuable on its own, but combined they can be used in identity theft. If an attacker obtains one of your user's social security numbers along with a specific corresponding birth date and home address that could be enough to obtain unauthorized credit cards and bank accounts under that user's identity. This PII may be just as good a target for an attacker as your company's financial or technical information.

Sometimes an IT staff member may come across a situation where he or she is called into an executive's office for an IT-related issue. It seems the executive accidentally deleted family photos, personal music, or other important personal information from the system and it falls on the IT department to recover that data. This situation is one where what you are supposed to do based on company policy and what you actually do diverges. The personal information stored on a business computer falls outside of company policies, so the company may not be required to retrieve it. Because the executive is high enough up in the company, however, you have to protect this information as if it is business-critical information.

Many people often use their business computer for personal use in violation of acceptable use policies, so there could be a significant amount of PII for your company's employees on these systems. You might find a user's personal financial information or even a resume that contains information that could be used against that person. What this means is that not only will you need to concern yourself with guarding your company's sensitive information, but also you need to secure the personally identifiable information of employees and customers.

So what might an attacker want from your company's information systems? That question is the one you have to ask yourself when designing a proper security plan, keeping in mind your organization's business model. An attacker might be intentionally targeting your information system trying to uncover company secrets, financial information, your organization's operational forecasts, PII of customers or employees, or a wide variety of other information. An attacker can use this information in a number of different ways, from selling information to your competitors to even falsifying an employee's or customer's identity.

The stealing of an organization's information is just one way an attacker can harm your organization. A more noticeable and immediate attack would be to disrupt company communications or way of doing business through a denial-of-service (DoS) attack on a target. A DoS attack can be done in several ways, but each has the same intended outcome: to prevent a computer system from performing the tasks for which it is intended. DoS attacks are commonly implemented against high-value websites, such as financial institutions, government entities, or other websites critical to a business' day-to-day operations. By overwhelming a website with so many false requests that it cannot respond to or process valid requests, the attacker makes the website unavailable to legitimate users. DoS attacks against a retail operation's website can cause a significant loss of revenue even if the attack lasts only a short amount of time.

During the holiday shopping season of 2009, Wal-Mart, Amazon.com, and several other e-commerce websites were hit by a DoS attack. The attack lasted only an hour, but during that time customers were not able to access these websites or they were extremely slow. It is unknown how much revenue was lost during this time, but since the attack took place during the holiday shopping season, even a small amount would be more than any of the companies wanted to lose.

In the earliest days of hacking, this exploit was often done just for the thrill of it—sort of like a passage into adulthood or moving up to the big leagues. Novice hackers, often called *newbies, script kiddies,* or *ankle biters,* probably still do this. But something you always want to keep in mind is that attackers are not generally just trying to break into systems for the challenge of it. Most attacks are executed by bad guys for financial gain. Bad guys want your valuable data, and they are willing to break into your systems to get it.

What will the attackers do with this data once they have it? That depends on what data they are able to get away with. If an attacker is able to steal business forecasts from your company, he or she may be able to sell this information to your competitors or even blackmail your company to keep the information confidential. The selling of intellectual property has become a booming business on the Internet, with major criminal organizations and possibly even countries taking part. There is a major market for people who want to sell an individual's personal information for identity theft and a company's secrets to the highest bidder. These black market identity brokers sell information ranging from a person's social security number to employment history to medical history to bank account information. Identity thieves will usually buy PII in bulk through these black markets and use the information for identity theft. Most any type of information imaginable concerning an individual or organization is available for the right price.

Here is an example of a possible threat against your personal information being stored on a company's systems. Have you ever received an email from a retailer suggesting a new product that you may be interested in? If so, have you ever thought about how the retailer is able to figure out what you would like? Many retail operations maintain a database of customer information that they use to monitor and predict customer shopping habits. These databases hold information about customers, like the customer's home address, date of birth, shipping addresses, possibly social security number, and credit card information, that, although not intended for such use, could be used for identity theft.

A major security concern is the customer credit card information that is sometimes held in these databases. When someone buys something from online retailers, their e-commerce web application allows the customer to save his or her credit card information with other personal information to facilitate future purchases. Saving this information makes future purchases much more convenient for the customer—and that much easier for an attacker to get information about the customer. By having all this information in one central location, all an attacker has to do is penetrate the single location and then he or she may have enough PII to steal the customer's identity. A major regulatory compliance initiative called the Payment Card Industry Data Security Standard (PCI DSS) has been implemented to ensure that credit card transactions are processed securely and customer data is held securely in order to prevent breaches of this information.

Another, more prevalent reason for an attacker to want access to your systems has nothing to do with information at all. Sometimes bad guys simply want control of the computer system itself. These systems can then be used to store and distribute potentially illegal information, such as copyrighted material or the PII of individuals to be used or sold. This one computer may not hold any important information, but its location on your network could allow it to be a pivot point into your internal, more secure network.

Interestingly, the bad guys who want your systems may not even want your most powerful systems. What could someone possibly want with a secretary's feeble workstation from a small office in the middle of nowhere, when much more powerful, well-placed, and well-connected targets are out there? These powerful systems often hold and process your organization's more important data. Because the powerful system handles the more important data, there is commonly an increased security focus on that system. This increased security makes the powerful server a harder target for the bad guy to compromise when compared to the lowly workstation. The bad guys do not want to get caught, so they are ready, willing, and able to take over an easier target, which is a less powerful system. A smaller, more vulnerable system is a nice target for an attacker. Compromising 10 or 20 easy, smaller systems brings more CPU cycles, more storage space, and more bandwidth to add to the attacker's distributed repository.

The attacker's goal is to add this machine as a node in the *botnet*. The attacker will install malicious software on the computer, giving the bad guy complete and continued access to the compromised system. The compromised system will then call to a system on the Internet, the *bot master*, which is used to control the other systems in the botnet, to receive instructions on what to do next. While the infected machine, known as a *zombie*, is attempting to make contact with its control point, it will more than likely attempt to infect other machines on your network as well, adding to the botnet's power base. This is how a botnet becomes so dangerous. The power of the individual machine is not so important; the number of machines the botnet master controls is. In the world of botnets, quantity surpasses quality.

There is an underground market for these botnet resources that not many people outside the security community are aware of. These botnets can be used as weapons against competing entities or governments, or used as vast distributed data stores for information or as a way of making money. *Spammers*, people who produce and distribute spam email as a business, use botnets as a way of distributing spam emails to people. Since the spam emails are being bounced around off of many infected computers in the botnet, stopping the emails from being sent is very difficult. As soon as one node in the botnet goes offline, another will pick up where the original node left off. Spammers sell their services to businesses, and much of the spam you receive is sent from computers that are part of a botnet—and the computers' owners haven't a clue that their computers are spam servers.

One of the main hurdles to overcome when implementing a security plan in your organization is that most of what security does is sometimes very difficult for your organization's management to understand. Quantifying the savings the security team provides is difficult. Because you can only provide estimates as to how much money the security program may have saved if attacks had happened, it is difficult to accurately determine how much a security program saves a company during a year. Security is usually only thought of when something goes wrong, like when a server goes down unexpectedly, or during a virus outbreak, or when critical data goes missing. Hopefully by understanding your organization's goals, you can better communicate its security needs to management before your organization becomes the target of an attack.

# Overview of CIA

In order to best understand and compare the different types of business models that will be discussed in this chapter, let us determine the commonalities among the majority of security programs. The concept that will be used to differentiate among these business models is a concept that security professionals should be aware of. That concept is the security triad, CIA. *CIA* in this reference stands for *Confidentiality, Integrity, and Availability.* The goal of a security program and its team members is to protect the confidentiality, integrity, and availability of the organization's valuable information assets. These are the core principles on which information security is based. Without a thorough understanding of these concepts and how they relate to your environment, you will not be able to assess your security program's needs accurately. Here is a quick recap of these concepts:

- **Confidentiality** You have secrets; your competitors have secrets; everyone has secrets. Keeping these secrets secret and ensuring that unauthorized individuals cannot access them is a key security concept. If an organization's confidential information is released to the public, this release could violate company policy as well as any regulatory compliances that those policies may have to meet. The most common way to keep information confidential is to use strong access controls, for instance, a form of cryptography, to encrypt the data.

- **Integrity** Imagine you get an email from a coworker telling you to order 10,000 widgets. How can you be sure the email wasn't modified in transmission? What if the original message instructed you to order only 10 widgets? If this email was modified from its original during transmission, this would be an example of a violation of integrity. Protecting the integrity of the information requires that the information (assumed to be correct information) cannot be, and has not been, inappropriately modified. Integrity protection disallows the inappropriate modification of data; integrity validation verifies that the data has not been modified. Both protection and validation are often required in strong security environments. Putting proper access controls in place is a way to protect data integrity. Most access controls cannot only restrict access to those authorized users or applications, but also help maintain strict logs of who does what with the information, which is known as an *audit trail.*

- **Availability** An old joke that used to go around security circles was that if a system is unplugged and locked in a closet, then that system is as secure as you are ever going to get it. Although this is true, unplugged and locked-away systems do nothing to help you run your operations. If no one can get to the information, then, of course, that information is secure from any attack, but it is absolutely useless to you, too. Making sure the critical information you need is accessible when you need it is the basis of availability. There are many ways to maintain availability, such as redundant systems, but how you keep this information consistently available is determined by you and your environment.

In the following chapters, these concepts will be used to better explain the security needs of the different types of business models. All of these principles need to be taken into account when planning your security policy, but some will have more weight in your decision making than others. These are not exact representations of all business models, so you will need to analyze your specific environment and determine what's best for you. The metrics that will be used to show the importance of the Confidentiality, Integrity, and Availability will be High, Medium, and Low. This is not meant to be a scientific calculation, but more of a differentiation of how important each of the facets of the triad of security is and an overview of what aspect of security each of the business models will want to focus on.

# Government

Long gone are the days when governments ran on pen and paper. Now most government information is stored on computers, and the work of the government is performed on global networks. This modernization of government processes has made governments more efficient and more capable of providing greater and better services to their nation's citizens, but modernization has also made governments' valuable information assets more exposed to attack. In the past, for a nation to be attacked, an army had to travel to the foreign country to conduct a physical war. Now, a nation can attack another nation without ever leaving its own borders. This global network, the Internet, has made the world a much smaller place, giving people the ability to share information in ways that, at one time, could not even be imagined. But that ease of sharing information has made it easier for the bad guys to try to take what is yours.

In many ways, a government is like a corporation. A government provides services and must answer to its citizens, much like a corporation provides services to its customers and answers to its shareholders. National governments have many parts and a few of them discussed here. The next sections focus on the parts of government or its departments that protect its citizens and on the parts or departments that provide services for the nation's citizens.

## Military

The old adage used to be that that an army marches on its stomach. But for the new 21st century soldier, a country's military lives and dies based on the information it has. In this age of televised wars, someone can turn on a news station and watch a war taking place in real time. As a member of a military IT support team, the key security aspect to focus on is availability. In a war zone, if you can't get to key information or if superiors do not have access to key information, missions may fail and people may lose their lives. The military does have secrets, with multiple classifications of sensitivity of the data that you need to protect (confidentiality). The military must also acquire accurate data and protect the accuracy of that data (integrity). But these important factors will sometimes need to take a back seat to the priority of ensuring the military's information is available to those who need it.

The commanders in a modern war have access to a vast amount of information, significantly more than at any other time in history. That information is very often provided in near real time. As a result, the modern military's network has to process data at an incredibly high rate in order to keep up with the demands of decision makers. Redundant systems are going to be one of the keys to maintaining availability. Many factors can cause a system to become nonoperational in a combat environment. These systems often need to run for extremely long periods of time, in very harsh physical environments without the properly required maintenance. The extremely hot, dusty conditions of a desert can be very detrimental to a computer system. Sand buildup and overheating can cause your systems to not function as long as they should. Redundant systems can help mitigate the issues that could arise from a system failure.

An effective way to gain an advantage over your enemy during a war is to disrupt their lines of communications. In the olden days, in order to disrupt communications, you would disrupt enemy supply lines or kill the messengers who were transporting messages. Nowadays, implementing a denial-of-service (DoS) attack against an enemy is the most cost-effective method for disrupting lines of communications. This method of attack has been recently employed during limited international skirmishes. During Summer 2008, an ongoing conflict flared between the countries of Georgia and Russia. While physical battles were also being fought between these two countries, several Georgian computer systems were hit with a distributed DoS attack. This attack brought down several Georgian websites used by its government. Although the perpetrators of this attack were never confirmed, the example shows that the disruption of computer systems can be used as a weapon.

A harder, but more effective way to gain an advantage during war is to intercept enemy communications. Today's modern, digital wars make intercepting enemy information a little more difficult due to the high levels of encryption being employed both for voice and data communications. Most military communication, regardless of the classification level, is encrypted to some degree when traversing through hostile territories.

In a deployed environment, the military does not usually have a preexisting information system infrastructure to function on, so they have to build a new one. This network must be built quickly and satisfy the demands of the, usually very stressed, decision makers. Because these new networks need to be set up rapidly and in adverse environments, there is a higher likelihood of security being side stepped, in order to complete a mission objective—the real reason for the network in the first place. During these times of initial deployment, a security professional must remain extremely vigilant to ensure that proper security procedures have been followed and security standards have been met, but the professional must also be aware that the mission's objectives come first.

|  | Confidentiality | Integrity | Availability |
|---|---|---|---|
| **Military** | Medium | Medium | High |

## Three-Letter Agencies

The term *three-letter agency* is predominantly a U.S. term that refers to U.S. government agencies that are known by their three-letter acronyms, often agencies that provide protection services. Examples of three-letter agencies within the United States are the Central Intelligence Agency (CIA), Federal Bureau of Investigations (FBI), and National Security Agency (NSA). These examples fit nicely because they all have three-letter acronyms, but the term is used even by agencies that have more or less than three-letter acronyms or even by agencies that are not normally known by any acronyms. Non-U.S. examples of what could be considered three-letter agencies would be Britain's MI5, Iran's Ministry of Security (MOIS/VEVAK), and Germany's Federal Intelligence Service (Bundesnachrichtendienst). Even though these agencies are part of the government, they function in a very different way than the military. The role of these types of agencies is to protect the government from internal and external threats. One of the agencies may be sanctioned to perform espionage and intelligence work outside of its country's borders. Another may have jurisdiction when dealing with internal threats to a government and its citizens, like monitoring and stopping major criminal activities.

The key security concerns for the business models that govern agencies like these are ensuring that sensitive information remains confidential, and that no one can tamper with that information. Much like the military, these agencies employ a classification scheme to specify the level of security that needs to be placed on different information assets. Examples of classifications are *Unclassified, Secret*, and *Top Secret.* These classifications not only denote how valuable the information is, but also define who can have access to the information. You need to have a specific and comparable security clearance to access information at a specific classification level. How you secure that information within those specific classification levels is determined by a concept known as *categorization of data* and *need to know*. What this means is that you are only able to access the least amount of information that is required for you to perform your duties. This is a good, overall security strategy for limiting what people have access to at bare minimum and is also referred to as *the principle of least privilege*.

Since these agencies do not officially take part in front-line warfare for a government, the methods used to defend national security are a little more covert. The intelligence-gathering arms of these government agencies are extremely concerned with the confidentiality of their information. This includes the encryption and classification of data at rest, which means while the data is being stored on a system, and the secure encryption of data in transit, which is when data is being moved between systems. If secrets are being passed from a hostile environment back within the country's borders, these agencies are usually concerned that no one can intercept and read or change the data being sent.

| | Confidentiality | Integrity | Availability |
|---|---|---|---|
| **Three-letter agencies** | High | Medium | Low |

## Social Services Infrastructure

The social services infrastructure of a government is how a government provides services to its citizens. This includes not only major services like electrical power and emergency services, but also agencies that most of us wouldn't think of like the postal service. These major and minor services that we rely on, but don't always think about, are also susceptible to attack. With some exceptions, these types of infrastructure groups are not as concerned with keeping their information secret as they with are ensuring their services remain available.

As long as you have paid your bills, when you turn your light switch on you expect your lights to come on. You don't really think about the complexity of the process that takes place behind the scenes to get that electrical power to your house. Electrical power plants need to be running properly, power lines need to be up, and relay stations need to step up or down to the voltage required. If just one of those pieces goes bad, you wouldn't have power at your home, office, medical facilities, or other vital locations. All of these systems that make up a country's power grid rely on computers to operate smoothly—computers that are susceptible to attack. What if the redundant systems went offline as well? The resulting power failure could affect anywhere from a few city blocks to large parts of the country. If something were to happen to a nuclear power station's information system, the result could be a catastrophic accident that would have a significant effect on the area around it. It has become a reality that events in cyberspace can affect things in the real world.

Most people know what would happen if the country's electrical grid went offline, but there are several other governmental functions that rely on computers to function smoothly. Because we depend on computers so much as a society, causing an interruption in service to social services could have far-reaching affects. For example, what if the postal service failed to operate? What affect would that have on a country? The postal system uses computers to sort and route mail efficiently and also for billing. Many people still receive their paychecks in the mail and conduct their day-to-day lives via mail. Many small businesses and even some large businesses rely on the postal service to operate. If an interruption in service occurred, even for a short period of time, there could be lasting, widespread repercussions felt throughout an organization or nation. If someone does not get his or her paycheck on time, that person may not be able to pay a bill to a company on time, which could mean that company is late paying its bills, and so on, and so on. One small delay could trickle down throughout society.

Another example is electronic voting. This technology is not as widespread as of present, but more and more countries are looking to electronic voting as a method for their citizens to cast votes in elections. If an attacker is able to compromise these machines unnoticed, then the attacker would have the power to slant the results of that election. There have been several tests performed on electronic voting machines, with mixed results as to the security of these devices.

The need to keep these services available to the countries' citizens is the primary requirement of the social services infrastructure. What happens if the police can't answer a call, the fire department put out a fire, or the power doesn't work in your city?

|  | Confidentiality | Integrity | Availability |
|---|---|---|---|
| **Social services infrastructure** | Medium | Low | High |

# Commercial Entities

When discussing commercial entities, we are focusing on actual businesses. Businesses are organizations that function by producing something or providing a service to customers in exchange for capital. There are many different types of businesses, each type focusing on providing different goods or services, but they all are in business to gain a profit from what they produce. Each of these types of commercial entities will need to focus on different aspects of security in order to maintain secure operations.

## Retail Services

When working in a retail-centric environment, two key security concepts need to be enforced. The first is the availability of the information systems, in this case, the systems and services that allow for transactions to be completed. A customer must be able to purchase the products, and the business must be able to complete these transactions to produce revenue. There is a direct relationship between how long a system is unavailable and how much money the business loses. The moment the business starts losing money because of security-related incidents, like their e-business website going down or an inability to produce their product, all eyes will be on you, the security professional for the organization.

If the retail business processes credit cards, the business must comply with the Payment Card Industry Data Security Standards (PCI DSS). The PCI DSS standards were established by credit card companies in order to enforce standards for the secure processing of credit card information and to lessen the likelihood of theft of credit card information that can lead to credit fraud, theft of funds, and identity theft. Prior to the establishment of these standards, most major credit card companies each had their own program in place for the processing of their specific credit cards. Keep in mind that the end goal of a retail business should not be to simply become compliant, but to secure your valuable information assets as well. Being compliant with a security standard is a good start, but too many business see compliance as a stopping point in the development and enhancement of their security posture, which is where it really only begins. Retail businesses need to go above and beyond these standards to establish a mature and comprehensive security posture.

|  | Confidentiality | Integrity | Availability |
| --- | --- | --- | --- |
| **Retail** | Medium | Low | High |

## Manufacturing/Production

Imagine that the manufacturing company you work for has just developed a way to produce widgets 25 percent cheaper than your competitors can, while providing comparable or superior quality. Within six months, your company will be able to dominate the widget market by underselling your rivals. Would you consider the process with which you manufacture these widgets to be valuable information? Would your competitors consider it valuable? On a large enough scale, even a small, per-unit cost reduction can make a huge difference to potential buyers since these small changes can add up very quickly when purchasing in bulk.

As time goes on, more and more manufacturing plants will become automated with less actual human interaction involved in the production of their products. This increases the risk of someone either unintentionally, or even intentionally, incorrectly configuring the manufacturing devices and information systems that drive them. Misconfigured systems can stop production and may introduce vulnerabilities into the systems, which could then provide an avenue for attack.

|  | Confidentiality | Integrity | Availability |
| --- | --- | --- | --- |
| **Manufacturing/ production** | High | Low | Medium |

## Banking

More and more people never really even see the money they have. Your money is actually just a series of numbers on some ledger, in some program, on some computer system, somewhere in cyberspace. More often now, companies use direct deposit to pay their employees, so the money is transferred electronically from one bank to another. When people pay for items at stores, they often use debit or credit cards to pay for their merchandise. Paying off credit card bills these days can be done via electronic transfers and online banking. Because all of these transactions and all of this financial information is transmitted and stored electronically, it is susceptible to a wide variety of attacks.

So what exactly does a bank do, and how does the bank make money? Most people just look at a bank as some place you securely store your money, but how is it that banks are able to give us returns in the form of interest for that money being stored? People commonly believe their money is in the bank, but their cash is not really in the bank. From a very simplistic perspective, the bank uses your money to loan to other people and businesses. The banks collect revenue from those loans from the interest they charge on the loan. So in the background of the banking industry, money is being moved around from account to account, ledger to ledger, and even bank to bank without you ever really knowing where your money is. This means that there are multiple points, whether the data is in transmission or at rest, where that data may be vulnerable to attack and compromise.

So what does an attacker want from a bank? The most obvious thing is to steal money. Wire transfers between banks are conducted all the time. Intercepting one of these transmissions, or gaining the ability to redirect one of these transmissions to another account, would be a very lucrative business for a bad guy. Of course the banks understand this, so the banks make the interception of these types of transmissions very difficult, due to the high levels of encryption generally used for these types of transmissions.

A possible way to compromise banking information would be to compromise information either at the source or at the destination. If you maintain information about your financial assets on your personal computer, then it is at risk of being compromised. One of the easiest things to do is use a spreadsheet to track your home finances. A lot of people do this, and it is a simple solution to managing finances that does not require buying an actual application to manage your money. The problem here is that the data at rest is usually not encrypted, and if it is, it uses very weak encryption. So an attacker going after your personal machine may be able to get financial information or PII that would let them access your personal or business financial information, allowing him or her to steal your identity and exposing you to fraud that puts you as a banking customer, and the bank, at serious risk.

|  | Confidentiality | Integrity | Availability |
|---|---|---|---|
| **Banking** | High | Medium | Low |

# Universities

Look at how a university operates. A college or university can be a very unusual and trying place for a network security professional to work. You have two contradicting requirements in this environment. On one hand, you need to maintain a level of open access, sometimes beyond that of standard business requirements, for your large and transient student network population, and on the other hand, you must ensure that the systems that are used by university administration personnel are secure. This may differ from standard business requirements because of the nature of a university. A university is a teaching institution designed for the open exchange of ideas and learning. In order to accomplish this, you may be required to allow students more access to the systems used for teaching than you think secure. In most every other organization, your student network users don't use the network as the service provider at their homes. Because many college students live in dorms on the campus and their internet connectivity rides across your networks, you need to provide them with a level of connectivity that is on par with most home service providers. This, in itself, is not really an issue, but add to it that the users will more than likely need access to some of your internal systems, and the actual implementation of security can become an issue.

By normal security standards, this makes for a complex environment to put proper controls in place. For example, just walk through a campus and count how many students are working on personal laptops in classes, libraries, or Internet cafes. Most universities have large, wireless networks in place. You can bet that many of the student computers are probably using the wireless network and are on your network. More than likely these computers are not managed by your university's IT staff and, therefore, are all possible threats to your network. That is not to say that every single one of those students, facility, or staff members is willfully trying to do harm, but from the security team's perspective, these client systems are unmanageable, and they are all possible threats to your information systems. Unless the university has protective and proactive security measures in place that validate users attempting to gain access to your network and determine the antivirus and patch level of a system, like a Network Access Control (NAC) system, you have no idea if the machine has been recently or ever patched, or if the antivirus definitions are up to date. If the system entering your network is not fully patched or its antivirus is out of date or nonexistent, these systems could introduce vulnerabilities to your network because they are easier targets for compromise.

A university computer system, in its simplest form, can be broken down into two different networks: the student network and the school administration network. This means that a university has to deal with two networks, and each has their own security issues that need to be taken into consideration. What you may want to keep in mind is that not only is a university an institution for teaching, but it is also a business, and that business has sensitive data. Behind the scenes at a college or university, away from the students and teaching population, is a backend network that handles student accounts, financial aid information, payment of university staff, student grades, cafeteria lunch menus, and so on. If a bad guy was able to gain access to this network, he or she would have access to a large amount of very sensitive information about past and present students, faculty, and staff.

The student network comes with its own perils. Normally, these networks are wide open with only a limited amount of restrictions, depending on the university. This network can include Internet hotspots, the school labs, and the dormitories. The student network is where your unmanaged computer threat really needs to be addressed. In these environments, you are not so much worried about someone stealing your sensitive information, as you are with these systems being a pathway, virus carrier, or a pivot point into your network. Depending on how the networks are segregated, the student network may have some limited access into the management network.

|  | Confidentiality | Integrity | Availability |
| --- | --- | --- | --- |
| **Universities** | High | Low | Medium |

# How Does Your Company's Business Model Affect You?

Once you understand your environment and its needs based on its business model, you want to start looking at the actual ways to add security. As a good starting point, you may want to monitor activity on your local network and the devices that run on it. Since this monitoring can generate a significant amount of data in the form of event logs from systems, you may want to consider a piece of software called a *Security Information and Event Management (SIEM)* system. A SIEM acts as a central repository for logs generated by systems and allows you, via logical rules that you would determine, to pick out specific events of interest. From a centralized location, you can then view information from a wide variety of devices and link events from multiple devices into a possible attack on your network. SIEMs can be very helpful in maintaining regulatory compliance and aiding in the overall security of your environment.

If you decide that a SIEM tool can help you provide better security for your environment, then what? A SIEM tool is very powerful and can do many things to help you better secure your environment, but you have to know what you want the SIEM tool to do. Know where your most valuable information assets are. Understand the relative importance of protecting the confidentiality, integrity, or availability of those assets. You should understand whether you should be more concerned with the confidentiality of your company's information than the availability of that information, or vice versa. Remember that a SIEM tool is not a magic bullet that will solve all your security problems and automatically bring you into compliance. Understanding the business model you work in will help to identify where your security priorities should begin. These issues need to be well thought out and understood before you can get the most useful information from your SIEM.

# Summary

As you can see, businesses are run in many ways and each of these business models carries with it certain security concerns that need to be taken into account. The examples given here are high-level business models. Your environment may vary from the examples given, depending on your environment's business strategy. By looking into each of these business model examples, you can see how they share certain commonalities, such as the need to ensure that the security measures that are put in place do not hinder normal operations. Also take note of the different aspects of security in which each of these business models weigh in heavier than others. By having a clear understanding of the business model you are trying to secure, you should have a better understanding of what to prioritize in your security strategy and, from that, the best ways to implement the overall security plan.

# CHAPTER 2 | Threat Models

A s you saw in Chapter 1, different businesses have different types of sensitive data that they need to pay particular attention to when considering how best to protect and secure their information systems and information assets. The reason a piece of data or hardware has an increased level of sensitivity is because it has a heightened level of value, in real dollars, as compared to other information assets. This increased value may be because its *confidental* nature gives your organization a competitive advantage, like having the recipe for the secret sauce. An asset may have heightened value because of the threat of regulatory fines or lawsuits if the information is exposed, like credit card numbers or other personally identifiable information. An asset may have increased value dependant on the *integrity* of the information and/or its availability, such as a database that adjusts a controlling system on a production line. If the data that defines the mixture for your widget production machine is corrupted or misconfigured, accidentally or willfully and maliciously, your output—the widgets—will be no good and you now must scrap the batch. The details of the mixture may not be a secret, but its integrity or data accuracy must be strictly maintained while the production system cranks out tens of thousands widgets every hour. Or, if the same controlling system fails and a breach of *availability* occurs, the production line simply stops. Not only are you not making money producing your widgets, but also you are incurring costs for raw materials that may be spoiling, paying hourly wages to workers who aren't working, missing customer deliveries, and possibly even losing your customers as a result of the late deliveries.

A firm recognition of these information assets with their heightened value and, therefore, special security concerns, is a fundamental component of properly securing your environment. As you understand your information systems, taking inventory of each and every information asset, you should recognize that each and every one of those assets has some value to the organization. If an asset within the inventory has no value to the organization, you should eliminate that asset. If the asset has no value, it cannot be considered an asset. Instead, it has become a liability; you are spending money to maintain and protect something that may take attention away from real assets that have real value in a critical situation, things that may introduce vulnerabilities into your information system—the open doorway that lets the bad guys come in. If an asset has no value, it is a liability. Get rid of it. Shut down the system. Securely delete the file(s) or database(s). Properly remove it from your inventory. Once you have removed unnecessary items, you can conclude that every information asset in your inventory has value to the organization.

Further, as you fine tune this picture of your assets through risk analysis and business impact analysis, you will begin to recognize which assets have greater value and are, therefore, deserving of greater security attention and protection. Remember, your job as a security professional is to protect the confidentiality, integrity, and availability of these valuable information assets. The level of protection and the amount of money your organization should be willing to spend to protect an asset should be aligned with the amount of money your organization will lose if that asset is compromised (confidentiality or integrity) or lost for any reason (availability).

This chapter will review the various types of vulnerabilities and attacks that could affect your valuable information assets. Understanding the nature of these various angles of attack or loss is important, but what matters even more is understanding how to recognize when your information systems are being attacked. How do you know when an attack is underway? What should you be looking for? What would the footprints look like? How will you recognize the attack when it happens and then know what you need to do to respond to the security incident?

The answers to these questions are the hooks into your information systems that you will connect to and monitor with a SIEM system. You will build your filters and rules on your SIEM system of choice around these types of events on the network to alert you of potential or certain attack, failure, exploit, or loss. Initially, you may experience numerous false-positive alerts, but over time, with developed experience, investigation, and fine tuning, you will reduce the number of false-positives and begin to get a handle on the true-positive security events that your security team should focus on.

# The Bad Things That Could Happen

You just finished installing your new Security Information and Event Management system and have connected to the console. Systems and applications are slowly being reconfigured to forward all logs to the collectors and connectors that feed into your SIEM system. The SIEM database is beginning to gather enough information to begin analyzing. You are grinning like a ten-year-old with a full bag of candy as you click through various multicolored screens on the console, with practically every type of bar chart, pie chart, and line graph available. You are amazed at what this thing can do! Uh-oh. Wait a second. You remember that you are actually supposed to use this tool to figure something out. What was it again? Security events. Just how are you supposed to do that?

You have to determine the ways that you will be able to use this new-fangled SIEM system to spot quickly, amid tens of thousands of normal events, the relatively few unusual and potentially threatening events that are the signs of a security event, and then recognize when to escalate that security event to the status of security incident.

## Vulnerabilities

Start by examining your IT systems for the weaknesses that would attract pesky attackers like pollen attracts bumble bees. Then figure out how to get reports of those weaknesses into the SIEM system so they can be correlated and directed to your attention as security events. You will need to identify existing systems, like routers or firewalls, and may need to identify needed security systems, like a vulnerability scanner or an intrusion detection system (IDS), to sense and then report to the SIEM system on the weakness.

Following are some relatively easy targets to get started with in your search for weaknesses on your IT systems.

## Vulnerable Protocols

Computers and networks and the protocols that allow them to communicate aren't new. Many protocols have known vulnerabilities and many have already been replaced with more secure versions. If you're trying to secure your environment, you should have policies in place to disallow the use of known vulnerable protocols. Have your routers feed their logs into the SIEM system, and on the SIEM system, filter on these vulnerable disallowed protocols. You will want to know quickly if and when these show up on your networks. Security systems, like a Snort IDS system, can be added to critical segments to monitor for these disallowed protocols, even if the protocol is used only on that one segment and doesn't traverse a router. Have these network IDS systems feed into your SIEM system to monitor traffic on these critical segments.

## Misconfiguration

Vulnerabilities can be introduced into otherwise secure systems if the secure configurations of those systems get altered. *Misconfiguration* is a change to a configuration that introduces some undesirable features or vulnerabilities. Sometimes it is accidental or even an oversight. Sometimes bad guys misconfigure systems intentionally to introduce vulnerabilities or to avoid detection of other malicious activities. It is not uncommon for an administrator to accidentally select a check box he didn't intend to when poking around on a system. Or the administrator is testing something and forgets to restore all changed settings back to their previous state. Some examples of accidental system misconfiguration that lead to increased vulnerability include turning off the personal firewall on workstations or servers or starting a web server service on a system that should not be running a web server. Configure your SIEM system to filter on firewalls being turned off and new services being enabled on systems that should not be running those services. You might consider using a configuration management and verification system like Tripwire to monitor critical systems. These systems are configured to identify and report on changes to specific configuration settings and can even identify changes to files and folders on critical systems.

## User Awareness and Mistakes

Many vulnerabilities are introduced into the IT environment by the end users. How do you stop that from happening? One way is to lock users out of the network. But you can't do that. The network is there to be a resource for users. But as those same users are motoring along on the corporate network being productive, they often make simple mistakes that increase the network's vulnerability and risk to your information systems.

One classic example is a user who walks away from her computer and leaves the system unlocked. Another user might see this exposed system and become curious enough to poke around a little. This unauthorized user, just browsing around on network shares to see whatever she can find, might attempt to access content that the original user does not have permission to access. The unauthorized user will often bump into multiple Access Denied errors. These errors can be detected by feeding the file server logs into the SIEM system and filtering on multiple Access Denied errors.

Another example is when a user receives an email that is actually a phishing attack. In this day and age, you expect users to know better, but on occasion, someone may still be asleep, or not really be thinking, and will click on a dirty hyperlink in an email from some unknown sender. Doing this, of course, connects the browser to a malicious website to download malware onto the user's system. The successful phishing attack can often be detected by filtering on an HTTP protocol request to *Internet dark space* (public IP addresses that have not been assigned) or to known bad websites and IP addresses. Many firewalls can be configured to block requests to these addresses through a dynamically updated blacklist filter and can report to the SIEM on rejecting outbound requests to those blacklisted addresses.

These are only a few examples of some obvious targets of a SIEM system and how to tune the SIEM system so these events can be escalated quickly. As your Security Operations Center (SOC) team spots security events and implements changes that eliminate vulnerable protocols, misconfiguratios, and user mistakes, you can tune your SIEM system to react more quickly when the more severe breaches occur.

## Malicious Intent

Beyond the use of risky protocols, misconfigurations, and user errors and omissions, another primary source of risk to information technology systems occurs when an attacker specifically targets your enterprise for any number of reasons. Sometimes they want to sell your trade secrets to the competition. Sometimes they are compiling and selling your customers' personally identifiable information (PII) to commit identity theft. Sometimes they are disgruntled employees just getting even for some perceived insult or injustice. Perhaps they want to know who gets paid how much in the organization. Whether for money, fame, jobs, revenge, or something else, whatever their reasoning, attackers may specifically adjust their sights and place the bull's eye squarely on your IT system. Take these threats very seriously.

### Internal Threats

Most system designers believe they understand threats internal to the organization because they have some vision, and perhaps even control, over those intranet wires and devices. It is that dark, scary, unknown network lurking just beyond the external firewall that is filled with the most horrifying, unimaginable threats. Yes, point the security systems outward. Most networks are built with security systems pointed outward, defending against the external threat, and producing a hard, crunchy outside, but allowing for a soft, chewy inside.

In various surveys taken in 2009, enterprises estimated that internal threats accounted for somewhere between about 50 percent and 90 percent of all IT-related security incidents. Although that is a pretty wide range to settle into, one glaring conclusion can be reached. Inside attacks are a real threat and need to be addressed in an organization's security program. As a security professional, you must remember that some of those people you share your days with, perhaps share meals with and extend a level of trust to, will look you in the eye and smile warmly and then covertly search for ways to violate company policy to implement a security breach.

> **NOTE**   For more information on the sources of security threats, see "The Top 10 Security Threats of 2010" at http://www.networksecurityedge.com/content/top-10-information-security-threats-2010 and "The Top Five Internal Security Threats" at http://www.malwarehelp.org/security-the-top-five-internal-security-threats-2008.html.

Employees often know where the company gems are hidden and that knowledge can become tempting. Sometimes employees develop the notion that they helped to build this value for the organization; therefore, some of it rightly belongs to them. Since it hasn't been offered up to them yet, they have the right to simply help themselves. Others just see an opportunity when no one is looking; they believe they can get away with it, so they take advantage of a hidden chance. Still others develop a resentment over time and for their own reasons and want to damage the organization so it will be forced to feel their pain.

Resist the temptation to conclude simply that your coworkers can be trusted just because they are your coworkers. In addition to that hard, crunchy external shell of security systems pointing outward, you must also implement sensors and countermeasures to detect and prevent internal violations. Viewed in this academic light, and using this somewhat cold logic, you can manage the urge to blindly trust coworkers and can implement appropriate security controls with a focus on internal threats, without introducing any unintended insult.

Following are several techniques commonly used to deter and detect internal malicious activities within an IT system and organization:

- **Separation of duties**   Don't give any one individual enough authority and access to carry out an act of fraud. Don't let the same person place orders, receive materials, perform inventory audits, and balance the nightly books. One person being responsible for the whole inventory control process allows too much access and opportunity for theft and fraud. Employees with that much access may get a bright idea, one that turns malicious. Break up and assign full process tasks like these to different individuals. If a desire to commit fraud remains, it will at least require collusion between two or more persons, putting the perpetrators at much greater risk, and making it easier for you to detect any malfeasance.

- **Job rotation**   Have the multiple persons performing different process tasks trade jobs regularly. If one bad apple is cooking the books, as the next worker rolls into that job, it increases the chances of detection.

- **Security awareness training**   Repeated security awareness training for all employees will often convince potential, internal bad guys that they cannot get away with whatever malicious activity they may have been considering. You are telling them that the security team is paying attention and that all coworkers are aware and may be watching, now that they all know what to look for.

- **Strict permissions on all resources**   Apply access control lists (ACLs) to IT resources following the principle of least privilege.

- **Implement auditing on critical data, applications, and system configuration and logs**   Finally, you can feed audits into a SIEM system for 24/7 automated monitoring and alerting. Configure auditing, also called *system access control lists (SACLs)*, on important information assets to track who is accessing or trying to access these valuable assets. Track changes to your infrastructure systems in case someone in the know doesn't want you to see what he might be doing. The bad guy may disable sensors or stop or edit (scrub) the logs. You'll want to know whenever that happens.

### External Threats

External threats are often easier to detect and defend against than internal threats because most networks are implemented with the security systems pointing outward. With the majority of your security systems pointing outward, if well tuned, the alarms should all fire when the bad guys begin to make their approach. External threats can be nothing more than a script kiddie probing to see if he can get away with defacing your website, or a well-funded, very focused team of professional hackers who are determined to obtain your customer database in order to steal money from identity theft activities or to extort "security consulting services" money from the organization. The more common attack falls somewhere in the middle of these two extremes, but the risks include the full range of threats.

External threats include the manual, human attack, where the attacker systematically probes and then tosses exploits at your systems, and programmatic attacks, like viruses, worms, and other scripted exploits. Manual attacks are slower in their progression and often are more focused and subtle. Automatic attacks are usually noisy; fire rapidly, and have a high rate of unsuccessful probes and attempted exploits.

## Recognizing Attacks on the IT Systems

Whether they are internal or external, automated or manual, focused or browsing, many attacks present identifiable characteristics that can be detected by your IT systems, fed into your SIEM system, and quickly correlated to notify the security team that something fishy is happening. The following is a summary of many of these identifiable events within attacks and some insights into how you might tune your systems to detect them quickly. An attack will not have all of these features, and multiple events can easily occur simultaneously or in a different order than presented here, but this section should be a good guide for your initial security and SIEM system tuning, as well as for the development of content within the SIEM system.

## Scanning or Reconnaissance

Before the bad guys can attempt to inject exploits into your systems, they will typically perform some reconnaissance to identify as much of the layout of your networks and the specifics of the systems on those networks. Following are the techniques they will use to do this:

- **Footprinting**   Used to identify the structure of the IT system, and IP subnets and systems on those subnets. There are many hacker tools designed to perform footprinting; however, the signature of such probing is consistent. The footprinting scan will usually be performed from the same source IP and will target many different destination IP addresses, often the entire range of a class C address (254 consecutive host IP addresses)

- **Fingerprinting**   Once a map of your network has been created (as good a map as can be discerned by the bad guy), showing different nodes on the network, the attacker will try to identify the nature of the nodes. By targeting a single system and probing for specific ports and services, an attacker hopes to identify the system of the targeted node. This helps her identify the juicy targets on your network—juicy for their valuable information assets, or for their known vulnerabilities that she can then exploit.

  An attacker wants to learn details, like the device type, the operating system on the node, the patch and service pack level, and the services and applications that are installed and running on the node. Fingerprinting scans are commonly performed from the same source IP address, targeting a single destination IP address, but probing many different ports on that destination system.

Footprinting and fingerprinting are very often automated, but can also be performed manually for that finer, gentler, and less detectable touch.

## Exploits

Once the bad guy has a rough idea of the network's layout and has identified one or more juicy targets that offer up potential vulnerabilities or valuable assets, he is ready to begin throwing exploits at the system in hopes of achieving a successful compromise. In some cases, the attacker does little or no reconnaissance. An automated attack will simply begin targeting any systems it can find with one or more exploits. This is how a worm travels a network and performs its malicious acts.

Some attacks are directed at preventing access to the valuable information assets that keep your company functioning, like a denial-of-service (DoS) attack. Other attacks seek to gain undetected control of your systems for pillaging and deeper penetration. Following are descriptions of various attacks and ideas on how you might spot their presence on your systems and wires.

### Viruses

A *virus* is malware that is written into or injects itself into executable code. When the infected executable is launched, the virus code is executed at the privilege level of the user who launched the executable. The virus code replicates itself, along with implementing whatever malicious activities are defined in the virus code. Most systems today run antivirus (AV) software and perform periodic AV scans of the system files as a spot check. AV software also typically performs AV scans when files that could contain viruses are used or executed (in real-time). Rely on your AV applications and management systems and alerts to identify virus infections. Usually in a well-developed IT environment, a small number of infections are considered a security event, not an incident. Escalate the event to incident level and scale up the nature of the response as the number of infections increases.

## Worms

*Worms* are self-propagating malware that target known vulnerabilities in applications or services. These guys can propagate rapidly and hit hard. Consider any worm infection to be an incident. Regular patching of the operating system and applications to eliminate known vulnerabilities in the software, along with running antivirus software will help to defend against and detect worm attacks. Just like viruses, rely on your AV systems and alerts to identify worm infections. Scale up the nature of the response as the number of infections increases, especially if this number increases rapidly.

## IP Spoofing from the Outside

Many types of attacks on internal systems from external sources require the malicious packets to present (or *spoof*) an internal IP address as the source address. Private IP addresses are limited to being used only on your internal networks and cannot be used on nodes on the public Internet (RFC 1918). If the external interface on the border firewall receives an inbound packet containing a private source IP address, the packet cannot be legitimate and should be rejected at the firewall. This is called an *ingress filter*. In addition, this event should be forwarded to the SIEM system to identify an attempted attack.

## IP Spoofing from the Inside

If the internal interface on your border firewall receives an outbound packet with a public source IP address*, it cannot be a legitimate packet. Because the packet originated on your private network, it cannot legitimately have a public source IP address. The firewall should reject the packet and report the event to the SIEM system. This is called an *egress filter*. This type of attack is even worse than spoofing from the outside because it implies that you have an attacker on your private network. Even worse, it is probably *not* one of your employees launching an attack on a public system; it is probably a compromised system on your network that is under the control of some attacker and is attacking a public system.

---

* A private network behind a border firewall may use public IP addresses. In this case, the term "public source IP address" means a source address that is not within the range of IP subnets used on your private network behind your border firewall.

### Distributed Denial-of-Service (DDoS)

In this attack, many different source IP addresses are targeting the same destination IP address and demanding service at such a high rate that the target system is so overwhelmed attempting to service these nonlegitimate requests, it is unable to service legitimate requests. Unfortunately, the signature for this attack resembles normal server operations. One systemic indication of the DDoS attack could be provided by a behavioral IDS sensor that recognizes an excessively high rate of demand on a port or protocol for a server or the breaching a threshold and fires off an alert. A second nonsystemic indication could be provided by the clients or help desk reporting the failure of the DDoS'ed services on the server. The human reports of system failure would be a further indication of a security breach when correlated with the behavioral IDS alert for excessive use of a port or protocol.

### Buffer Overflow and SQL Injection Attacks

These two different, yet similar, types of attacks target vulnerabilities that are typically introduced into systems by developers through poor coding of user input fields for programs. If the program expects user input, the input must be validated for proper format and length. If the input is not properly qualified and restricted, bad guys can often take advantage of this weakness and perform several different types of attacks. First, all user input fields should include code to qualify that the provided input matches the nature of the expected input for that field. If the input falls outside these qualifications, the application should reject the input. To identify attempted buffer overflow and SQL injection attacks, monitor the application servers for application errors related to the rejected input (error reporting must be programmed into the application) and SQL errors on the back-end database. When multiple input rejection errors occur, coming from the same source (client), it is at least an indication that a user is in need of training (a security event), but it may also indicate an attack is underway (a security incident).

### Password Attacks

Bad guys may be trying to crack passwords to gain unauthorized access to systems and resources by trying many different combinations of characters to discover the password. These attacks are usually performed by password-cracking applications. All systems should have an account lockout security feature configured for multiple failed logon attempts that occur for the same user. Monitor systems for multiple failed login attempts, especially on infrastructure systems like firewalls, routers, DNS servers, and on critical resource servers where you may be hosting the more valuable of your valuable information assets.

### Attacks on IDS/IPS Systems

Knowledge-based intrusion detection and prevention systems contain the signatures of known attacks and monitor the network or individual hosts watching for these known attack signatures. Behavioral-based IDS/IPS systems track the typical behavior of a system or network and then alert you if that behavior changes beyond some preconfigured threshold of tolerance. IDS and IPS systems are known for their high number of false-positive alerts, but the systems can be fine-tuned over time to reduce that number. Monitor these systems closely for their alerts. Also monitor and investigate packets destined for the IDS/IPS sensors. Typically, the only legitimate source of packets being sent to these sensors should be from their management systems. Packets from other sources might very easily be from an attacker attempting to disable the sensors from spotting one or more attacks.

### Other Systems Under Attack

Attempting to exploit vulnerabilities on systems is often like shooting in the dark. The attacker is never quite sure which shots (exploits) will affect the target and how the target system will react to the malicious packet(s). The results of a failed exploit attempt are often unexpected, and systems under attack will often begin to behave erratically. Monitor otherwise stable systems that begin to act up, like when an application or the operating system locks up or when the system reboots unexpectedly.

## Entrenchment

If an attack is successful, often the next phase for the attacker is to entrench to ensure that he has an easy way to return to the system, even if the system is rebooted or a patch is applied that fixes the vulnerability he just successfully exploited. The attacker will configure or install backdoors to regain access and bypass the built-in security systems. He will often configure the system in such a way as to avoid being detected when violating normal security components and accessing the system.

Following are several tricks and techniques bad guys use to ensure their continued presence remains undetected when accessing your now compromised system.

**Disable operating system and application updates.**   So you don't inadvertently remove the vulnerability just exploited, the attacker will often disable your ability to patch the operating system and/or applications. Patches, of course, fix known vulnerabilities in system software and applications. You need to monitor systems for patch installation. You may notice a drop in traffic from your system(s) to the Windows Update website or your internal patching servers. Another technique to keep you from your patching and updating services is to reconfigure your name resolution settings to redirect DNS queries to a DNS server under the attacker's control. This way the attacker can add host address (A) records for these security services with mappings to websites of his choosing, websites that definitely do not provide legitimate patches. Monitor outbound destination port 53 DNS queries going to IP addresses that are different from your intended DNS servers. These outbound DNS query packets to port 53 should only go to your legitimate DNS servers. Track changes to the hosts file on systems to protect against name resolution alteration, as well.

**Disable antivirus and antispyware updates.**   To avoid having his so carefully installed collection malware detected and quarantined and an alert sent to you, the bad guy may disrupt the system's ability to connect to the antivirus (AV) and antispyware (AS) patching servers used to download updated signatures for AV and AS applications.

Monitor your systems for the installation of updates. You may monitor for a drop in traffic from your systems to the AV and AS update websites or from your internal, centralized AV/AS management system. Again monitor for outbound port 53 DNS query traffic going to different DNS servers.

**Disable forwarding logs to syslog or the SIEM system.**   If the bad guy can disrupt your ability to monitor the system, he will have a longer run on the system. Configure your SIEM system to identify when a reporting system hasn't provided logs in a timely manner.

**Make system configuration changes.**   To open up new backdoors and ensure his ability to regain access to the server, the bad guy will often make configuration changes on the now compromised system. These changes may include adjustments in the registry and in the host-based (personal) firewall. Configuration monitoring tools like Tripwire may be used to monitor these settings for changes. These configuration changes typically are also reported in the system event logs. Tune your SIEM system to identify system configuration changes to security components on critical systems.

**Install new service(s) and/or stop service(s).**   To open new doors, the bad guy may start an existing service or install a new service with a known vulnerability that he can exploit as a back door. The attacker may open up several new vulnerabilities in case one or more are detected and shut off or patched, and he may stop or disable services related to security systems or monitoring systems to avoid detection. Once again, configuration monitoring tools like Tripwire may be used to monitor these settings. Tune your SIEM system to identify system configuration changes to security components on critical systems.

## Phoning Home

As part of, or after, the entrenchment phase of an attack, an attacker commonly wants to install more tools and malware on your system for pillaging and for deeper penetration into your IT systems. Since uploads into your environment are almost always disallowed at the external firewalls, the attacker must make the compromised system, your IT asset, perform a download of his rootkit or collection of malware.

Following are several techniques bad guys often use to phone home to get their latest and greatest collection of tools and malware onto your compromised system.

**Reset the browser's default home page.**   When a browser loads a website, scripts and executables can be triggered to run on the client system. If the bad guy can change the browser's default home page setting, the very first thing that happens when the user innocently launches the browser is that a fresh batch of malicious software gets downloaded and possibly even installed on the system. If the bad guy spoofs the look of the legitimate default home page on his web server, this malware refresh may occur over and over again. To protect against this happening, first, systematically lock down the default home page enterprise wide, and then monitor for changes and attempted changes to the default home page setting.

**Use known bad or blacklist IP addresses.**   Bad guys need to keep their resources available on the Internet, so they can have a compromised system reach out to them and participate in the malicious activity. In some cases, their resource server is a web server dishing up malware to anyone who makes a connection. In other cases, the server may be a legitimate Internet server hosting public IRC chat rooms. The attacker uses a chat room to update and manage his army of zombies, or bots, for some eventual DDoS attack. While the protocols and mechanisms used to communicate and distribute malware may vary from server to server, many of the servers on the Internet that host these malicious activities are known, and their IP addresses get added to what is commonly called the *black list*. There are numerous security websites on the Internet that maintain a current black list and make the list available for download to your security systems. Many IDS systems include blacklist checking and alerting and most firewalls include the ability to update the black list automatically, and to monitor for, and reject, packets destined for blacklisted addresses. Monitor your networks for outbound packets with a destination IP address that is on the black list.

**Use of dark IP address space.**   Many of the public IP addresses on the Internet are either reserved for special uses or simply haven't been issued to legitimate systems yet. These unused public IP addresses are collectively called *dark IP address space*. To avoid being tracked down, and to avoid relying on legitimate ISPs for their less-than legitimate business on the Internet, the bad guys often find ways to mount a host system on the Internet using an untraceable address within the dark IP address space. Just like the black list, use your IDS systems and firewalls to monitor and alert on all traffic destined for this never good, dark IP address space.

**Use of a good destination IP address, but with unusual behavior.**   Often the attacker's external resource system has not yet been identified and has not yet been added to the black list, so the destination address on the packet going to this server may not be a usable parameter to alert on. Once a server has been added to the black list, attackers often need to move the server to a different IP address to continue doing their dirty deeds. Monitor for big uploads and big downloads, especially after hours. These incidents may often prove to be false positives, like a legitimate remote user performing a backup, but they may also be the signature of significant data loss. It is worth checking out. Also in the last few years, many professional attacks have been originating in China, Eastern Europe and the former Russian republics, the Baltic states, and the "-stan" countries. Tracing the source IP address to one of these geographic locations should increase the significance of any unusual behavior to a security professional.

## Control

At this point, the bad guy knows the lay of your network; he has identified one or more target systems and has successfully exploited one or more of these systems; he has covered his tracks, ensuring his ability to regain access to the servers; and he has contacted his external repository for a fresh and complete download of his favorite dirty tools and malware. Now that he is firmly in control of the compromised systems, he will be moving about on these systems to identify and collect valuable data, and will perhaps be connecting to other systems, usually nearby. He is in control and is now in the pillage phase. Most of the activities seen in this phase have been seen before.

- **IRC**   This protocol is often used as a communications medium between the bad guy and his collection of compromised systems, called *zombies*. The bad guy will use IRC chat rooms to isolate the bad guy from his zombies, because he can sign up for a free account and remain anonymous. The zombies are programmed to monitor a specific chat room and watch for a key phrase or member and then obey the encrypted communications, often by using key words, rather than cryptography. The IRC protocol is usually not needed and, therefore, disallowed on corporate networks. Monitor routers and firewalls for the attempted use of the IRC protocol.

- **Known bad ports**   Many worms, viruses, and other malware use specific ports to communicate. While these ports may be coincidently selected for client-side ephemeral port use, you should alert on these ports known to be used by malware. Then prove out the false-positive alert for innocent and legitimate use when they occur.

- **Unexpected/atypical protocols**   The traffic and protocols used on the organization's network will often settle into a relative standard and predictable list. Trigger alerts when something that is known to be bad or atypical occurs on the wires.

Also look out for the signs discussed previously: known bad IP addresses, blacklisted IP addresses, dark IP address space, and the use of a good destination IP address, but unusual behavior. Any time you are alerted to poor performance, unexpected server behavior, and other indications of systems under attack, monitor system event logs being fed into the SIEM system.

## After That...

Once the bad guy has pillaged to his satisfaction on a compromised system, he can use the system, which is trusted on your network, to launch new attacks on systems deeper within your network. This is called *pivot and attack*. Now, instead of attacking from an untrusted source server outside your environment, where your guard is high, he is attacking from within, with some level of privilege and trust that he established through successful exploits on the other systems. From this new and trusted vantage point, he will repeat the whole formula:

- Scan
- Exploit
- Entrench
- Phone home
- Control
- And then, once again, pivot and attack

# Summary

There are several ways that vulnerabilities can be unintentionally introduced into IT systems. These include the use of vulnerable protocols, unintentional system misconfiguration, and user and administrator errors and omissions. These vulnerabilities are all correctable once they are discovered.

When your valuable IT assets become the target of malicious activity, from the inside or from the outside, there are recognizable telltale signs of the malicious activity you can be on the lookout for. Whether the goal of the attacker is denial of service, control of systems, or theft of valuable data, you need to know what to watch for. You must design your security systems to spot these attack signatures quickly to minimize the losses to the organization.

As you consider the many aspects of threats to your IT environment and the different stages of the many types of attacks, consider which systems are in place, or are needed, as well as where and how these systems are placed, to identify the attack signatures. You'll need to tune these sensor systems to identify and record the security events, often in the form of system logs. Then you need to implement the proper monitoring of these systems, preferably by feeding these logs into your SIEM system. Finally, on the SIEM system itself, you'll need to build content, filters, logic, conditions and criteria, along with correlation rules to identify and escalate quickly the likely true-positive security events and incidents to the top of the stack for faster response.

# CHAPTER 3 | Regulatory Compliance

One of the forces driving the growth of Security Information and Event Management systems is the relatively recent governmental and industrial regulatory compliance requirements for businesses. Because government entities and industry leaders have concluded that businesses and organizations all too often fail to protect sensitive information appropriately, causing damage (losses) to individuals and to other organizations, governments and industry leaders have imposed standards of compliance, along with potentially severe penalties for failure to comply, in an effort to reduce losses and to protect innocent victims. Not only must an organization now comply with these numerous and new security requirements, but also they must show evidence of their compliance, which requires self-auditing, monitoring, and reporting.

For many organizations, especially those that previously only had an operations mindset (availability at all cost), this philosophical revolution about how to manage IT systems and the many new facets of security controls has been overwhelming. Organizations that are subject to the laws and regulations are expected to implement *prudent security* throughout their IT system, with increased security for the more sensitive information assets. This focus on increased security, of course, targets different types of information assets depending on the nature of the business and the law(s) or regulation(s) it is subject to, for example:

- As the rate of identity theft increases, organizations that keep information on their customers or their employees must protect what is called personally identifiable information (PII). Almost 10 million U.S. residents were victims of identity theft in 2008. This number is up nearly 22 percent from 2007, according to Javelin Strategy and Research (as of February 2, 2009). Many companies have individuals as customers, and virtually every company has employees, so this requirement applies to almost every organization. PII generally includes information like name, address, phone number, date of birth, and social security number. Just this information is enough to be dangerous already. If a bad guy can also associate a driver's license number, vehicle identification number, credit or debit card numbers, bank account numbers, other business account numbers, or PINs, passwords, or access codes, the individual is in real trouble.

- Financial institutions must implement additional security mechanisms, beyond just "prudent security," to protect and validate the protection of their customer's PII.

- In the medical industry, organizations must protect all medical information related to patients.

- In retail organizations, credit card numbers must be protected.

- In publicly held organizations, the integrity (accuracy) of the business's financial information must be protected and validated to provide truth in reporting.

This can seem like too many new and discrete functions to add to an already overburdened IT operations department. Organizations need tools to help them meet this seemingly endless list of compliance requirements. SIEM to the rescue!

Through feature-rich monitoring and reporting functions, SIEM can help with many aspects of compliance. It never gets tired or bored. SIEM systems can help with log management and archival (event collection), system maintenance and monitoring, validation of monitoring, incident detection, active response, and even proof of all of the above. The major SIEM vendors typically can provide compliance-related configuration and reporting packages to tune the SIEM system for the organization's particular compliance needs, facilitating a faster and easier implementation, as well as providing real-time, in-your-face vision on those most critical information assets.

At first glance, this imposed security compliance within an organization is both a good thing and a bad thing. The benefit of compliance is that improved security within the organization will translate to fewer losses due to security breaches and a more efficient utilization of the valuable information assets. Companies are doing the right thing as they operate with due diligence and due care and prudently protect the confidentiality, integrity, and availability of these valuable information assets. This is all-good; run a tighter ship. The negative aspect of compliance is the cost associated with new hardware systems and software tools and the staff needed to install, configure, maintain, monitor, and respond to incidents identified by the new security systems. With proper consideration, you should be able to dismiss the bulk of the bad news regarding the cost required to implement and maintain prudent security. While SIEM systems do not provide the typically desired *return on investment* (ROI) that the bean counters are looking for, they can provide financial benefits through *loss avoidance* due to improved IT system and use efficiency, a reduction in fines and penalties that may be imposed for noncompliance, and fewer losses from security breaches. The losses that can be reduced include the cost of defending against lawsuits and their punitive damages that may be awarded after a security breach. Another significant loss that can be reduced is the trust lost when it becomes public that company is unconcerned about or incapable of protecting not only its own valuable information assets, but also the valuable information assets of its customers and vendors.

Consider then that a properly configured and monitored SIEM system can reduce the costs associated with compliance. With its automated and continuous monitoring, dismissal of false-positive security events, alerts and potential response to true-positive security events, auditing and reporting, a SIEM system simplifies many of the sticky tasks of legal and regulatory compliance.

In this chapter, you will review several of the most prevalent *compliance regulations* as well as several industry and government recommended *security best practices* lists. Because almost all of these regulations and laws rely on a basis of prudent security, this discussion will be followed by an overview of what security components are typically required as part of *prudent security*.

# Compliance Regulations

Today most organizations are required to comply with one or more legal or industry regulations. It is the goal of these laws and regulations to compel business owners and department heads to perform *due diligence* (understanding the risks to valuable information assets) and *due care* (taking reasonable action to minimize the loss of these valuable information assets due to those risks). Monitoring and validation (auditing and reporting) of adequate security systems are also typically required.

Following are descriptions of several of the laws and regulations that affect many organizations:

- Sarbanes-Oxley Act (2002) - SOX
- Gramm-Leach-Bliley Act (1999) - GLBA
- Healthcare Insurance Portability and Accountability Act (1996) - HIPAA
- Payment Card Industry Data Security Standard - PCI DSS
- California Senate Bill 1386 (2003) - CA SB1386
- Federal Information Security Management Act (2002) - FISMA
- Cyber Security Act of 2009 (SB 773) - not yet ratified

 **NOTE**   This overview is provided as a general reference and should not be used to determine any level of compliance with any guidelines, regulations, or laws.

## Sarbanes-Oxley Act (2002) - SOX

Sarbanes-Oxley addresses the requirement for truth in financial reporting for all publicly held companies that are regulated by the Securities and Exchange Commission (SEC). SOX became law after several large and publicly held companies failed, costing their investors and all U.S. taxpayers billions of dollars. These companies were "cooking the books," providing false information in their required public reporting to the SEC. The executives of the companies were lying to the public to create the false impression that they were doing well financially, when in reality, they were losing and wasting large volumes of money.

An organization cannot protect and validate the accuracy (integrity) of information if its IT system is not secure. Therefore, SOX requires prudent security of the IT system as a foundation and requires the organization's executives produce truthful and accurate financial information.

## Gramm-Leach-Bliley Act (1999) - GLBA

GLBA targets U.S.-based financial institutions and international financial institutions that do business with any U.S.-based financial organization. Organizations like insurance and securities companies, as well as commercial and investment banks, are all deemed financial institutions under GLBA. The act requires that these institutions protect the security and confidentiality of their customer's private information adequately against "reasonably foreseeable" internal or external threats. It also requires that financial organizations tell their customers what information is collected, with whom the information might be shared, and how it is secured.

Organizations cannot ensure the protection (confidentiality) of their customers' private information if their IT system is not secure. GLBA requires prudent security of IT systems so the organization can adequately protect its customers' information.

## Healthcare Insurance Portability and Accountability Act (1996) - HIPAA

HIPAA was originally designed to manage health insurance coverage for workers when they changed employers (HIPAA Title I). It was enhanced in 2003 (HIPAA Title II) to include the protection (confidentiality) of patient information, including medical records and financial information. This body of sensitive information is referred to as *protected health information (PHI)*.

The HIPAA regulations require administrative, technical, and physical safeguards to ensure the confidentiality, security, and integrity of PHI. It also requires written policies and procedures, a designated privacy officer responsible for developing and implementing those policies and procedures, integrity and confidentiality controls, access controls, testing, and auditing of security measures, as well as reporting and incident response.

## Payment Card Industry Data Security Standard - PCI DSS

PCI DSS targets businesses that store, transmit, or process credit or debit card-holder data. The standards also apply to all network infrastructure components, servers, messaging systems, and applications included within or connected to a cardholder data environment. PCI DSS was originally developed by Visa and MasterCard to prevent credit card fraud and identity theft, but has been voluntarily adopted by other credit card companies like Japan Credit Bureau (JCB), Discover, Diners Club, and American Express.

PCI DSS includes a security specification containing 12 separate areas of controls with numerous specific requirements within each area.

The twelve major areas are:

- Install and maintain a firewall configuration to protect data.
- Do not use vendor-supplied defaults for system passwords and other security parameters.
- Protect stored cardholder data.
- Encrypt transmission of cardholder data across open, public networks.
- Use and regularly update antivirus software or programs.
- Develop and maintain secure systems and applications.

- Restrict access to cardholder data by business need-to-know.
- Assign a unique ID to each person with computer access.
- Restrict physical access to cardholder data.
- Track and monitor all access to network resources and cardholder data.
- Regularly test security systems and processes.
- Maintain a policy that addresses information security for employees and contractors.

## California Senate Bill 1386 (2003) - CA SB1386

CA SB1386 requires that if you hold any computerized, personally identifiable information (PII) on any person who resides in California, you must report to the individual any breach of security that may have exposed his or her PII data. This state bill obligates any agency, person, or business throughout the world that holds PII data on Californians to abide by this law. Although this bill was one of the first strongly worded articles of legislation that required such notification, almost all other states, as well as the U.S. federal government, have passed similar types of legislation.

## Federal Information Security Management Act (2002) - FISMA

FISMA applies to federal agencies of the U.S. government. It is a federal law that requires federal agencies and departments to develop, document, and implement a security program for information and information systems that supports the agency's mission and assets. This requirement includes any organization that does business with U.S. federal agencies, including contractors. While it was originally signed into law in 2002, FISMA became effective on March 6, 2006, and all federal information systems were required to be in compliance by March 9, 2007, as defined by the Federal Information Processing Standard (FIPS) Publication 200 (FIPS 200).

FISMA defines many of its specifications through a number of Federal Information Processing Standards (FIPS). It also takes advantage of the series of NIST Special Publication 800 documents. FISMA encourages the use of its requirements and standards by state, local, and tribal governments as well as private sector organizations.

## Cyber Security Act of 2009 (SB 773)

Although this act has yet to be ratified, it could become one of the most powerful laws affecting IT. It provides for a broad range of authority for the President of the United States, giving him (or her) full control over U.S. organizations that maintain critical infrastructure, or interact with the Internet, in order to protect the functionality and security of the Internet with respect to the interests of the United States.

If this act is ratified, the President can declare federal and private information systems or networks as "critical infrastructure" and can then require demonstration of compliance with new standards for these critical infrastructure networks.

If this act does get passed into law, just hope the President does not declare your IT system "a critical infrastructure or information system or network." If he does, you should probably start shopping for a SIEM.

# Recommended Best Practices

There are many sources of guidelines, baselines, and standards related to IT security and compliance. Most of the sources referenced in Table 3-1 are government or educational institution sources. Hardware and software vendors typically have product specific "recommended best practices" for security as well. Check the vendor's website for these. Prudent security often either recommends or strongly suggests the use of these and the manufacturer's recommendations on the secure configuration of your IT systems.

| Source | URL |
| --- | --- |
| International Organization for Standardization / International Electrotechnical Commission ISO / IEC 27002:2005 Previously BS 7799, then ISO 17799 | http://www.iso.org/iso/home.htm You can purchase the ISO / IEC 27002:2005 for about US$200. |
| National Institute of Standards and Technology (NIST) Special Publication 800-53 Revision 3, Information Security | http://csrc.nist.gov/publications/nistpubs/800-53-Rev3/sp800-53-rev3-final.pdf |
| NIST Special Publication Series | http://csrc.nist.gov/publications/PubsSPs.html |
| Federal Information Processing Standards (FIPS) | http://csrc.nist.gov/publications/PubsFIPS.html |
| Computer Security Incident Response/ CERT Coordination Center Carnegie Mellon University/Software Engineering Institute | http://www.cert.org/csirts/ |

**Table 3-1.**   Recommended Best Practices

# Prudent Security

For virtually every law and regulation in IT security, you must first establish a *security baseline*, that is, a stable, trusted environment. Upon that stable base, you can impose the additional, topic-specific objectives of the law or regulation. If your environment is not secure, how can you protect or validate the integrity of your valuable information assets? How can you protect confidentiality? Without underlying and constant prudent security, you have no foundation to build solutions for these higher-level security objectives.

It is important to remember that your compliance responsibilities may also transfer to your personnel, contractors, customers, and vendors if they store, process, or transmit your sensitive information. This may mean you are responsible for ensuring these employees and third-party entities are also implementing prudent security and are in compliance with regard to your information and the applicable laws and regulations.

The following is a list of security objectives commonly thought of as components of a prudent security program in an organization. Many aspects of these objectives are specified, along with additional requirements, within the various regulations as they pertain to that regulation's security focus.

**Assign a Specific Individual or Group Responsible for Security/Compliance**    Senior management must commit to supporting the security program, and assign an individual or group to be responsible for the design, implementation, and ongoing management of this program.

The security officer should not be subordinate to operations in any way because of the conflict of interest. As you read in Chapter 1, operations' mentality is typically "availability at all cost." The security team's mentality should be "If it isn't secure, pull the plug. Get it off the network." While the latter concept should be considered carefully before actually pulling the plug, it should be an available option in the face of a security breach.

**Implement Environmental (Physical) and Operational Security**    If the bad guys can just walk right in unnoticed, how can you ever secure your information assets? Create a physical perimeter boundary that requires some form of authentication to pass through. You could use a security guard, a swipe card or smartcard ID badges, a PIN code, or even biometrics.

Within the perimeter boundary, define security zones that relate to the sensitivity of the IT assets the area may contain. Each boundary into more sensitive areas should require additional authentication. Each authentication attempt should be logged, and the logs should be reviewed for violations. (Wouldn't this be an excellent job for your new SIEM system?)

Personnel should be trained to remain aware of potential physical security breaches and to notify the appropriate personnel with their observations.

Finally, it goes without saying that the safety of personnel is paramount. Ensure the environment is safe and free from hazards like fire and electrical shock. In addition to protecting your personnel, you will also be protecting your IT assets.

**Identify, Categorize, and Protect Sensitive IT Assets (Systems and Data)**   As the security professional responsible for protecting your valuable information assets, you must first understand which assets are most worthy and least worthy of your protection. Every IT asset must be considered in this appraisal—that includes files, folders, databases, storage media, servers, workstations, switches, routers, and everything else that makes up your IT system. Rank each asset on a scale.

The value may be based on many factors. Consider if the asset were lost. This might mean a loss of availability, of confidentiality, or of an asset's integrity. If you ever hear, "We don't know what the numbers are supposed to be, but they're not correct," you have lost the integrity of the data. Then consider the financial impact of that loss.

Consider the following costs:

- Cost to replace and install asset
- Cost to develop the trade secret
- Value as a trade secret in future sales (17 secret herbs and spices!)
- The amount the competition would pay to get asset
- Lost productivity due to the asset being unavailable
- Damage to the organization's reputation
- Fines, penalties, or lawsuits resulting from the loss
- And many more....

**Define Policies and Procedures Regarding IT Security**   Policies define the structure of the security program and the security posture of the organization. Procedures define the actions required regarding the security program. Collectively, policies and procedures form the basis of all security activity and all security awareness for personnel. These policies and procedures should be required reading, along with a signed agreement by all personnel for compliance.

Management, at all levels, should be responsible for enforcing policies and procedures. Although the security team are few in numbers, managers are responsible for, and have a vision of, every office, department, location, etc. They are trusted and distributed and have the authority to affect the environment and the behavior of personnel. Policies and procedures define the standards that the workers must abide by and managers use to gauge the actions of the workers against.

Acceptable use policies should cover the range of user activities—Internet use, e-mail use, computer use, widget machine use, etc., and should include the term "grounds for termination" for failure to comply.

**Follow Vendor, Industry, and Government Security and Configuration "Best Practices"**   No need to reinvent the wheel. Learn from trusted sources on how to configure applications, operating systems, networking, and security devices securely. Once you understand their recommendations, and the reasons for those recommendations, adjust your configurations as required for your specific installation. Document the deviations from the recommendations: what is different and why. During a compliance audit, a good answer is "I based the configuration on the manufacturers' recommended best practices."

**Provide Ongoing Security Awareness Training to All Employees**    The security team may consist of 5 people. Your organization may have 5,000 employees. The security program will get a lot more traction if all 5,005 people are aware of the rules (policies), have agreed to abide by the rules, and will help to enforce the rules.

Security awareness training should be based on the organization's policies and procedures. Training should occur at least annually for all personnel. Supplemental security awareness training should be performed for all personnel with elevated privilege, such as laptop users (Yes. Using a company laptop is an elevated privilege that warrants additional security awareness training.) and managers and administrators of applications, databases, servers, or networking devices, etc., as well as any personnel found to be violating any policies or procedures (the ones who didn't get fired!).

**Design Systems and Applications with Security Built In**    Have you ever heard "It would be easier if we just did it this way"? This is often a bad plan. Every program, connection, device, or system that is added to the IT system should have security "baked-in" during its design, development, testing, installation, and ongoing maintenance routines. Security components are much more effective and efficient if the system is intrinsically secure, without the need for some marginally effective, after-thought security band-aid.

Personnel in any kind of design or development work should be trained with this concept in mind. Quality assurance and testing personnel should be trained to validate the designed-in security components of in-house systems and applications and to identify the security components that are missing.

**Separate Development, Quality Assurance, and Production Systems and Processes**    A developer tries to think of everything to make his or her application or system do the right things. But the developer already understands how a user should employ the system. While developers often do a fine job, they often don't consider what happens when a user "clicks here," because they know that users should never need to click here, for example. What if a bug or vulnerability exists in the program? This could lead to a loss of confidentiality, integrity, or availability of valuable information assets.

Quality assurance (QA) personnel, separate from the developers, should test the system and validate functionality and assurance that the system operates securely. Shortcomings should be resolved by developers, and then the system should be retested by QA personnel until it is functional and secure.

Production should only ever have access to approved applications and systems for implementation, and developers should never work on production systems. If this segregation of roles is lost, oversight is lost, and the potential for a security violation—whether unintentional or intentional, or perhaps even fraud—is created.

**Secure Sensitive Data in Transit and at Rest (Encryption)**    By implementing access controls and privilege based on the principle of least privilege, you allow access to valuable information assets to only those who need access. That is excellent. But what happens if a bad guy gains control of a server through exploiting a vulnerability? Or drops a sniffer on a wire where the data may be flowing? You have lost the confidentiality and integrity protection of the information asset. Ouch.

All information assets categorized at or above a specific level of sensitivity should be encrypted in transit (using Secure Sockets Layer (SSL) v3 or Advanced Encryption Standard (AES) or Virtual Private Networks (VPNs)) or while at rest (using disk or volume encryption). Specify encryption technologies with strength that aligns to the relative value of the data (greater strength typically equals greater cost).

If this data is transmitted, stored, or processed by third parties, require and validate that they protect your data at the same level of security that you do.

**Implement Unique User IDs per User and per User's Role**   Each user is assigned a unique user account with a unique authentication mechanism, like a password or token device. If a user requires elevated privilege, say for administrative purposes, that user is assigned a standard user account and a separate administrative user account. Users only use the administrative account to run the administrative processes. Otherwise they should always use the standard user account.

Regularly review user accounts and disable or remove unneeded accounts.

**Implement Strong Authentication Techniques**   Authentication is a two-step process:

1. **Identification**   A user provides some claim of identity, like a username, with some form of identity proof, like a password.

2. **Authentication**   An authentication system that has knowledge of the user account and the identity proof validates the provided information as accurate.

Proof of identity typically can be provided in three forms:

- **Something you know**   Passwords, passphrases, etc.—weakest
- **Something you have**   Token device, smartcard, etc.—stronger
- **Something you are**   Fingerprint, retina scan, etc.—strongest

Authentication systems can be strengthened further by requiring two or more of these forms of authentication in combination. This is called multifactor authentication. Authentication systems can also be strengthened by requiring mutual authentication; the user proves his or her identity to the authentication agent, and the authentication agent proves its identity to the user.

Users should be trained to never share their identity information with others and, furthermore, to jealously guard its secrecy. The bad guy does bad things, but the system records show that your user account did the bad things. So you're fired.

**Implement a Strong Password Policy**   When it comes to passwords, or better yet passphrases, typically, longer is better. Character complexity, requiring a mix of upper- and lower-case letters, numbers, and symbol characters, strengthens passwords. Passwords should not be easy to guess, like a pet's name or your phone number. Passwords should be changed regularly for every user, system, application, etc., wherever they are used. Passwords should never be shared or be written or typed in plain text.

**Provide Access Using the Principle of Least Privilege**   When granting access to any IT asset (this is called *authorization*), grant only the least amount of privilege necessary for the user to accomplish his or her required task(s), and not one ounce more. It is better to grant too little access and need to loosen it just a little, than to provide too much access and lose the confidentiality, integrity, and/or availability of the valuable information asset.

Regularly review levels of privilege granted. As users are promoted, change responsibilities, or transfer within an organization, remember to remove previously granted but now unnecessary privilege. This retention of previous and unnecessary privilege is called *authorization creep*.

**Implement Access Controls on All IT Assets**   Secure all information assets so only the fewest number of users who need access have access. Nobody else can access the asset. This best practice is typically accomplished through physical controls (if the bad guy can't get to it, he can't take it, break it, or manipulate it), or through the use of unique user accounts, strong authentication, and access privilege granted at the lowest possible level, but sufficient to accomplish the required functions.

**Configure Systems Securely Before Implementing Them in Production**   If you put a system on the wire, and then begin to lock it down, it may already be compromised by a bad guy before you get the chance to keep him out. He may have planted a Trojan to open a back door or have cracked the administrative password. Secure every system *before* you connect it to the network.

Next, follow the manufacturer's recommendations on security best practices guidelines, combined with other industry and government best practices guidelines, along with specific configuration requirements to satisfy your implementation needs.

Disable or delete all unnecessary user accounts, applications, services, and protocols. Reduce the privileges on all remaining accounts, services applications, and protocols following the principle of least privilege.

**Patch Operating Systems, Devices (Firmware), and Applications in a Timely Manner**   All software is buggy and filled with vulnerabilities. Vendors typically patch their software to fix these vulnerabilities when they are discovered. If you aren't applying patches when they are released (of course, you should test the patches before applying them to production systems), your systems have known vulnerabilities and are ripe for the picking. Game over.

You should be patching operating systems (OS) and applications, as well as the firmware on all network nodes, like routers, managed switches, modems, firewalls, and IDS/IPS devices. If the device doesn't include an automated procedure, you must include it in your policies and manual procedures to check for, test, and apply patches regularly. The more often you do this, the more secure your systems are.

**Implement Antivirus and Antispyware Applications on All Nodes, and on IDS and IPS Systems and Update Definitions Frequently** A lot of bad guys are out there with a lot of bad software. Virtually every node could be infected and compromised through malware. You must implement malware protection on every system possible. Further, malware and attacks are routinely adjusted, either programmatically or manually, to change their signatures. Antivirus and antispyware vendors are continually updating their signature databases to detect the new malware. IDS/IPS vendors are continually updating their signature databases on attacks. Just like not patching an OS, if you don't update your malware and attack signatures… (How did that go? Oh, yeah…) … "ripe for the picking."

**Implement Properly Configured Perimeter/Boundary Security Systems (IP Tables, Firewalls, Proxy Servers)** Connectivity between your known and relatively trusted intranet and all other networks should be restricted to the fewest number of paths. These *choke points* should be controlled by boundary security devices that restrict the traffic to the minimum types required to allow necessary functions. Block all inbound ports except those you need to support for external clients. Even then, restrict the inbound traffic for a port to the one, or the fewest, server(s) that provides that service to external clients. This is called a *reservation,* or *many-to-one connection.*

Implement an *ingress filter.* This filter drops all inbound traffic with a source IP that exists within your network because this could only be a spoofed packet—an inbound attack.

Implement an *egress filter*. This filter drops all outbound traffic with a source IP that exists external to your network. This packet is even worse. These packets probably mean you have one or more compromised systems that are participating in an attack on someone else.

Configure *point-to-point sockets* (one IP address and port number to one other IP address and port number), also called *pinhole connections*, whenever possible.

Log all boundary device traffic and review the logs regularly. (Ooh. Another excellent use of a SIEM system!)

**Monitor All IT System Access (Auditing)** If you can't see it and know that it is good, it might be really, really bad. Because your job is to disallow "really, really bad" things on IT systems, you must know what is happening in all places and at all times within the IT system.

All existing devices that can log events should be sending logs to a central system for review and archival purposes. On other devices and segments where this function does not exist, you should implement monitoring sensors, like intrusion detection sensors (IDS) or intrusion prevention sensors (IPS). Network IDSs/IPSs can be installed on critical or otherwise *dark segments* (segments with no monitoring capabilities, those without vision). Host IDSs/IPSs can be installed on critical systems. Application, database, and file system auditing should be configured for the most sensitive information assets.

Most monitoring devices must be configured with details of what to watch for, and what to ignore, like attack signatures or unapproved protocols or traffic from trusted, friendly sources. These monitoring sensors should be configured to disallow all traffic sent directly to the sensor, except that from the administrative console (a pinhole connection). This setting protects the sensor from compromise by a bad guy.

Most IT security laws and regulations set minimum time periods for archival of these logs. Many require integrity protection and integrity validation of the logs. Your log archival system should accommodate these requirements.

All of these events and logs would easily overwhelm a human, or even a team of humans. An automated system, like a SIEM system, should be used to parse, analyze, and alert or respond efficiently, as appropriate.

**Provide Automatic Alerting Systems on Violations of IT System Assets**    For alerts to occur in an IT system, monitoring and triggering on specific events is required. Some devices provide this functionality on the front-end, the device itself. Many devices do not. In this case, these devices must send their logs to a system that can monitor and trigger on specified events. That sounds a lot like a SIEM system.

The more critical or valuable the IT asset is, the more triggers, and the more finely tuned the triggers should be. The goal is to alert on true-positive events, not to trigger on false-positive events. Too many false-positive alerts consumes security team resources unnecessarily and dulls the initiative for decisive response, like crying wolf.

**Implement Incident Response to All Breaches of Security**    Most IT security laws and regulations require some level of incident response (IR). To implement this properly, an IR team, called a *Computer Security Incident Response Team (CSIRT)* is required. This team should be made up of professionals with a wide range of practiced skills, from departments including IT security, IT operations, penetration testers (white hat hackers), legal, human resources (HR), and management. Specific roles and assignments should be made to individuals, and those individuals must be skilled, trained, and rehearsed on their roles on the CSIRT team. In addition, they should cross-train with other roles on the team, in case of personnel turnover, absence, or even worse in the face of some event.

Now that you have the team sorted out, you need to document specific plans and procedures for the various types of incidents that might affect your organization. A fairly common list of incidents that warrant discrete plans are:

- Break-in to IT environment
- Theft or loss of IT asset
- Malware outbreak, small to medium (virus, spyware, worm, malware Bot, or BotNet)
- Malware outbreak, medium to large
- Unauthorized access
- IT asset misuse
- Unauthorized disclosure

- Willful attack (manual or automated exploit attempts, denial-of-service (DoS) attack, distributed DoS attack)
- Other type of incident

IR plans and procedures should be rehearsed and tested regularly. IR actions should be made only with the approval of management. Each incident should be qualified regarding whether there may be a chance of intent to prosecute. If there is a potential intent to prosecute, implement predefined and more strict investigative and forensic analysis methodologies. These methodologies include considerations regarding search and seizure, chain of custody, legal aspects, HR aspects, and involvement with law enforcement officials.

After each event a final report should be made to management and a debriefing meeting should take place with the CSIRT team to review what happened, what should have happened, lessons learned, and proposed refinements and additions to policies and procedures, roles, and responsibilities, CSIRT team tools and members, security sensors, countermeasures, etc.

### Test Security Systems and Processes Regularly

"We have a BotNet outbreak on segments 101 and 102. Why didn't the IDSs pick up the original attacks?"

"Oh. We haven't been getting any data from that IDS for about three months."

Don't let this happen to you. Know your IT security system. Know when something isn't working right and get it fixed. Validate the accuracy and completeness of the information when the devices are reporting. Verify that the configuration of IT security systems haven't been modified inappropriately.

Perform testing at various levels of sophistication regularly to validate IT security system and security team processes. Perform internal audits to verify that personnel are adhering to policies. Periodically manually spot-check the logs of various critical IT assets to be sure the triggers on their alerting systems are tuned and functioning properly.

# Summary

Legal and regulatory compliance is here to stay, and it has made a powerful impact on the way businesses and governmental entities operate on a daily basis, and the way management, IT, and even personnel view IT systems and assets. Compliance requirements have dramatically improved the overall security posture and wellbeing of regulated IT systems. Ultimately, this is a good thing for to IT systems and security.

The next challenge is to maintain and manage these new security standards and systems properly over time. Many Security Information and Event Management systems are specifically designed to assist IT security and compliance personnel with satisfying these numerous and complex collections of compliance requirements.

# PART II | IT Threat Intelligence Using SIEM Systems

# CHAPTER 4 | SIEM Concepts: Components for Small and Medium-size Businesses

As discussed in previous chapters, the art and science of implementing Security Information and Event Management on your network requires a number of moving pieces. Perhaps those of you responsible for the security of small and medium-size business have already reached the conclusion that SIEM is beyond your grasp. While understating the potential complexities associated with implementing and managing a SIEM solution would be irresponsible, with proper expectations and planning you can achieve your goals and set out on the correct path toward a SIEM-like solution.

As commercial SIEM offerings become more mature and vendors expand their offerings, the question of whether it is more desirable for small and medium-size businesses to "roll their own" solution or to acquire the entry-level version of a full-blown commercial SIEM product becomes more difficult to answer offhand. Like all other product segments, commercial SIEM offerings began as customized solutions requiring enormous amounts of time, effort, and cash to acquire, implement, and administer over time. Today, many SIEM vendors offer entry-level products at price ranges that may be equivalent to the cost of employing engineers dedicated to researching, implementing, and maintaining a custom solution. It is also possible that your organization may not need every SIEM feature and you may be able to address your requirements using one or more of the components described in this chapter.

In this chapter, we will look at the component pieces of a SIEM and some of the available tools that you could deploy to perform these individual tasks using a home-built solution. We will also discuss the offerings of SIEM vendors that may also be appropriate for organizations in this size range.

## The Homegrown SIEM

To justify creating your own homegrown SIEM, you need to be able to acquire, implement, configure, and integrate all of the components of a SIEM from individual parts, and without exceeding the cost of a fully baked commercial offering. Because open source (freeware) tools for all of the component functions are available for download—and since, in theory, you might have surplus hardware lying around to implement these free tools on—the question may be "How much time do I need to dedicate to this?" At the very least, the effort comes at the cost of other things you could be accomplishing, and if you are paying someone on your staff to do the work, you have some measurable hard cost in the form of that person or persons' fully burdened salary. Because the completed end solution will be central to the maintenance of your security going forward, you want a solution that is still useful should the individuals who built it eventually leave the company. Therefore, you need to factor in the time and effort necessary to create a full set of documentation for your unique SIEM implementation.

Where cost sensitivity is greatest—as perhaps it may be among smaller organizations—some basic needs can possible be met by implementing single components in a very low-cost configuration. In this scenario, you would most likely first implement first a simple syslog server as described in the next section, giving you the ability to at least retain a given amount of logging information that you could manually review as situations warrant. Some of the syslog server options available on the Internet today include reporting and other advanced features, so as an option this path may result in a fairly robust end result.

# Log Management

Log management is the first key to any SIEM solution. If you are not collecting at least some of the *events* that your network produces, you will not be able to extract any *information* from those events and, therefore, you will not likely achieve any *management* of your *security,* without which SIEM functionality will be impossible to achieve.

Log management, using the simplest analogy, can be imagined as a large box into which information about things that happen on your network ("log messages") are stored. If no further functionality were added to process and data-mine the logs being held in the box, you would at least have the luxury of going back and rifling through them should the need or desire arise.

When beginning to consider log management needs, you will want to define the boundaries within which your solution will be constrained. The basic questions you need to answer that will allow you to define those boundaries are:

■ *How long must you retain the logs?* This first question brings up questions regarding data retention and data destruction. Industry regulations or laws may require you to retain certain types of data for a given period of time (*data retention*). You may also have legal and functional drivers that dictate how you dispose of information after a given period of time (*data destruction*). The period of time you retain log information will be no shorter than the former and no longer than the latter.

■ *How much log information will you be required to retain?* Even on a small network, the amount of log and event information that can be produced will rapidly overwhelm the likely amount of storage available if it is not limited. Set to their highest logging levels just a handful of network devices can easily produce millions of event messages per day. In large businesses, it is not at all unheard of to deal with hundreds of millions or even billions of messages per day. You will want to define what a reasonable amount of data storage is for your environment, and in combination with your data retention and data destruction requirements, use that information to decide what kind of data you need to retain.

■ *What kind of information system logs are you required to retain (and eventually analyze)?* Event information comes in many sizes and shapes, and a critical key to both the issue of log management and also the ultimate usefulness of your SIEM solution is in choosing what kind of information you will retain. Log information can be produced by virtually every device on your network and, in the case of servers and workstations, could be produced by both operating systems and applications. Furthermore, each log source can usually be tuned to provide a record of virtually everything it is doing or of only the most basic status information.

Log management can be structurally the simplest component of the overall solution in a generic environment, but it can quickly become a more complicated task as varied sources of information are included and higher levels of functionality, such as filtering, correlating, and reporting, are enabled. For the purpose of this chapter, we will focus primarily on the syslog standard for log information, but we would be remiss if we did not touch on the other types of information that your network produces as well.

## Syslog

*Syslog* is an industry standard method for devices to record and report events that they perform or situations they encounter (see RFC 5424). Most network devices—such as routers, switches, firewalls, and hosts—are capable of producing a stream of syslog messages that can be sent to a central location for processing and/or storage. Devices can typically be configured to lower reporting levels (fewer messages) or higher reporting levels (more messages). You will need to consider what types of syslog messages you are interested in from each type of device and configure those devices appropriately.

Every syslog message should follow the format in the RFC, so some basic filtering can be performed at the syslog server level without undue difficulty. It is important to note, however, that beyond the basic header information in a syslog message every vendor is free to format the message body as it chooses, leading to syslog messages that say the same thing very differently.

## Alerts

Some types of devices on your network may use proprietary methods of delivering event information. Typically, these may include such technologies as antivirus and Intrusion Detection/Prevention System (IDS/IPS) devices. As you inventory the devices and technologies on your network, you will want to identify which, if any, you have that do not send event information in syslog format.

## Flow Data

*Flow data* is produced by network devices and provides information on specific streams of data between endpoints. For example, a client system on your network that has requested a web page from a server on the Internet might produce hundreds of syslog messages from a router in the path as it handles each individual packet, but it would produce only a single flow message that includes information on the two devices (the IP addresses of the client and the server), the amount of data transmitted, and the service that the connection used (such as HTTP over port 80). Flow data is a very useful method for gathering high-level views of the traffic that is transiting your network.

Flow information is produced in such vendor-specific formats as NetFlow (Cisco Systems), J-Flow (Juniper), or QFlow (Q1Labs), as well as the sFlow standard (RFC 3176) supported by multiple vendors. Typically, you will only be able to collect flow data with a commercial SIEM product or "flow collector" product. Some of the flow collector products provide data analysis tools themselves and could provide value independently or as part of a SIEM system.

A number of freeware flow collectors are available such as The Cooperative Association for Internet Data Analysis's (CAIDA) cflowd, mindrot.org's flowd and flow-tools, which can be found at splintered.net. Commercial flow collector products are available from router and switch vendors as well as from third parties. Lancope's Stealthwatch is a line of flow collector appliances that will gather flow information in most or all formats, and IBM Tivoli's Netcool Performance Flow Analyzer and Arbor Networks' PeakFlow are all fine tools but come at a significant cost.

## Vulnerability Assessment Data

If you have used a Vulnerability Assessment (VA) tool on your network, the information produced is also very useful to your SIEM efforts. VA data will tell you which systems are likely to be vulnerable to what sorts of attack vectors; therefore, you will want to keep this information handy when it comes time to try to make sense of the event information you have collected.

VA information is particularly useful when trying to verify whether an attack detected by a device such as an IDS sensor is targeting a system that could be compromised by it. Quite often an IDS alert of (for example) an attack designed to compromise a Windows server will, in fact, be directed at a Linux server on your network and can, therefore, be largely ignored. Conversely, in situations where an attack is specifically targeting a system that is potentially vulnerable, VA information not only allows you to be immediately diligent about remediating the affected system but it also indicates the attacker may know more about your network than you would like him or her to.

## Let the Collection Begin

Now that you have an idea of the types of information that may be available on your network, it is time to put some planning into log collection. Following are some basic questions you will want to answer before moving forward:

- Which devices will you collect events from?
- Which events will you collect?
- How long will you keep the logs?
- Where will you store the logs?

## Which Devices Will You Collect Events From?

Looking at a diagram (or at least a sketch) of your network, you can determine which devices are critical to your operation, such as core corporate servers containing sensitive corporate and/or customer information. You will definitely want to gather at least some log information from these devices.

Moving out from these, determine which network devices provide access to these assets. Firewalls, routers, and switches transport traffic to and from these systems and will be among the first candidates to provide logging information.

Devices designed for sensing abnormal traffic—such as Intrusion Detection Systems—are also sources you will definitely want to gather information from.

The endpoint devices from which employees of your organization access the sensitive information on your network are the last basic system layer you will want to gather information from. While you can gather log information directly from each of these devices, it may be beyond a reasonable scope to install and collect log information from each laptop and desktop in your company. In this case, you may still be able to gather event information from systems that provide centralized control of some aspects of these devices, such as management stations for antivirus, virtualization, and other mechanisms. If you use Citrix in your environment, for example, this can be a great place to get event information regarding endpoint activity. SNARE is a common tool for generating and aggregating event messages from endpoints, including agents that can be installed on endpoint systems and a server for collecting these events. The SNARE agents are available as open source tools and can be downloaded at snare-server.com.

## Which Events Will You Collect?

The volume of events that a single device can produce may be far beyond your needs and abilities to collect. An edge firewall, for example, can be set to provide *debug-level* log output containing far more information than you are likely to desire or be able to apply toward any reasonable security effort, and the sheer volume of which could raise the necessary amount of storage media to unreasonable levels. The log information most commonly utilized from devices such as firewalls, routers, and switches—the "connectivity" devices that create the mesh of your network—usually relate to the source, destination, and service of the traffic they handle. Other useful device management information, such as records of administrators logging onto devices, configuration changes, and software changes, is also desirable. Most vendors will have combined these types of log information to a common logging level that can be enabled on the device in question.

Some forms of event information contain relatively large amounts of information in relatively small amounts of space. Flow data is one of these event sources, containing summary information about entire communication sessions in a single message, whereas the equivalent information might require the retention of perhaps thousands of syslog messages describing the handling of individual packets. Flow data is quite often further reduced by *sampling*—having the network device in question only send one out of a given number of possible messages to the storage device. Although sampling will not provide a record of each individual network connection, it can be a valuable source of information in constructing a holistic view of network behavior with a reasonable amount of effort. Sampled flow data will quite often provide a clear sign of compromise by indicating at which point normal network behavior is suddenly and dramatically altered.

## How Long Will You Keep the Logs?

Determining how long you will keep records of network operations is the act of defining an optimal balance among several competing needs and desires. On the one hand, a maximum length of time will provide the best possible data set for several desirable goals such as identifying growth trends for capacity planning, discovering and remediating long-standing issues of network security, and identifying and quantifying breaches in policy by current and past employees. On the other hand, retaining years of data beyond what is required by law and industry regulations can open your organization up to costly and potentially damaging discovery should you find yourself in the unfortunate position of having to open your records up for investigation by external entities.

Given that the risk of negative financial and legal implications from retaining too much data for too long—or too little for not long enough—is more likely to cause stress and anxiety at the management and shareholder level, it is generally recommended to base your data retention policies on the regulatory and legal statutes that your organization is bound to adhere to. These parameters will generally provide more than enough of a window for you to implement and exercise the security diligence that you desire from your SIEM efforts. Remember, when designing and operating your storage solution, that it is just as important (your lawyers may say "much more important") for you to ensure that data is completely and irrevocably destroyed from all forms of storage as it passes out of the determined retention window.

## Where Will You Store the Logs?

The answers to the preceding questions will largely determine how much storage you need to achieve your goals. However, depending on the level of your enthusiasm in answering those questions, you may find that the math is producing numbers that exceed your appetite for managing RAID arrays and tape archives (and/or your management's appetite for spending money). Within the boundaries of the answers to the preceding questions, you will find that you have a respectable amount of leeway to limit the amount of information you will need to gather and store. A reasonable effort at weighing the value of certain types of information (like that debug-level deluge coming from your firewall) will likely reduce the numbers to something manageable, but on the other hand, do not be overly surprised if the volume remains significant even after your best efforts at reduction. Some of the logging solutions you have at your disposal may provide some additional space savings through included compression techniques.

# Logging Solutions

There are a wide range of logging solutions available on the market, including dedicated syslog server solutions, SNMP collectors, flow collectors, and solutions that combine some of these functions. As you look for more sophisticated solutions that are capable of gathering event and other information from broader ranges of sources, you may very well find yourself wandering into the space that only purpose-built SIEM products can address.

## Open Source Syslog Servers

Among the most common solutions is the standard syslog daemon that comes installed with almost all variants of the UNIX operating system. This is the tried-and-true journeyman's log server, requiring only the efforts of a willing engineer and enough hardware to provide it the space it needs.

A variety of improved syslog server daemons are also available for free from the open source community. These typically provide additional functionality not part of most default syslog daemons found on common *x*NIX distributions.

MetaLog is an open source syslog solution that provides advanced features such as the ability to filter messages based on "facility, urgency, program name and/or Perl-compatible regular expressions," according to its SourceForge description, and can trigger actions based on patterns found, such as the firing of user-generated scripts.

Syslog-NG is a fairly mainstream open source upgrade to the traditional syslog daemon and is included in several UNIX distributions, either as the default log server or as a package with a documented upgrade path.

## Commercial Syslog Servers

A fairly wide range of vendors provide commercially supported logging solutions, many with advanced features up to and including event correlation and reporting. We recommend you search vigorously and download the trial or open source versions of some of these products to get a feel for what is available on the market to help you compare offerings. Some good examples are discussed here.

Kiwi Syslog Server from network management company SolarWinds is a very popular Windows-based syslog server providing many basic log management functions in a single package. Kiwi Syslog Server accepts syslog messages over UDP and TCP and also receives SNMP traps as well. LogRythm is another commercial syslog server with a similar range of features. EventLog Analyzer from ManageEngine (the

Enterprise IT Management division of Zoho Corp) is a web-based, log management software product available as an annual subscription, or it can be purchased outright.

Splunk is another commercial-logging solution billed as an "IT Search" solution that is embedded in products such as Cisco System's IronPort. With a web-based interface, Splunk is fairly intuitive to set up and manage and makes for a good example of what is out there. Figure 4-1 shows the first part of the Splunk web interface and to gives you a sense of its look and feel.

Splunk takes the reasonably user-friendly approach to interface design by making the initial experience easier on the less practiced admin. You can set up your Splunk server to receive live syslog feeds, monitor the local machine, or drop in existing log files simply enough through the Index Data tab. Figure 4-2 shows how you begin defining log inputs in Splunk.

**Figure 4-1.** Splunk web interface

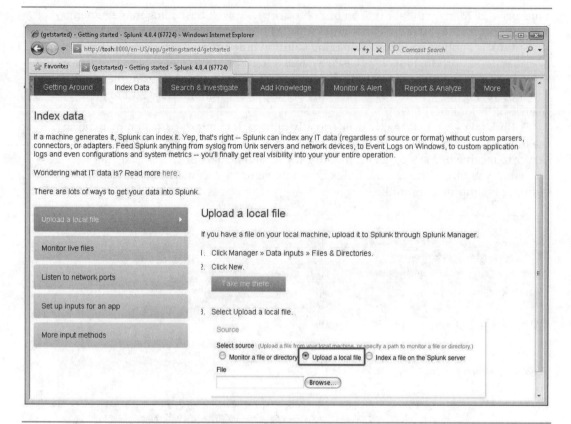

**Figure 4-2.** Defining log inputs in Splunk

Like many similar logging products, reporting capabilities are part of the base product and, in Splunk's case, are relatively straightforward to use. The usual types of data-representation formats are available from drop-down menus on the screen as well as options to export the report results as a flat text, comma-separated, XML, or JSON file for further analysis. One of the nice things about Splunk's web interface is that any report can be shared as a URL, allowing other people in the organization to see specific reports that the system administrator creates for them. Figure 4-3 shows an example of that interface.

All of these products have substantial commercial pedigrees and are likely to contain the types of features you should expect from a relatively turnkey logging solution.

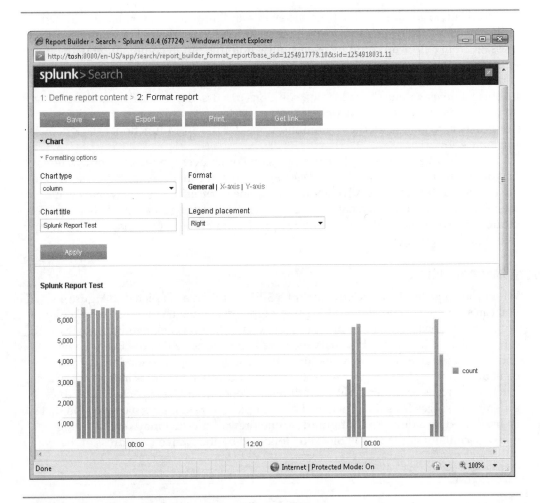

**Figure 4-3.** Splunk's reporting interface

# Event Correlation

Having logs and event information in hand is a good and wonderful thing compared to having no records at all. Now you can, for example, look back and determine whether traffic that should not be allowed based on your policy has traversed your firewall. Inversely, you can make sure your policy has remained in effect over a given period, thereby satisfying the requirements of regulatory regimes.

However, to get more value from the events and information you have collected, it will be necessary to relate them to each other: to "co-relate" them. For example, a syslog message from a firewall could by itself signify nothing, but in combination with other event messages from a router, a database server, and an intrusion detection sensor, it could indicate an attack against a vulnerable system. Much of this functionality might be obtainable using one of the logging solutions discussed previously, but depending on the complexity of your environment and your desire for advanced capabilities, your needs may extend beyond these solutions. Consider the SIEM functional stack depicted in Figure 4-4.

The *Event Layer* is where you collect logs and other event messages from systems on your network. The *Normalization Layer* is where you convert related messages that are formatted differently to a common syntax. The *Correlation Layer* is where events are related to each other to create incidents, and the *Reporting Layer* is where output is created and/or actions taken based on the processing of the events that have been input into the SIEM system.

## Event Normalization

When you consider the basic structure of a SIEM solution as depicted in Figure 4-4, you can see where some of the difficulties might arise when trying to achieve a higher order of functionality with simpler products such as log servers. Event messages can be collected in standard formats such as syslog and SNMP at the Event Layer and then stored in a common repository easily enough. Since no standard for the content of the event messages themselves exists, however, products in the same class (such as firewalls or routers) but from different vendors can be expected to produce different messages for similar events. For example, when stopping a connection that is disallowed by a device's configuration, one firewall product may send a syslog message containing the word "blocked" followed by the source IP address of the

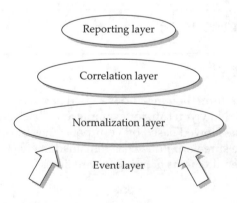

**Figure 4-4.** The SIEM stack

connection that was disallowed, whereas another firewall product could send a syslog message containing the source IP address first followed by the word "dropped." SIEM products address this by "normalizing" event messages after they have been received so they mean the same thing to the internal logic of the SIEM. Creating and maintaining this Normalization Layer over a wide range of product vendors and versions is a significant effort even for companies who specialize in producing SIEM products and can rapidly become more than a small or even large enterprise can manage on its own.

## Correlation Rules

Although in heterogeneous environments normalization is required before correlation is possible, if your environment is simple, you may be able to skip the normalization step. Since we have addressed the issue of normalization, let's talk about correlating that data. Some open source tools such as the Perl script SEC (Simple Event Correlator) provide sufficient documentation such that an engineer familiar with Perl could create custom correlation rules to trigger actions such as alerts. SEC users have further created a Ruleset Repository where you can download some preexisting correlation rules for use with your home-built SIEM solution. The number of correlation rules already created for this and other open source correlation tools are not likely to satisfy every need for most organizations, but where sufficient time and expertise is available, they can provide basic templates you or other engineers on your staff can draw from in creating new rules.

Many of the most simple types of attacks against your network can be detected with fairly simple correlation rules, which may satisfy the bulk of your needs, but as the sophistication level of the risk you are trying to detect increases, the potential complexity of the correlation rules increase as well. These correlation rules are some of the "secret sauce" developments that commercial SIEM vendors spend significant ongoing resources on creating and maintaining. Your need or desire for these more advanced detection capabilities may be among the factors that drive you to consider commercial SIEM solutions. If, on the other hand, you are the kind of person who has both the knack and the experience to design complex event correlation rules, you may find yourself in high demand in the market (drop us a line, we're always interested in folks like you).

## Commercial SIEM for SME

As mentioned earlier, many of the commercial SIEM vendors have released products in the lower price ranges, which could well fall into the budgets of small and medium-size businesses. The entry-level Cisco MARS SIEM appliance, Q1Labs' QRadar, and the commercial version of OSSIM sold and supported by AlienVault are just a few of the offerings that could prove to be similar in cost to the engineering resources necessary to assemble and configure a passable open source SIEM solution. As with all commercial solutions to technical challenges, the advantage of continuity of support and the ability to leverage the lessons learned at a large number of other sites (instead of always having to learn them through your own painful experience) weigh on the side of acquiring a turnkey product when the costs are similar to brewing your own. The usual counter argument is that you will have the ultimate flexibility of building any customization into your own solution if you build it from open source or whole cloth. (The counter-counter argument is that even turnkey solutions need significant configuration to fit a given environment, so it isn't like you're going to be bored either way.)

If you do choose to acquire a commercial product for your small business, however, be careful to estimate as liberally as possible your need for performance and capacity. Many entry-level product offerings have very limited capacity, so without careful planning, you may easily find yourself upsizing rapidly beyond your projected budget.

## Active Response

It is quite possible that a well-deployed SIEM solution could identify an attack while it is underway. Logic would seem to dictate that the SIEM should, if possible, stop the attack automatically. In some cases, this may be desirable, but it is imperative that you think through the implications of stopping an attack in progress before enabling this sort of functionality.

Some SIEM products, such as the Cisco MARS, have built-in capabilities to identify the path of an attack and take some sort of action in response. This response could come in the form of a command to a network device such as a router, switch, or firewall to block a traffic stream involved in the attack or to knock an offending endpoint device off the network.

Even if you want to actively respond, *many* companies will not allow you to make changes to the configuration of network devices without going through change-control systems and other checklist-rich corporate processes first. And, by definition, these processes are anything *but* real-time. Although those of us who focus entirely on the tactical act of securing the information systems we ritually obsess over may righteously object to this type of plodding corporate linearity, it is worth bowing to the assumed wisdom of the organizational leadership—and not only because they can fire you. Though it may be true that the attacker you can see on your network could disrupt your business and cause you harm, accidentally cutting your company off from the transactions that fill the accounts your paychecks are drawn from could make you responsible for doing the same thing or worse.

Before granting your SIEM the power to perform any sort of automatic mitigation of the attacks it thinks it detects on your network, consider the words of an executive that this author met with in the early days of a SEIM startup: "If your product is capable of automatically stopping an attack, I will have to ask you to leave the building now."

# Endpoint Security

Many SIEM systems have the capability to perform endpoint security. *Endpoint security* is the managing the security of the many endpoints (typically client nodes) on the network from a centralized location or management system, as well as managing the security of the network by protecting it from the endpoints. The endpoints on a network include laptop computers, desktop computers, and personal computing devices such as connected smart-phones and PDAs.

Following are the main areas of endpoint security that you should consider:

- Patching the operating system and major applications
- Antivirus and antispyware updates
- Firewalls—making sure they are on and configured properly
- Host Intrusion Detection Systems (HIDS) and Host Intrusion Protection Systems (HIPS)
- Configuration management
- Management of removable media, such as USB drives and CD and DVD burners
- Network Access Control (NAC) (which may also be called Network Access Protection (NAP))
- Network Intrusion Detection Systems (NIDS) and Network Intrusion Protection Systems (NIPS)

Included in the following sections are descriptions of many different tools and techniques used to satisfy these various objectives of endpoint security in small and medium-size businesses or departments. These tools should be relatively affordable and typically do not require an extensive budget to maintain and operate after purchase.

## Securing the Endpoints

In order for any network to be secure, you must be certain that the client systems remain secure. All it takes to lose your network to the bad guys is for a single system to become compromised. This is the attacker's foothold and pivot point to dig deeper into the network because he or she now is operating from one of your trusted systems. In the absence of an expensive and elaborate SIEM system, many more affordable products can help you manage the security of these endpoint systems. The products available target different and essential facets of endpoint security.

### Patching the Operating System and Applications

Most vendors of the major operating systems, like MS Windows and Red Hat Linux, and major applications, like MS Office and Adobe, have a secure and automated updating system built-in. These built-in patching systems should be used whenever possible. In the corporate environment, with regard to the more popular Windows platform, Microsoft provides, free of charge, the Windows Server Update Services (WSUS). This system allows for a hierarchical construction. The top tier contains one or more WSUS servers used to download updates securely from Microsoft's Update servers. Here, the updates can be tested, and once approved, deployed to a second tier of WSUS servers. This second tier of WSUS servers is used for increased capacity, load balancing, and geographic distribution to the Windows systems throughout the network.

For your Red Hat systems, you can subscribe to the Red Hat Network, an automated OS updating service. Using the Red Hat Network from Red Hat provides automatic updates for a fee, but you can subscribe to Information Services & Technology (IS&T) and receive free Red Hat updates.

Beyond these, for critical devices (firmware), operating systems, and applications that do not have built-in patching systems, you might consider scheduling visits to the vendors' websites and manually checking for updates.

In addition to these automated and manual techniques, running a vulnerability scanner, like QualysGuard, Nessus, GFI LANguard, SAINT, Microsoft's MBSA, and Retina, against your systems can help to identify missing patches. Of course, you will then need to initiate the download and deployment of those missing patches.

## Antivirus and Antispyware Updates

It has become standard operating procedure to have antivirus and antispyware (AV/AS) software on every system. These client applications can operate independently and perform automated updates of their signature database, or they can operate in a managed configuration. The management software, which usually performs a single download of the signature updates and then provides internal distribution, monitoring, and reporting capabilities, typically must be purchased for an additional fee.

Many free AV/AS products are available, like Spyware Doctor from PC Tools, Avast! Antivirus, AVG, ClamWin, and Avira AntiVir, to name a few. These generally operate in independent mode only and may be slower to update signatures for the newest malware.

The more enterprise-caliber AV/AS will cost you money, but these tools generally are faster to update their databases with new signatures and often have centralized management system capabilities. These include products like McAfee's VirusScan Enterprise, Symantec's AntiVirus Enterprise, and Sunbelt's Vipre Enterprise. AVG sells a Network Edition and an even more affordable Small Business Server (SBS) edition.

## The Personal Firewall

These days most operating systems include a personal firewall and usually assist with default, recommended configurations, since most end users aren't sure what types of traffic should be allowed or denied. In the Windows world, for computers that are members of an Active Directory domain, the enabling and specific configuration of the personal firewalls can be managed through Group Policy Objects (GPOs).

For something with a few more bells and whistles, third-party firewall software can be downloaded, installed, and configured on systems. Many products are free, but many must be purchased. Free personal firewalls include PC Tools Firewall Plus, Comodo's Firewall and Antivirus, and Sunbelt's Personal Firewall. Of course, commercial products are often more feature rich and better supported. Several affordable personal firewalls include ZoneAlarm Pro, Outpost Firewall Pro, Tiny Personal Firewall, and eConceal Pro.

## Host Intrusion Detection Systems (HIDS) and Host Intrusion Protection Systems (HIPS)

HIDS/HIPS utilities differ from AV/AS applications in that they do not scan files looking for malicious code as an AV application does. HIDS tools monitor the system and watch for risky behavior by processes—"risky" being based on signatures of known malware actions and attacks. Risky behavior by a process might be the modification of contents in the memory location for a different process, modifying systems files, or an attempted **del \*.\*** action by a process.

HIDS/HIPS tools are often overlooked on systems. However, Microsoft provides a free HIDS/HIPS application called Windows Defender. Defender can be configured to alert (HIDS) or quarantine applications (HIPS) that spawn processes.

Another free HIDS product is Open Source Tripwire, which catalogs system files by calculating a hash value and then monitors those files for changes. If a change occurs, Tripwire sends an alert to report the modification.

Another HIDS/HIPS system is OSSEC, owned by Trend Micro. This free product can be used to protect a large number of platforms by monitoring system files, performing log analysis, and detecting rootkit installation. OSSEC can simply report or be configured to perform active response and protect the system. It can be used independently on systems in a centrally managed configuration for a larger enterprise.

## Configuration Management

The goal of configuration management in IT is to ensure that systems do not get reconfigured unless it is needed, planned, tested, known by all affected, and fully approved. Configuration management is typically implemented through administrative policies, but can be enforced through monitoring systems that catalog the configuration of targeted critical systems and monitor these configurations for changes. This is similar to a component of HIDS/HIPS operations, such as the OSSEC and Tripwire tools.

## Managing Removable Media

A major threat to an organization is unauthorized disclosure of confidential information. Countermeasures that address this problem are referred to as Data Loss (or Leakage) Prevention (DLP) solutions. With small and unnoticed USB drives, a user can walk out of a secured office with tens or hundreds of gigabytes of sensitive and valuable data. The user might not even realize the severe risk and incredible loss to the organization just introduced, if the media gets lost or stolen. This removable media, ranging from the rare floppy disk, to CD-R and DVD-R media, to tens of GBs in USB thumb drives, smart phones, and PDAs, to hundreds of GBs on USB disk drives, must be carefully controlled at the network's endpoints.

This security measure should start with strict organizational policies and user security awareness training, but should also be managed using technical controls. In the Windows world, optical disk drives can be locked, and USB drives can be disabled by GPO. For additional control on Windows and Linux systems, third-party tools can be used to secure these removable media components. Tools like DeviceLock, InterGuard's DataLock, GFI's EndPoint Security, and Lumension's Device Control, to name a few, can be deployed to help to manage DLP on the endpoints of a network.

# Protecting the Network from the Endpoints

So far you've looked at how to secure the many nodes, or endpoints, on a network, with the objective of securing the endpoint system. The tools and techniques described work well on systems that are always on the network. But what should you do to protect the network when you add new systems to the network, or when you have transient systems connecting to your network off and on? One dirty machine can infect the entire network. There are a few tools and techniques you can use to protect your network from the endpoints, just in case.

## Network Access Control (NAC) or Network Access Protection (NAP)

A relatively new capability that can be used on a network is a system that will isolate new nodes from the core network and then interrogate the new node and establish its degree of security health. If the new node is healthy in a security sense, the node is allowed to connect to the core network. If the new node isn't healthy, the new node is quarantined and gets connected to a remedial segment where security applications and updates may be installed on the new node to improve its security health level.

A node's health is typically characterized by its OS patch status, whether it is running a reasonably configured firewall, and whether it is running AV software with recent signature updates. Some NAC systems can check for HIDS on a new node and can perform vulnerability scans on new nodes.

You must somehow initially isolate the new, incoming node. You generally do this by capturing the inbound new connection at a boundary chokepoint, like at a virtual private network (VPN) server, at the dynamic host configuration protocol (DHCP) server, or at an 802.1x port-based authentication device (often used to connect wireless networks to wired networks and with dial-in servers (RADIUS)), as well as on 802.1x switches.

Cisco Systems devices can include the components to implement NAC, if you're administering a Cisco house. Microsoft introduced their version called NAP in Server 2008. NAP is a free collection of features in Server 2008, but it requires some pretty substantial configuration and hardware (servers and possibly network devices) to get it up and running. Several vendors have entered the NAC market, like NetClarity's' Network Access Control Module.

Trusted Computing Group's open source project called the Trusted Network Connect (TNC) defines an architecture to validate endpoint security for multiple platforms and vendors' systems. PacketFence is an open source project that implements NAC. HUPnet (Helsinki University Public Network) is another free NAC tool that captures the new node on a NAT server boundary chokepoint. NetPass is an open source NAC that can be downloaded at SourceForge.net. FreeNAC is an open source NAC project that uses VLAN Management Policy Servers (VMPS) communicating with switches.

## Network Intrusion Detection Systems (NIDS) and Network Intrusion Protection Systems (NIPS)

Another mechanism that can be employed to help protect the network from dirty endpoints is the network IDS/IPS. These are often deployed inline at network chokepoints to monitor traffic and identify known attack signatures or traffic anomalies, like a spike in certain protocols. These can simply alert (NIDS) or respond (NIPS) to the detected malicious traffic on the network. The signature database requires regular updates. The behavior-based detection engine that watches for anomalies typically must be configured with *thresholds* (tolerance or deviation limitations) to trigger on.

These can be software add-ons for server-based proxy servers or firewall devices, but can also be hardware devices added to the network. NIPS products include the TippingPoint IPS, NSFocus NIPS, Cisco's Adaptive Security Appliance (ASA), Radware's Defense Pro, IBM's Proventia product line, McAfee's Network Security Platform, and Juniper Networks, which makes several different NIPS devices.

Free IDSs include the ever-popular Snort by Martin Roesch; EasyIDS (based on Snort); Untangle, which provides an open source NIDS; and the Bro NIDS, which is released under the BSD license. In addition, the Prelude Hybrid IDS, which includes a collection of IDS sensors, also performs a bit of correlation—like a mini, free SIEM system.

# IT Regulatory Compliance

Over the past 20 years, a range of regimes have arisen to regulate information systems. To date, each of these has arisen to protect a specific type of data for a specific business purpose: HIPAA for medical records, SOX for accounting records, and PCI for credit card information. As this book is going to print, the Cybersecurity Act of 2009 is being considered in Washington, DC, and whether this particular act or another like it passes into law, the time is approaching when broader regulations will come into play. These issues are discussed at length in Chapter 6, which we recommend you study. For our purposes here, we would like to provide just the underlying lessons to keep in mind regarding regulatory compliance.

All forms of compliance ask the fundamental question related to diligence:

*Have you taken the steps to perform your responsibilities to securely manage the information in your control—which a reasonable person would expect of someone in your position?*

In other words, if you had to defend your actions in this regard in front of a jury of your peers, would you be comfortable stating that you had used available best practices and sufficient effort to perform your duties? If you cannot imagine yourself making that statement with no more than the expected trepidation that such situations warrant, you should soon take the time to ponder the questions that could follow such a statement and what your answers might be.

While studying the specific regulations that apply to your environment—and/ or hiring consultants or advisors who are intimate with them—is the critical step in diligently performing your responsibility to your company regarding compliance, the techniques and technologies related to SIEM provide answers to the most stomach-churning rebuttal that you could be presented with in such a (hopefully imaginary) confrontation:

*Prove it.*

*You say you have followed best practices as far as separating sensitive and mundane data? You posit that the configuration of the security devices protecting your trove of customer data has been kept in alignment with the requirements of your industry? You want us to believe that there was no leakage of Personally Identifying Information (PII) from your network during the period in question?*

*Well, the court will be interested in looking at the evidence.*

Of the technologies discussed so far in this chapter, many are examples of the security best practices that you are likely to find mentioned in regulations that apply to your business. The security of the endpoint systems that your fellow employees use to access the sensitive data at the center of the compliance issue should be made reasonably secure from infection by viruses and other malware. You should probably make reasonable efforts at implementing technologies that will have a good chance of detecting an intrusion should one occur, and if you can reasonably detect sensitive data as it is leaking from your network, you should without a doubt deploy such safeguards.

But without a method of logging the ongoing activity of the devices that handle the data in question, the answer as to whether these safeguards have been continuously effective between any two points in time is an academic debate. As you sit awaiting the decision of those who are judging your diligence, in the aftermath of an incident where—despite your best efforts—the information in your care has been misused, the last thing you want the outcome to hinge on is an academic debate.

The number one tool that will provide you with some ability to answer confidently to the interrogation … er … "questioning" that is likely to follow any real or perceived breach of security at your site is, therefore, a log server. Being able to demonstrate via syslog records that the traffic across your network has followed the rules laid down by the regulation in question is your best first step in proving that you have done what is expected of you.

The reliability of your log server will be the most important feature when it comes to demonstrating diligence, and two features of log servers make for the best reliability: TCP transport and encrypted storage.

- **Reliable transport of syslog messages**   Syslog is, by default, delivered by the UDP mechanism—officially *User Datagram Protocol* but often also accurately described as the *Unreliable Delivery Protocol*—where the syslog client sends a syslog message to the syslog server but does not require a verification of receipt from the server. Upgraded syslog servers can use TCP transport for syslog messages, where the client and the server perform a "handshake" to confirm that each message has been accurately received. Failure to complete a handshake will result in the client system resending the original message.

- **Encrypted storage of syslog messages**   In systems where a syslog server performs some sort of encryption of its own database of stored messages, there is much higher likelihood that the data stored is unaltered from its original state. Therefore, should the occasion arise to use these stored messages to demonstrate diligence in regards to regulatory compliance, the value of this data will be much higher than if it were stored in a less secure format.

There are currently efforts underway through the IETF to establish standards for the signing of syslog messages, which would establish a foundation of reliability to the underlying structure of syslog. Future versions of syslog servers and clients that incorporate whatever standard may emerge from these industry efforts will be well worth considering for use in your shop.

## Compliance Tools

When contemplating how to address your regulatory compliance requirements, a great deal of value can be had by stepping back and gaining an understanding of the overall framework of the regulations you are subject to. Depending on the regime, the majority of the intent behind the regulation itself, as well as the activities needed to achieve and demonstrate compliance with it, may be outside the realm of SIEM, or even outside the realm of IT entirely. In any case, one of the best first steps in planning your compliance strategy is to leverage the hard work and experience of others who have trod the path before you. A simple search online for **compliance checklist** and the name or acronym of the regulation you are concerned with will usually amply reward you. There are copious amounts of preexisting documents that will both allow you to get a 30,000-foot perspective on what you are facing as well as help structure your efforts.

Many products are available to help with your compliance efforts, particularly around reporting and process management. You will find many of these referred to under the label of "Governance, Risk and Compliance" (GRC), a market segment that is growing rapidly as IT and information security regulation becomes more common. In this space, there are companies such as TruArx, CIO Controls, BWise

CornerstoneOnDemand, and others providing solutions from Software as a Service (SaaS) offerings to modular software frameworks to guide compliance efforts and produce reports.

As mentioned, while products in this space may provide functionality that is similar to a SIEM, they often also provide value to compliance efforts in addition to what a SIEM can provide. The TruArx suite of products, for example, touts functionality to define, manage, and distribute written policies. CIO Controls' solution allows for inputs as diverse as the post-processed output of a SIEM to the clipboard auditing of physical workspaces and business procedures. BWise offers a very modular structure of nine separate components including auditing and risk analysis tools as well as best practices templates gleaned from customer experience in different industries, while CornerstoneOnDemand offers a pure SaaS solution that centers on the human resources–oriented aspects of managing compliance efforts.

Some of the commercial products discussed in the log-management section earlier in this chapter provide various reporting capabilities that can be used to help with demonstrating compliance. Splunk, for example, includes both compliance checklists and a complete PCI application covering all 228 subitems of the PCI Data Security Standard.

In your efforts to address regulatory compliance, be prepared to either perform significant customization to your solution or pay to have someone else do the work. Even high-end SIEM systems with preinstalled compliance modules typically require nontrivial amounts of customization to address the specific regulatory compliance needs of any given company fully.

# Implementation Methodology

Each of the tools and technologies mentioned so far can be implemented independently and will provide measurable value in themselves. It is conceivable that savvy technical staff will be able to achieve a respectable level of integration among various components, at least at the reporting level. However, it must be made clear that people have gone to the effort to start companies that do nothing other than build and maintain SIEM products, and other companies have paid good money to buy these products and have them customized to fit their environments, for a very good reason:

*It takes an enormous amount of effort to create a fully featured SIEM.*

When you consider the range of different possible sources of event information that a SIEM may have to consume and normalize (every firewall formats syslog messages differently, for example), the volume of data that must be handled (easily billions of events per day), the complexity of correlation rules, and the effort needed to present results in a highly consumable manner, you begin to see how much effort you could expend on your home-grown SIEM without achieving a noticeable percentage of the function of a commercial product.

If you make some good choices early on and set your sights on appropriate goals, however, you can achieve a measure of success with free or low-cost tools and a reasonable amount of effort.

As mentioned earlier, some syslog server programs provide the ability to correlate events and trigger actions, such as sending emails under certain conditions or causing a script to run. When you know what you are looking for in advance, this can be a way of achieving a level of SIEM-like function with a single tool. With a moderate amount of effort, you may have the capability to enable many of the SIEM features you are hoping to achieve by carefully configuring a good logging solution.

By combining some of the pieces mentioned already in this chapter, you can achieve fairly rich SIEM features from a home-brewed solution. An open source syslog server combined with the SEC Perl script and a reporting tool like Groundwork gives you all of the basic tools to build a customized implementation, and a reasonable amount of online documentation is available from other people's efforts to give you a running start.

There is at least one fully featured open source SIEM available—OSSIM—that you can download and install for free from alienvault.com. This software can also be purchased with full support, the creators have founded a company called AlienVault that sells commercial versions of the technology, providing you a path from your home-built SIEM to a fully supported commercial solution. OSSIM has a very large user community so you won't be breaking new ground going this route. OSSIM is described in detail in Chapters 8 and 9.

# Tools Reference

Here are some tools to help in your quest to build your own SIEM. Some of these tools have been mentioned previously in this chapter.

| Type of Tool | Tool |
| --- | --- |
| Commercial SIEM vendors with entry-level products | EMC enVision, Cisco MARS, Q1Labs, eIQ Networks, AlienVault, Trigeo Network Security, NitroView ESM |
| Commercial logging products | Syslog-NG, Metalog, Msyslog, Sysklogd, Sysklogd-sql, Snare, Logcaster, InTrust, LogLogic |
| Open source event correlator | SEC (Simple Event Correlator) OSSIM (Open Source SIEM) |
| Reporting tools | Plixer International Scrutinizer, flow analyzer, Fluke Networks, NetFlow Tracker |
| Compliance tools | TruArx, BWise, CIO Controls, CornerstoneOnDemand |

# Summary

Although SIEM products are, in general, still thought of as tools for only larger organizations, that distinction is fading relatively quickly. Over the coming several years, the cost/benefit line between buying a commercial solution and building all or part of a SIEM from open source or commercial pieces will continue to blur, drawing more and more SME (small medium enterprise) organizations to adopt the technology using commercial products. In the meantime, there exists today a rich selection of tools that can perform all or some of the features of a full SIEM at little or no cost, other than the time and energy to learn, install, configure, and customize them. For the engineer who is qualified and enthused about the topic, it is a very good time to experiment with the available freeware tools and build a knowledge base that will serve well as this market matures.

As is the case in large enterprises, we have for better or worse entered the age where virtually all of the functions of information security required by organizations in the SME range are met by the features of a SIEM. Reporting, alerting, complying, auditing, and simply confirming that your security is staying the way you last configured it are all functions that operate best when there is a central source for log storage, analysis, and reporting. While the past decade or more of SME security has been primarily the realm of the firewall and antivirus, the coming decade will be the realm of the SIEM.

# CHAPTER 5 | The Anatomy of a SIEM

A SIEM can be compared to a complex machine in that a SIEM has several moving parts, each performing a specific job, that need to work properly together or else the entire system will fail. There are variations on the standard SIEM, with additional specific parts, but a simple SIEM can be broken down into six separate pieces or processes. These individual pieces are the source device, log collection, parsing/normalization of the logs, the rule engine, log storage, and event monitoring and retrieval. Each of these parts can work independently of the others, but without them all working together, the SIEM as a whole will not function properly.

# Source Device

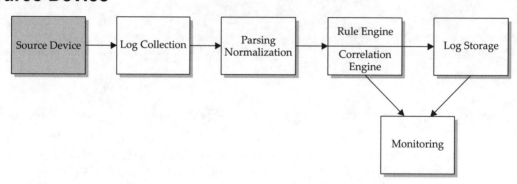

Most people don't realize the sheer volume of logs that are generated every day through their normal day-to-day activity. Just the act of a user opening a web browser and checking his or her email generates logs from a multitude of different devices: The user's computer, along with the various routers, switches, and firewalls that the user will have to traverse to reach the website, and then the website itself that holds the user's email inbox all generate logs that show exactly what the user did and where the user went. Depending on what it is you are looking for, some of this information is not very useful, and some of the information is very useful.

The first part of a SIEM is the source device that feeds information into the SIEM. A *source device* is the device, application, or some other type of data that you want to retrieve logs from that you then store and process in your SIEM. The source device can be an actual device on your network, such as a router, switch, or some type of server, but it can also be logs from an application or just about any other data that you can acquire. The source device is not an actual part of the SIEM, when looking at the SIEM as an application you purchase, but it is a vital piece of the overall SIEM process. All systems on your network are there to process some type of information for you and your users. Your web, email, and directory services servers all process information generated by your users. Without the source device and the information that these devices generate, your SIEM is just a nice application that does nothing.

Understanding what is present in your environment is going to be very important in your SIEM deployment. Knowing what sources you want to retrieve logs from in the early stages of establishing your SIEM architecture will save you a significant amount of headache and heartache. Since the source is the first stage of the SIEM process, if you can determine that right from the very beginning, it will make deployment that much easier when moving down the line and configuring the other pieces.

## Operating Systems

Microsoft Windows, variations of Linux and UNIX, AIX, Mac OS X, and so on—the list of the different types and flavors of operating systems being used in today's enterprises is pretty long. Most of these operating systems have different underlying technologies and are adept at performing different tasks, but one of the things that they all have in common is that they generate logs. These logs show all your system statistics: who logged in, who did what on the system, and basically anything else that you can think of that users do or that the operating system itself does. Chances are if you do something on a workstation or server, that information is being logged by the system; most people are unaware this even happens. The logs generated by an operating system about the system and user activity could be very useful when conducting incident response on a possible security incident or diagnosing problems and misconfigurations.

## Appliances

Most appliances are black box systems, where the system administrators do not have direct access to the underlying operating system, but instead only administer the device via a device-specific interface. This interface could be web-based, command-line based, or run through an application loaded on the administrator's workstation. The operating system that the network device runs may be a standard operating system, such as Microsoft Windows or a flavor of Linux, but it may be configured in such a way that you cannot use the standard operating system methods to examine the logs being generated.

A prime example of an appliance is a router or a switch. Network devices fall into the appliance category, because regardless of the vendor, you never really have direct access to the underlying operating system, you only have access to the command line or web interface used to manage the router. These devices store their logs internally on the system or can usually be configured to send logs out via syslog or FTP.

## Applications

Running on top of the operating systems are the applications that are used for a wide variety of functions. In a standard enterprise environment, you may have Domain Name System (DNS), dynamic host configuration protocol (DHCP), various types of web servers, various types of email systems, and a multitude of other types of applications. These application logs contain detailed information about the status of the application, such as system statistics, errors, or informational messages. Would some of these applications logs be useful to you? Are you required to maintain these logs to be compliant with a law or industry standard?

Besides off-the-shelf applications, you may be using home-grown or custom-built applications in your environment. These in-house developed applications may cause some difficulties when trying to bring them into your SIEM. The application may not be coded in a way that it generates logs or it may generate logs that are in its own proprietary format. This makes it difficult, but not always impossible, to bring these logs into the SIEM properly.

## Determining Needed Logs

Once you know what is present in your environment, you need to determine what you want logs from and why. You want to make sure to retrieve logs from sources that could provide you with important information in order to better secure your environment and possibly aid in diagnosing issues as they arise on your network. The other reason for log collection and retention is due to regulatory compliance, such as PCI and SOX, which requires you to maintain copies of logs from devices for a specific period of time.

One thing you might want to consider is that not all logs are needed from all devices. This mentality probably goes against most security professionals' way of thinking, because they believe if you have logs from everything you will know exactly what is going on the network. Although true, what you really want is to maintain a balance between the amount of logs you have versus the amount of logs that can be processed by the SIEM and then used by you. You will want to take into consideration the finite resources most administrators have to work with and maximize the effectiveness of your SIEM. More than likely, you will not have an unlimited amount of storage space or processing power, so you will need to determine what types of logs you need from what types of devices. For example, are you required to store DNS logs for operational support or regulatory compliance? These logs may give you some information that could help during specific security incidents, but will the cost of processing and storing them be worth it? Bottom line here is just because you can pull the logs from a device, doesn't mean you will really need to.

Another reason to be prudent with what device logs you bring into your SIEM, at least initially, is that by bringing too much into your SIEM at once, you can easily overwhelm your incident handlers with superfluous information and make it that much more difficult to detect real problems or security incidents in your environment. If you have so many logs coming into your device with nonuseful information, the key piece of information needed to determine an actual security event may be buried.

## Determining Needed SIEM Resources

Once you have determined what source devices you will want to retrieve logs from for your SIEM, you will want to evaluate how much of your SIEM resources to devote to the processing and storing of these logs. There are a few things to take into account when determining the required resources:

■ What is the source device's priority? How important is the data that you will be pulling from this device in order to maintain your overall security posture?

- What are the size of the logs generated during a specific period of time? This information will be used to determine how many resources this source will consume on your SIEM, specifically the amount of storage space that will be required to hold these logs.

- At what rate does this source generate logs? This information along with how large the logs for the source device are can be used to determine what the network utilization will be when collecting the source's logs.

- What are the network links like between the source and the SIEM?

- Do you need the logs in realtime or can you set up a batch process at specific times during the day?

The above information can very useful in generating an approximation of the required resources, but it will not give you an exact number. There are too many variables, however, to determine accurately the exact amount of resources you will need for your SIEM system. The number of users on your network, your environment's maintenance schedule, and numerous other variables can have a significant impact on the volume of logs generated per day. With the information you have gathered in hand, it is highly recommended that you add some buffer to your required resources, in case of an emergency. When something bad happens on your network, such as a worm outbreak or denial-of-service attack, there could be a significant increase in the number of logs being generated.

# Log Collection

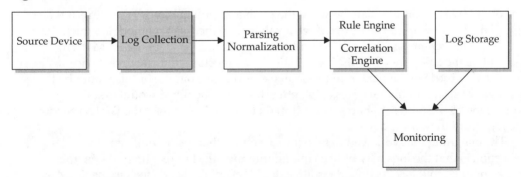

The next step in the device or application log flow is to somehow get all these different logs from their native devices to the SIEM. The actual mechanics of how the logs are retrieved vary depending on the specific SIEM that you are using, but at its most basic, the log collection processes can be broken down into two fundamental methods of collection: Either the source device sends its logs to the SIEM, which is called the *push method*, or the SIEM reaches out and retrieves the logs from the source device, which is called the *pull method*. Each of these methods has positives and negatives when used in your environment, but they both succeed in getting the data from the source device into the SIEM.

## Push Log Collection

The push method has the benefit of ease of setup and configuration at the SIEM. Usually you just need to set up a receiver and then point your source device at this receiver. A common example of this would be syslog. When configuring the source device using syslog, set up the IP address or DNS name of a syslog server on your network, and the device will automatically start sending its logs via syslog to the syslog receiver. In this example, the syslog server would be a receiver on the SIEM.

The advantages of using the push method for log collection, including ease of setup and configuration, come with some disadvantages, however. For example, using UDP syslog in your environment introduces some security vulnerabilities that you will want to take into consideration when designing your SIEM deployment. The inherent nature of using standard syslog over UDP means that you can never ensure that the packets reach their destination, since UDP is a connectionless protocol. If a situation occurs on your network in which utilization becomes extremely high, such as when a virus aggressively propagates throughout the network, you may not receive the syslog packets to your SIEM.

Another security issue that could arise is that if you do not put proper access controls on the SIEM receiver, a misconfigured system or malicious user could flood your SIEM with false information, making it harder for real events to float to the top. If this was an intentional attack against your SIEM, a crafty bad guy could falsify packets and inject garbage data into your SIEM. For this reason, understanding which devices are sending their logs to the SIEM is essential.

## Pull Log Collection

The easiest way to differentiate between the push and pull methods is looking at which end of the log flow initiates the act of retrieval. Unlike the push method, in which the source device sends logs to the SIEM without any interaction from the SIEM itself, the pull method requires the SIEM to initiate the connection to the source device and actively retrieve the logs from the source device. An example of this would be if the logs are stored in flat text files on a network share. The SIEM would establish a connection to the network shares using stored credentials and read the flat text file for the logs from the source device.

The one thing that you need to take into account when using pull-type log collection is that the logs may not be coming into the SIEM in real time. When you think about push log collection, the source device normally sends logs to the SIEM as soon as it generates them, but with a pull connector the SIEM needs to reach out to the source device and pull in the source device's logs. The pull log collection may be batched to run at certain time periods, which could mean every couple of seconds or every couple of hours. This time period is generally user configurable, but you will want to check the default configuration for your SIEM when setting up the pull log collection.

## Prebuilt Log Collection

Depending on the type of SIEM you will be using, there are usually prebuilt methods available for getting logs from specific devices or applications. For example, you may be able to point the SIEM at a server running an instance of an Oracle database, give the SIEM database credentials, and the SIEM will have the authentication methods and logic built-in to pull specific information from the Oracle database.

This example makes it very easy to get logs from the source to the SIEM, but what if you have a custom application that you want to receive logs from and there isn't a predefined method for log collection built in to your SIEM from that specific device or application? At this point, you really only have two options as to what you can do. The first is to change the logs from the source format into something your SIEM will understand. An example would be if you are running an application on a server and the application stores its logs in a flat file format on the server. You may be able to use a secondary application to read this flat file and send the logs off via syslog, which most SIEMs should be able to accept. In the case of a Windows server, another way to work with nonstandard logs would be to write logs to the Windows Event Log and pull the Windows Event Log into your SIEM.

## Custom Log Collection

With all the different devices in your network, you may have some sources that do not have standard log collection methods included in your SIEM. The second method of retrieving logs from a nonstandard source is to build your own method to collect the logs. Building your own log collection and parsing method can be labor and time intensive, but if done properly, it will mean the logs will be pulled directly from their native system into the SIEM. A benefit of creating your own collection method would be that you would have control over all the retrieval and parsing processes that take place. The flexibility to pull in logs that are not directly supported significantly expands the functionality of your SIEM. However, having control over the retrieval and parsing process may be a disadvantage. You need to understand the log format that you want to bring into the SIEM and also understand the fields available in your SIEM. This knowledge is necessary in order to properly parse the original log format and put the information into the proper fields so the SIEM will understand it.

## Mixed Environments

Most environments will have more than one device, which means you will need multiple methods of log collection. Let's say you have a Cisco ASA, a Snort IDS running on a RedHat Linux server, and a Windows 2003 Server that you need to pull logs from. The Cisco ASA will store logs internally so you will be able to use syslog to send the logs to another system. The Snort IDS can store its logs to a MySQL database while the RedHat server stores its logs in a flat file on the server itself. Then Windows

Server 2003 stores its logs in the events logs on the local server. These four different types of logs could require four different methods of log retrieval for your SIEM.

For the Cisco ASA and Linux server, you could have the source devices send their logs via syslog to a receiver in your SIEM. You would need to configure access into the MySQL database to retrieve the Snort IDS logs. Lastly you will want to pull the Windows event logs from Windows Server 2003. In this example, you need a minimum of three different types of connectors to collect the logs from these devices. You may be able to combine devices to use the same collection method and, therefore, minimize the number of methods being used for log collection.

## Parsing/Normalization of Logs

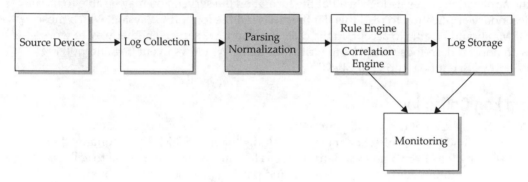

Now that the logs from the multitude of devices and applications in your environment are being forwarded to the SIEM, what happens next? At this point, the logs are all still in their native format so you have not really gained anything, other than a centralized repository for your logs. What needs to happen in order to make these logs useful in the SIEM is to reformat them into a single standard format that is usable by the SIEM. The act of changing all these different types of logs into a single format is called *normalization*. Each type of SIEM will handle the act of normalization in different ways, but the end result is to have all the logs, no matter what type of device or manufacturer, look the same in the SIEM.

These two systems, a Windows Event Log in Figure 5-1 and a Cisco ASA in Figure 5-2, both show a user logging into the device. The way various systems log similar actions is dependent on the vendor. As stated previously, you need to understand the format and details contained within the event. This is where the SIEM's log normalization really helps.

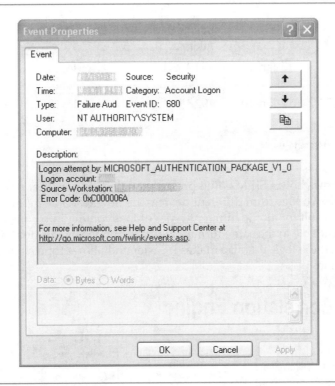

**Figure 5-1.** Windows event log

| Priority | Hostname | Message |
|---|---|---|
| Local4.Info | 192.168.1.1 | :%ASA-sys-6-605005: Login permitted from 192.168.1.18/42925 to INSIDE:192.168.1.1/ssh for user "aiel" |

**Figure 5-2.** Cisco ASA syslog message

| Time | Date | Source Device IP Address | Event Message | Event ID |
|------|------|--------------------------|---------------|----------|
| 22:54:53 CST | 17-Jan-10 | 192.168.1.1 | User login | ASA-sys-6-605005 |
| 22:54:53 CST | 17-Jan-10 | 192.168.1.18 | User login | Security: 680 |

**Table 5-1.** Correlated Events

Table 5-1 shows how a SIEM could present both logs to you after normalization. As you can see, the two logs from different devices are now readable in the same format. This is the end result for all the different types of logs coming into your SIEM; they all should be readable in the same format. Normalizing the events not only makes it simpler to read these logs, but also makes it easier and allows for a standard format of rule generation.

# Rule Engine/Correlation Engine

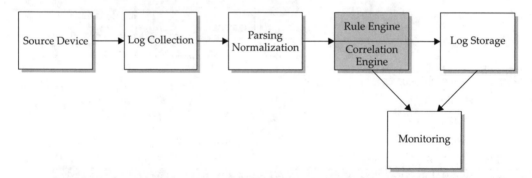

The rule engine expands upon the normalization of events from different sources in order to trigger alerts within the SIEM due to specific conditions in these logs. The method of writing the SIEM rules usually starts off fairly simply, but can become extremely complex. You typically write the rules using a form of Boolean logic to determine if specific conditions are met and examine pattern matching within the data fields.

Let's say you wanted to have an alert trigger off of anyone logging into a server with local administrator-level credentials, as shown in Figure 5-3. If you had a variety of different server OSs in your environment, you would need to look for different triggers in logs dependant on the OS that signals when a local administrator account

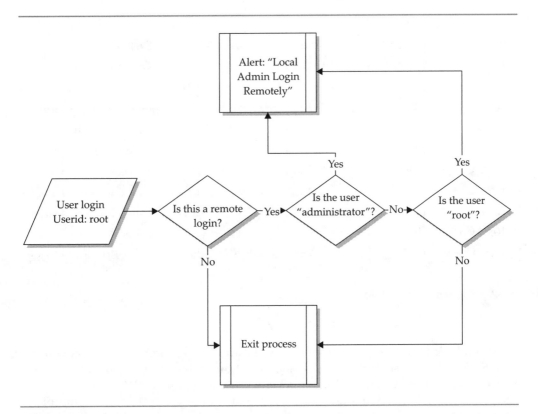

**Figure 5-3.**    Administrator login rules

was used to log in locally. For a Windows Server, you would want to look for the username "administrator" and on a Linux server, you would look for the username "root" to indicate that a local administrator had logged into the server. With a SIEM, instead of having multiple rules trigger for the different types of administrator logins, you can write a single rule using the SIEMs internal logic to trigger a rule based off of multiple variables.

## Correlation Engine

The correlation engine is a subset of the rule engine. What the correlation engine does is to match multiple standard events from different sources into a single correlated event. Correlation of standard events into a correlated event is done in order to simplify incident response procedures for your environment, by showing a single event that is triggered off of multiple events coming from various source devices.

| Time | Event Number | Source | Destination | Event |
|------|--------------|--------|-------------|-------|
| 10:10:01 CST | 1035 | 192.168.1.200 | 10.10.10.25 | Failed login to server |
| 10:10:02 CST | 1036 | 192.168.1.90 | 10.10.10.21 | Successful login to server |
| 10:10:03 CST | 1037 | 192.168.1.200 | 10.10.10.25 | Failed login to server |
| 10:10:04 CST | 1038 | 192.168.1.91 | 10.10.10.35 | Failed login to server |
| 10:10:05 CST | 1039 | 192.168.1.10 | 10.10.10.2 | Successful login to server |
| 10:10:06 CST | 1040 | 192.168.1.10 | 10.10.10.3 | Successful login to server |
| 10:10:07 CST | 1041 | 192.168.1.200 | 10.10.10.25 | Failed login to server |
| 10:10:08 CST | 1042 | 10.10.10.54 | 192.168.1.201 | Failed login to server |
| 10:10:09 CST | 1043 | 10.10.10.34 | 192.168.1.10 | Failed login to server |
| 10:10:10 CST | 1045 | 192.168.1.200 | 10.10.10.25 | Successful login to server |

**Table 5-2.**   Standard Events in SIEM

If you look at the example in Table 5-2, it shows multiple login events coming into your SIEM over a 10-second period. By looking at this, you can see login failures and login successes from several sources to several destinations. If you look closely, you can see a pattern of a single source failing to log in to multiple destinations, multiple times, and then all of the sudden you see a successful login. This could possibly be a brute-force attempt against that destination server, but unless you have a really good memory, you may have forgotten that the first event happened.

Let's expand upon this example and say that instead of just 10 events in a 10-second period, you have 1000 events in 10 seconds. Manually picking out the events from all the background noise in the system that could show a possible malicious event that spans multiple events is extremely difficult. You need a way to remove all the unrelated information in your logs and just track the specific events that could indicate a malicious event spread across multiple events.

For the possible brute-force compromise, you would need to logically match up a number of failed login events with the same source address to the same destination address and then a successful login to the destination server from the original source over a specific timeframe, as shown in Figure 5-4. This is what the correlation engine does for the SIEM: It groups individual events, which can make up a part of a possible malicious incident, into a single event displayed on the console of an operator monitoring your environment. So, instead of having to scour through your logs attempting to find individual events and the relationship among those events, you can use the SIEMs built-in logic to gather your network events into a correlated event.

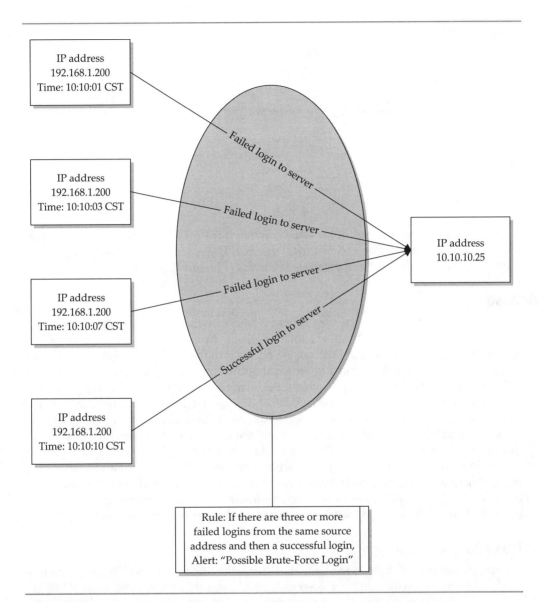

**Figure 5-4.**   Correlated event example

Taking the events from Table 5-2, you would need to write a rule to trigger from the events that make up login/logoff activities. The logic for this correlated rule might look something like the pseudo-code shown here, depending upon the SIEM system your organization uses.

```
If [(failed logins >= 3) and then (Successful Login)] from the same source
within 20 seconds = Possible Brute Force Compromise
```

# Log Storage

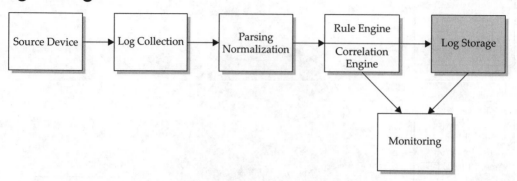

To work with the volumes of logs that come into the SIEM, you need a way to store them for retention purposes and historical queries. There are typically three ways that the SIEM can store its logs: in a database, a flat text file, or a binary file.

## Database

Storing logs in a database is the way most SIEMs store their logs. The database is usually a standard database platform such as Oracle, MySQL, Microsoft SQL, or one of the other large database applications being used in the enterprise. This method allows for fairly easy interaction and retrieval of the stored data because the database calls are part of the database application. Performance should also be fairly good when accessing the logs in the database, depending on what hardware the database is running on, but the database application should be optimized to run with the SIEM.

Using a database is a good solution for log storage, but a few issues may arise depending on how the SIEM implements its database. If your SIEM is an appliance, you will normally not have a lot of interaction with the underlying database, so provisioning and maintenance is typically not an issue. But if the SIEM is running on your own hardware, you may need to administer the database yourself. This can become challenging if you do not have a qualified DBA in your environment.

## Flat Text File

A flat text file is just a standard text file that stores the information in a fairly human-readable format. The file needs to be some type of delimitated file, be it comma, tab, or some other character, so the information can be parsed and read properly. This storage method is not used very often, because it is not designed to scale to large environments. The other issue you will run into is performance. The act of writing to and reading from the text file is going to be slower than the other methods.

You don't really get a lot of positives when using a flat text file to store your data, but it does make it easy for external applications to access this data. If your logs are stored in a text file, it is not difficult to write your own code to open the file and retrieve the information to be used in another application. Another benefit is that since the text file is in a human-readable form, it makes it very easy for an analyst to search through the file. You can open the file and use GREP or some other text file searching tool to pull out the information you are looking for without opening a management console.

## Binary File

The binary file format is a file using a custom format to store binary information that is used only by the specific SIEM to store information. The SIEM is the only application that knows how to read and write to this highly proprietary file.

# Monitoring

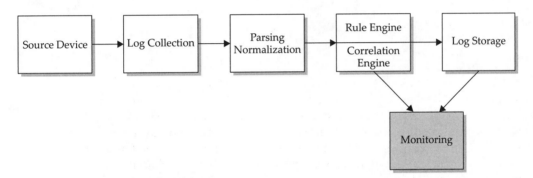

The final stage in the anatomy of a SIEM is the method of interacting with the logs stored in your SIEM. Once you have all the logs in the SIEM and the events have been processed, you need a way to do something useful with the information—otherwise the logs are just in the SIEM for storage purposes. A SIEM will have an interface console, which will either be web-based or application-based and loaded on your workstation. Both interfaces will allow you to interact with the data stored in your SIEM. This console, be it web- or application-based, will also be used to manage your SIEM.

This interface into the actual SIEM application will allow your incident handlers or system engineers a unique view into your environment. Normally, in order to view the information that the SIEM gathers, incident handlers or engineers would have to go to the different devices and view the logs in their native formats. The SIEM makes viewing and analyzing all these different logs much easier because the SIEM normalizes the data. Within the SIEM's management and monitoring console, you will be able to develop the content and rules that will be used to pull out the information from the events being processed. This console is going to be your main way of interfacing with the data that is stored in your SIEM. Think of it as the interface into a database, where you can use the SIEM's internal language to query the data stored there.

# Summary

A SIEM is composed of many parts, each doing a separate job. Remember, each of these systems can run independently of the others, but without them all running in unison, you will not have an effective SIEM. Depending on the system you are using, there may be more pieces added to that specific SIEM, but each SIEM will always have the basic underlying systems as described in this chapter. By understanding each part of the SIEM, what each piece does and how it works, you will be able to manage your SIEM effectively and troubleshoot issues as they arise.

# CHAPTER 6 | Incident Response

A s an organization and its IT department mature in their level of sophistication, a natural and needed extension of the security program is an incident response program. Typically, once an organization has established itself as being capable of sustaining its operations and satisfying its primary objectives (like making a profit), management turns toward protecting the valuable assets that have been developed to allow that level of success. Of course, firewalls and ACLs are probably already in place within the IT system for basic levels of protection, but what about protection from those sudden and unexpected security breaches? Herein lies the need for an incident response (IR) program.

# What Is an Incident Response Program?

The IR program is a subset of the organization's overall security program that deals with those unexpected violations to the policy defined as "acceptable and expected use" of the IT systems. The primary goal of an IR program is to develop a team, infrastructure, and procedures to identify security breaches quickly and then to adjust the IT environment rapidly to minimize or halt the losses of IT assets, while also minimizing the impact on the organization's primary objectives (like keeping the revenue-generating functions operational). Ideally, this means the IR team must stop the security breach or attack without slowing or shutting down the organization's main functions.

One possible, but usually undesirable, response to a security breach is to pull the plug on all systems. This certainly stops the attack and any losses to IT systems, but it also blocks the organization's ability to perform. During an extreme incident, where losses are reaching critical proportions, this response may be considered and may be the correct response. But with this as a response, the bad guy has just performed the ultimate denial of service (DoS) attack, so, in most cases, a bit more balanced and measured response is required. Defining and managing this balanced response is where the need for a carefully planned and documented IR program comes into play.

## Grown from the Security Program

Whether it is a legal or regulatory requirement or the need to maintain the organization's ongoing profitability, protecting the organization's valuable information assets is vital. Upper management usually drives the development of a security program. The security program is typically defined by written policies and procedures that communicate the organization's rules and establish the framework for implementing and managing the organization's desired security posture.

When an information system is being developed for initial functionality, for most, that development includes the obvious and basic security components. These basics include a current diagram of the network, firewalls at least at the boundary connections to the outside world, user accounts, access control lists (ACLs) on network resources, antivirus protection, regular patching of operating systems and applications, and so on.

In some cases, the initial network design may even include security devices like intrusion detection/protection systems (IDS/IPS) and vulnerability scanners. But the security structure is largely homogenous, generally protecting everything at a common security level. Although a good start, it certainly doesn't take into consideration the range of values that different assets can have. To protect the confidentiality, integrity, and availability of the organization's valuable information assets, one of the first steps is to understand which assets are the most valuable, warranting the highest level of protection. The following steps are typically taken in developing this understanding of each asset's value:

1. *Identify all information assets.* Assets can be very different in their nature. One asset may be a MS Word document, a file that contains the secret sauce recipe for example. Another asset is the server that holds this file, along with other files. Another asset to consider is the layer 2 switch that forms the backbone of the segment that hosts the file server. The server room, with its air temperature and humidity controls, its clean and redundant power supplies, and its secure access system is yet another valuable information asset that needs to be considered. Develop an inventory of all assets that make up the IT system and support the objectives of the organization.

2. *Assign value to each asset.* The value of the asset isn't just what you paid for it. The value includes factoring in delivery and installation costs and replacement cost (what you paid for an asset two years ago may be different than what it would cost today). But that's still not all you need to consider when assigning a value to the asset. You need to consider the impact on the organization if the asset were lost in one way or another. If a particular server were to catastrophically fail, would production stop? For how long? How much revenue would the organization lose if production stopped for that period of time until repairs could be completed and production is resumed? This is one component of identifying an IT asset's value. How much would the company lose if the secret sauce recipe were to be exposed, stolen by the competition? What would be the fines, penalties, and lawsuits if a database were stolen that contained data on all of your customers and employees, including personally identifiable information (PII—used by bad guys to commit identity theft) and medical records? It is just a database file, but it could be worth tens or hundreds of millions of dollars.

3. *Categorize each asset to simplify the protective hierarchy design.* A comprehensive valuation of all information assets is a large project and may result in an inventory of thousands of items, each with potentially a different value. To simplify the resulting security structure being designed to protect these assets at an appropriate level, create several categories (typically three to five different categories) that represent various levels of value and required protection for assets in that class. For example, instead of having 8,000 different levels of protection, one for each different valued asset, you define four categories, or security zones, to design security systems for in which you distribute the

8,000 assets, for instance, critical, protected, restricted, and public. Using this example, you can design your network security structure to include the four security levels, or security zones, to store and process data for the matching classification.

This way, as the enterprise matures and develops, the IT security program has an established foundation to rely on. The security program may already have a developed disaster recovery and business continuity program. As the security program grows and matures, a security team and security operations center (SOC) will likely be created to assist with the security aspects of the information system's design and monitoring. The IT assets, and their value, are known. You have a network diagram with some security systems in place. You may even be blessed with a system to monitor all of those systems—a Security Information and Event Management system (SIEM). You will put all of these resources to good use as you develop your IR program.

## Where the IR Program Fits In

The security team will be required to deal with a vast amount of information being fed into the security operations center, even if that SOC is one guy monitoring the IT systems from one workstation. Input comes from security systems, system logs, end users, and even the helpdesk. This inbound information will need to be sorted with regard to its significance relative to the organization's state of security. There are generally five basic categories used to classify information items and events flowing into the SOC:

- **Normal operations**  Even when things are working as they should, systems are busy doing their routine and legitimate work and writing routine action logging items into the system event logs.

- **Security events**  Items that may be unusual and warrant a little closer look or have the potential for escalation to security incident. The goal of the SOC team member is try to identify and rule out false-positive security events—things that may look unusual, but after inspection, do not pose increased security risk to the organization. The SOC team member may also be responsible for resolving low-scale, true-positive security events, like a simple, single instance malware detection alert on a workstation. Even this will trigger some level of incident response, like running a full AV scan on the affected system and focused monitoring of the organization to verify that it is a single instance event. But a low-risk, easily handled item like this does not constitute a full-blown security incident.

- **Security incidents**  Events that cannot be ruled out as false-positive security events or resolved easily get escalated to security incident status and to the IR team. The first job of the IR team member is to try to verify the event as a false-positive and consider refining the alerting mechanisms. If the event cannot be classified as a false-positive, the incident response system is set into motion. More details on what that means will follow in this chapter.

- **Disasters**   Commonly considered a security incident that renders one or more critical organizational functions inoperable for one day or more. Disasters might include a flood, fire, or earthquake that disables production for a period of time, from a few days to a few weeks, but the organization is often able to recover.

- **Catastrophes**   Commonly considered a security incident that destroys one or more critical organizational functions. Catastrophes might include a flood, fire, or earthquake that destroys a critical component like a primary production facility required for production. Organizations are often unable to recover from catastrophes.

Remember that security is tasked with protecting the confidentiality, integrity, and availability of an organization's valuable information assets. Events like power outages and fires, while not exactly security breaches like theft or unauthorized access, can be considered security incidents since they can affect the availability of information assets.

# How to Build an Incident Response Program

Senior management recognizes the need for a certain level of protection for the valuable systems and processes that keep the organization functional. Whether it is to protect trade secrets and keep the shareholders happy, protect the identities of government agents working abroad, or comply with government or industry laws and regulations, the need for an IR program becomes apparent at some point as an organization matures. At this point, senior management develops a comprehensive security program in the form of written documents to define the program: policies, procedures, standards, baselines, and guidelines. These written documents are collectively referred to as *policies* throughout this chapter. The IR program gets its mandate and structure through these policies.

The components of an IR program include these policies, a team of individuals with some specialized skill sets, a collection of security tools, an understanding of the current network design, and an understanding of the inventory of information assets and their value, as described earlier in this chapter. Since no IT system is ever static but constantly in a state of change, the IR team must also remain aware of proposed and current changes to the systems. Finally, the IR team must understand the socio/political aspect of their role as the team interacts with other teams or departments within the organization.

## The IR Team

The IR team, often referred to as a *Computer Incident Response Team (CIRT)* or *Computer Security Incident Response Team (CSIRT)*, is made up of personnel with a broad range of specialized skills. Realize that during a security breach, the organization is experiencing loss and response times must be short. The IR team is often receiving only fragments of information; some of the information that appears significant is a part of the breach, and other pieces of information that appear equally significant are often not related, potentially causing misdirection. In spite of being fed only spotty and often misleading information, bold conclusions and decisions must be made and acted upon quickly. Wrong decisions could cost the organization dearly. For these reasons, it is often the most talented and seasoned individuals with the various required skill sets who are drafted to participate on the IR team.

Following is a sample list of roles, or professional disciplines, that are commonly required on a well-developed incident response team. Each role may require one or more individual to cover the load (scale, location, etc.), and skills required (Windows, Linux, routers, ERP systems, DBA, etc.). In smaller organizations, one person may be tasked with multiple roles. There may be need for cross-training and backup personnel to handle situations when one or more IR team members are unavailable.

The core IR team typically includes:

- **CISO**    The decision maker and liaison with the rest of the organization's management team.
- **IR team lead**    Strong management and decision-making skills, coupled with security and network engineering skills, knowledge of the organization's IT network and hierarchy (org chart), and an understanding of the value and location(s) of the IT assets.
- **Security professional/Security analyst**    Skilled with security systems, network systems, and attack tools and methodologies. This guy or gal runs the SIEM system.
- **Network engineer/architect**    The guy with the operational "big picture" of the organization's IT system.
- **System engineer**    Should have specialized skills on various hardware, operating systems, applications, and/or devices.
- **Human resources**    In case the incident involves misdoings by an employee.
- **Legal department**    In case the incident introduces legal ramifications, including potential for prosecution, compliance or legal violations, or has contractual implications.
- **Compliance officer**    In case the breach causes or risks compliance failure or triggers new compliance requirements.

Supplemental or optional IR team members may be drawn into assisting with an incident as necessary. These supplemental roles may be employees or outside contractors and include the following:

- **Forensic investigator**    Skilled in digital forensics and forensic methodologies, including chain of custody and search and seizure procedures, aligned to present findings and evidence in court
- **Developer/hacker**    Skilled in scripting, coding, compiling, and decompiling, along with knowledge of attack tools and methodologies
- **Helpdesk**    To assist with coordination of activities regarding end users and endpoint systems

■ **Other representatives from critical departments or factions of the organization**   Knowledge of the priorities, assets, procedures, personnel, and structure of their respective areas

The members of this team are generally provided advanced and more frequent training to keep their skill sets high and well polished, and are often compensated at a higher rate, at least partially due to the potential 24/7 responsibilities they are subject to.

Some of these roles can be satisfied using internal personnel and skills; sometimes it makes sense to contract certain skill sets on an "as needed" basis. Maintaining the latest training and tools for these highly specialized skill sets can be very expensive. If your IR team does plan on using contracted labor during an incident, the contractor or firm should be predefined, with signed agreements concerning confidentiality, service level, and pricing already in place. In the face of an incident, you don't want to get caught up in having to locate a professional with the required skill set and immediate availability, and then having to negotiate and execute a contract before you can put those skills to work.

## Useful Tools for the IR Team

The IR team is often an exception to many of the security policies targeting the average user. This team will often need to perform unscheduled network and system scanning and probing, and will often require tools that would be otherwise disallowed on enterprise computing systems. The tools often used and needed by IR team members include:

■ **SIEM system**   The Cadillac security tool, for log aggregation and correlation against standard and customized rule sets.

■ **IDS/IPS systems**   Both wired and wireless. Used to detect known attacks based on previously seen attack signatures and to detect anomalous behavior on the IT systems. The IPS is configured to implement specific defenses against recognized attacks.

■ **Configuration monitoring systems**   To send an alert when a system configuration is modified without proper notice and authorization.

■ **Sniffers**   To perform packet captures.

■ **Scanners**   To footprint and fingerprint networks and remote systems.

■ **Forensic tools**   To manage forensic investigations, recover deleted, hidden, and encrypted content, search remote file systems for sensitive data like PII, and to collect digital evidence, when appropriate.

■ **Hacking tools**   Tools used by the bad guys to bypass system security and gain unauthorized access, like password crackers and exploit databases. This optional and controversial collection of tools must be carefully managed and focused, when allowed in the enterprise. These tools should only be used in carefully chosen situations and only after receiving upper-management approval.

■ **Antivirus and antispyware tools**    From a different vendor than what is used on the IT systems (using a different signature database increases the chances of early detection of malware).

■ **Access to administrative consoles of many systems**    To verify (and potentially adjust) configuration attributes. (Security personnel are often disallowed from having administrative access to systems, but they often are provided read access to the administrative consoles of critical systems. In other words, you can monitor the system, but you can't change it. You'll need to tell someone else to make any required changes.)

■ **Alternate connectivity to the Internet**    To bypass enterprise firewalls and proxy systems. Used to access potentially blacklisted websites to research attacker tools and techniques.

■ **Known clean systems**    Hardened, fully patched with fresh antivirus and antispyware definitions and a limited number of services and applications other than the required monitoring and analysis tools (running services and applications introduce vulnerabilities into the system). Bad guys often try to disable the functionality of monitoring systems to remain undetected. These IR team systems need to resist those malicious attempts.

## Socio/Political Aspects

The security / IR teams have very different mandates than other departments within the organization. The mandate and mentality of production and most management is usually "Maintain availability of the production systems at all costs." The mandate and mentality of security teams is "If it is not secure, disconnect it from the IT system." These opposing creeds tend to keep most personnel within the organization estranged from the security team personnel.

Expect that, as a member of the security or IR team, you will not be met warmly by the majority of other personnel. This often translates to resistance and confusion when you must closely and suddenly interact with members of other departments. To minimize the complications and diffuse any tensions, be sure you have the appropriate management approvals before contacting the networking team and telling them to down one or more interfaces on the core router, for example. Take your recommendation through the proper channels, and have those approval details in hand when making your request.

## The Price Tag

Ouch. All these skilled professionals, all these tools, and all the advanced training—obviously staffing and maintaining this IR team will not be cheap. For the commercial sector, the price tag for the IR program must all be cost justified. It is a difficult challenge trying to prove an IR program's worth to accounting types who are usually programmed to only understand one thing: "How much money will this make for the company?"

Facing that mentality, the IR team will never be properly funded, potentially crippling the efforts and effectiveness of the IR program itself. The security program, and its subset, the IR program, must be presented to show not the revenue and profits that the programs will generate, but the money they will save the organization by minimizing or eliminating losses. The same asset valuation procedures used previously can be used here to show the losses an organization can incur if one, and only one, security breach is successful. Detail the losses the organization will incur if production is shut down for 24 hours due to a successful DoS attack. Show the costs to legally defend the organization if the customers decide to file a class action lawsuit for failure to protect their PII when a database gets exposed. Show the business your company will lose if the competition learns your trade secrets through a compromise and can now produce products as good and inexpensively as yours. In the commercial world, you must justify the cost of the IR program by showing how much money you can save the organization through loss avoidance.

Justifying the price tag for the IR program is not so much a problem in the government world. When human lives are at stake, you can't cost justify. When you are protecting the balance of a nation's economy, you can't cost justify. The government is held to a higher standard and simply must be prepared for IR. Government IT systems are often the most developed and sophisticated with mature and well-exercised incident response programs.

# Security Incidents and a Guide to Incident Response

Each security incident is unique, requiring its own formula for resolution. But most incidents have several stages and actions in common.

On a typical midsized network, events can occur several thousand times per second. These events are the logging systems of every computer, device, and application of interest that are documenting their normal operations. Security systems, such as centralized antivirus, IDS and IPS systems, vulnerability scanners, and configuration management systems, are constantly monitoring and spitting out alerts. This massive volume of event information, of course, is impossible for a human to review and interpret to identify unusual, aberrant, or clearly noncompliant behavior or actions. The SIEM system is designed to do just this for the security operations team. Whew!

## A Typical Escalation Flow to Security Incident

When unusual, aberrant, or clearly noncompliant actions are detected in a SIEM system, they are escalated to security events. Security events are also reported to the security operations team (SOT) by end users or system administrators who spot something unusual and report it, or by helpdesk personnel who recognize security issues while resolving something in the general user population. These security events are often assigned to Tier One Security Operations, or *Tier One SecOps*. Tier One SecOps performs a limited investigation of the event in an attempt to rule the event as a false-positive security event; it may be an unusual event, but it does not increase the risk of a security breach. If the event can be ruled a false-positive, it is typically documented, with a potential to make adjustments to the filtering system(s) that sent the alert based on the false-positive event, so it doesn't get alerted again.

If the event can be ruled as a true-positive, but a routine, low-threat security event, like a limited and mild virus infection that can be resolved easily by well-exercised helpdesk procedures, Tier One SecOps may trigger the resolution and then additionally monitor to confirm the small scale, limited risk characteristic of the event. (In the case of the small scale, one-off virus infection, be sure the end user is advised as to the possibility that any recent backups, shadow copies, and restore points may also be infected. All external storage devices that the user has accessed from the infected system, such as USB drives and removable media, should also be scanned and verified as clean before using them on any system.)

If the event cannot be ruled a false-positive and isn't easily resolved by Tier One SecOps, the event gets escalated to Tier Two SecOps where a more detailed investigation can be performed. Tier One must get back to the business of monitoring the enterprise via the SIEM system. Tier Two SecOps repeats the actions of Tier One, only allocating more time to review the event in greater depth and detail, once again attempting to prove the event a false-positive. Tier Two will often increase the level of monitoring to acquire additional information about the event and often consults additional external resources targeting malware, vulnerabilities, and current malicious activities being reported on the Internet. If the event remains questionable or can be confirmed as a true-positive security incident, the security event is escalated to the IR team.

One of the first actions an IR team member will perform after being notified of a security event is to understand as much as is known about the event—get a summary from Tier Two of who, what, when, where, and how. Because some time has passed since the first alert, has there been any change in the system? Has the event grown in scope? Are any similar events occurring elsewhere within the IT systems? Ideally, there will be no indication of growth, and the IR team member still hopes to be able to rule the event a false-positive.

Now it's time for the IR team member to begin his or her investigation. The IR team member will also consult additional external resources targeting malware, vulnerabilities, and current malicious activities being reported on the Internet, triggering further monitoring and perhaps additional team members into action in an attempt to rule this event as a false-positive or to declare an incident and sound the alarms!

## Finally! An Incident

If and when a security event gets escalated to security incident, the dynamics and demeanor of the environment changes dramatically. One of the first actions taken when a security incident is declared is to contact the appropriate personnel on a prescribed Notify List. This may start with a call to SecOps to fire up all monitoring systems and focus on the area where the event occurred. This call is usually followed quickly by an initial report to the CISO and then to the immediately available IR team personnel. The call list may continue and include emergency services to be called when appropriate, such as fire and medical. The affected department and location management personnel may be contacted, as well as service providers as appropriate, such as your ISP or the vendors and support personnel of affected systems.

The actions to be taken typically include:

1. Implement all relevant monitoring systems focused on the area of the event. The goal is to identify the history, behavior, scope, growth, target(s), source(s), assets, losses and potential losses, and other changes related to the event. You will also want to identify whether the attack is from an internal or external source, whether the nature of the attack is targeted or random, and whether the attack is being performed manually (usually slower) or programmatically (often events occur very fast).

2. Determine initial estimates of these parameters related to the event, and advise the CISO.

3. Identify theories (to be verified or dismissed if proven incorrect), and propose possible initial responses to stop or mitigate losses. Because of only receiving small fragments of information at this early stage of the incident, many of your initial theories will be incorrect. This is natural. Coordinate IR team members to investigate and research, as necessary, to confirm theories or prove the theories incorrect, to develop understanding of the incident, and to identify appropriate potential countermeasures.

4. Pursue approval to take action believed to be helpful in stopping or reducing the losses. Escalate the severity of those responses as the severity of the attack and the losses increases.

5. Continue with the heightened monitoring and ongoing research and investigations.

6. Prove or disprove new theories, and adjust the recommended and approved countermeasures accordingly. The goal is to stop the losses (stop the bleeding), and restore basic functionality (stabilize the patient). Countermeasures that get approved and implemented must be carefully monitored to verify their effectiveness. Adjust those countermeasures as necessary.

7. Report the incident status regularly to the CISO.

8. As correct countermeasures are put into place and adjusted, with losses stopped and system functionality returned, the goal is to return to normal operations, signifying the end of the incident.

9. After normal status has been restored, a final report to management should be generated summarizing the incident timeline, conclusions reached, correct actions, incorrect actions, affected systems, current status, and a summary of known and estimated losses. Finally, the report should include a summary of recommended new or reconfigured countermeasures intended to mitigate whatever vulnerability was exploited to produce the incident in the first place.

These are the basic and common functions that typically occur during the course of a generic security incident.

## Incident Response Procedures

Most events that could escalate to the level of security incident can be categorized into one of about six different classifications. You might consider that events that cannot fit into the following six types of incidents get lumped into a seventh, generic "Other" category. Each organization must develop their own customized procedures to address systematic incident handling and accommodate their individualized and specialized resources and security concerns. Even when using your custom procedures, the nature of most incidents is difficult to predict, so be prepared to recognize the need to adjust these procedures when the situation warrants. Make the proposed adjustments to procedures only after acquiring the CISO's approval to do so.

Sample descriptions, along with logic and procedure flow diagrams for the seven categorized incidents, are detailed as follows:

- Loss or theft of IT device
- Malware outbreak
- Inappropriate use
- Unauthorized access
- Unauthorized disclosure
- Willful attack
- Other security incident

### 1. Loss or Theft of IT Device

Loss of devices could include single or multiple device failure (availability) for any number of reasons, including power outage or a fire in the facility. However, this type of loss is usually planned for in the disaster recovery plan, is handled by the disaster recovery team, and often doesn't constitute a security incident. A security incident loss or theft of device commonly occurs through break-in, or through loss of portable devices, like laptop computers, USB drives, or even optical or backup media. If the computer was a laptop, consider whether additional devices were also stolen within the laptop case, such as USB drives, optical media, and authentication token devices. Disable all accounts and connectivity associated with the lost or stolen devices. Monitor these disabled accounts and connectivity for attempted access. Attempted access after the loss may lead you to the device. If the missing device is a smart phone or PDA, many of these devices on enterprise systems include a remote wipe functionality to allow you to purge all data contained on the remote and missing device.

If any of the lost or stolen devices are recovered, consider them to be tampered with and compromised: *Do not allow their use on the network.* These recovered systems should be returned to SecOps for careful analysis. These systems should be scanned for viruses and other malware, signs of tampering (configuration changes), or even rootkits. If properly handled, even a compromised system can be isolated from all network connectivity (air-gapped), and the user's data files may be recovered after being carefully scanned and confirmed clean. The data on the missing device, even when returned, should be considered to be exposed since the data was not in the control of the organization for some period of time, so a compliance officer should be involved in the analysis and report.

The losses incurred primarily include disclosure of sensitive data, in addition to the loss of the substantially less valuable hardware or media itself. Figure 6-1 shows the logic and flow of a common response to this type of incident.

## 2. Malware Outbreak

A malware outbreak does not include small-scale virus detection that can be handled by routine Tier One SecOps or helpdesk procedures. A malware incident is usually triggered when some threshold is reached, such as when a predefined number of systems is detected as having the same or similar virus or malware. A critical component of a multisystem malware infection response is to identify if, how, and how rapidly the infestation is growing. Self-propagating worms can spread like wildfire and require constant, real-time monitoring and appropriate adjustment to your response. You must understand the transmission method used by the malware and interrupt that process. Interview users of the infected systems to verify that one or more of the documented transmission methods coincide with user actions and the behavior of the infected system. Containment actions could include shutting down systems, segments, or entire locations. Response is scaled up as necessary to contain and eradicate the infection. Remember that typically all response actions must be approved by the CISO and coordinated with other affected department heads.

Eradication typically requires research to identify the type of infection (which virus or worm your systems are infected with) and the eradication mechanism(s) typically documented on many antivirus and malware support sites. Eradication may require performing one or more recovery actions, like updating signatures, patching the operating system or applications, downloading and executing a specific malware removal kit, correcting registry and other configuration components, and deleting infected files. Eradication tools and techniques should be tested on a small scale before deploying them enterprise-wide. Any eradication procedures must be monitored to verify their effectiveness at completely removing the malware and its malicious artifacts.

You will want to consider any increased vulnerability and exposure of sensitive data as a result of a successful infection. Often malware will plant back doors on systems for later unauthenticated access, or alter the configuration of a system to entrench, disallow patching or signature updates, or to steer the system to malicious sites by altering the hosts file or DNS configuration. It is possible that before removal of the infected system from the network, data may have been accessed and transmitted to another system. Often a review of the logs of relevant systems is warranted to understand what sensitive information may, or may not, have been exposed.

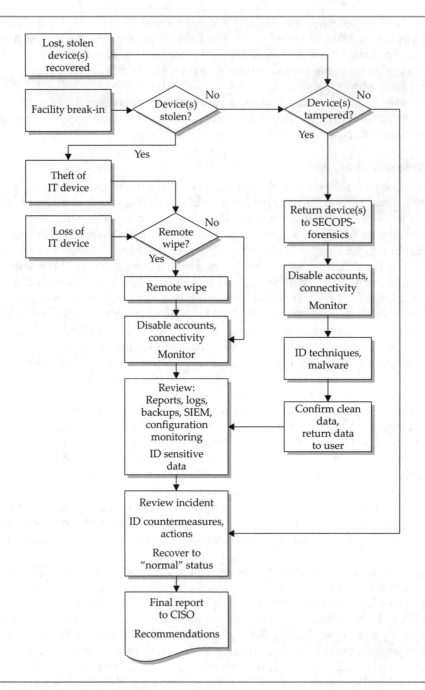

**Figure 6-1.** Loss or theft of IT device

Consider the possibility that backups from the infected systems are themselves infected. Scan backups to verify they are free from infection, or disallow their restoration onto any system. Disable volume shadow copies and disable system restore functions, again with the consideration that they, too, may be infected. All external devices and removable media that has been connected to the infected systems must be scanned and declared clean before you should allow their use on any system.

Losses incurred by malware infections range from just being a nuisance to complete system and multisystem compromise. It doesn't get much more critical than this. A sample incident response procedure for a malware outbreak is provided in Figure 6-2.

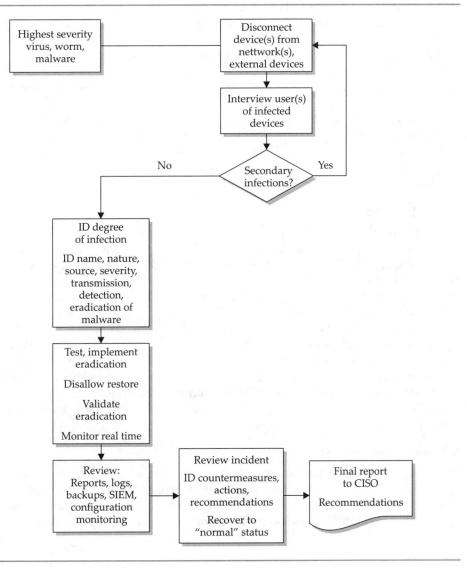

**Figure 6-2.**   Malware outbreak

### 3. Inappropriate Use

Misuse occurs when authorized users perform actions that violate the organization's policies or its security controls. Misuse includes inappropriate browsing, the storage or distribution of inappropriate content on the organization's computing systems, installation of unapproved software, using the company laptop for personal business, or using the company printer to print nonbusiness documents. Since this incident is usually related to one or more employees, the HR and Legal department IR team members should be closely involved in the investigation and response to the incident. If litigation or prosecution is a potential objective, forensic investigations and methodologies should be implemented during the investigation and evidence collection. You may need to bring in a forensic investigator for additional evidence collection.

While in a perfect world it should never happen, inappropriate use could legitimately be unintentional if the user is unaware of policies that define acceptable use of IT resources. Security awareness training would be the countermeasure in this case.

Losses could include data leakage, damage to the organization's reputation, fines, and even lawsuits. Response for inappropriate use, unauthorized disclosure, unauthorized access, and willful attack follow a similar procedure. Figure 6-3 details a sample of incident response for inappropriate use and the three other security incidents that follow.

### 4. Unauthorized Disclosure

This might be intentional or unintentional unauthorized disclosure, which should be determined during the course of the investigation and incident response. Examples of unauthorized disclosure include the failure to shred sensitive documents or optical media before disposal, sending sensitive data via email to a supplier in violation of the data protection security policy (for good intent or bad intent), and selling trade secrets to the competition (definitely for bad intent).

Consider whether the incident has the potential to be a criminal act. If so, forensic methodologies should be utilized during the investigation and evidence collection. You may need to bring in a forensic investigator for additional evidence collection.

Losses include data leakage, and could include fines for compliance violations or lawsuits from disgruntled employees, customers, or shareholders. The preceding Figure 6-3 presents the logic and flow for a sample unauthorized disclosure security incident.

### 5. Unauthorized Access

This breach involves an authorized user circumventing security controls to gain access to data or resources he or she is not privileged to access. Examples of unauthorized access include a user logging into a different user's account to gain access to otherwise disallowed resources. This breach could occur when users share passwords, or when

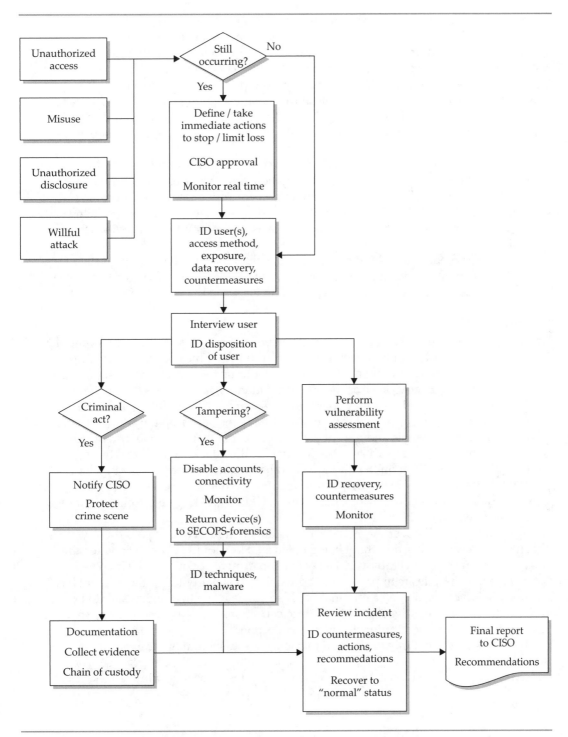

**Figure 6-3.** Inappropriate use, unauthorized disclosure, unauthorized access, and willful attack

users do not secure their passwords properly. This breach could also occur by way of social engineering, where a legitimate user is tricked into exposing his or her credentials, or providing access to otherwise restricted resources. Another example would be the unauthorized installation of a wireless access point on the network to provide Internet access to wireless systems, for example, because someone wants to browse the Internet on their laptop while at the outside smoking area. There is a chance that unauthorized access is unintentional, when a legitimate user is unaware of policies that may restrict access to certain resources, like the use of a fax machine for personal purposes.

Since the unauthorized access usually involves an authorized user (an employee), you typically need HR involved in the investigation and response. Consider whether the incident has the potential to be a criminal act. If so, notify the Legal department, and forensic methodologies should be utilized during the investigation and evidence collection. You may need to bring in a forensic investigator for additional evidence collection.

Losses are primarily data leakage, but could include system compromise if the credentials exposed provide administrative privilege. An example of incident response for unauthorized access is shown in the preceding Figure 6-3.

## 6. Willful Attack

The bad guy has focused his malicious intent on your IT systems. Willful attacks should be taken very seriously and handled very carefully. If negligible losses are occurring (so far), you may consider allowing the attack to continue to covertly gain insights into reconnaissance intelligence, such as the attacker's identity, target, and what tools and techniques are being used. You may collect evidence in hopes of building a case for prosecution. But if you choose not to respond immediately and stop the attack, be sure you are watching the whole and only attack vector(s), and that you have the emergency shutoff switch handy, and ready to push, just in case the attacker has a breakthrough. You might just be focusing on the diversion and be missing the real attack elsewhere.

Willful attacks can come in many forms, including a denial of service (DoS), a distributed denial of service (DDoS), password cracking, and targeted exploit attempts against systems vulnerabilities.

You might even discover the attack is being launched from one of your own systems that has been compromised without being detected. HR should be involved when the attacker is found to be an employee. The Legal department should also be involved since there may be a desire to prosecute, if possible. Consider whether the incident has the potential to be considered a criminal act. If so, forensic methodologies should be utilized during the investigation and evidence collection. You may need to bring in a forensic investigator for additional evidence collection.

If successful, the willful attack could introduce losses including the exposure of sensitive data, data loss, and complete single and multiple system compromise. The preceding Figure 6-3 demonstrates a sample incident response to a willful attack.

### 7. Other Type of Security Incident

When a violation of policy occurs, or some other form of IT loss occurs through a breach of security that is not covered by the preceding six categories of security incidents, disaster recovery, or business continuity programs, you should follow a generic response plan and adjust it as necessary to mitigate losses to the organization. You will need to develop a comprehensive list of losses from the incident as the details are uncovered during the investigation and after the conclusion of the incident.

As the nature of the "other" type of incident is revealed, you may find that one of the preceding incident response logic and procedure flow diagrams may provide some applicability and guidance. Consider developing and documenting a response plan for this new type of incident. Figure 6-4 presents a generic, "other" type of security incident logic and procedure flow.

# Automated Response

Some security systems can be configured to automatically adjust to increase security when the system detects a threat. These automated response systems generally fall into the category of an intrusion prevention system, or IPS. Knowledge-based IPS systems rely on recognizable, known attack signatures. Behavior-based IPS systems target attacks that do not yet have a signature. Behavior-based IPS systems typically track defined parameters to establish a base line of "Normal" behavior. They kick in the automated response when a configured deviation from "Normal" behavior for the monitored parameter is breached. Thresholds can be configured for both spikes and drops in the monitored parameter. Monitored parameters could include the number of bytes of a specific protocol, traffic to or from specified ports, bandwidth consumption on a specific interface or link, or bandwidth consumption to or from a specific server, and much more.

There are network-based IPS systems (NIPS) that monitor the network and make response-based adjustments to network devices like firewalls and routers (packet filters). The most common response triggered when a NIPS detects (or thinks it detects) an attack is to block the identified traffic from the untrusted system in a session or from the identified source of the attack (the perceived attacker), typically operating at layers 3 and 4 of the OSI model.

Intrusion prevention can be put to work on individual systems as well. These systems are called host-based IPSs or HIPSs. These systems reside on, and monitor, a single, usually critical system, and watch processes running on the system for aberrant or threatening behavior. If detected, the HIPS terminates the suspect process and typically quarantines the executable that initiated the offending process to disallow its being executed again. Microsoft's Windows Defender program is a form of a HIPS system.

In some ways, this automatic response can be a good thing. In some ways the automatic response can be a bad thing.

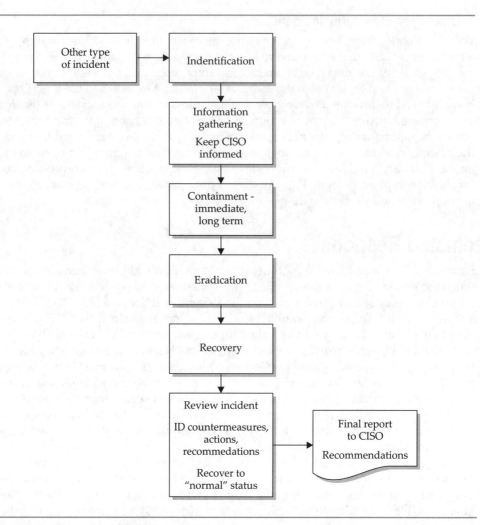

**Figure 6-4.** Other type of incident

## Automated Response—a Good Thing

The automated response system is a tireless security professional, watching potentially hundreds of thousands of packets every hour, 24/7. IPSs can monitor dozens to hundreds of parameters simultaneously. When configured correctly, they rarely miss a true-positive hit, and their response time can be milliseconds to a few seconds, much faster than any human response.

This combination of relentlessness, accuracy, and speed in performance is a powerful addition to an organization's security structure. But don't decide to implement an IPS system in your environment just yet. Read on.

## Automated Response—a Bad Thing

The negative aspects of running an IPS system in your environment are not insurmountable, but should be carefully considered before implementing one. You may find the positive aspects outweigh the negative ones, and you may be willing to accommodate the downsides.

First, both the IDS and the IPS are prone to a high level of false-positive alerts. Often, legitimate network or system activity will appear like malicious behavior to the IPS. One example of a false-positive alert would be a threshold set on FTP downloads from your FTP server. During normal activity, the server (that we just made up) pumps out approximately 500MB per hour in FTP file transfers on average. You have a threshold set for plus or minus 50 percent, defining normal FTP download activities between 250MB per hour on the low side and 750MB per hour on the high side. Last night, your company released a 100MB service pack update for your premier software product. When the news of the service pack hits the streets, or when the default automatic update download time occurs in the application, suddenly your FTP server is on track to pump out 5GB per hour. Boom! The automated response feature of your IPS shuts down all port 21 traffic from your most diligent customers, in its well-intended attempt to protect your IT systems.

One way to reduce this high frequency of false-positive responses from the IPS is to fine-tune the system to make exceptions for known good traffic. You could identify the source IP addresses that your customers use for their updates and set your IPS to ignore traffic from these known "friendlies." But these IP addresses may change over time, so you must readjust your exceptions. All good. But if you define too general or broad an exception (like a class C subnet, instead of the ten known friendly IP addresses for a customer), you may have just set your IPS to never trigger on an actual attack. So the difficulty and ongoing demands of tuning out the false-positive traffic the IPS properly identifies, without tuning out true-positive events, is a second problem with IPS systems.

Many enterprises have strict policies and restrictions on performing configuration changes on production systems. Only after a proposed change is reviewed, tested, approved, and scheduled can a configuration change be made. Often this change control is implemented to satisfy legal or regulatory compliance requirements. So if your IPS thinks it sniffs an attack and adjusts the rule on the firewall, you have just violated one or more of your compliance requirements. Herein lies automated response problem number three. However, even with this complication of unscheduled and unexpected configuration changes on production systems, some organizations have developed a reasonable, and if done correctly, compliant solution. The solution is to identify a limited set of responses that you configure your IPS system to perform. Run these configuration changes through the structured change approval board, and identify them as predefined, preapproved, automatic, and (possibly) temporary configuration changes. In this way, automated response does not cause a change-control compliance violation, and you get to reap the benefits of the IPS's super-human monitoring and response time.

The fourth downside of an automated response can be significant. Imagine that the bad guys have figured out that you're running an IPS system, and they know how to trigger it. All the bad guys have to do now is throw a few of the right type of packets in your direction causing your IPS to kill a certain type of otherwise legitimate traffic, and they have successfully executed a very efficient denial of service attack on your system. As your IPS responds to the perceived threat, the IPS will stop otherwise desirable services. So the automated response system is now used against you as an easy, built-in, DoS attack.

Consider the pros and cons that can be achieved by using automated response before designing, recommending, purchasing, and implementing these security systems.

## Summary

The Computer Security Incident Response Team (CSIRT) is a natural and essential development in a maturing IT environment. It is a group of well-trained and talented personnel, but is often not well-received by other departments within the organization. When the heat is on in the face of a security incident, this team works with small glimpses of the big picture, but even so, must quickly and accurately understand that picture so the appropriate and measured response can be implemented to minimize the losses to the organization.

To aid the difficult decision making needed during the incident, preplanned procedures should be documented, rehearsed, and followed. Adjustments and deviations from the predefined procedures will often be required, so good communications with your CISO are essential. Remember to get approval for each action taken during an incident response, especially the deviations from the documented procedures.

A worthy reference you can access in this regard is the National Institute for Standards and Technology Special Publication, Series 800, Document 61 (NIST SP800-61) Computer Security Incident Handling Guide. This guide can be found on the NIST website at http://csrc.nist.gov/publications/PubsSPs.html.

# CHAPTER 7 | Using SIEM for Business Intelligence

As you have learned from previous chapters of this book and from discussions with professionals and management within your industry, there are many reasons to deploy a SIEM within your organization. For the most part, SIEM is thought of as a Security Incident and Event Management system, as the name specifies, performing normalization, detecting anomalies and malicious behaviors, sounding alerts on noteworthy events, enabling actions of various kinds, and creating reports and graphics to depict what is happening on your network in real time or for historical reference for either compliance requirements or specific organizational policies. These SIEM actions are great ways to improve the security posture of the organization. The SIEM system provides a robust and reliable system to negotiate among events reported by disparate vendors, into a fantastic and easy-to-understand view of your entire network.

While this is typically the primary function of a SIEM, think outside the box for a moment and consider all of the tasks that the SIEM system is performing. These intelligent functions can be put to work for another, very useful purpose. Not only can you utilize SIEM technology to support your internal security requirements, but also you can use its database, alerts, reports, analytics, and network and asset knowledge for Business Intelligence (BI) to improve your business's internal processes and your position in the industry relative to your competition.

This chapter describes BI and its accompanying technologies and processes, along with some terminology that will be useful as you undergo this endeavor. Then you will walk through answers to some of the common questions that companies ask and particular challenges these organizations face, when it comes to using SIEM to provide useful BI in their environments. Finally, you will walk through a few of the objectives and goals when expanding your SIEM implementation to support some BI functionalities.

# What Is Business Intelligence

*Business Intelligence (BI)* refers to using the collective knowledge and analysis of your current business processes to produce better business processes and decisions. It includes an analysis of the skills, processes, technologies, applications, and practices within an organization. BI technologies draw from a data warehouse of corporate data on historical and current business operations to produce predictive views of the business. The process of developing business intelligence includes common functions such as reporting, analytics, data mining, business performance management, benchmarking, and predictive analytics.

As you break that broad view of BI down a bit, you begin to realize that BI is not simply a system of deployed technology; it is much, much more. Yes, of course, BI includes technologies and applications to support the required objectives initiated by upper management. However, BI uses employees' skills and organizational processes to support better decision making at all levels within the organization. This support comes from understanding what is important to the various departments within an organization, like sales figures, inventory counts, shipping costs, and, above all, resource utilization. That resource can be either human or technological. But either way, several important factors to consider during business decision making include:

- How are the resources being used?
- Are they being used as efficiently as possible?
- Does the organization need more resources?

## Business Intelligence Terminology

As with many specialized processes, business intelligence comes with a collection of terms that may not be commonly known or used outside of this niche. Following are several terms that you should know when working in the area of BI:

- **Analytics**   The process of determining an optimal or practical approach to making a decision based on current data. Decisions based on past experiences, rules of thumb, or other qualitative aspects are not considered analytics, as no quantitative data is involved to support any claims. Analytics includes the study of data using statistical analysis to discover and understand historical patterns to predict and improve performance in the future.

- **Benchmarking**   The process of comparing current business processes and performance metrics, including cost, cycle time, productivity, or quality, to another set of business processes and performance metrics that are widely considered to be an industry standard or best practice. Benchmarking provides a snapshot of a business's current performance and helps management understand where its metrics stand in relation to a particular standard. The result of this benchmarking process provides actual data to assist in making changes to systems, processes, or operations that make the organization more efficient and effective.

- **Business analytics (BA)**   Includes the skills, technologies, applications, and practices needed for constant iterative examination and investigation of past business performance to gain business insight and to drive business planning.

- **Business Performance Management (BPM)**   A set of processes that enable an organization to optimize its performance. BPM provides a framework for organizing, automating, and analyzing business methodologies, metrics, processes, and systems to improve business performance.

- **Dashboards**   Visualization tools that assist business users in determining how well various business units are performing by identifying trends and patterns in large amounts of corporate data. Dashboards represent a collection of Key Performance Indicators (KPIs).

- **Data integration**   Combines disparate data from different sources to provide users with a cohesive view of these data. This process enables an organization to fully utilize and understand the information gathered within their data warehouse.

- **Data mart**   A subset of an organization's data contained within the data warehouse, usually oriented toward a specific purpose or subject to support business needs and answer business questions. Data marts are analytical data stores designed to focus on specific business functions for a particular department within an organization.

- **Data mining**   The process of extracting various patterns from existing data. Data mining is an important tool that transforms the collection of data into quality information to assist in an organization's development and success. Data mining takes the raw and disassociated data and combines it within a specific context or relationship to produce helpful information for users.

- **Data warehouse**   A repository of an organization's vast, electronically stored data. Used to facilitate reporting and analysis.

- **Key Performance Indicators (KPIs)**   A measure of the performance of significant or critical processes, commonly used to assist an organization in defining and evaluating how successful these processes are, typically in terms of making progress toward the long-term organizational goals set by stakeholders.

- **Management by Objectives (MBO)**   The process of defining specific objectives within an organization where management and their employees agree to accomplish those stated objectives. Typically, both parties are rewarded for successful attainment of the objectives.

- **Metadata**   Provides information about data managed within an application or environment and usually defines the structure or schema of the primary data. Metadata is commonly described as "data about data." The following information is an example of metadata. "There are 300 records in the Parts database."

- **Online analytical processing (OLAP)**   An approach to answer analytical queries quickly in order to accomplish relational reporting and data mining. Typical usage of the OLAP processes are in business reporting for various areas like sales, marketing, management reporting, business process management (BPM), budgeting, and forecasting.

- **Predictive analytics**   Finds patterns in historical and current transactional data to identify risks and opportunities for the organization. Assists in capturing relationships among many factors to allow for the assessment of risk or potential risk associated with a specific set of conditions, helping to guide decision making in an organization.

- **Scorecard**   A strategic performance management tool utilizing a semistandard report used by managers to keep track of the progress and completion of activities by individuals within their department. Scorecards aid in the ability to achieve the organization's targeted goals, incorporating methodologies around Key Performance Indicators (KPIs).

- **Strategy map**   A visual representation of the strategy of an organization that illustrates how the organization plans to achieve its vision using a linked chain of continuous improvements.

# Common Business Intelligence Questions

There are many reasons why organizations will want to deploy BI solutions within their environment. With the time that it takes to implement this level of intricacy within their business and its processes, this solution will provide answers to certain questions. After all, implementing BI, as the definition in the previous section explains, is not just about incorporating technology. It is about providing information and creating a framework of processes and procedures to empower individuals at all levels to make appropriate and improved business decisions for the overall betterment of the company. It also assists in providing views at many levels of business to improve upper management's vision, enabling everyone to stay the course, or right the direction of the ship if necessary.

Ultimately, all BI processes need to adhere to business objectives, whether those objectives are to gain market share, break into new markets, or determine what internal cost units are performing above or below expectations set by management. And, of course, as an organization begins the process of incorporating BI processes into its environment, any and all of these objectives may be required and should be constantly verified and measured to ensure success.

## Answers to the Common Business Intelligence Questions

The following are some common questions that companies may have when deciding what the best route is for providing the required views and analytics to determine how to make better business decisions. Using data as a resource to confirm current conditions within the organization and provide the capability to forecast trends for the future, the first set of questions are common to the technological aspects of BI. The initial questions relate to how to garner and securely store important data, and how to provide an efficient and effective technological framework to make the important data accessible to those who need it. The specific questions include:

- What types of data does the organization need to accomplish its stated objectives?

- Who within the organization needs access to this data to make better, informed decisions?

■ Where is the data going to be stored that provides confidentiality, integrity, and availability?

■ How is the data going to be tailored or normalized to provide a common format for easy analytics across the organization?

The next set of questions is aimed at deciding what to do with the data to make better and more informed decisions. These questions are intended to determine what the organization is going to do with the data accumulated from the data sources, whether externally obtained or provided by internal IT devices. They include:

■ How does a company identify new market trends and opportunities to obtain competitive advantage?

■ How can a company determine if marketing strategies are effective?

■ What is the company's support statistics per region?

■ How does an organization identify underperforming cost centers and provide insight as to how to increase performance?

■ How does a company identify high-performance cost centers to replicate applicable processes accordingly?

In the following sections, you will explore various functions provided to answer the above questions utilizing common BI techniques and the SIEM implementation's infrastructure and technologies.

**What types of data does the organization need to accomplish its stated objectives?**     To determine what types of data the organization needs to accomplish its stated objectives, you must first identify those objectives. These objectives will be different from one business to the next and depend on the industry that your organization is involved in. However, there are some common objectives that many organizations will want to meet when determining how BI will be incorporated into their infrastructure. Some of the common objectives include:

■ Increasing profitability

■ Increasing resource efficiency

■ Increasing customer satisfaction

■ Determining attainment of MBOs

■ Determining KPIs for the organization

Now that you have established a set of business objectives, your next question is, How can SIEM assist in obtaining these objectives? One of the recurring themes that will be exposed within this chapter is the use of SIEM as a data warehouse. This data warehouse gives individuals within the organization the ability to access the various types of data and mine the metadata for specific types of attributes. These attributes will be relevant to the managerial capabilities and decision-making abilities of the various members of your organization.

To determine if the organization is increasing its profits, efficiencies, and customer satisfaction, some data sources that should be considered are *Enterprise Resource Planning (ERP)* technologies that may be currently employed and *Customer Relationship Management (CRM)* platforms that are in use by the organization. Many SIEM vendors provide defined and supported integration packages for several major ERP and CRM applications that facilitate the use of the data from the application within the SIEM system. These are often add-on packages that can be used to import and analyze the ERP and CRM events within the SIEM system specifically to address these particular business objectives. If the SIEM system vendor you have currently employed does not provide the required packages (which may also be referred to as *connectors* or *agents*) for these applications, most SIEM vendors will include the ability to make custom connectors or agents to obtain the required events from its applications.

Although ERP and CRM applications are dependent upon internal resources, an organization may want to receive information regarding market position and competitive advantage within their respective markets. This information can be obtained by utilizing data from external sources such as the Security and Exchange Commission's (SEC) Electronic Data-Gathering, Analysis, and Retrieval (EDGAR) system. All publicly held companies are required to submit quarterly and annual reports to the SEC. These reports include financial information about the companies, market forecasts, and other related information. The EDGAR system performs automated collection, validation, indexing, and acceptance of submissions by these publicly held companies. The EDGAR database is available to the public for a fee via the Internet. Each day, you could download the data gathered by EDGAR on your competitors, suppliers, distributors, and companies that are working on new and related technologies, via a specific, supported application called FastCopy or using FTP. Then a custom connector or agent can be created to parse the data and import it into the SIEM application for correlation against various marketing objectives.

The data integration provided by the many SIEM applications, by default, allows for the information obtained by the multiple data sources within your organization to be sent to a centrally located data warehouse. Once the business data has been collected and normalized into the data warehouse, it can be correlated by the SIEM system. Multiple types of views can be produced in a process of data mining for those who require a vision into departmental specifics or of the entire organization.

To assist in the evaluation of Management by Objectives (MBOs) and Key Performance Indicators (KPIs), SIEM can correlate the various events from ERP and CRM applications to verify the various MBOs specified. This analysis and reporting, often in near real-time, can assist in exposing performance on objectives that individuals or teams are responsible for, such as order to fulfillment, order and payment history for various customers, and measuring production benchmarks. Again, since the SIEM product is capturing the ERP and CRM events, you can determine how long it takes to receive an order and process and complete the order to fulfillment and delivery. You can also determine how quickly those orders are being paid for and how many outstanding orders are still in process. These now very timely and visible MBOs provide a framework for KPIs that the organization will detail and measure against. Having a rapid and clear vision of the overall organization allows for rapid and clear decision making when an adjustment is needed within the business processes. Making the data warehousing, correlation, and reporting capabilities of SIEM available as a Business Intelligence tool for management can be very useful in determining, measuring, and providing feedback regarding the status and completion of the organization's objectives.

It is always a good idea to obtain as much information from as many data sources within the organization as possible, as this leads to better visibility and provides for better decision making. If the data is not a complete picture of all of the tasks behind the various processes, then there is no way to establish, identify, or measure the capabilities and shortcomings of the organization, which can lead to continued poor performance and less production, ultimately hurting the most important business objective—the bottom line.

**Who within the organization needs access to this data to make better, informed decisions?**    The obvious answer to this question would be the managers of the various departments who are responsible for ensuring the objectives set out by the organization are met. You can take this a step further, however. In understanding what MBOs are and how they are measured, mid-level managers and even the various individuals within the organization who are responsible for actually performing the tasks related to the MBOs can use the SIEM displays and reports to verify the progress of each of their stated objectives. This vision can help individuals also gain an understanding of how the various tasks they are required to perform can affect, for the good of or for the detriment of, the organization as a whole. This provides the organization's employees with the sense of being connected and a member of a team as it pertains to the vision of senior management and stakeholders, and how the smaller, specific tasks performed by individuals impact the achievement of the stated business objectives.

While this may seem like a trivial acknowledgement from the stakeholders to the other individuals within the organization, it is important that everyone is on the same page and working toward the same goals. If a cog in the machine is not working in harmony, whether intentional or not, the entire process has the potential to fail.

This data can be viewed by the individuals who require it through the use of OLAP methodologies and the SIEM's data-mining capabilities to create benchmarks, strategy maps, scorecards, and dashboards of the various facets of the organization's processes and people, to providing the organization and its members with a comprehensive view or vision of the entire system. It can be a beneficial vision, even to those who do not make direct decisions about the company's direction. If a production worker realizes that his or her task is taking longer than allocated within the entire process, and then determines how he or she can improve the process to improve performance, the entire process is better off.

**Where is the data going to be stored that provides confidentiality, integrity, and availability?**    The data stored within the data warehouse is highly sensitive and valuable to the organization. Its confidentiality, integrity, and availability need to be protected. This should be one of the primary missions for information security professionals implementing SIEM for Business Intelligence.

The *confidentiality* metric ensures that the organization's secrets remain secret and are accessible only to those individuals who have a legitimate business need and are authorized to have access to that information. While this may seem evident to most, the various cryptosystems incorporated into SIEM systems are often overlooked. Sensitive data must be protected while in transit (over the wire) and while at rest, stored on a hard drive, or SAN. Confidentiality of data is integrated into almost all SIEM platforms, by default, using various cryptographic elements like SSL and digital certificates for secure communications to ensure that only individuals who are supposed to access the data residing within the data warehouse can access it.

The infrastructure of the data warehouse must also provide a means to protect and verify the *integrity* of the data held within the data warehouse. This means that the data cannot be tampered with or inappropriately modified. As stated previously, the integrity of valuable data is also one of the primary missions for information security professionals responsible for an organization's critical data. What good is learning the valuable secret if the information provided by the secret is incorrect, leading to poor business decisions. Integrity protection and verification of data stored by the SIEM system is typically integrated into SIEM platforms by default. Encrypting the data provides integrity protection. If you cannot read or understand the information, you cannot intelligently modify the data. Hashing functions provide integrity protection of data. Hash values are calculated on new data and then again when the data is accessed later. If the hashes are different, the data has been inappropriately modified and should not be trusted, for instance, hashes of the various rows and columns within the database ensure that specific details have not been modified.

For any information system to function as required, the data must be *available* when it is needed by authorized individuals. This means that the systems used to store and process the data, the security controls protecting the data, and the communication channels used to access this data must all be functioning correctly. Again, availability is an integrated mechanism within almost all SIEM platforms by default. Redundancy of critical system components, like power supplies and hard disks, are utilized by SIEM vendors. SIEM systems commonly work with specific fault tolerant databases to ensure the storage and processing of the information is valid and available.

Although it is not the function of a SIEM to provide availability among network components or to connect the devices or applications required to obtain the desired information, a SIEM system data warehouse should provide a highly available, central data repository. It is the responsibility of the security professional, perhaps you, to design a network architecture with sufficient availability, fault tolerance, and redundancy among the devices feeding the SIEM system components and among the SIEM components themselves.

**How is the data going to be tailored or normalized to provide a common format for easy analytics across the organization?** So now that you know what type of data the organization requires, who needs access to that data, and how you are going to store that information, the next thing you must look at is the format of the data itself. As you have seen, SIEM applications can receive information from a myriad of different data sources, like routers, firewalls, IDSs, IPSs, servers, workstations, switches, and so on. On a busy network, large amounts of data are continuously being streamed into the data warehouse, often in very short periods of time. To organize this large amount of fast-moving data into something that can be quickly processed, the SIEM system must recognize each different type of input and convert it into a standard format. Some SIEM vendors call this formatting process normalization. The SIEM system parses the data stream from the various data sources and reorganizes it into a common schema within the SIEM database. This process is inherent in almost all SIEM applications available. The ability to create a custom parser for source devices should be a requirement when you are defining the specification for a new SIEM system.

Many SIEM vendors also provide the ability to modify the database schema, to a certain extent, to accommodate unexpected and new data sources. This allows the data warehouse to store and process details and attributes contained within events from various devices and applications that the SIEM system originally could not retain. As new IT devices and business management applications hit the market over time, this could become a critical issue when selecting the right SIEM system for your organization.

**How does a company identify new market trends and opportunities to obtain competitive advantage?**    Using the SIEM system to receive input from internal systems and applications is probably the more common approach and mentality when implementing a SIEM system. However, if you turn the focus of the SIEM system toward external sources, particularly sources related to your market, or markets of interest, you can begin to gain Business Intelligence to recognize emerging market trends and external business opportunities rapidly. Accessing these external data sources is usually accomplished through paid subscriptions to commercial data warehouses. One of the most useful commercial data warehouses that can be accessed is EDGAR. While you can access the entire EDGAR database manually for free, for the purposes of SIEM and BI, you'll probably want automatic and programmatic access to the data warehouse. EDGAR provides electronic data on publicly held companies (those traded on stock exchanges) in multiple types of subscriptions including multitiered, EDGAR Online, the EDGAR Public Dissemination Service (EDGAR PDS), and even EDGAR data via FTP downloads. The EDGAR service collects and not only provides the business information required by the U.S. SEC, but also has some built-in mechanisms to ensure that data is properly captured, processed, and available for dissemination. The SEC's EDGAR PDS system includes redundancy and failover capabilities to help ensure your organization can receive data when needed.

To support simultaneous, encrypted dissemination of submissions, immediate verification, and authentication, the EDGAR PDS system uses FASTCopy from RepliWeb, Inc. FASTCopy uses a proprietary protocol based on the Transmission Control Protocol (TCP) that supports compression and authentication during transfer. The FASTCopy product employs a variety of security-enhancing functions that limit the use of remote server commands. Therefore, the SEC and Keane Federal Systems Inc., who developed EDGAR and maintains the EDGAR database for the SEC, require that

FASTCopy dissemination commands be the only available remote server commands supported from the PDS sites to ensure the security of the PDS and the disseminated data.

Most of the available SIEM systems provide the capabilities to create connectors/agents to parse the file downloaded from the EDGAR system for pertinent information that can aid in identifying new markets as well as obtaining an advantage over your competitors and providing many benefits to an organization's customers. Some of the details contained in the TXT or HTML files that are sent to your organization via the EDGAR PDS include:

- Submission type
- Submission company name
- Submission date
- Acceptance date
- Income statements
- Balance sheets
- Cash flow statements
- Stockholders' equity
- Legal proceedings affecting the company
- Risk factors affecting the company, from the point of view or opinion of the company
- Market information, from the point of view or opinion of the company

By using this data obtained from the SEC's EDGAR system, along with the principles of predictive analysis, an organization can exploit patterns found in historical and current transactional data to identify opportunities. Using the correlation capabilities of the SIEM application, your organization can look at many inside details from your competitors. Gather that information on 100 of your competitors, 100 of your suppliers, 100 of your customers, and 100 of your distributors; then correlate all that data and present it within displays and reports to observe trends, pitfalls, opportunities, and new directions.

This information can assist in determining what area of your industry your competition is moving or expanding into. An executive can also track how quickly the competition is moving in a specific direction, and predict when your organization can or should move in the same direction, or a different direction. Some other important information that can be gleaned from this data is if a merger has been submitted, to whom, and when it should be completed.

There are vast benefits that can be achieved just from the data obtained by EDGAR PDC, the U.S. Census Bureau, as well as other government agencies and private companies that provide industry-specific information and data such as Gartner. Whether the information is about competition, populations, spending patterns and trends, R&D directions, salaries, or mergers and acquisitions, the chances are very good that a SIEM system can assist in identifying new market opportunities. SIEM does this by enabling a view into various details garnered by the different data sources, information like SEC filings or disposable income per capita in a particular area of the country. The SIEM can also assist in obtaining a competitive advantage in that it can correlate historical data to ascertain trends and present the relationships among the various data sources to provide a variety of results to allow for an informed decision by the company's stakeholders.

Using the SIEM's inherent alerting capability, you can send notifications to individuals to advise them that various patterns are emerging from the data being received by the SEC. Teach your SIEM how to read your competitors' 10-K and 10-Q and other SEC filings and you could discover a great deal of information about your market. This information can provide insight into the industry landscape and allow your organization to modify its product offerings or services to account for these changes.

**How can a company determine if marketing strategies are effective?**    As previously discussed within the answer to the question regarding the types of data an organization needs to accomplish its stated objectives, you learned that ERP and CRM applications can be integrated quite simply into the SIEM environment through the use of connectors/ agents. To determine if the company's current marketing strategies are effective, you can parse and normalize data garnered from the ERP and CRM applications within the SIEM system. The SIEM will then correlate this information to assist in understanding if customer orders, current and past sales, and delivery and acceptance of products to specific areas are helping to ensure your organization is spending its marketing budget accurately.

While this seems like a difficult task, with the tools built into most SIEM systems, it really is not. Using the internal functionality of a SIEM system and its correlation capabilities, your organization can create reports on pre-marketing-campaign sales versus post-marketing-campaign sales, or determine how many orders turn into actual sales and how quickly a monetary transaction takes as a result of a marketing campaign. Using business analytics theories to create trending and delta reports documenting sales before and after a marketing campaign has been dropped into the specific locations and demographics will help your organization determine what, if any, results were yielded because of the campaign. Using the information gathered and correlated by the SIEM, your organization can also determine if the monetary gain from a marketing campaign outweighs the expenditures required to provide the marketing campaign and correctly record it for future reports.

The SIEM can also alert the appropriate individuals within the organization to the fact that a marketing campaign is successful or not, when an allocated budget has been spent, and the gains garnered from that expenditure have been met or not. These notifications can be in the form of an email displaying the status of a specific pattern of activity being observed by the SIEM system.

Again, this can be accomplished by using the inherent correlation and data warehouse functionalities of a SIEM system and the SIEM's capability to obtain information from various device sources. Whether those data sources are network and security devices, or business applications, or feeds from external sources, if the SIEM can obtain these feeds, it can assist in many different aspects of not only networking and security, but also Business Intelligence as well.

**What are the company's support statistics per region?**   You read previously that a SIEM system can incorporate many different data sources such as ERP, CRM, external feeds, and the various networking/security devices currently supporting your network's infrastructure. A SIEM solution is like putting together a puzzle; you can not get the entire picture until you put all of the pieces together. As stated previously in this chapter, the more information that your SIEM can obtain, the better picture the SIEM can paint of your environment. This picture will ultimately provide your organization with extraordinary insights into complex issues that will help not only security professionals, but also business leaders.

To answer this particular question on regional statistics, another data source must be introduced. This piece is the customer support and services applications or portals that allow your organization to assist in customer support issues, tracking those issues through resolution. While these products tend to have their own reporting functionality, you cannot get correlation, data warehouse, data mining, predictive analysis, or OLAP capabilities from within these applications. This type of functionality is generally not what customer support and services applications provide.

Using a SIEM system, not only can you can record and track customer support incidents through resolution, but also you can correlate customer sales and contact information from the CRM, as well manufacturing, processing, and delivery of products to the customer through the ERP system. Within this process, the SIEM can alert you about issues within your customer support process—for instance, if, resolution is taking too long, how many issues a certain customer has, if returned products are taking too long to send to remedy a customer's complaints, or if the return merchandise authorization (RMA) items have not yet been received and are overdue. You can get a full 360-degree view of all of the details for every one of your customers, including their transactions within your organization. This view provides all the information needed for predictive analysis to determine many of the components required for an organization's success: are the company's current objectives being met, or does your organization need to shift gears to follow up-and-coming trends, to name a few.

**How does an organization identify underperforming cost areas and provide insight as to how to improve performance?**   Now that you have learned about the external data sources and the various applications that are typically available, you can add yet another piece to the puzzle. All SIEM systems have a networking configuration component. This is where you will configure your internal networking components into manageable, separate, and distinct areas, like the production process within a manufacturing company. You can configure various cost areas, like cost centers, within the SIEM application to depict what is happening within your environment. Such cost areas could include design, manufacturing, specific product lines, specific marketing campaigns, and packaging and shipping. Each of these cost areas can be configured within an ERP system and be incorporated into the SIEM system. These functionalities include things like correlating information between the ERP and the various components within the production process such as design. You can correlate the time it takes for an individual to complete the design of a product, along with the technology used, such as Internet activity, personnel usage (number of hours), and database and application access to name a few.

With this information in hand, as an organization, you can determine what capacity of your technological infrastructure is being used and the time it takes to complete the design process. This information enables department managers to determine the effectiveness of not only the individual performing the design tasks, but also the technologies required and used to complete that design task. If it appears that the individual is spending vast amounts of time performing research, the organization can determine if the problem is network latency within the design department, or perhaps that individual is browsing the web for pleasure. The pleasure browsing could even be confirmed within the SIEM system from firewall or proxy server logs.

Another prime example of gaining Business Intelligence includes monitoring the manufacturing of components. Remember, if you can get data into the SIEM, you can correlate and compare time, efficiencies, and other aspects of the manufacturing process. If your organization manufactures widgets, for example, you could use the SIEM system to determine, based on industry benchmarks, the efficiency of the individuals and technology in the manufacturing widgets. This information can be extremely beneficial to management.

If you expand upon the widgets manufacturing example, the organization must obtain the design specifications, acquire raw materials, and process those materials into the required sizes for the widgets. Then an individual must assemble the various pieces of the widget. After assembly has taken place, another individual will paint or coat the widget to satisfy the details of a specific order. Next might be a quality control inspection to ensure the widget is functioning properly, which your customer may require. After the quality assurance process is complete, the widget must be packaged and shipped to the customer. All of these production stages can be monitored and reported on using SIEM. Even after delivery of the finished product to the customer, using the SIEM application you can track any customer support issues that may arise.

As you can see from this sample process of manufacturing widgets, many valuable corporate resources—technological and human—are being consumed to perform these specific tasks to complete the design, manufacturing, packaging, and delivery of this widget. Using SIEM, you can correlate all of the data being obtained from the devices used during production and from an ERP application where individuals are assigned their tasks and also assigned a timeframe for completion, along with the input of the actual time it took to complete these tasks.

Here is where you can determine if a single process is taking too long, and by correlating the time ascertained from the ERP system, you can get a view into the production of your widgets. If there is a benchmarked time from order to shipping of 24 hours (3 full 8-hour days) and you see from viewing status reports from the SIEM application, that the average time taken to complete this process is actually 32 hours, first, the expected cost of manufacturing the widgets has increased, and second, it may indicate there is some solvable problem occurring. In any case, the increased production time is costing the organization money. The company can use the data found within the data warehouse to determine, through correlation of other devices and applications used within the manufacturing process, where the inefficiencies are, and perhaps even how to correct them.

Some examples of the inefficiencies that could be ascertained include, is the design department taking too long to produce and move the custom widget design specifications through to the (theoretical) widget routing machine? Using SIEM, your organization can see the types of constraints that are present during this process. Again, is the designer spending too much time browsing the Web? Or is the download time for large files to the widget router taking too long? If the problem is technological, in that the widget router is not receiving the data quickly enough, perhaps a technological solution, such as a dedicated fiber line or more processing and/or memory on the machine controlling the widget router, is required.

Maybe you have discovered that the design department and the widget router are moving as fast as predicted and that the manufacturing process is taking too long. Again, using the ERP data and the various technological inputs, you gain visibility into the manufacturing process. Perhaps you discover that after the widget routing is completed, the assembly process is taking too long. By correlating the time-tracking capabilities of your ERP system, and input from the devices that the assembly department uses, you can determine if, again, the resource issue is technological or human, presenting opportunities and direction for corrective management to intervene.

If the constraint appears to be a longer than expected lag time between how long it takes for the assembly department to obtain the finished widget materials and complete the assembly of the widget, then you can utilize the SIEM to determine what is causing the backlog within this process. Perhaps the individuals are taking the appropriate benchmarked time to assemble the widgets, but the backlog persists. This analysis could provide the ammunition you need to hire more assembly personnel to decrease the overall assembly time for the widget orders. Using the SIEM, you might uncover the fact that the assembly personnel are simply taking too long and more training is required.

At any part of this process, these principles can be applied. You can also, based on information gathered from the ERP and customer support applications, accurately monitor which widget product seems to be failing in the field, and which customers are having the most difficulty with particular widgets. You can then correlate that information using the SIEM application to correct the appropriate aspects of the manufacturing process, or perhaps to educate the customer on the proper use and installation of the widget in question through adding content to the user guide, or adding a notice flag affixed to the widget.

Either way, this analysis into the data being obtained from the ERP and customer support systems and correlated with the technology required to complete a specific process or the entire process can benefit any organization. By using a SIEM system, with its inherent capabilities, you can analyze not only the network and security devices to ensure an appropriate security posture and response, but you can also utilize the data being supplied by almost any business application to correlate and determine if a cost area is underperforming, be alerted to any potential poorly crafted and inefficient processes, and increase visibility into the available options to make any process within an organization more efficient.

**How does a company identify high-performance business areas to replicate applicable high-efficiency processes accordingly?**    In answering this question, you can look at the above response in how to determine a poorly performing cost center. If your organization has multiple cost areas or business units that provide similar functionality within the company, by determining whether an area is performing efficiently and effectively, you can take the same technology and personnel, and apply those processes to a less productive business area to increase performance.

Taking the widget manufacturing theme again, your organization not only produces widgets, but also produces cogs. Although the end product is different, the processes to create this cog may be similar, if not the same, as the processes required to create the widget, in that the cog needs to be designed, cut, assembled, painted, packaged, and then delivered to the customer. And, of course, you need to track any customer issues with a specific cog model or palate of cogs.

In your analysis of your widget manufacturing process, you have found that the various business areas seem to be performing well and that all is running smoothly. However, you have discovered some issues within the development and manufacturing of your cogs. In defining an internal benchmark for your processes, based on the success of your widget manufacturing processes, you can apply the characteristics of the high-efficiency business areas to poorly performing business areas. Again, if you have the data being sent to the data warehouse and you have your SIEM monitoring and potentially alerting you to underperforming processes, you can quickly remediate those issues and apply known good practices to those underperforming areas.

In general, the more information you are able to provide the SIEM system, the more visibility you can gain, whether it is related to marketing, sales, production, or customer support resolution, into your organization and the activities that it performs. The SIEM provides the ultimate means to culminate data from the various data sources into a data warehouse, where it can be easily maintained and secured by an existing IT and security personnel.

# Developing Business Intelligence Strategies Using SIEM

So now that you have been exposed to some common BI questions along with how SIEM can accommodate their solutions within your environment, you will learn how to utilize an existing SIEM implementation to garner BI analysis of your organization. The topics that you will learn about in the following section of this chapter are

■ How to utilize SIEM to achieve your BI objectives

■ Using data that your organization currently possesses

■ What other companies are doing with SIEM and BI

What you will gain from this chapter is the ammunition you may need to begin the process of expanding your SIEM solution to provide BI for your organization.

## How to Utilize SIEM for Your BI Objectives

Before you determine what type of information you require from the various applications within your network to enable BI initiatives within your organization, you must determine your objectives. These objectives will drive the type of data required and define which applications used within your organization you can gather that data from.

As mentioned before, the objectives you establish might be some of the more obvious and typical objectives provided within this chapter, or they might be more specific to your industry and organization as a whole. These objectives may be handed down to you from management, or provided by you to assist in expanding the role of a SIEM in your organization. However these business objectives are identified and defined, you must be sure they are reasonable and achievable. Make sure you look for the following when establishing your objectives as they relate to BI:

■ **Low hanging fruit**   Make sure you can obtain the objectives relatively quickly and with little overhead or resource consumption. This gives your organization some quick wins. When you attain these quick wins, you will gain the leverage you may need to obtain the resources and funding from upper management required for a larger implementation of SIEM and BI projects in the future. Prove that you can produce positive results with a small amount of resource consumption, and your organization will gain confidence that SIEM can help them improve business.

■ **Business objectives versus technical objectives**   Ensure that this expenditure of time and money is applicable to, and will result in, meeting some sort of business objective. While this seems like common sense, this issue is often overlooked by technical individuals, as this process is not just about implementing technology, but business processes as well. To change the culture of an organization, there must be some sort of business need that can be accounted for by using the SIEM to enable BI analysis. Speak to management in terms of business needs and business objectives.

■ **Upper management support**   As mentioned throughout this chapter, implementing BI in any organization is not just about the technology used. The improvements suggested through newly gained BI will often require incorporating new processes or sometimes require improvements to existing processes. These changes need to be delivered to, and reviewed, understood, and supported by, upper management. The change process must be monitored by individuals who have the power to promote and implement these changes throughout the organization. There must be a solid, undeniable requirement for the people within the organization to follow these new processes, along with consequences if they do not. Remember to communicate effectively with the individuals within the organization, and show them that not only will these new processes help the organization to be more profitable, but also the results can provide the necessary data, hopefully positive feedback and results, to upper management. Upper management will use this data to assist in determining new, and verifying existing, MBOs and KPIs for the various departments. These refined MBOs and KPIs can result in more allocation and distribution of valuable resources within the various departments that may need them. Whether these resources come in the form of increased personnel, or technology, the lives of those who will follow these processes should become easier and more productive.

## Using the Data that Your Organization Currently Possesses

Next is a bit more detail on a topic that has already been discussed within this chapter. As stated previously, recognize that the more information you can provide the SIEM application, the more relevant and meaningful the resulting output will be toward your goal of improving your Business Intelligence.

SIEM has the capability to obtain information from a myriad of data sources such as ERP, CRM, network and security devices, physical devices, and many external sources as well. The challenge is to get that information into the SIEM by using the connectors/ agents that are available from the SIEM vendor. Many of the connectors/agents for various major application and device manufacturers are already created by your SIEM vendor. However, in the event that your SIEM vendor does not have a connector/ agent available for the applications currently in use by your organization, many SIEM vendors provide the capability to create custom versions of these connectors/agents. This custom connector or agent functionality is pivotal in gathering event feeds from new and perhaps even usual or unexpected sources, and then formatting those event feeds into a common schema for processing by the SIEM system. Included with the SIEM application is the capability of storing these formatted events in a centrally located and administered area known as a data warehouse.

This integration of data from the various internal and/or external data sources provides a multifaceted, or a 360-degree, view of your organization as it pertains to the organization's security posture and compliance requirements. This improved vision also facilitates BI capabilities to enable managers to determine the capabilities, efficiencies, and effectiveness of their individual departments. This integration and common access to the organizational data stored in the data warehouse also provides key stakeholders with visibility and clarity into the current position of the organization in terms of market share, customer success, sales, and internal cost area proficiencies. The transparency that the integration provides enables individuals from within the organization, from the CEO down to the production-line worker, to assess the organization's current production capabilities to determine KPIs as well as their own personal MBOs.

The conclusion is that SIEM can provide BI competencies on top of its innate security and compliance capabilities. The discussion now must go more deeply into the data that your organization currently holds and how you can get that information into your SIEM system, enabling BI initiatives to facilitate your organization in better decision-making capabilities.

You should begin by listing the various applications that your organization currently uses that may track or otherwise provide insights into routine business activities. No matter the types of information being provided by these applications, consider which details are most important to the people who use the applications.

If your SIEM vender has created a connector/agent that you can use to obtain the information being generated by the various applications that your organization uses, it is good practice to view that information from within the SIEM console. This allows you to view the events that have been captured by the connector/agent to get a clear understanding of how the SIEM system is parsing those events and then formatting and displaying them. Understand what is being provided by default or automatically. Then you can begin to build and refine the SIEM content (parsers, rules, alerts, etc.) required to better understand your environment.

If your SIEM vendor does not provide a connector/agent to obtain the information being generated by the various applications your organization uses, and you must build custom connectors or agents, you must first understand how to manually parse the log files being acquired from the business applications and other nonstandard devices or systems. It is important that you understand the log line formats, the different attributes and what they mean to the application, and the commonalities among those attributes. If it does not appear that the log files are capturing the required information for your BI purposes, some more logging features may need to be enabled from the application itself to provide those attributes.

Another important aspect is to understand how much information is being captured by the application's logs. As you add more event sources to the system and data warehouse, keep in mind the network bandwidth consumption and the data warehouse's disk space requirements. It is easy to overlook these two aspects and cause yourself more problems than you'll resolve. The primary purpose of this exercise is to get very familiar with the log format, available logging options, and the attributes that you require from the application in order to build the custom connector/agent to feed those logs to the SIEM for further analysis and correlation.

If, at any point, you are having difficulties with transmitting the log files to the SIEM, enabling extended logging capabilities at the application, or receiving specific attributes within the application logs that are required to provide the BI analysis desired, you may need to talk to the application developers, or obtain a Software Developer Kit (SDK) from the vendor of the application in question. This SDK, along with other supporting documentation provided by the SIEM vendor, will assist in developing your custom connector/agent.

Of course, when you have successfully created your custom connector/agent, you will need to define the correlation rules, and also views and alerts, as appropriate, for those events being parsed, to get the most benefit from your specific applications.

## What Other Companies Are Doing with SIEM and BI

One of the best ways to determine how you can utilize SIEM for BI analysis is to identify process-related benchmarks. These benchmarks provide a means of determining and ultimately comparing what your organization is doing to others to see where you can implement and incorporate other best practices into your business processes. Information like this is often available from the manufacturers and vendors of your production applications, systems, and devices. Your organization isn't the only customer of those vendors that wants or needs to measure their productivity.

Next, you should consider the various ways in which BI has been implemented by other organizations along with three BI implementation initiatives. The three types of BI initiatives are strategic, analytic, and operational. These BI initiatives are both iterative and complementary to one other. When you incorporate these three initiatives into your organization, as it pertains to BI, you will see how the SIEM tool can be used to provide the required results.

When discussing *strategic* initiatives, the principle goal is to enhance the operations of the company as a whole, as well as the distinct departments and business units that fabricate and supply the company's products or services. During this initiative, management sets the strategic path that is then implemented at the various levels of the organization. The objectives ascertained within the strategic planning initiative are provided to the organization and measured using various types of BI functionalities such as reports, scorecards, and strategy maps. This foundation provides key performance measurements and allows a vision to be established and communicated throughout the organization.

The next initiative is the *analytical* phase. Within this initiative, an organization is attempting to identify the source of an issue once it has been uncovered during the production or business process. To determine the location or cause of any problems within the process of developing, producing, or delivering your organization's goods or services, you will employ various types of BI functionalities such as dashboards, OLAP, predictive analytics, and ad hoc queries into the data captured to assess these discrepancies or shortcomings. The results obtained within the analytical process will help drive the operational initiatives that will be discussed next. Another benefit of this analysis is that it will assist in determining whether your company has the resources, capabilities, and capacities to effectively obtain the objectives sought by management and developed within the strategy initiative.

The *operational* initiative facilitates the day-to-day decision making that happens within the individual departments of an organization. The function of the operational initiative enables the objectives that were established by management within the strategy phase to be attained. The operational phase also provides information to those who are responsible for analyzing the processes performed when there are problems within the production or delivery of your company's products or services.

When you apply these three BI initiatives to your processes, remember that they are intended to be iterative, in that they are to be monitored and adjusted constantly, and new goals and objectives must always be created. There must also be processes in place to measure existing goals to ensure they are being attained. As you can see, these three initiatives work in conjunction with each other. There may not be a complete separation of duties, as key individuals may be responsible for addressing a single part, or potentially all of these actions, within an organization.

# Summary

Using the inherent capabilities of the SIEM system, such as accepting custom feeds, normalization, correlation, reporting, and visual representations of data through the use of various dashboard functions, allows a business to detect marketing, production, and sales transactions for patterns and trends. These patterns include things like the business health and direction of your competition, population and spending statistics, as well as marketing specifics detailed through the use of data obtained from the Census Bureau. These capabilities and this improved vision is often sought by organizations but often left unsatisfied. As long as the information is there, the SIEM system can provide a consistent interface to these processes and transactions and can correlate them to find the hidden patterns among various data sources to enable your organization to flourish.

A few examples of how SIEM can aid with the development of Business Intelligence have been presented, but allow your insights, needs, and creativity to run with this. The SIEM tool can become a powerful data-mining utility, in addition to being a powerful security management utility.

# PART III | SIEM Tools

# CHAPTER 8 | AlienVault OSSIM Implementation

In this chapter, we will discuss the Open Source Security Information Management (OSSIM) project, developed by AlienVault.

# Background

OSSIM offers an attractive approach to SIEM. As its name implies, OSSIM is open source and, therefore, free to download, install, modify, and operate. The free version has some limitations, involving performance, storage, and support; however, when you outgrow the free version, the professional version can fill your requirements. Especially for those looking to install their first SIEM, this tool is highly recommended. Chances are that once you see all the tool has to offer you will stay with it and eventually upgrade to the professional version.

 **NOTE** AlienVault does not consider OSSIM to be a full SIEM. Their distinction is based on the lack of long-term forensic storage of events in the free OSSIM. As we will discuss later, their Professional SIEM version solves that problem. For our purposes, however, the tool does qualify as a SIEM worthy of evaluation.

## Concept

The concept of OSSIM is simple—don't reinvent the wheel. There are many proven open source tools available, and OSSIM looks to leverage and forge them into a powerful one-stop solution for your security operations. On top of the open source tools, AlienVault has added a robust collection infrastructure, correlation engine, and risk assessment, reporting, and management tools that are very impressive. The result is a cohesive platform that offers data abstraction and allows the security analyst to monitor millions of events and focus on the few "needles in the haystack" that really matter. Customizability is emphasized as users are allowed to pick and choose how to deploy the technology, which tools to use, and how to configure and tune the device to meet their individual needs.

## Open Source Tools

Open source tools offer increased flexibility and allow organizations to reduce cost and leverage the talent of thousands of programmers. Most organizations already use some sort of open source security applications. OSSIM allows for the continued use of those tools. More than 15 best-of-breed open source tools are compiled into OSSIM, some of the more notable ones are briefly described next.

### Snort

Snort is the premier open source IDS available today. A customized version is built into OSSIM and provides alerts concerning attempted network attacks.

## OpenVAS

OpenVAS is a General Public Licensed (GPL) version of Nessus, a popular open source vulnerability scanning tool. This tool is used to provide vulnerability scans of network assets and add that valuable information to the OSSIM database. Nessus is still supported through a plug-in.

## Ntop

Ntop is a popular open source network traffic–monitoring tool. The tool provides invaluable information about traffic on the network, which can be used to detect abnormal or malicious traffic in a proactive manner.

## Nagios

Nagios is, you guessed it, a popular open source network device–monitoring software tool. This tool is used to monitor network devices and services for up time and provide alerts in the event of outages.

## PADS

The Passive Asset Detection System (PADS) is a unique tool. The tool silently monitors network traffic and logs host and service activity. This data can be monitored by OSSIM for network service anomalies.

## P0f

The p0f tool is used for passive operating system fingerprinting (discovery of operating system type and version). This tool silently listens to network traffic and identifies operating systems communicating on the network. This information is useful in the correlation process.

## OCS-NG

The Open Computer and Software Inventory Next Generation (OCS-NG) provides cross-platform asset management capability. This tool provides an automated way to keep track of what you have and provides the security analyst with that information as needed.

## OSSEC

OSSEC is an open source host-based intrusion detection system (HIDS). The tool provides cross-platform log analysis, file integrity checking, rootkit detection, policy monitoring, and real-time alerting and active response. This tool helps protect the OSSIM itself.

## OSVDB

The Open Source Vulnerability Database (OSVDB) project maintains up-to-date information about vulnerabilities and is incorporated into OSSIM and used during the correlation process and provided to the analyst as required.

### NFSen/NFDump

Netflow is an important artifact of network traffic and is extremely valuable in the correlation process. NFDump allows for the processing of Netflow v5, v7, and v9. NFSen provides a graphical web-based interface to NFDump. Both NFSen and NFDump have been integrated into OSSIM and have been customized to work with the other tools.

### Inprotect

Inprotect is a web-based interface for Nessus, OpenVAS, and NMAP. Inprotect has been integrated into OSSIM and provides the ability to define scan profiles, schedule scans, and export the scan results to different formats.

## Functionality

OSSIM is more than the sum of all its parts; a synergy is created by the way AlienVault have laced the tools together. The following diagram shows how all the tools work together (from the lowest to the highest level).

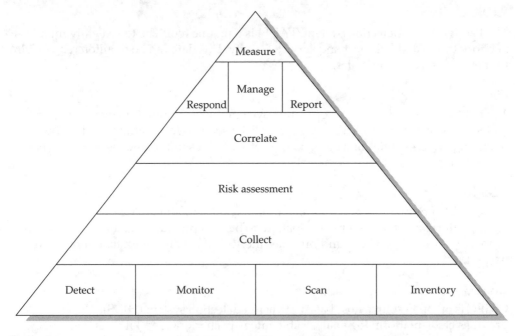

### Detect

AlienVault defines a *detector* as any program that listens on the network, monitors files or logs looking for signs of attacks, and issues alerts accordingly. There are basically two types of detectors: pattern based (signature) and anomaly based.

**Pattern-based (Signature) Detectors**    Pattern-based detectors use a signature of known bad behavior and alert when activity matches that signature. Most of the security devices in place today are pattern-based (or signature-based). OSSIM comes with a couple of pattern-based IDSs/HIDSs included. However, the true power of OSSIM is in its ability to interface with many external (commercial and free) devices through an agent, plug-in technology. Currently more than 2390 plug-ins are available to interface with nearly every security or other application available. The plug-ins are customizable and new ones can be created as needed.

**Anomaly-based Detectors**   Anomaly-based detectors have a baseline of known good behavior and alert on anomalies or deviations from that baseline. Anomaly-based detectors are the only types of detector that can identify zero-day (or previously unknown) attacks. Anomaly-based detectors offer a strong complement to pattern-based detectors. Several anomaly-based detectors are built into OSSIM.

## Monitor

OSSIM uses monitors to provide perspective on network traffic and quickly find changes in the network. Along with detectors, OSSIM uses monitors for correlation. There are three types of monitors: Network, Availability, and Customized.

**Network Monitoring**   Network monitoring is done by building usage profiles and performing session analysis. The Ntop tool produces three types of monitoring:

- **Network usage information**   This information deals with network statistics like number of bytes transmitted over a period of time.
- **Service activity information**   This information deals with the statistics of services like pop, http, smtp, ssh, etc.
- **Real-time session monitoring**   This information provides a picture of active sessions, in real-time, and which hosts are participating on which ports. The Ntop tool may provide this information through sniffing, or network flow data may be imported from Cisco routers and other devices.

**Availability Monitoring**   Availability monitoring is used to detect denial of service (DoS) attacks or other network outages. The Nagios tool interacts with a special plug-in to include this data in the correlation process and present it to the user as appropriate.

**Customized System Monitoring**   You can also customize a plug-in to detect just about anything you are interested in and then act accordingly. For example, you may trigger a vulnerability scan of a host that that you suspect is compromised and further adjust the correlation, risk, and reliability properties based on the results.

## Scan

Network vulnerability scans are critical to the correlation process. These scans attempt to simulate attacks and determine if a network device is vulnerable to a particular attack. The OpenVAS tool is used to perform this task, and the data is inserted into the database and used by OSSIM.

## Inventory

One of the fundamental questions in network security is, What do you have? It is a question that is often overlooked or not taken seriously until there is an incident. At that point, it is too late and security operations teams then loose valuable time trying to track down basic asset and owner/user contact information. OSSIM employs multiple agent-based and agent-less tools to provide automated asset inventory collection. Then you can manually insert or adjust the information on the server.

## Collect

The purpose of the collection infrastructure is to capture and normalize all disparate security device information and provide it to the server for further processing. This function is very important because of the varying data formats used by security device vendors. After the data has been collected and normalized, it can be used in conjunction with other data from other sources, now in the same format, to discover potentially malicious traffic emanating on your network. There are basically two ways to get information from a security device: push or pull.

**Push**    In a push scenario, data is pushed from the security device in the native format of the device. This is often done by SNMP or SYSLOG format and no changes are made to the software running on the security device. This technique is often useful for appliances and other devices that are difficult to install additional software on.

**Pull**    In a pull scenario, a software agent is installed on the security device and is used to pull data from the device to a collection sensor or server. An agent uses plug-ins to parse information from a particular format (varies for each device vendor). This technique is often used on servers and workstations where it is easy to install software.

**Prioritization**    When events arrive at the server, the priority levels are normalized and placed into a standard AlienVault format from 0 and 5. The administrator may adjust these default values through a normalization table and prioritization policy. For example, higher priority may be given to internal events over external events.

**Collection Policy**    It is possible to establish a priority and collection policy at the sensor level to filter and consolidate events prior to sending them to the OSSIM server. This powerful technique allows the administrator to throttle events and manage what would otherwise be an overwhelming event flow on some networks.

## Risk Assessment

Risk assessment is the process of measuring risk and attempting to determine what is important and what is not. This risk assessment is meant to be an aide to the decision-making process. OSSIM calculates a risk parameter for each event. This calculation is based on the following three parameters:

■ Asset value (how much does it cost if compromised?)

■ Threat represented by the event (how much damage can be done to the asset?)

■ The probability that the event will occur (or get past mitigating factors)

The creators of OSSIM use this traditional definition to describe the calculation of risk (http://www.alienvault.com/community.php?section=Whatis):

*A measure of the potential Impact of a Threat on Assets given the Probability that it will occur*

Since the SIEM is positioned on the network with a unique view of the assets, threats, and network traffic (to help determine the likelihood of an attack); the SIEM may assign real-time risk values to an event that essentially say this event is highly likely to have happened, this event is probably a false positive, or this event is otherwise insignificant.

## Correlate

The most important aspect of any SIEM tool is the correlation engine. The job of the correlation engine is to reduce *false positives* (false alarms) and prevent *false negatives* (where intrusions go unnoticed). This is truly where the magic happens. OSSIM was built to provide "context of the attack." To do this, five variables are considered: alerts, vulnerabilities, inventory, anomalies, and the network. OSSIM performs three types of correlation, which are described next.

**Logical Correlation**   Logical correlation takes place through a set of predefined and customized rules that perform Boolean logic on any number of event conditions. A tree of conditions is built based on rules. As the event is tested against the tree of conditions, the priority of the event is increased as conditions are met. Additional events may be generated by the correlation engine and recursively added to the correlation process.

**Inventory Correlation**   Inventory correlation takes place when an asset's characteristics are measured against a particular threat. For example, if a blaster worm is detected attacking an Apache web server, the event may be discarded as a false positive.

**Cross Correlation**   Cross correlation performs a cross-check between IDS data and vulnerability data. This allows for the increased priority of events based on whether the asset is vulnerable to that exploit or not.

## Respond

OSSIM is capable of responding automatically to a given event or set of events. Responses include sending an email or sending a network change directive, such as adjusting a firewall or switch configuration. It should be stated that this type of activity should be well thought-out and poses a risk to network operations. That said, OSSIM offers tools to help you do this if you need to.

## Manage

Once an attack is detected, collected, assessed for risk, correlated, and validated by the analyst as real, a ticket may be generated to track the incident through resolution. Tickets may be generated from several places: Alarm Panel, Forensic Console, and the Risk Dashboards. Each ticket contains information about the owner of the incident, the events contained in the incident, the current status of the incident, and history of the incident. The ticket is stored in a database that can be searched for trending analysis and reports can be drawn from that data.

## Report

From time to time, an analyst will need to produce reports for analysis or management. OSSIM contains a robust report engine with many canned reports and the ability to customize and create reports for specific purposes.

## Measure

Dashboards are provided to visually present data in a manner that is easy to digest. Again, OSSIM comes with standard dashboards, and you have the ability to create your own. Existing dashboards include Executive views, Compliance views, Map views, and Network Diagram views, to mention a few. Each analyst can select and work with the dashboards that allow him or her to complete required tasks more efficiently. The dashboards offer various viewpoints at different levels of your organization.

 **NOTE** The measure function allows for higher-level functions like compliance. In fact, OSSIM has a built-in compliance module that measures elements of ISO27001 and PCI compliance.

# Commercial Version

As previously mentioned, AlienVault offers a commercial version of OSSIM, called the *Professional SIEM*. This solution is more appropriate for high-volume production environments. The AlienVault Professional SIEM offers several benefits.

## High Volume Storage

AlienVault calls this *Security Event Management (SEM)*, which is part of their Professional SIEM offering. SEM allows for long-term storage in a dedicated, robust database. Further, this version digitally signs and time-stamps events as they are stored in the database. This ensures the integrity of the data in a forensically sound manner, which may be necessary when presenting evidence in a court of law.

## Scalability

Using the AlienVault Professional SIEM, you may design distributed and hierarchical deployments of the SIEM components. This facilitates monitoring of large organizations with multiple locations. On the extreme end of this scalability is what is called *Managed Security Service Provider (MSSP)*, which is the ability to monitor multiple clients (remotely) within the SIEM.

### Increased Performance

The AlienVault Professional SIEM has several optimizations and load distribution layers. According to AlienVault, this allows a boost of performance that is 30 times faster than the free OSSIM version.

### Increased Reliability

For those organizations that require a commercial license and the level of support and accountability that come with that, the AlienVault Professional SIEM may be for you. Even though both versions are thoroughly tested by AlienVault and the OSSIM community, naturally, as with all open source solutions, OSSIM may be less stable and more prone to bugs.

### Appliance Form Factor

The AlienVault Professional SIEM comes in both software and hardware-appliance forms. The appliance provides additional performance and stability.

# Design

When designing your SIEM implementation with OSSIM, first you need to know what the components are and how they fit together.

## Architecture

OSSIM has four components: sensors, management server, database, and frontend. These building blocks are typically put together as shown in Figure 8-1.

### Sensors

A sensor is the lowest-level component and serves as an interface between other security devices and management server(s). The sensor is a combination of a collector agent and a set of detectors and monitors. The agent uses plug-ins to parse traffic from other security devices and send the data to upstream management server(s). In addition, the sensor may also

- Serve as a security detector by performing pattern-based or anomaly intrusion detection
- Serve as a network vulnerability scanner
- Perform network monitoring

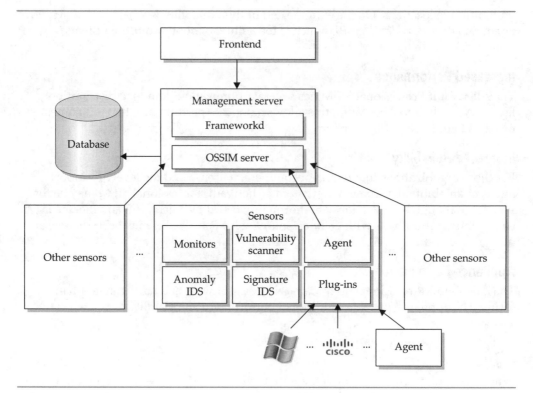

**Figure 8-1.**    OSSIM architecture

## Management Server

The management server includes two components:

- *Frameworkd,* which serves as a daemon that controls other components
- *OSSIM server,* which processes the events received from sensors

The server is responsible for normalizing, collecting, prioritizing, correlating, and assessing risk. In addition, some maintenance functions are performed, such as backups, inventory, and scheduled processes.

## Database

The SQL database stores all the information required for OSSIM to function. It should here again be noted that the OSSIM only stores data required for real-time correlation and forensic analysis. For long-term storage, the AlienVault Professional SIEM should be used.

### Frontend

The frontend or console provides a user interface to OSSIM. The interface is web-based and very impressive indeed (as you will see in the next chapter). The collection of data and integration of otherwise orthogonal tools is noteworthy.

## Deployment Considerations

Before deploying OSSIM, several things should be taken into consideration.

### Topology

OSSIM is flexible and may be installed in a traditional manner, as shown in Figure 8-1, or in a more complex manner with several hierarchical levels of servers. Also, all of the components may run on a single server or may be split up and run on multiple servers.

### Functionality of the Sensors

Since sensors have several built-in functions, the role of each sensor should be planned in advance. Whether scanning, performing IDS, or network monitoring, the time to figure this out is prior to installing the device.

### Collection Requirements

Give some thought to the types of security device information you need to collect. The required plug-ins should be verified or created as needed. Decide if an agent will be installed or if the security device will push the events to the sensor in a raw (native) format for parsing by a plug-in at that point.

### Storage Strategy

Decide whether some events will be stored, and if so, for how long. By default, 100 days of events are stored in the forensic events database. However, only 20 million events (total) may be stored. You can adjust the days of storage in the Main | Backup screen of the configuration panel. You should also decide whether the database will be stored locally on the server or remotely on a separate device.

## Implementation

As part of the implementation process, we will discuss requirements, the installation process, profiles, and changes to the system after installation.

# Requirements

Prior to installation, the following requirements need to be met.

## Hardware Requirements

In general, the stronger your hardware, the more data and traffic it can handle. At a bare minimum, the system should have at least

- 2GB RAM
- 25GB HD
- 32- or 64-bit processor (64-bit is preferred when available, but not necessary)

## Network Interface Cards

There should be at least two Network Interface Cards (NICs) in the machine where the OSSIM will be installed. One NIC will be used for sniffing and passive activity. The second NIC will be used for scanning and other activities. The second NIC may also be used to manage the device; however, if available, a third NIC may be used for that purpose. The latter option is preferred as then you can place the management interface on a separate management network.

 **NOTE** When it comes to the type of NIC, select a NIC that supports the e1000 driver. This driver is widely accepted and compatible with the Debian GNU/Linux platform (which OSSIM is built on).

## Network Traffic

When it comes to collecting network traffic, you have several options.

**Network Span Port** The most common way to provide network traffic to a monitoring device is to use port mirroring or a Switch Port ANalyer (SPAN). Nearly every managed switch on the market has this ability. However, there are some things to consider first. Typically, the switch will take the full duplex (send and receive) traffic and combine it into the send channel of the SPAN port. This effectively cuts the bandwidth to the monitoring device in half. Therefore, on saturated networks, the SPAN port may drop packets. You can monitor this in the switch's performance statistics and manage accordingly. For example, if the amount of traffic to be sent to the SPAN port cannot be reduced, then another method may be required.

**Network Tap**   Network taps may be placed between two network devices, for example, between a server and a switch, or a router and a switch, or a router and a firewall. There are two types of Network taps: Aggregator and Full-Duplex. The Aggregator Network Tap, like the SPAN, combines send and receive traffic into a single send port to the monitoring device. However, some buffering is used to improve performance over a SPAN port. The Full-Duplex Network Tap sends both of the full send and receive data streams to the monitoring device. This requires a special NIC on the monitoring device that has dual-receive capability.

**Hub**   This is, by far, the least preferred option. However, in low-bandwidth situations, it may be the only option available due to equipment constraints. This type of configuration is prone to packet collisions and may effect the fidelity of data received.

### Understanding of Network Topology

One of the most important requirements before installing any monitoring or SIEM device on a network is to understand the network topology. You take internal, external, DMZ, encryption, extranet, and remote access factors into consideration before deciding where to place a device and how to configure the SIEM to get the most out of it.

## Installation Process

Once you get to this point, the actual installation is simple.

### Installation Media

OSSIM is updated regularly. The system is distributed by an installation CDROM (ISO image). Ensure you have the latest ISO image by going to http://www.alienvault.com/opensourcesim.php?section=Downloads.

---

 **CAUTION** The installer disk will delete anything presently on your hard drive.

## BIOS Configuration

Ensure the machine's BIOS settings are configured to boot from CD-ROM. Insert the CD-ROM and boot the machine. You should see an AlienVault boot screen. Press ENTER to start the install.

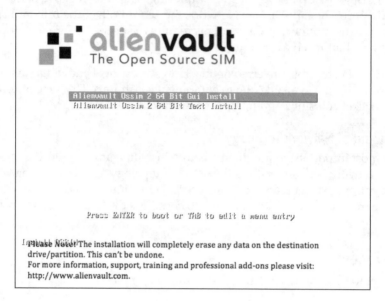

## Language

Select the language to be used for the installation process and installed system.

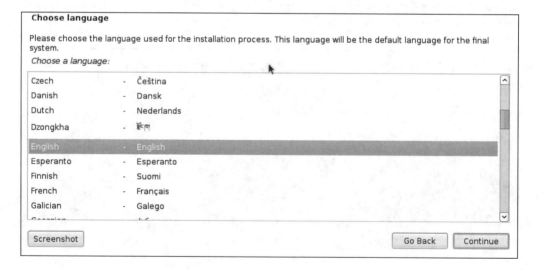

## Location

Select the location (Country) for the system.

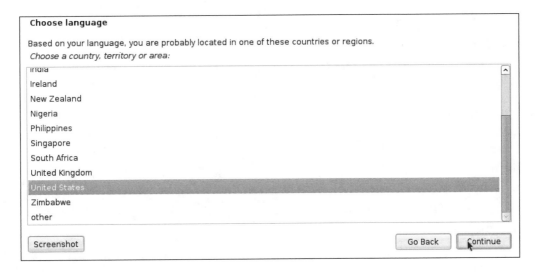

## Keyboard

Select the keyboard layout.

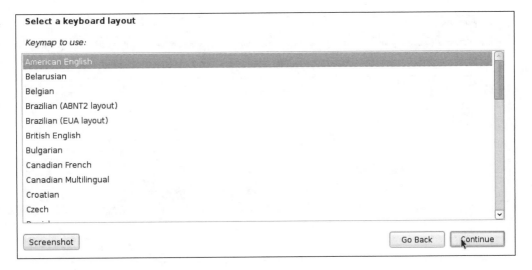

## Profile

Select the profile to be installed (all profiles are selected by default).

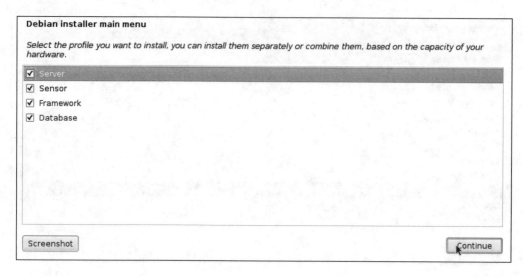

## Network IP

Select the interface to be used for management and provide an IP address.

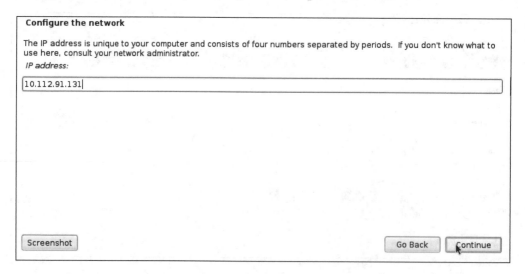

## Netmask

Enter the network mask.

---

**Configure the network**

The netmask is used to determine which machines are local to your network. Consult your network administrator if you do not know the value. The netmask should be entered as four numbers separated by periods.

*Netmask:*

| 255.255.255.192 |
|---|

| Screenshot | | Go Back | Continue |
|---|---|---|---|

---

## Gateway

Enter the network gateway.

---

**Configure the network**

The gateway is an IP address (four numbers separated by periods) that indicates the gateway router, also known as the default router. All traffic that goes outside your LAN (for instance, to the Internet) is sent through this router. In rare circumstances, you may have no router; in that case, you can leave this blank. If you don't know the proper answer to this question, consult your network administrator.

*Gateway:*

| 10.112.91.129 |
|---|

| Screenshot | | Go Back | Continue |
|---|---|---|---|

## DNS

Enter the DNS server(s), separated by spaces.

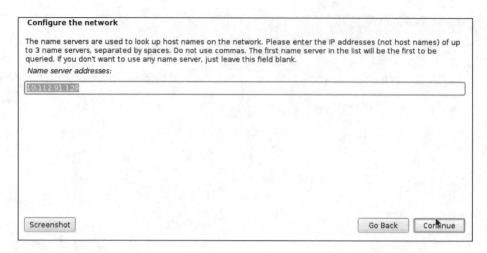

## Hostname

Enter the hostname.

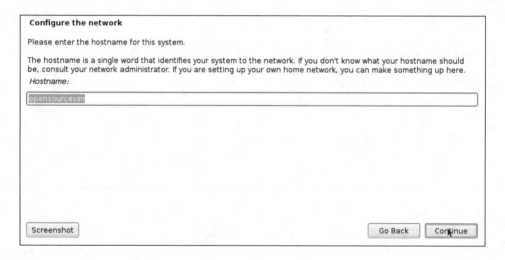

## Domain Name

Enter the domain name (suffix).

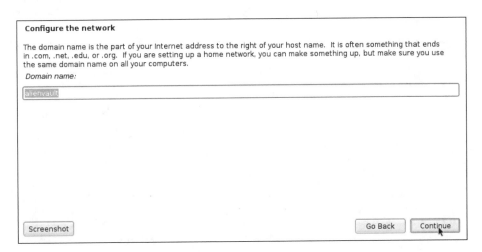

## Time Zone

Select the time zone.

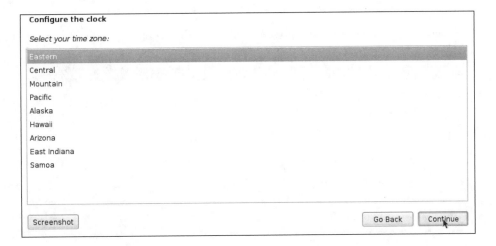

## Partitioning

Select partitioning method (we will use the default method: Guided).

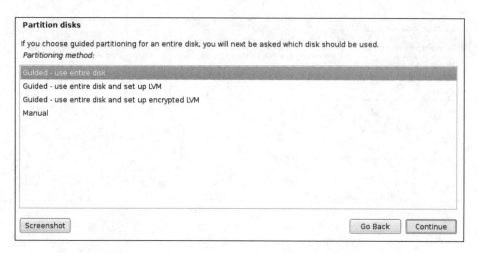

## Partitioning (*continued*)

Select the disk to partition. Remember, all data will be erased on this disk!

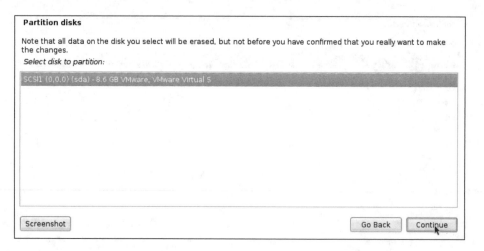

## Partitioning (*continued*)

Select the partitioning scheme (we will use default method: All Files In One Partition).

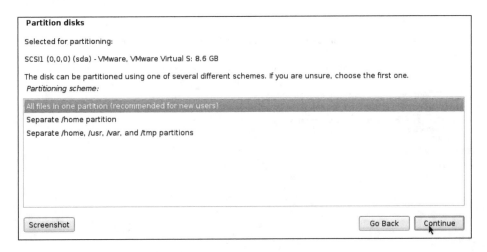

## Partitioning (*continued*)

Press Finish Partitioning And Write Changes to Disk to complete partitioning.

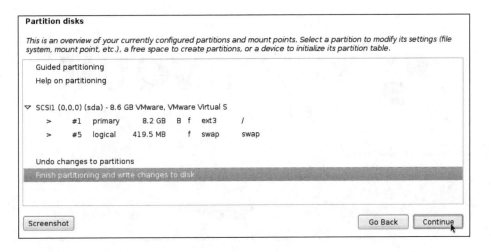

## Partitioning (*last one*)

Select Yes to confirm you want to write the changes to disk.

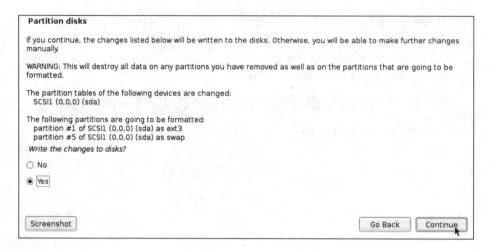

## System Installs

Watch as the system files are installed.

## License

Enter the license key (this is for the commercial SIEM; you can leave this blank for the OSSIM).

**Alienvault Cd Installer**

*Please, introduce the key for Alienvault Professional server (leave in blank for opensource version)*

| |
|---|

| Screenshot | | Go Back | Continue |
|---|---|---|---|

## Sniffer

Select the interface to sniff from.

**Install the base system**

*Select interfaces in promisc mode.*

☐ eth0 (admin)

| Screenshot | | Go Back | Continue |
|---|---|---|---|

## Network to Monitor

Select the network to monitor in CIDR format.

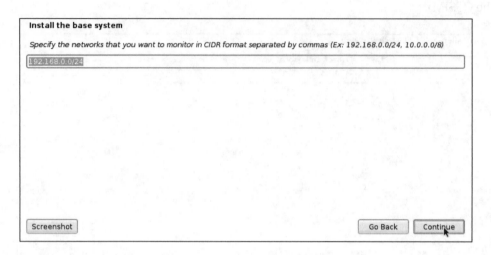

## Root Password

Provide a good root password, to be used from the console and ssh.

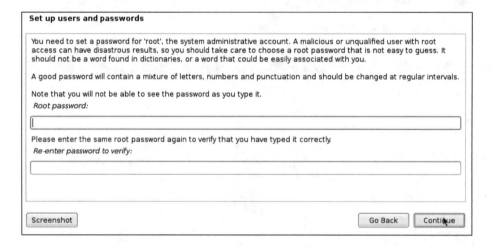

## Detectors

Select the detectors to be used.

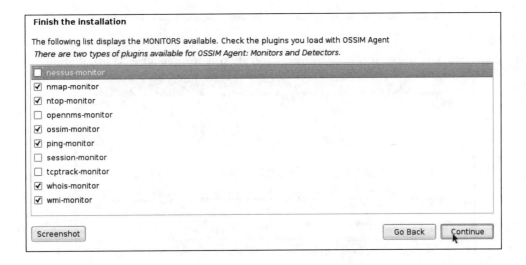

## Monitors

Select the monitors to be used.

## Reboot and Log In

Reboot and log into the web interface at http://servername/ossim/ (enter username: **admin** and password: **admin**).

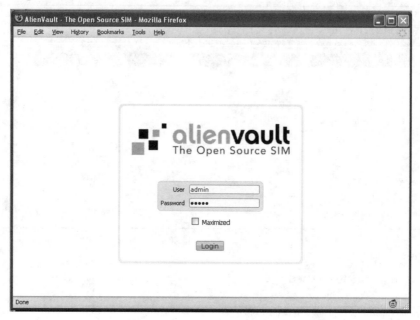

## Welcome

Read the welcome screen for useful information about your new OSSIM installation.

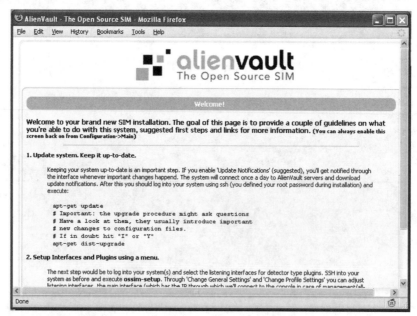

### System Configuration

After the installation, you may wish to make some changes to the configuration. You may use the following command from the console prompt:

```
ossim-config
```

After making the desired changes, run the following command to update the appropriate applications:

```
ossim-reconfig
```

From time to time, AlienVault will provide updates to the OSSIM system. You may obtain those updates by entering the following commands on the console:

```
apt-get update; apt-get dist-upgrade;
```

## Profiles

After installation, all profiles will be enabled. The system allows you to change the profile by issuing the `ossim-setup` command from the console. The following profiles are available.

### All-in-One

The All-in-One profile calls for all of the system components to run on one machine. This is the default configuration.

### Sensor

The Sensor profile turns the machine into a sensor that is responsible for collecting logs from other devices and sending them to a server after normalizing them. Snort, Ntop, p0f, PADS, and Arpwatch are enabled on the sensor profile.

### Server

The Server profile turns the machine into a server that collects events from subordinate OSSIM sensors, processes those events, and stores them in the database. The Server profile also includes maintenance and external task such as backups, online inventory, or launching scans.

### Database

The Database profile will build a MySQL database to store events, inventory information, system configurations, and other information generated by OSSIM.

## Modifications After Installation

You may modify your OSSIM installation through the console commands (shown previously) or from the Configuration menu on the web console. From there, you will be able to adjust all of the system components as needed.

# Web Console

Much care was given when developing the OSSIM web console to incorporate as much of a security analyst's needs as possible. A robust collection of user interfaces is presented in the web console (see Figure 8-2). A brief overview of the web console follows. A detailed description, including how to use the web console, will be given in the next chapter.

## Dashboards

Dashboards are provided to summarize data and get a quick snapshot of the security posture. They are meant to be a starting point for deeper analysis. The broad array of views and crisp data representations are truly astonishing. There is no doubt they are commercial grade! The Dashboard page has two subpages:

- **Dashboards**   Various dashboards presenting executive views, networks, tickets, security, vulnerabilities, inventory, and compliance
- **Risk**   A set of risk maps and metrics

## Incidents

The Incidents page shows events that have been categorized as an incident. The incidents page has three subpages:

- **Tickets**   Events categorized by an analyst as incidents
- **Alarms**   Events categorized by OSSIM as potential incidents
- **Knowledge DB**   Past events, categorized as incidents

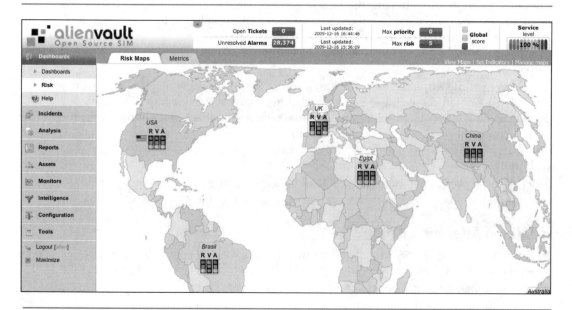

**Figure 8-2.**   OSSIM web console

## Analysis

The Analysis page presents the events that have been processed by OSSIM. The analysis page has three subpages:

- **Security Database**  Security events gathered from the various sensors
- **Vulnerabilities**  Events gathered from the vulnerability scanner
- **Anomalies**  Events gathered from the various anomaly detectors built into OSSIM

## Reports

The Reports page provides access to all of the canned and custom reports. The Reports page has two subpages:

- **Asset Search**  Allows for the searching of information from all assets
- **Reports**  Allows for various reports such as events, alarms, business compliance, vulnerabilities, tickets, metrics, and user logs

## Assets

The Assets page lets you display and edit OSSIM Asset groups. This page is critical to how OSSIM processes events and performs correlation and other actions. The Assets page has two subpages:

- **Assets**  Contains lists of host, host groups, networks, network groups, and ports
- **SIEM Components**  Provides information about sensors, servers, and databases

## Monitors

The Monitors page presents data from the three types of OSSIM monitors. The Monitors page has four subpages:

- **Network**  Shows network statistics and flow
- **Availability**  Shows availability of critical systems
- **System**  Shows the status of custom system monitors
- **Inventory**  Provides an interface to the built-in OCS-NG inventory application

## Intelligence

The Intelligence page is where the policy and rules are defined that control the correlation engine. As stated before, this page is where the magic happens. The Intelligence page has four subpages:

- **Policy/Action**  Contains the policies and actions for OSSIM
  - **Policy**  This is where many types of policies are managed, from host to network to sensors to servers to ports to plug-in groups.
  - **Action**  This is where custom actions are defined, for example, to send an email or scan a host with nmap after a sequence of events occur.

- **Correlation Directives**  Contains the heart of the correlation rules, the logical directives

- **Cross Correlation**  Contains the cross references among IDS, OSVDB, and OpenVAS events

- **Compliance Mapping**  Contains mapping of ISO27001 and PCI DSS standards

## Configuration

The Configuration page is where you modify the OSSIM configurations. The configuration page has three subpages:

- **Main**  Contains configuration parameters for all OSSIM components

- **Users**  Contains user management functions

- **Collection**  Contains the priority and reliability policies for plug-ins

## Tools

The Tools page provides an interface to perform miscellaneous task with OSSIM. The Tools page has three subpages:

- **Backup**  Contains the Backup manager and allows you to restore from backups

- **Downloads**  Provides links to various tools, including the OSSIM agent for Windows

- **Net Scan**  Allows you to launch a nmap scan

# Summary

In this chapter, we have discussed the OSSIM product by AlienVault. The OSSIM, which is based on open source tools, is free and an alternative to the commercial solutions discussed in this book. AlienVault also produces a commercial version that you may grow into. The system is highly configurable and comes full of options. We walked through the basic installation process and discussed the main web interface and the options in this chapter. In the next chapter, we will get into operating the SIEM and using it for analysis.

# CHAPTER 9 | AlienVault OSSIM Operation

I n this chapter, we will discuss the operation of OSSIM to include the interface and analysis. We will now take a detailed look at some of the interfaces.

# Interface

At the top of the interface, a status bar shows useful system statistics (clickable for drill down).

# Dashboards

Let's start by looking at the dashboards panel.

## Executive Summary

The executive dashboard gives a security posture overview, with several clickable graphics.

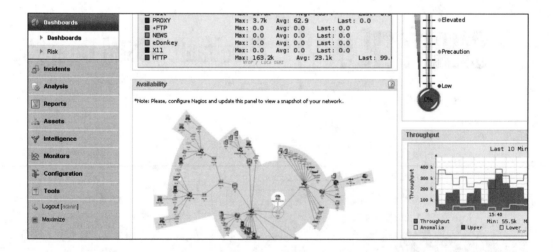

## Network

The Network dashboard provides useful network statistics and drill-down capability. Here we see the protocols used in the network and a historical timeline of their use.

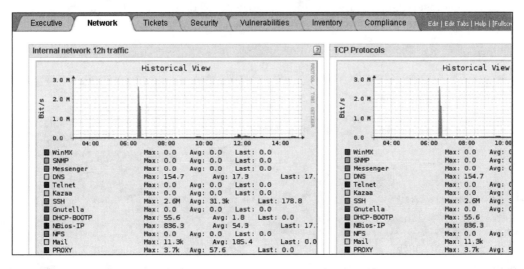

## Tickets

The Tickets dashboard provides useful information about open and closed tickets. This is useful for tracking the average time to closed tickets.

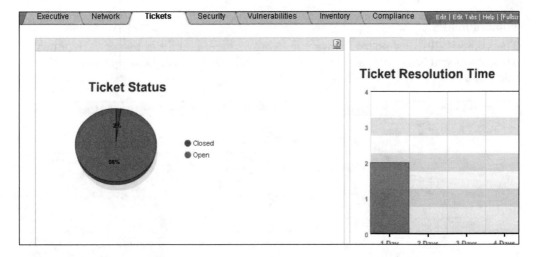

## Security

The Security dashboard presents top talker information in a clickable and graphical format. For example, the Netbios promiscuity screen shows the systems that send or receive the most Netbios traffic. Further down, a cloud diagram is shown, where the larger the IP address, the more traffic it has seen.

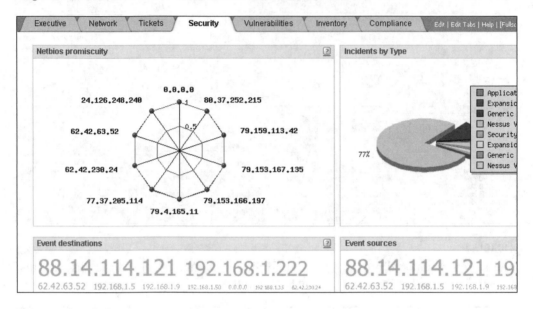

## Vulnerabilities

The Vulnerability dashboard allows you to browse vulnerabilities by network or host. This dashboard is useful when determining which networks or hosts to focus on first and clean up.

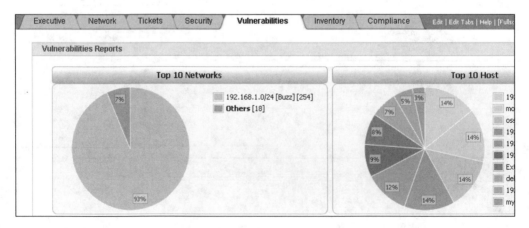

## Inventory

The Inventory dashboard presents useful information about host and software installed.

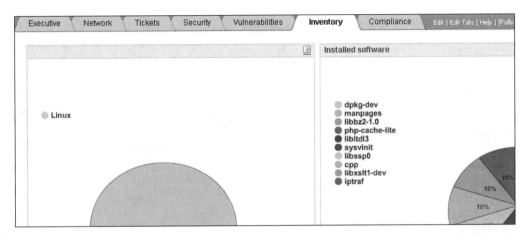

## Risk Maps

The Risk Map dashboards provide regional or global risk maps, allowing for easy assimilation. Indicators may be set, providing a visual signal of the network or asset being monitored. Each indicator shows the calculated risk, vulnerability, and availability.

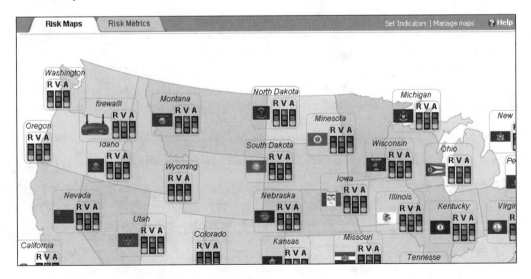

## Incidents

The Incidents panel is where analysts spend much of their time, monitoring and handling events.

### Alarms

The Alarms console provides high-level, correlated notifications of suspicious events that warrant further investigation, giving the analyst a starting point to begin the investigation. The calculated risk level for each alarm is shown in the color-coded box, with possible values from 0 to 10, 10 being highest.

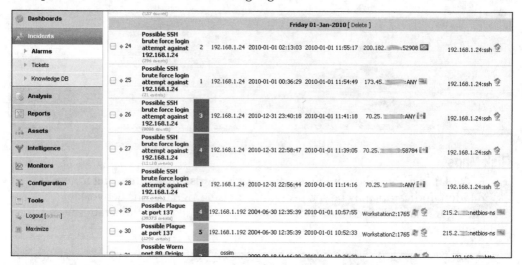

**NOTE** The foreign IPs are obscured to protect the innocent.

You can drill down on each of the alarms to get a more detailed view. In this case, we have expanded the 26th alarm, to see the subevents contained within it. In this particular alarm, we see that three subevents triggered the alarm.

Again, you may click on a subevent and see more details, in this case the raw events. With this particular event, we see there were several brute-force attempts to log into the SSH server.

**Alarm Detail ID2471966**

| # | Id | Alarm | Risk | Date | Source | Destination | Correlation Level |
|---|----|-------|------|------|--------|-------------|-------------------|
| 1 | 2471966 | ▣ **Possible SSH brute force login attempt against 192.168.1.24** | 3 | 2010-01-01 11:41:18 | 70.25.▮▮▮ ANY [◆] | 192.168.1.24:ssh | 5 |
| | | **Alarm Summary** [ Total Events: 1000 - Unique Dst IPAddr: 1 - Unique Types: 2 - Unique Dst Ports: 1 ] | | | | | |
| 1 | 2471965 | **SSHd: Invalid user** | 1 | 2010-12-31 23:44:12 | 70.25.▮▮▮ANY [◆] | 192.168.1.24:ssh | 5 |
| 2 | 2471964 | **SSHd: Invalid user** | 1 | 2010-12-31 23:44:10 | 70.25.▮▮▮ANY [◆] | 192.168.1.24:ssh | 5 |
| 3 | 2471963 | **SSHd: Invalid user** | 1 | 2010-12-31 23:44:10 | 70.25.▮▮▮:ANY [◆] | 192.168.1.24:ssh | 5 |
| 4 | 2471962 | **SSHd: Invalid user** | 1 | 2010-12-31 23:44:10 | 70.25.▮▮▮ANY [◆] | 192.168.1.24:ssh | 5 |
| 5 | 2471961 | **SSHd: Invalid user** | 1 | 2010-12-31 23:44:10 | 70.25.▮▮▮:ANY [◆] | 192.168.1.24:ssh | 5 |
| 6 | 2471960 | **SSHd: Invalid user** | 1 | 2010-12-31 23:44:10 | 70.25.▮▮▮:ANY [◆] | 192.168.1.24:ssh | 5 |
| 7 | 2471959 | **SSHd: Invalid user** | 1 | 2010-12-31 23:44:10 | 70.25.▮▮▮:ANY [◆] | 192.168.1.24:ssh | 5 |
| 8 | 2471958 | **SSHd: Invalid user** | 1 | 2010-12-31 23:44:10 | 70.25.▮▮▮:ANY [◆] | 192.168.1.24:ssh | 5 |
| 9 | 2471957 | **SSHd: Invalid user** | 1 | 2010-12-31 23:44:10 | 70.25.▮▮▮:ANY [◆] | 192.168.1.24:ssh | 5 |

## Tickets

Tickets are used by the analyst to track suspicious events or incidents.

| Ticket | Title | Priority | Created | Life Time | In charge | Submitter | Type | Status |
|--------|-------|----------|---------|-----------|-----------|-----------|------|--------|
| ALA179 | AV Possible SSH Scan from ossim against dell | 2 | 2010-01-12 17:42:16 | 8 Days 21:29 | Pablo Vargas | OSSIM admin | Generic | Open |
| ALA178 | Possible SSH brute force login attempt against 192.168.1.24 | 3 | 2010-01-12 13:38:54 | 9 Days 01:33 | OSSIM admin | OSSIM admin | Generic | Open |
| VUL177 | nessus: SSH protocol version 1 enabled | 2 | 2009-12-25 18:13:45 | 26 Days 20:58 | OSSIM admin | nessus | Nessus Vulnerability | Open |

Sidebar navigation: Dashboards | Incidents ▸ Alarms ▸ Tickets ▸ Knowledge DB | Analysis | Reports | Assets | Intelligence | Monitors | Configuration

Top tabs: Tickets | Report    Types | Tags | Email Template    ? Help

Filter Simple [change to Advanced] — Class: ALL | Type: ALL | Search text in all fields | In charge | Status: Open | Priority: ALL

You can click on a ticket for detailed information. This ticket reveals a discovered vulnerability, whereby the SMB shares are accessible by a NULL connect attack.

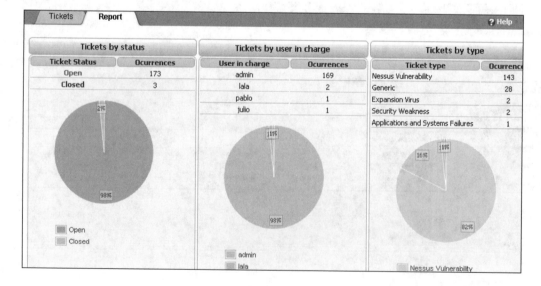

## Ticket Reports

Quick reports may be generated on tickets from the Report tab (inside the Tickets console).

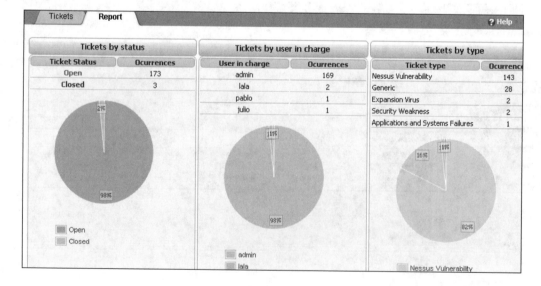

## Knowledgebase

This is one of OSSIM's unique and powerful features: its ability to build knowledge.

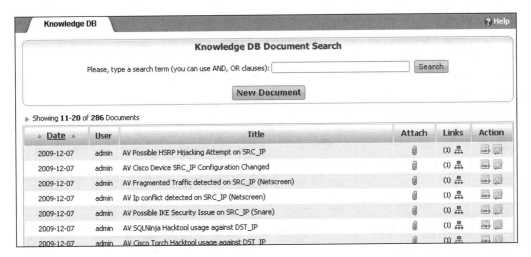

As can be seen here, historical knowledge can be retained. You may click each document for details. It is good practice to start the document title with a description of the organization or network being monitored. In this case, the *AV* stands for *AlienVault*. You may use whatever designation you like. This helps provide a quick context when monitoring several organizations or networks.

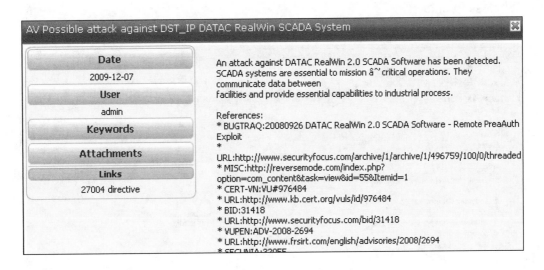

## Analysis

The Analysis panel is where you normally land if you click on a higher-level view.

### SIEM Events

SIEM Events are stored in a database and may be searched and filtered as required. For instance, a search may be performed of Unique Events, sorted by TCP Protocol, by clicking that link in the Summary Statistics box on the right-hand side.

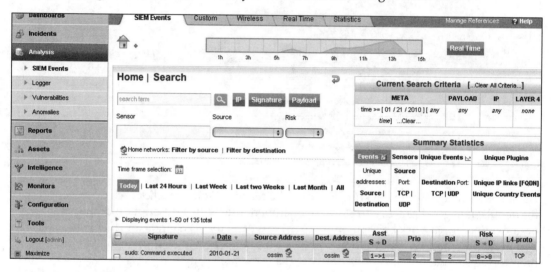

### Wireless Events

The Wireless tab contains all events received by wireless devices.

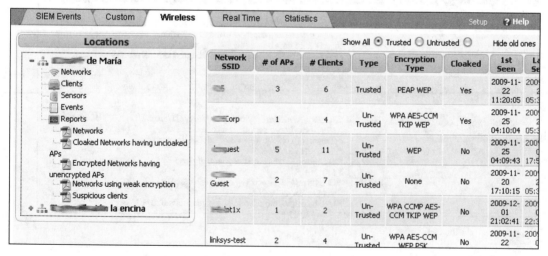

## Real Time Events

The Real Time tab contains the most up-to-date information (last 15 events received). You may hover over the Event Name to see more detailed information, such as the event priority, reliability, network interface, and network protocol.

| Date | Event Name | Risk | Generator | Sensor | Source IP |
|------|-----------|------|-----------|--------|-----------|
| 2010-01-21 15:07:50 | sudo: Command executed | 0 | sudo | ossim | ossim |
| 2010-01-21 13:50:00 | rrd_threshold: ntop global IP_DHCP-BOOTPBytes | 0 | rrd_threshold | ossim | N/A |
| 2010-01-21 13:45:00 | rrd_threshold: ntop global IP_DHCP-BOOTPBytes | 0 | rrd_threshold | ossim | N/A |
| 2010-01-21 13:44:41 | sudo: Command executed | 0 | sudo | ossim | ossim |
| 2010-01-21 13:44:19 | sudo: Command executed | 0 | sudo | ossim | ossim |
| 2010-01-21 13:44:18 | sudo: Command executed | 0 | sudo | ossim | ossim |
| 2010-01-21 13:43:57 | sudo: Command executed | 0 | sudo | ossim | ossim |
| 2010-01-21 13:43:46 | sudo: Command executed | 0 | sudo | ossim | ossim |
| 2010-01-21 13:43:41 | sudo: Command executed | 0 | sudo | ossim | ossim |

*pause   Done. [0 new rows]*

## Vulnerabilities

On the Vulnerabilities console, you may view detailed reports from the vulnerability scanner. In this case, you can see a Nessus report of our network, which shows the host(s) names at the top, their open ports, and a detailed list of vulnerabilities found.

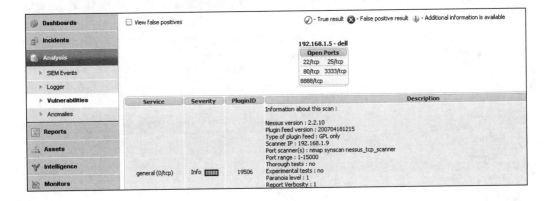

## Anomalies

In the Anomalies console, you will find events from the anomaly detectors. Here, we see that several hosts triggered Ntop alerts because their network traffic levels crossed Ntop configured thresholds (refer to Chapter 8 for a description of Ntop).

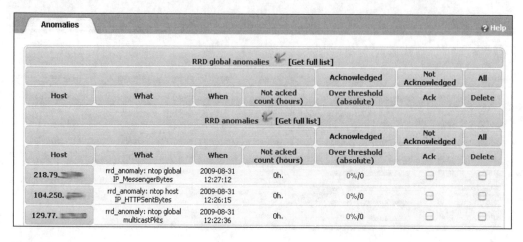

## Reports

In the Reports console, you can generate preconfigured or custom reports. As you can see, several "Top 10" or "Top 15" reports are available in several formats (PDF, RTF, and email).

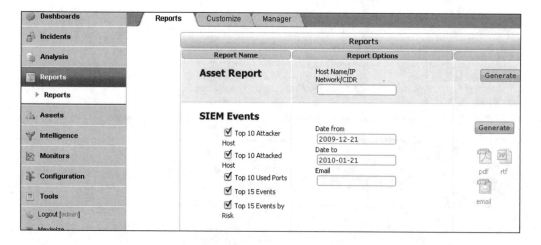

# Assets

Next, let's take a look at the Assets panel.

## Hosts

The Host console provides detailed information about the host being tracked by the SIEM. This console can be used to add or remove a host from the SIEM.

| Hostname | IP | Asst | Thr_C | Thr_A | Sensors | Scantype | Alert | Per |
|---|---|---|---|---|---|---|---|---|
| Workstation28 | 192.168.4.10 | 3 | 30 | 30 | ossim ossim-server | Nagios | 0 | 0 |
| Workstation2 | 192.168.1.130 | 3 | 30 | 30 | ossim ossim-server | None | 0 | 0 |
| Webserver3 | 12.0.1.13 | 2 | 310 | 310 | ossim ossim-server | None | 0 | 0 |
| Webserver2 | 12.0.1.12 | 2 | 310 | 310 | ossim ossim-server | None | 0 | 0 |
| WebServer1 | 12.0.1.11 | 2 | 310 | 310 | ossim ossim-server | None | 0 | 0 |
| VPN-Router | 12.0.1.100 | 2 | 310 | 310 | ossim ossim-server | None | 0 | 0 |
| SMTP-Server | 12.0.1.14 | 2 | 310 | 310 | ossim ossim-server | None | 0 | 0 |
| prueba uno | 192.168.1.10 | 2 | 31 | 31 | ossim ossim-server prueba | None | 0 | 0 |

Tabs: Dashboards | Incidents | Analysis | Reports | Assets ( Asset Search, Assets, SIEM Components ) | Intelligence | Monitors | Configuration | Tools | Logout [admin]

Top tabs: Hosts | Host groups | Networks | Network groups | Ports | Inventory

HOSTS — New | Modify | Delete selected | Duplicate selected | Apply

## Networks

The Networks console provides detailed information about the networks tracked by the SIEM. This console can be used to group hosts into appropriate networks and provide proper organizational context on reports and other SIEM screens within.

Top tabs: Hosts | Host groups | Networks | Network groups | Ports | Inventory

NETWORKS — New | Modify | Delete selected | Duplicate selected | Enable/Disable **Nessus** | Enable/Disable **Nagios** | Apply

| Name | IPs | Asst | Thr_C | Thr_A | Nessus | Nagios | Sensors | Description |
|---|---|---|---|---|---|---|---|---|
| Buzz | 192.168.1.0/24 | 3 | 30 | 30 | ✓ | ✓ | ossim | |
| Chicago-Office | 10.0.3.0/24 | 2 | 310 | 310 | ✗ | ✗ | ossim ossim-server prueba pruebadk Sensor_10.255.254.1 test alberto 2 | |
| DMZ-Network | 12.0.1.0/24 | 2 | 310 | 310 | ✗ | ✗ | ossim ossim-server prueba pruebadk | |

# Intelligence

Next, let's look at the Intelligence panel.

## Correlation Directives

The Correlation Directives console is used to control the correlation engine. As you can see, the rules are listed in the center and then detailed information about each rule is provided on the right.

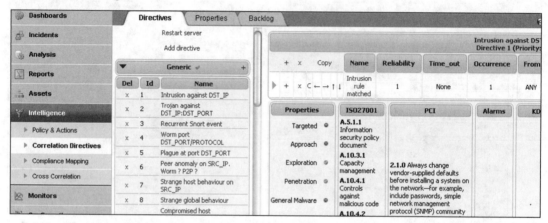

You may click the small right-facing arrow next to each rule for details about that rule. In this case, you see the rule is comprised of several smaller rules that track events from snort or Ntop devices.

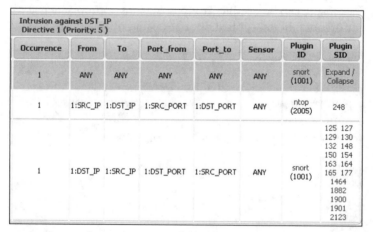

| Occurrence | From | To | Port_from | Port_to | Sensor | Plugin ID | Plugin SID |
|---|---|---|---|---|---|---|---|
| 1 | ANY | ANY | ANY | ANY | ANY | snort (1001) | Expand / Collapse |
| 1 | 1:SRC_IP | 1:DST_IP | 1:SRC_PORT | 1:DST_PORT | ANY | ntop (2005) | 248 |
| 1 | 1:DST_IP | 1:SRC_IP | 1:DST_PORT | 1:SRC_PORT | ANY | snort (1001) | 125 127<br>129 130<br>132 148<br>150 154<br>163 164<br>165 177<br>1464<br>1882<br>1900<br>1901<br>2123 |

Intrusion against DST_IP
Directive 1 (Priority: 5 )

## Correlation Backlog

The Correlation Backlog console is very interesting and provides all of the rules still in various states of correlation. The rules will stay in this queue until they time out or complete, which is useful to an analyst, allowing him or her to be proactive and detect attacks in progress, even before the final rule triggers. An analyst can also use this console fill in the gaps of another triggered rule and as a leaping off point for further investigation.

| Directive Name | Directive Id | Count | Edit |
|---|---|---|---|
| New directive | 8000 | 154017 | View/Edit current directive definition |
| test permisos sensor 1.1.1.1 | 54728 | 45777 | View/Edit current directive definition |
| New directive | 14 | 9145 | View/Edit current directive definition |
| Copy of New directive | 26 | 9145 | View/Edit current directive definition |
| Possible portscan against DST_IP | 11 | 6569 | View/Edit current directive definition |
| Recurrent Snort event | 3 | 876 | View/Edit current directive definition |
| Possible Trojan against DST_IP:DST_PORT | 2 | 682 | View/Edit current directive definition |
| AV Possible Cisco VPN brute force login attempt against SRC_IP | 11005 | 45 | View/Edit current directive definition |
| An important host (SRC_IP) has changed its OS | 18 | 39 | View/Edit current directive definition |
| Possible Worm port DST_PORT/PROTOCOL | 4 | 36 | View/Edit current directive definition |
| Possible Plague at port DST_PORT | 5 | 36 | View/Edit current directive definition |

Directives | Properties | **Backlog**    ? Help
The backlog contains all those directives matched who either haven't reached the last correlation level or haven't timed out yet

## Compliance Mapping

The Compliance Mapping console provides a map between directives and ISO/PCI standards. For example, here you can see a mapping between the PCI DSS 1.1.1 and a peer-to-peer (P2P) directive.

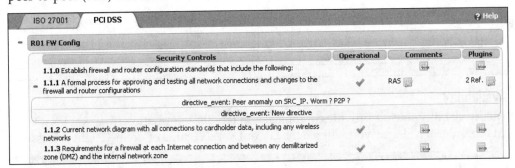

ISO 27001 | **PCI DSS**    ? Help

R01 FW Config

| Security Controls | Operational | Comments | Plugins |
|---|---|---|---|
| 1.1.0 Establish firewall and router configuration standards that include the following: | ✓ | | |
| 1.1.1 A formal process for approving and testing all network connections and changes to the firewall and router configurations | ✓ | RAS | 2 Ref. |
| directive_event: Peer anomaly on SRC_IP. Worm ? P2P ? | | | |
| directive_event: New directive | | | |
| 1.1.2 Current network diagram with all connections to cardholder data, including any wireless networks | ✓ | | |
| 1.1.3 Requirements for a firewall at each Internet connection and between any demilitarized zone (DMZ) and the internal network zone | ✓ | | |

## Cross Correlation

The Cross Correlation tab provides the mappings between vulnerability data and event plug-ins. This mapping is one of the strengths of the SIEM—its ability to correlate across plug-ins from different sources. Those associated may be edited or modified from this screen.

**Plugin reference** | Correlation Rules | Edit Rules    ? Help

(0-25 of 4543)  Next 25 ->

| Plugin id | Plugin sid | Reference id | Reference sid |
|---|---|---|---|
| snort | BACKDOOR subseven 22 | nessus | nessus: SubSeven |
| snort | BACKDOOR subseven 22 | ovsdb | 1 |
| snort | BACKDOOR ACKcmdC trojan scan | services | 1054 |
| snort | BACKDOOR subseven DEFCON8 2.1 access | nessus | nessus: SubSeven |
| snort | BACKDOOR QAZ Worm Client Login access | services | 7597 |
| snort | BACKDOOR netbus active | nessus | nessus: NetBus 1.x |
| snort | BACKDOOR netbus active | nessus | nessus: NetBus 2.x |
| snort | BACKDOOR netbus getinfo | nessus | nessus: NetBus 1.x |
| snort | BACKDOOR netbus getinfo | nessus | nessus: NetBus 2.x |

## Monitors

Next, let's move to the Monitors panel.

### Network

The Network console provides network statistical information from Ntop. Notice how the traffic is broken down into GBytes of traffic and then by protocol (FTP, web proxy, HTTP, and DNS). Each host is clickable so you can obtain detailed information.

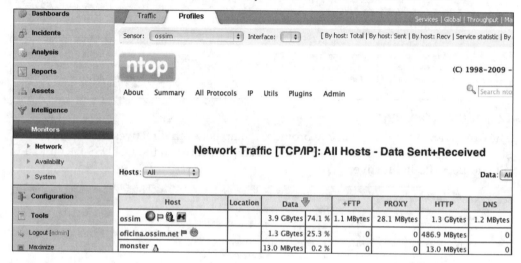

### Availability

The Availability console provides graphical and tabular information from Nagios. On this console, at a glance, you will see the UP or DOWN status of defined network assets.

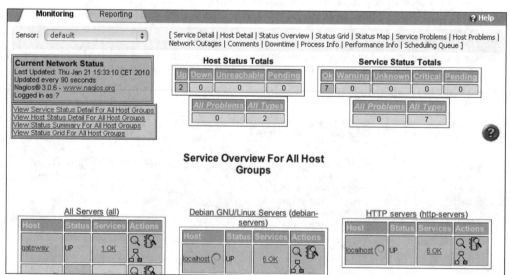

# Analysis of a Basic Attack

Now that you've taken a test drive around the interface, it's time to get busy doing analysis.

The best place to start is inside the Alarms console. Scanning down from present day to recent days, you see something interesting, a series of alarms on the evening of December 31.

From this, you can already see the types of alarms: Possible Plague on port 137 and Possible Worm on port 139/tcp. You can see the risk values ranging from 1 and 5. Let's drill down on the second alarm shown (34) by clicking the plus sign on the left-hand side.

Now you can see the subalarms that comprise the higher-level alarms. Analyzing from the bottom up, you discover that the first events started at 17:49:01, and it appears that several other levels of correlation kicked in as more events arrived. From the Alarm Summary statements, the first alarm fired after 17 events, the next level of correlation fired after 300 events, and so on, up to 20,000 events. This shows some of the power of the SIEM to aggregate like events and reduce data to a manageable form. You can drill down even further to see events within an alarm by either clicking the plus sign or selecting the risk number.

| # | Id | Alarm | Risk | Date | Source | Destination | Correlation Level |
|---|-----|-------|------|------|--------|-------------|-------------------|
| 1 | 2311184 | ◇ Possible Worm port 139/tcp | 5 | 2009-12-31 17:51:40 | prueba uno:1765 | Ext Gateway:netbios-ssn | 5 |
| | | **Alarm Summary** [ Total Events: 20000 - Unique Dst IPAddr: 20000 - Unique Types: 1 - Unique Dst Ports: 1 ] | | | | | |
| 2 | 2291183 | ◇ Possible Worm port 139/tcp | 5 | 2009-12-31 17:49:24 | prueba uno:1765 | Ext Gateway:netbios-ssn | 4 |
| | | **Alarm Summary** [ Total Events: 2000 - Unique Dst IPAddr: 2000 - Unique Types: 1 - Unique Dst Ports: 1 ] | | | | | |
| 3 | 2289182 | ▣ Possible Worm port 139/tcp | 2 | 2009-12-31 17:49:08 | prueba uno:1765 | Ext Gateway:netbios-ssn | 3 |
| | | **Alarm Summary** [ Total Events: 300 - Unique Dst IPAddr: 300 - Unique Types: 1 - Unique Dst Ports: 1 ] | | | | | |
| 1 | 2289181 | **Spade: Closed dest port used** | 0 | 2004-06-30 12:35:41 | prueba uno:1765 | 192.168.1.47:netbios-ssn | 3 |
| 2 | 2289180 | **Spade: Closed dest port used** | 0 | 2004-06-30 12:35:41 | prueba uno:1765 | 192.168.1.46:netbios-ssn | 3 |
| 3 | 2289179 | **Spade: Closed dest port used** | 0 | 2004-06-30 12:35:41 | prueba uno:1765 | 192.168.1.45:netbios-ssn | 3 |
| 4 | 2289178 | **Spade: Closed dest port used** | 0 | 2004-06-30 12:35:41 | prueba uno:1765 | 192.168.1.44:netbios-ssn | 3 |
| 5 | 2289177 | **Spade: Closed dest port used** | 0 | 2004-06-30 12:35:41 | prueba uno:1765 | 192.168.1.43:netbios-ssn | 3 |

Now, you can see the raw events that triggered this subalarm. The Spade anomaly detector has supplied these events, due to "Closed dest port used." This means the destination port is closed, but the suspicious machine keeps attempting to connect to that port.

If you want to see the log of the correlation engine, as the levels of correlation occurred, you can click the name of the correlation rule, in this case, Possible Worm Port 139/tcp. This brings up a log report from the correlation engine; by scrolling to the bottom, you can see when each level occurred. Since you clicked the first rule, you expect to see five levels of correlation performed.

```
       directive_event: Possible Worm port DST_PORT/PROTOCOL, Priority: 4
       Rule 1 [2009-12-31 17:49:01] [1104:1] [Rel: 1] 192.168.1.10:1765 ->
       192.168.1.11:139
       Rule 2 [2009-12-31 17:49:01] [1104:1] [Rel: 3] 192.168.1.10:1765 ->
Log    192.168.2.15:139
       Rule 3 [2009-12-31 17:49:08] [1104:1] [Rel: 5] 192.168.1.10:1765 ->
       192.168.1.47:139
       Rule 4 [2009-12-31 17:49:24] [1104:1] [Rel: 10] 192.168.1.10:1765 ->
       192.168.7.223:139
       Rule 5 [2009-12-31 17:51:40] [1104:1] [Rel: 10] 192.168.1.10:1765 ->
       192.168.78.189:139
```

At this point, diving into the correlation engine to see what is happening is worthwhile:

1. First, click the Intelligence – Correlation Directive menu on the left side to go to the Correlation Directive console.

2. Next, click the Backlog tab since, chances are, the correlation directive you are dealing with is still in the processing queue. Sure enough, you find your directive there. You could have also found this directive in the list of directives on the Directives tab.

3. Now that you are looking at the directive in question, let's expand all of the rules by clicking the right-facing arrows on the left side.

| | | | Name | Reliability | Time_out | Occurrence | From | To | Port_from | Port_to | Sensor | Plugin ID | Plugin SID |
|---|---|---|---|---|---|---|---|---|---|---|---|---|---|
| + | x | Copy | | | | | | | | | | | |
| + | x | c ← — ↑ ↓ | Rare dest connection | 1 | None | 1 | ANY | ANY | ANY | 25,135,137,139,445,1433,1434 | ANY | spp_anomsensor (1104) | ANY |
| + | x | c ← — ↑ ↓ | Too many rare connections (15) against same port | 3 | 180 | 15 | 1:SRC_IP | ANY | ANY | 1:DST_PORT | ANY | spp_anomsensor (1104) | ANY |
| + | x | c ← — ↑ ↓ | Too many rare connections (300) against same port | 5 | 1200 | 300 | 1:SRC_IP | ANY | ANY | 1:DST_PORT | ANY | spp_anomsensor (1104) | ANY |
| + | x | c ← — ↑ ↓ | Too many rare connections (2000) against same port | 10 | 1800 | 2000 | 1:SRC_IP | ANY | ANY | 1:DST_PORT | ANY | spp_anomsensor (1104) | ANY |
| + | x | c ← — ↑ ↓ | Too many rare connections (20000) against same port | 10 | 43200 | 20000 | 1:SRC_IP | ANY | ANY | 1:DST_PORT | ANY | spp_anomsensor (1104) | ANY |

Worm port DST_PORT/PROTOCOL
Directive 4 (Priority: 4 )

As expected, there are several correlation rules. Because all of the parameters remain the same except for occurrence, each level is triggered based on repetitive events arriving. Notice how the labels 1:SRC_IP and 1:DST_PORT are used, these mean same previous source IP and same previous destination port, respectively. Also notice that events from the spp_anonsensor (Spade anomaly detector) plug-in drive this correlation directive.

4. Back to the Alarm console, you can continue your analysis by clicking the time of the alarm to see what other events came in at that time. This gives you context and allows you to see what the correlation engine saw at that instant in time.

As expected, you see many packets coming in during that timeframe. Notice also how the calculated risk is growing on the right-hand side.

| | Signature | Date | Source Address | Dest. Address | Asst S → D | Prio | Rel | Risk S → D | L4-proto |
|---|---|---|---|---|---|---|---|---|---|
| ☐ | directive_event: Possible Trojan against DST_IP:DST_PORT | 2009-12-31 17:29:22 | prueba uno:1765 | ossim-server:139 | 3->3 | 4 | 3 | 1->1 | TCP |
| ☐ | directive_event: Possible Trojan against DST_IP:DST_PORT | 2009-12-31 17:29:22 | prueba uno:1765 | ossim-server:139 | 3->3 | 4 | 3 | 1->1 | TCP |
| ☐ | directive_event: Possible Trojan against DST_IP:DST_PORT | 2009-12-31 17:29:22 | prueba uno:1765 | ossim-server:139 | 3->3 | 4 | 4 | 2->2 | TCP |
| ☐ | directive_event: Possible Trojan against DST_IP:DST_PORT | 2009-12-31 17:29:22 | prueba uno:1765 | ossim-server:139 | 3->3 | 4 | 4 | 2->2 | TCP |

Notice at the top of the Alert screen, there is a search panel that will assist you further.

| all events | |
|---|---|
| with | |
| 192.168.1.10/ | Source \| Destination \| Source/Destination |
| as: | |
| show: | Unique Events \| Portscan Events |
| Registry | |
| lookup | ARIN \| RIPE \| APNIC \| LACNIC |
| (whois) in: | |

5. By selecting the Source link, you see all of the events in the database from this IP as a source.

| | Signature | ▲ Date ▾ | Source Address | Dest. Address | Asst S → D | Prio | Rel | Risk S → D | L4-proto |
|---|---|---|---|---|---|---|---|---|---|
| ☐ | directive_event: Possible Worm port DST_PORT/PROTOCOL | 2009-12-31 17:49:01 | prueba uno:1765 | ossim-server:139 | 3->3 | 4 | 3 | 1->1 | TCP |
| ☐ | directive_event: Possible Worm port DST_PORT/PROTOCOL | 2009-12-31 17:49:08 | prueba uno:1765 | ossim-server:139 | 3->3 | 4 | 5 | 2->2 | TCP |
| ☐ | directive_event: Possible Worm port DST_PORT/PROTOCOL | 2009-12-31 17:49:24 | prueba uno:1765 | ossim-server:139 | 3->3 | 4 | 10 | 5->5 | TCP |
| ☐ | directive_event: Possible Worm port DST_PORT/PROTOCOL | 2009-12-31 17:51:40 | prueba uno:1765 | ossim-server:139 | 3->3 | 4 | 10 | 5->5 | TCP |
| ☐ | directive_event: Possible Plague at port DST_PORT | 2009-12-31 17:51:47 | prueba uno:1765 | ossim-server:137 | 3->3 | 4 | 10 | 5->5 | TCP |
| ☐ | directive_event: Possible Plague at port DST_PORT | 2009-12-31 17:53:30 | prueba uno:1765 | ossim-server:137 | 3->3 | 4 | 8 | 4->4 | TCP |

6. By clicking the Unique Events link, you get some statistics about the unique directives that have fired due to this IP. This helps you to understand the relationship to the other Alarm received: Possible Plague at port 137.

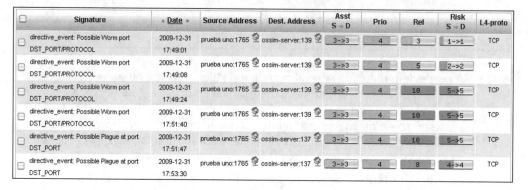

| **3 unique events detected among 20 events on 192.168.1.10/32** | | | | |
|---|---|---|---|---|
| **TCP Flags** | **Total Occurrences** | **Num of Sensors** | **First Occurrence** | **Last Occurrence** |
| directive_event: Possible Trojan against DST_IP:DST_PORT | 8 | 1 | 2009-12-31 17:29:22 | 2009-12-31 17:29:31 |
| directive_event: Possible Plague at port DST_PORT | 5 | 1 | 2009-12-31 17:29:36 | 2009-12-31 19:07:01 |
| directive_event: Possible Worm port DST_PORT/PROTOCOL | 7 | 1 | 2009-12-31 17:49:01 | 2010-01-01 10:24:29 |

7. At this point, you have enough to mark this Alarm as a potential incident and create a ticket for further tracking, assignment, and resolution. From the Alarm console, you can click the small notes icon on the right-hand side of the Alarm. This link creates a ticket for the suspicious Alarm and pulls all of its data into the ticket. At the first ticket screen, you can assign a type, in this case Expansion Virus. You can also adjust the priority (taken from the Alarm risk) if you like.

| Alarm Ticket | |
|---|---|
| Title | Possible Worm port 139/tcp |
| Submitter | OSSIM admin |
| Priority | 5 |
| Type | Expansion Virus |
| Source Ips | 192.168.1.10 |
| Dest Ips | 192.168.1.11 |
| Source Ports | 1765 |
| Dest Ports | netbios-ssn |
| Start of related events | 2009-09-18 11:11:33 |
| End of related events | 2009-12-31 17:51:40 |
| OK | |

Once the ticket has been created, you see basic information from the Alarm, along with attachments and links at the top of the ticket. You may subscribe (get email updates) to changes on this ticket by using the drop-down box to select your account and click the Subscribe button.

| Ticket | Incident | Status | Priority | Knowledge DB | Action |
|---|---|---|---|---|---|
| ALA181 | Name: **Possible Worm port 139/tcp**<br>Class: Alarm<br>Type: Expansion Virus<br>Created: 2010-01-21 21:21:53 (00:00)<br>Last Update: 00:00<br>In charge: **OSSIM admin**<br>Submitter: **OSSIM admin**<br>Extra: n/a<br>Source Ips: **192.168.1.10** - Source Ports: **1765**<br>Dest Ips: **192.168.1.11** - Dest Ports: **netbios-ssn** | Open | 5 | Documents<br>No linked documents<br>Related documents [ 2 ]<br>Link existing document<br>New document | Edit ticket<br>Delete ticket<br>New ticket |
| Email changes to: | OSSIM admin *(No email)* | | | | Subscribe  Unsubscribe |

At the bottom of the incident ticket, you find more information like status, priority, owner, description, and action taken.

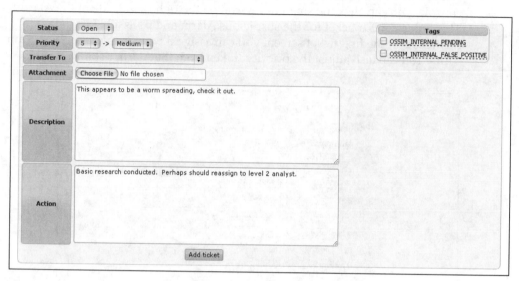

# Analysis of a Sophisticated Attack

Now let's look at a more sophisticated attack. Looking at the Dashboard console, you notice a burst of events and alarms in the last couple of days.

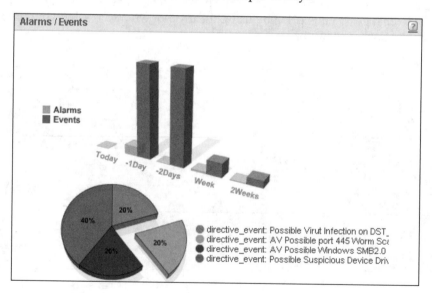

Next, you turn your attention to the Alarm console and see the following set of alarms:

| # | Alarm | Risk | Sensor | Since | Last | Source | Destination |
|---|-------|------|--------|-------|------|--------|-------------|
| | Monday 25-Jan-2010 [ Delete ] | | | | | | |
| ⬦ 1 | AV Possible Windows SMB2.0 Successful Denial of Service against 192.168.1.133 <br> (3 events) | 4 | ossim | 2010-01-25 13:12:00 | 2010-01-25 13:12:17 | Server-Win:47401 | 192.168.1.133:microsoft-ds |
| ⬦ 2 | AV Possible port 445 Worm Scan Behaviour on Server-Win <br> (4 events) | 2 | ossim | 2010-01-25 13:05:12 | 2010-01-25 13:11:36 | Server-Win:54004 | 192.168.3.157:microsoft-ds |
| ⬦ 3 | Possible Suspicious Device Driver installed on Server-Win <br> (15 events) | 3 | ossim Server-Win | 2010-01-25 13:09:09 | 2010-01-25 13:10:31 | 219.235.▨:62518 | Server-Win:instl_boots |
| ⬦ 4 | AV Possible Malicious PDF downloading suspicious executable <br> (6 events) | 3 | ossim | 2010-01-25 13:02:58 | 2010-01-25 13:08:36 | 70.38.▨:http-proxy | Server-Win:34374 |
| ⬦ 5 | Possible Virut Infection on Server-Win <br> (6 events) | 2 | ossim | 2010-01-25 13:03:09 | 2010-01-25 13:08:36 | 121.14.▨:2777 | Server-Win:1042 |

Looking at this set of alarms, you can see that they are in order, with the most recent alarms are at the top of the list. Just from this screen, you can surmise there was a virus infection (alarm 5), further files were downloaded (alarm 4), perhaps a rootkit was installed (alarm 3), another local host was scanned (alarm 2), and finally it looks like another local host was compromised from the first host (alarm 1).

**NOTE** The foreign IPs are obscured to protect the innocent.

Because the last events hit the two bottom alarms at the same time, let's review those two alarms (4 and 5) and get some idea of what happened here.

| = 4 | AV Possible Malicious PDF downloading suspicious executable <br> (6 events) | 3 | ossim | 2010-01-25 13:02:58 | 2010-01-25 13:08:36 | 70.38.▨:http-proxy | Server-Win:34374 |
|---|---|---|---|---|---|---|---|
| # | Id | Alarm | Risk | Date | Source | Destination | |
| 1 | 51 | ⬦ AV Possible Malicious PDF downloading suspicious executable | 3 | 2010-01-25 13:08:36 | 70.38.▨:http-proxy | Server-Win:34374 | |
| | | Alarm Summary [ Total Events: 2 - Unique Dst IPAddr: 1 - Unique Types: 2 - Unique Dst Ports: 2 ] | | | | | |
| 2 | 3 | ⬦ AV Possible Malicious PDF downloading suspicious executable | 3 | 2010-01-25 13:03:15 | 70.38.▨:http-proxy | Server-Win:34374 | |
| | | Alarm Summary [ Total Events: 2 - Unique Dst IPAddr: 1 - Unique Types: 2 - Unique Dst Ports: 2 ] | | | | | |

⬦ 2 Total events matched after highest rule level, before timeout.    **View/Edit** current directive definiti

| = 5 | Possible Virut Infection on Server-Win <br> (6 events) | 2 | ossim | 2010-01-25 13:03:09 | 2010-01-25 13:08:36 | 121.14.▨:2777 | Server-Win:1042 |
|---|---|---|---|---|---|---|---|
| # | Id | Alarm | Risk | Date | Source | Destination | |
| 1 | 60 | ⬦ Possible Virut Infection on Server-Win | 2 | 2010-01-25 13:08:36 | 121.14.▨:2777 | Server-Win:1042 | |
| | | Alarm Summary [ Total Events: 2 - Unique Dst IPAddr: 2 - Unique Types: 2 - Unique Dst Ports: 2 ] | | | | | |
| 2 | 12 | ⬦ Possible Virut Infection on Server-Win | 2 | 2010-01-25 13:03:15 | 121.14.▨:2777 | Server-Win:1042 | |
| | | Alarm Summary [ Total Events: 2 - Unique Dst IPAddr: 2 - Unique Types: 2 - Unique Dst Ports: 2 ] | | | | | |

⬦ 2 Total events matched after highest rule level, before timeout.    **View/Edit** current directive definition

As shown here, by expanding the two alarms (4 and 5), you can see the subalarms. After clicking a few of the subalarms, you determine that the first events received for these alarms were actually part of alarm 4.

You can display the events of an alarm by clicking the small green plus sign at the lower-left-hand corner of the alarm. Next to this plus sign is a note that says "Total events matched after highest rule level, before timeout."

Let's take a look at the events for alarm 4.

| # | Id | Alarm | Risk | Date | Source | Destination |
|---|----|-------|------|------|--------|-------------|
| 1 | 51 | ▓ AV Possible Malicious PDF downloading suspicious executable | 3 | 2010-01-25 13:08:36 | 70.38.▓▓▓:http-proxy ▓ | Server-Win:34374 ▓ |
| | | Alarm Summary [ Total Events: 2 - Unique Dst IPAddr: 1 - Unique Types: 2 - Unique Dst Ports: 2 ] | | | | |
| 1 | 50 | snort: "ET POLICY PE EXE or DLL Windows file download" | 0 | 2010-01-25 13:08:27 | 121.14.▓▓▓:2777 ▓ | Server-Win:1042 ▓ |
| 2 | 49 | snort: "ET CURRENT_EVENTS Nginx Serving PDF - Possible hostile content (PDF)" | 0 | 2010-01-25 13:08:21 | 70.38.▓▓▓:http-proxy ▓ | Server-Win:34374 ▓ |
| 2 | 3 | ▓ AV Possible Malicious PDF downloading suspicious executable | 3 | 2010-01-25 13:03:15 | 70.38.▓▓▓:http-proxy ▓ | Server-Win:34374 ▓ |
| | | Alarm Summary [ Total Events: 2 - Unique Dst IPAddr: 1 - Unique Types: 2 - Unique Dst Ports: 2 ] | | | | |
| 3 | 2 | snort: "ET POLICY PE EXE or DLL Windows file download" | 0 | 2010-01-25 13:03:05 | 121.14.▓▓▓:2777 ▓ | Server-Win:1042 ▓ |
| 4 | 1 | snort: "ET CURRENT_EVENTS Nginx Serving PDF - Possible hostile content (PDF)" | 0 | 2010-01-25 13:02:58 | 70.38.▓▓▓:http-proxy ▓ | Server-Win:34374 ▓ |

From the timestamps of the alarm 4 events, you can see that the first (bottom) event received came from Snort and showed a download of a hostile PDF from a server in Canada to the Windows server (ID 1). Next, moving up the list, you see that the Windows server then downloaded a PE (Windows executable file) from a server in China (ID 2). Moving up, you see that five minutes later, the same sequence occurred (IDs 49 and 50).

You can click on each of the Snort events to see details from that event. Let's look at the snort event: "ET CURRENT_EVENTS Nginx Serving PDF" (event ID 1) by clicking it.

| Payload | length = 1448 | |
|---------|---------------|---|
| Plain | 000 : 48 54 54 50 2F 31 2E 31 20 32 30 30 0A 43 6F 6E | HTTP/1.1 200.Con |
| Display | 010 : 6E 65 63 74 69 6F 6E 3A 20 63 6C 6F 73 65 0A 43 | nection: close.C |
| | 020 : 6F 6E 74 65 6E 74 2D 54 79 70 65 3A 20 61 70 70 | ontent-Type: app |
| Download | 030 : 6C 69 63 61 74 69 6F 6E 2F 70 64 66 0A 53 65 72 | lication/pdf.Ser |
| of | 040 : 76 65 72 3A 20 6E 67 69 6E 78 0A 58 2D 43 72 65 | ver: nginx.X-Cre |
| Payload | 050 : 61 74 65 64 2D 42 79 3A 20 68 74 74 70 3A 2F 2F | ated-By: http:// |

From this screenshot, on the right-hand side, you can see there was, indeed, a download from a nginx server, which is commonly used today by sophisticated malware authors.

You can also take a look at the other Snort event (ID 2).

| | | |
|---|---|---|
| 150 : 09 CD 21 B8 01 4C CD 21 54 68 69 73 20 70 72 6F | ..!...L.!This pro |
| 160 : 67 72 61 6D 20 63 61 6E 6E 6F 74 20 62 65 20 72 | gram cannot be r |
| 170 : 75 6E 20 69 6E 20 44 4F 53 20 6D 6F 64 65 2E 0D | un in DOS mode.. |

As expected, on the right-hand side, you can see this was indeed a Windows PE header.

**NOTE** Windows PE headers begin with the ASCII Text: "This program cannot be run in DOS mode." This text is presented if you try to run it from DOS mode.

Now switching to the events of alarm 5, you can see the effect of these downloads (again, click the plus sign in the lower-left-hand corner of alarm 5).

| # | Id | Alarm | Risk | Date | Source | Destination |
|---|----|-------|------|------|--------|-------------|
| 1 | 60 | Possible Virut Infection on Server-Win | 2 | 2010-01-25 13:08:36 | 121.14.___:2777 | Server-Win:1042 |
| | | Alarm Summary [ Total Events: 2 - Unique Dst IPAddr: 2 - Unique Types: 2 - Unique Dst Ports: 2 ] | | | | |
| 1 | 59 | snort: "ET TROJAN Virut Counter/Check-in " | 0 | 2010-01-25 13:08:34 | Server-Win:1045 | 58.53.___:7777 |
| 2 | 56 | snort: "ET POLICY Suspicious Executable (PE under 128)" | 0 | 2010-01-25 13:08:32 | 121.14.___:2777 | Server-Win:1042 |
| 2 | 12 | Possible Virut Infection on Server-Win | 2 | 2010-01-25 13:03:15 | 121.14.___:2777 | Server-Win:1042 |
| | | Alarm Summary [ Total Events: 2 - Unique Dst IPAddr: 2 - Unique Types: 2 - Unique Dst Ports: 2 ] | | | | |
| 3 | 11 | snort: "ET TROJAN Virut Counter/Check-in " | 0 | 2010-01-25 13:03:12 | Server-Win:1045 | 58.53.___:7777 |
| 4 | 8 | snort: "ET POLICY Suspicious Executable (PE under 128)" | 0 | 2010-01-25 13:03:09 | 121.14.___:2777 | Server-Win:1042 |

Moving up from the bottom of the screen, you can see a download from a server in China (ID 8). Next, the virus (called Virut) checked into the controller—a server in China (ID 11). Then, five minutes later, another binary is downloaded from the same server in China (ID 56). After this, you see the malware check into the controller for further instructions (ID 59). These events caused the correlation engine to fire a "Possible Virut Infection on Server-Win" event (IDs 12 and 60).

Let's see what happened next, moving up the stack of alarms and expanding alarm 3.

| | | | | | | | | |
|---|---|---|---|---|---|---|---|---|
| ☐ | = 3 | Possible Suspicious Device Driver installed on Server-Win (5 events) | 3 | ossim Server-Win | 2010-01-25 13:09:09 | 2010-01-25 13:10:31 | 219.235.___:62518 | Server-Win:instl_boot |

| # | Id | Alarm | Risk | Date | Source | Destination |
|---|----|-------|------|------|--------|-------------|
| 1 | 95 | Possible Suspicious Device Driver installed on Server-Win | 3 | 2010-01-25 13:10:31 | 219.235.___:62518 | Server-Win:instl_boots |
| | | Alarm Summary [ Total Events: 1 - Unique Dst IPAddr: 1 - Unique Types: 1 - Unique Dst Ports: 1 ] | | | | |
| 2 | 93 | Possible Suspicious Device Driver installed on Server-Win | 1 | 2010-01-25 13:10:31 | 219.235.___:62518 | Server-Win:instl_boots |
| | | Alarm Summary [ Total Events: 2 - Unique Dst IPAddr: 1 - Unique Types: 2 - Unique Dst Ports: 2 ] | | | | |
| 2 Total events matched after highest rule level, before timeout. | | | | | | View/Edit current directive definitio |

It appears that the malware installed a backdoor or kernel-level rootkit at this time. Let's expand the events of this alarm to conduct further analysis (again, click the plus sign in the lower-left-hand corner).

| # | Id | Alarm | Risk | Date | Source | Destination |
|---|----|-------|------|------|--------|-------------|
| 1 | 95 | Possible Suspicious Device Driver installed on Server-Win | 3 | 2010-01-25 13:10:31 | 219.235.___:62518 | Server-Win:instl_boots |
| | | Alarm Summary [ Total Events: 1 - Unique Dst IPAddr: 1 - Unique Types: 1 - Unique Dst Ports: 1 ] | | | | |
| 1 | 94 | Snare: A service was successfully sent a (start/stop) control. | 0 | 2010-01-25 13:10:31 | Server-Win:ANY | Server-Win:ANY |
| 2 | 93 | Possible Suspicious Device Driver installed on Server-Win | 1 | 2010-01-25 13:10:31 | 219.235.___:62518 | Server-Win:instl_boots |
| 2 | 92 | Snare: Privileged Service Called | 0 | 2010-01-25 13:10:31 | Server-Win:ANY | Server-Win:ANY |
| 3 | 86 | snort: "ET POLICY Suspicious Executable (PE offset 512)" | 0 | 2010-01-25 13:09:09 | 219.235.___:62518 | Server-Win:instl_boots |

From this sequence of events, you discover the download of the suspicious executable (ID 86). Then Snare (the host-based log monitoring tool) reported a privileged service call (ID 92). Snare then reports that a service was successfully sent a (start/stop) control (ID 94). This sequence of events caused the correlation engine to fire an event: "Possible Suspicious Device Driver Installed on Server-Win." This event (ID 93) was elevated in risk level when event ID 94 was factored into the equation (yielding ID 95). This is a good example of the power of the correlation engine to discern threats and properly identify them in a manner that gets the analyst's attention.

Now let's turn our attention to alarm 2.

| # | Id | Alarm | Risk | Date | Source | Destination |
|---|---|---|---|---|---|---|
| 1 | 98 | AV Possible port 445 Worm Scan Behaviour on Server-Win | 2 | 2010-01-25 13:11:36 | Server-Win:54004 | 192.168.3.157:microsoft-ds |
| | | Alarm Summary [ Total Events: 3 - Unique Dst IPAddr: 2 - Unique Types: 1 - Unique Dst Ports: 1 ] | | | | |

Displaying the events of this alarm (again, click the plus sign in the lower-left-hand corner, you see from list of events that the Windows server is now scanning other internal hosts.

| # | Id | Alarm | Risk | Date | Source | Destination |
|---|---|---|---|---|---|---|
| 1 | 98 | AV Possible port 445 Worm Scan Behaviour on Server-Win | 2 | 2010-01-25 13:11:36 | Server-Win:54004 | 192.168.3.157:microsoft-ds |
| | | Alarm Summary [ Total Events: 3 - Unique Dst IPAddr: 2 - Unique Types: 1 - Unique Dst Ports: 1 ] | | | | |
| 1 | 97 | snort: "ET SCAN Behavioral Unusual Port 445 traffic, Potential Scan or Infection" | 0 | 2010-01-25 13:11:35 | Server-Win:54685 | 192.168.2.182:microsoft-ds |
| 2 | 96 | snort: "ET SCAN Behavioral Unusual Port 445 traffic, Potential Scan or Infection" | 0 | 2010-01-25 13:10:35 | Server-Win:54004 | 192.168.3.157:microsoft-ds |
| 3 | 48 | snort: "ET SCAN Behavioral Unusual Port 445 traffic, Potential Scan or Infection" | 0 | 2010-01-25 13:05:12 | Server-Win:54004 | 192.168.3.157:microsoft-ds |

Finally, let's inspect alarm 1.

| | # | | AV Possible Windows SMB2.0 Successful Denial of Service against 192.168.1.133 (3 events) | 4 | ossim | 2010-01-25 13:12:00 | 2010-01-25 13:12:17 | Server-Win:47401 | 192.168.1.133:microsoft-c |
|---|---|---|---|---|---|---|---|---|---|

| # | Id | Alarm | Risk | Date | Source | Destination |
|---|---|---|---|---|---|---|
| 1 | 101 | AV Possible Windows SMB2.0 Successful Denial of Service against 192.168.1.133 | 4 | 2010-01-25 13:12:17 | Server-Win:47401 | 192.168.1.133:microsoft-ds |
| | | Alarm Summary [ Total Events: 2 - Unique Dst IPAddr: 2 - Unique Types: 2 - Unique Dst Ports: 2 ] | | | | |

♦ 1 Total events matched after highest rule level, before timeout.                                                      **View/Edit** current directive defin

It appears that the Windows server attacked another internal host with the SMB 2.0 Denial of Service attack. You can display the events of this alarm to verify it (again, click the plus sign in the lower-left-hand corner).

| # | Id | Alarm | Risk | Date | Source | Destination |
|---|---|---|---|---|---|---|
| 1 | 101 | AV Possible Windows SMB2.0 Successful Denial of Service against 192.168.1.133 | 4 | 2010-01-25 13:12:17 | Server-Win:47401 | 192.168.1.133:microsoft-ds |
| | | Alarm Summary [ Total Events: 2 - Unique Dst IPAddr: 2 - Unique Types: 2 - Unique Dst Ports: 2 ] | | | | |
| 1 | 100 | ping-monitor: host alive | 0 | 2010-01-25 13:12:17 | 192.168.1.133:microsoft-ds | Server-Win:47401 |
| 2 | 99 | snort: "ET CURRENT_EVENTS Remote SMB2.0 DoS Exploit" | 0 | 2010-01-25 13:12:00 | Server-Win:47401 | 192.168.1.133:microsoft-ds |

Here, Snort reports a "Remote SMB2.0 DoS Exploit" (ID 99), and then you see an event from the ping (host alive) monitor (ID 100). In order to verify this, let's click the "Ping-monitor: host alive" event.

| | |
|---|---|
| **Log** | Monitor Command: {ping-monitor: ping -c 1 192.168.1.133} , Monitor expresion evaluation: 0(arg2)  0(arg1) + 0(value)? , Command Response: PING 192.168.1.133 (192.168.1.133) 56(84) bytes of data. <br><br> --- 192.168.1.133 ping statistics --- <br> 1 packets transmitted, 0 <br> received, 100% packet loss, time 0ms |

Yep, as expected, this host is down and no longer returning pings.

At this point, you have enough information to confirm an attack on one internal Windows server. The attack began with the download of a malicious PDF from a server in Canada. Next, you verified the infection and subsequent downloads of files (from servers in China), the installation of a rootkit, and further successful attack across the network. There is no doubt you have enough information to start an incident ticket and take further action to contain and remediate the hosts involved.

# Summary

As shown, the OSSIM tool has a wide variety of user interfaces that enable an analyst to connect the dots and get to the root of the problem quickly. Once familiar with the interfaces, analysts can rely on the Dashboards and the Alarms console to get their attention so they can rise from the minutia of monitoring raw events streaming into the system.

The OSSIM is a worthy competitor to other free and commercial alternatives alike. The true value comes from the synergy of open source tools, the low entry cost (did I mention it was *free*), and the ability to scale up to the commercial version if needed.

# CHAPTER 10 | Cisco Security: MARS Implementation

The Cisco Monitoring Analysis and Response System (MARS) is a family of SIEM appliances produced by network equipment manufacturer Cisco Systems. MARS has been sold to more commercial customers than any other SIEM product and is second in technology adoption to the Open Source SIEM (OSSIM). Due to the company's dominant position in the network equipment market and the broad adoption of the technology, the impact of the product on security management as a whole may outlive MARS as a true SIEM product. In late 2009, the company announced the end of support for third-party devices, and industry analysts Gartner Group, Inc. removed the product from the annual SIEM Magic Quadrant for this reason. According to the company, MARS does have a roadmap into the future and indications are that the technology may eventually be integrated with other Cisco management products.

In this chapter, we will go over the architectural concepts embodied in MARS, look at the process of planning for and installing MARS, and cover the high points of the user interface. The goal is to create a general understanding of how MARS functions.

# Introduction to MARS

The MARS was initially designed with a focus on the mitigation portion of the SIEM spectrum. Therefore, that its particular strengths are be found in this area is not surprising. The acronym *STM* (*Security Threat Mitigation*) was coined to describe this intent. When deployed correctly, MARS is able to

- Identify an attack in progress.
- Show, in detail, the network paths involved in the incident.
- Identify devices in that path that could be used to halt the attack.
- In many cases, provide the specific commands to be applied to the device at that point that can stop the attack.

Like all SIEM solutions, the MARS also has the inherent capacity to provide forensic and reporting functionality and to serve as a focus of investigation into security and network operations issues, as well. Auditing of network policies, reporting on network and device usage, identifying trends for capacity planning and the typical range of SIEM functionalities are possible with the MARS.

It has been much reported by Cisco itself, its competitors, and the press that Cisco as of late 2009 has "dropped support for third-party devices" in the MARS. While it would be extreme hubris on the part of the authors to refute what the vendor itself has to say about such things, it is worth clarifying this statement slightly for the reader. MARS does have the ability to support event information from any device or application that supports syslog or SNMP, and a MARS user or integrator can create a "custom parser" to integrate the events from such devices. Because custom parsers are effectively interpreted—instead of being compiled efficiently into the product—such devices will not provide the performance of devices that are officially supported by the MARS, however.

Finally, due to rampant speculation in the market as to the future disposition of the MARS product family as of this writing, the reader might find some value in the completely unfounded opinions of the authors on the topic. It cannot be overstated that these opinions are not based on any type of inside information or oracular insight and are strictly our personal wild guesses and intuitions, that such opinions should not be used for planning purposes by any person or organization, do not represent the views of McGraw-Hill, Cisco Systems, the Government of West Blogonia, or any other organized institution, and are entirely *not* fit for human consumption in any fashion. That caveat made, the authors feel that Cisco will most likely continue to leverage the technology represented by the MARS product line into the foreseeable future. This may well be as the standalone product line currently being shipped. The technology could, at some future point, be embedded into other security management offerings from the company. It might be that the MARS functionality is included as part of some as-yet-unknown comprehensive "uber-network-management" suite that Cisco might deliver in the future. Whatever the future holds, it is our opinion that a customer who has a network that wholly or largely consists of Cisco equipment should not leave MARS out of consideration when evaluating SIEM solutions at this time.

## Topology, Sessions, and Incidents

To understand MARS, it is important to first understand some of the key concepts inherent in its architecture: topology, sessions, and incidents.

A key feature of the MARS is the ability to create a map describing the *topology* of the network. The MARS gathers configuration information from connectivity devices, such as routers, switches, and firewalls, and uses this information to create a topological map of the subject network such as you see in Figure 10-1. The information gathered includes routing tables and vulnerability assessment data as well as host identification. Individual atomic events are then mapped as they are received to this topology to re-create end-to-end *sessions* across the network (as shown in Figure 10-2). These sessions are then correlated in the context of existing *rules* configured in MARS to trigger *incidents* and, as appropriate, fire alerts indicating that a condition has been met.

As an example of a session, an individual syslog message from an edge router might indicate simply that a packet has been passed. Another syslog message from the perimeter firewall behind the router may indicate that an inbound connection has been allowed. An IDS alert from a sensor on the internal network might indicate that a known Windows 2000 attack has been detected passing the segment monitored by that sensor, and finally the recipient server itself might produce a log message indicating that it has received the connection. Now, each of these events, in and of itself, might not indicate anything particularly useful, but together they could represent a single connection coming in from an external host, past the edge router and firewall, and across the internal network to a specific internal host, indicating that this individual connection—or session—is, in fact, bearing a particular type of attack payload. The topology information may also indicate that the target host is potentially vulnerable to the detected attack (in this case, a Windows 2000 attack).

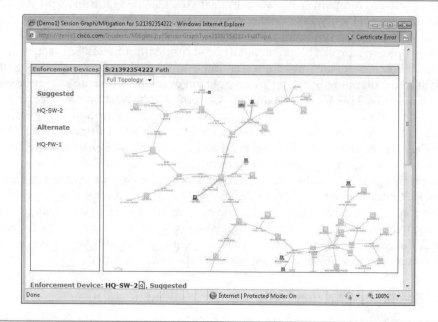

**Figure 10-1.** Network topology

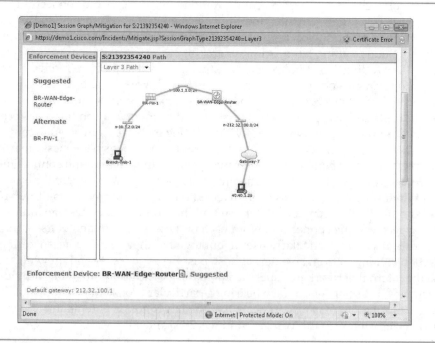

**Figure 10-2.** Network session

Now even the ability to see this potentially offensive connection may not warrant immediate concern and action by the human operators running the network. This host is possibly already patched against this particular attack or the attack might even fail for some other reason. However, if this session is followed by another session that indicates an unusual change in behavior by this same host—such as creating anomalous SQL connections to a database server—then these sessions together might well indicate that someone has scanned your network, identified a vulnerable host, compromised that host, and has turned it against you. The ability to see that this has just happened and perhaps do something about it would be a good thing.

Let's put the previous example together into a single sequence and look at how MARS would function in this context.

An attacker at Host A out on the Internet automatically scans a network monitored by a Cisco MARS. This generates hundreds of syslog events from the edge firewall and other devices on the network. The MARS correlates these events with the network topology map, creating dozens of sessions. As mentioned previously, although these events and sessions are not by themselves a useful indicator that there is real cause for concern, they could be precursors of something that is. Following this period of scanning, the same external Host A initiates a single connection to one of the scanned hosts, this time triggering an alert from an IDS sensor along the network path, creating another session in the MARS. Subsequently, events from devices on the network are correlated in the MARS to create sessions that indicate the historical behavior of the attacked host has changed. This sequence of sessions would match a default rule in the MARS, creating a High Priority incident. An operator investigating this incident would, in most cases, be offered at least one method of mitigating the attack, perhaps in the form of a configuration command for the firewall in the path between the external attacker and the compromised host that would break the connection between the two.

## Scaling a MARS Deployment

The MARS appliances can be deployed individually or in a "Local Controller/ Global Controller" distributed configuration. MARS appliances come in a range of sizes offering different storage and event-processing capacities, from the MARS 25R, which can handle 75 events per second (eps) and 1,500 NetFlows per second, and provides 250GB of storage, to the MARS 210, which can handle 15,000 eps and 300,000 NetFlows per second, and provides 2TB of storage. Where the largest MARS device is not sufficient to the needs of the application or where geographic or organizational concerns dictate, individual MARS devices can be deployed under the umbrella of a Global Controller MARS device. This generally provides an integrated framework that can be administered from the top down and/or regionally.

Cisco offers two Global Controller products based on the same physical chassis (which is also the same chassis as the MARS 210). The less expensive Global Controller, the GC2R can manage a maximum of five MARS Local Controllers (LC), and these LCs must be the smaller devices (specifically the MARS 20R to MARS 55 models). The other Global Controller available, the GC2, has the same physical chassis as the MARS 210 as well; however, it has no LC model capabilities and unlimited connections.

# Analyze Requirements

When planning any deployment of information security technologies, it is first necessary to review your information security policies. Your application of technology should reflect your organization's motivations as enunciated in these policies, and often the technology planning process provides the opportunity to review, or perhaps even create, such policies. We will discuss this topic in the following "Objectives" section.

An aspect of policy creation that is worth calling out on its own is a review of the unique threats your organization faces, which will be discussed following the "Objectives" section.

Finally, in planning for a SIEM deployment, it is necessary to start with an inventory of the technology already deployed on your network. This inventory will both determine what information sources are available to leverage in your deployment as well as provide the first opportunity to identify potential technology gaps that you may want to fill. We discuss this in more depth in the "Infrastructure Inventory" section.

## Objectives

In Cisco's operating manual for the MARS, an early section discusses policy in the context of "Objectives." Since this is a valid approach and to maintain some consistency with the material you will rely on when planning the deployment of a MARS device, we will use the same terminology here. The four areas of focus listed by Cisco under "Objectives" are as follows:

- Security Policy Objectives
- Monitoring Policy Objectives
- Mitigation Policy Objectives
- Remediation Policy Objectives

If you did not already have a written security policy, you now have a good reason to create one, and you have a logical framework to guide your efforts. For our exercise here, we will assume that you do not have one and will walk you through the logic of creating one. We will look at this written policy as a single document with the four major sections, as stated above, though, of course, in a complex environment, maintaining your policy as a set of discrete documents may be best.

The overriding theme of your security policy will be the Security Policy Objectives. In other words, you need to have an idea of what it is you are protecting, why you are protecting it, and how you plan to do so. In creating this set of statements, identifying the criticality of different portions of your information system is important—whether data sets, such as financial information that might exist on many portions of the network, or physical assets, such as your entire research facility.

Since monitoring is the purpose of your MARS, enunciating a policy of *who* will be doing the monitoring, what you are monitoring *for*, where you will be monitoring it *from*, and what you expect the *result* to be is a primary concern. In defining this process, you will find it necessary to take into account the relative locations of the individuals tasked with performing various monitoring tasks. What impact, if any, will the activities of these operators have on the function of the network itself? What foreseeable network conditions could impact the operators' ability to perform their tasks? At this stage, it will also be valuable to compare the parts of your network that are critical or that handle critical data with your network diagram to determine which devices will be able to report on the status of those critical components. What monitoring devices are available and what logging or reporting capabilities do these devices have? What gaps remain between the reporting capabilities that exist and those you feel are required to protect these critical resources adequately?

Because the MARS literally contains a "Big Red Button," which will allow direct mitigation of an ongoing attack against your network, your mitigation policy is extremely important. Though perhaps counterintuitive from a pure security perspective, on many networks the risk of interrupting legitimate network traffic (i.e., financial transactions) will be considered greater than the desire to immediately halt a confirmed network attack. To begin to create a specific policy in regards to *when* you will enact mitigation of an attack, you first need to identify *where* it will be possible to do so, *how* you will record the handling of the incident, *who* will have the final responsibility for authorizing the actual act of mitigation, and *which* groups and individuals will be notified before, during, and after the process.

Lastly, to use your MARS as a tool that can continually advance the state of security on your network as a whole, crafting policy guidelines for remediating issues discovered during operation will be necessary. As just noted, it is entirely possible that real, live, active attacks will be detected that will not be mitigated at once. Addressing these occurrences will require a more sophisticated and nuanced approach, which may include an analysis of the application, host, and associated network components in the context of critical business operations. As part of your MARS standard operating procedures, consider the implications of such scenarios and designate, in advance, the processes and methods operators will use to escalate such situations to appropriate technical and business resources, and how such resources will go about planning remediation that appropriately addresses the business and security risks involved.

## Unique Threat Concerns

The type of risk profile your organization faces as a function of normal operations will greatly determine the design and operation of your MARS deployment. A nuclear power facility, for example, faces a vastly different set of potential threats than a retail operation. Each MARS customer will want to design a capacity for monitoring and responding to the threats it faces that is appropriate to the scale of its security needs, and will want to embed these considerations into the documented policies just described.

If your company is subject to some sort of regulatory compliance, you will want to factor the associated requirements into your MARS deployment. Every top-level requirement of the Payment Card Industry Data Security Standard (PCI DSS), for example, touches on a feature that a SIEM could provide and should be reflected in the policy documentation described if your company is subject to PCI compliance.

If supporting a given PCI requirement with your MARS deployment is possible, you should consider enabling that functionality.

As a specific example of a regulatory requirement that your MARS could support, consider PCI DSS Requirement 1. The requirement reads: "Install and maintain a firewall configuration to protect cardholder data." If your firewall—and perhaps the routers or switches on the inside and outside of the firewall—are reporting to the MARS, then you could create rules in your MARS that will detect any traffic that is not specifically permitted by the approved configuration of that firewall. Thus, should the firewall configuration ever change through unauthorized access or administrator error, your operations staff would be immediately alerted to the change.

Each additional section of the PCI DSS 1.1 intrinsically or explicitly includes requirements that can be supported by a MARS SIEM, typically in a fairly clear manner as just described. To help you think about the manner in which the MARS or any other SIEM can work to support virtually any of the requirements that may apply to your unique situation, let's take a quick look at PCI DSS Requirement 9: "Restrict physical access to cardholder data." This requirement might seem like it has little to do with event data management, but if the physical space where cardholder data can be accessed from is itself secured by a physical access-control method, such as a card-swipe mechanism, then you have an opportunity to integrate this physical-access system with your MARS. If the authentication system on the backend of the system is capable of producing log messages natively or can be configured to do so, then it will be possible to match physical access with user login information from workstations inside that physical space.

## Infrastructure Inventory

Before you sit down to actually design the architecture of your MARS deployment, you will want to create a reasonable list of the software and hardware on your network that could be used as some part of the project. Since the MARS contains a significant focus on mitigation, it is logical to view hardware and software on your network in terms of reporting assets, mitigating assets, and supporting assets. *Reporting assets* can provide information to MARS, *mitigating assets* can both provide information to MARS as well as act as enforcement points to mitigate an active threat, *supporting assets* provide services to the MARS itself. Among the top list of supporting assets are an email server (required), NTP server (recommended), DNS server (required), and the PC you will do the initial management from.

The MARS documentation contains a very good sample chart for creating an Inventory Worksheet. Capturing the data contained in this worksheet will enable you to enumerate the assets that can be brought to bear to support your MARS deployment as well as ensure that you have the appropriate set of information about each asset. These categories are listed here:

- Device name
- Reporting IP address
- Management IP address

- Username/password
- Role in system/segment
- Required protocols
- Log settings/SNMP RO community
- Tunable (y/n)
- Notify (y/n)
- Notification format

# Design

With your inventory in hand and some policies enunciated, you are in reasonable shape to begin the actual design of your MARS deployment. Your task now is to turn your desires into a plan, leveraging the existing infrastructure to inform the MARS and enable you to achieve the goals stated in your policy documents.

As you go through this process, you may find that you need to choose only some of the possible monitoring devices to send data to the MARS so you can stay within the capacity of the MARS appliance that your budget dictated. Wisely selecting the devices that will send data to your MARS will be the difference between a successful implementation and one that leaves you (and, as importantly, your management) wanting.

Any SIEM deployment touches more of the network than most any other IT project. Since you will likely want to monitor devices and traffic flows all across your network you will find that every network device between your MARS and a given monitoring device must cooperate to make your project successful. This means you will want to identify all of the groups and individuals inside your organization who may be necessary for your deployment to be successful, including network operations management and anyone responsible for the operation of remote networks that you may want to gather data from. Corporate technical endeavors are almost always contingent on human issues, SIEM deployments more so than most. Make friends with the other stakeholders early and often and involve them in the planning process so you do not run into roadblocks when you try to actually deploy the MARS.

## Resources and Requirements

As an appliance, most of the physical resources needed to deploy the MARS will be the MARS itself. However, you will need a separate PC to perform the initial configuration beyond the application of an IP address and other basic setup such as applying the IP address and netmask for the MARS interface(s). If at all possible, you will want this PC to be on the same network segment as the MARS itself, to reduce the possibility of having to troubleshoot network issues when you already have enough other things to deal with. The PC itself should have Internet Explorer 7.0 or greater on it and the Adobe SVG Viewer installed (see the MARS documentation for additional IE settings).

If you are using a SAN to augment the storage of the MARS, you are best served by having it on the same network segment as the MARS itself. If the SAN you must use is located across your network, you should spend some cycles ensuring that there are no capacity or configuration roadblocks between the MARS and the SAN itself.

To best select the inputs to your MARS, you should evaluate the value of the logs and other events that are produced by the monitoring devices you are considering. Different devices and logging levels provide more or less useful information, so spending some time getting intimate with the event output of your devices will be time well spent at this point.

Also, while choosing devices to monitor with your MARS, consider the dual use of potential logging sources as both monitoring devices and mitigation devices. MARS will only suggest mitigation commands for devices that are already being monitored, so inasmuch as you plan to use the MARS as a Security Threat Mitigation (STM) device, you will want to give extra weight to monitoring network devices that make for natural traffic choke points. Any firewall devices are worth considering for mitigation purposes; switches at primary junctions inside the network and routers at WAN edges are obvious locations to perform mitigation of detected attacks and will generally also provide rich contextual information about network activity.

## Roles and Responsibilities

Your plan should include a list of all pertinent players—from management to network operations. The requirements for each role should be defined as clearly as possible to ensure that the efficient and comprehensive system of command and operations that is part of your normal business functions is reflected in the operation and management of your MARS.

# Deployment

The deployment of the MARS appliance itself is fairly straightforward. Like any standard network appliance all that is literally required is an AC power source (120/220), an Ethernet drop, and a valid IP address for the network it is being plugged into. All examples in this section will assume a single stand-alone MARS "Local Controller" installation.

## Installing the Device and Connect to Network

For initial deployment, it is necessary to have a keyboard and monitor available that you can connect to the appropriate ports on the back of the MARS appliance. After mounting the device in the rack, attaching the monitor, keyboard, and Ethernet connections, connect the power and turn the device on using the switch on the back.

The monitor will reflect what looks like—and largely is—a typical RedHat Linux boot script output. From the factory, this should result in a login screen as seen in Figure 10-3. Log in to the device with the username **pnadmin** and password **pnadmin** (for the computer-history geeks in the audience, this is a legacy from the time when that stood for "Protego Networks Admin").

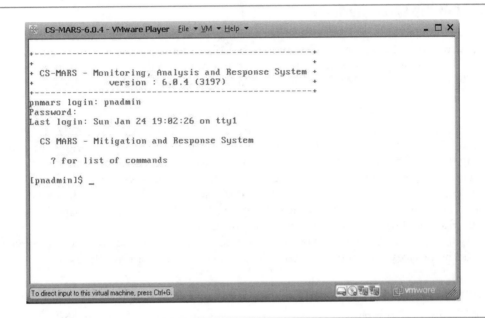

**Figure 10-3.**    MARS command-line interface

You will find yourself at what could be mistaken for a Bourne Shell prompt in a standard RedHat environment. While this is, in some essence, correct, there are only a very limited number of commands that can be issued from this prompt, which can be found by typing **?** or by reading the product documentation.

Your installation manual will walk you through several steps at this point, most importantly changing the default password and applying network setting. Although MARS is capable of using separate networks for data collection and out-of-band management, for our purposes, we will assume you will be using the primary network interface (eth0) for both. Issue the command to set the IP address and netmask for eth0 in the following format (where, of course, the address and netmask are the ones you want to use on your network):

**Ifconfig eth0 *192.168.1.100 255.255.255.0***

When you enter the command, you will be asked to reboot your MARS. Press ENTER to accept, and log in again when the login prompt appears. Next, set the network gateway for the device with the **gateway** command. If needed, you can also enter static routes from the command line at this point.

You can confirm network connectivity by using the **ping** command from the MARS command line to ping a host on your network that you know should return a response. If everything is good, you can move to a workstation connected to the network to continue the configuration of your MARS.

## Configuring the Web Interface

The MARS web interface works best with Internet Explorer version 7 or greater. You will also require the Adobe SVG Viewer to be able to see the topology maps embedded in the MARS interface; you will be prompted to download the SVG viewer the first time you log in to your MARS if the workstation you are using does not have it installed already.

Unless you have purchased a digital certificate for your MARS, you are likely to see an error each time you log in to the web interface. Click the OK To Proceed option when this error pops up in your browser to continue to the MARS interface. Log in using the same **pnadmin** username and the password you used at the console. You will be prompted to upload the license file or enter the license key that goes with your MARS before you can perform any other tasks. Go to the Admin tab, select System Setup, and enter the rest of the basic networking and administrative information (such as DNS server, hostname, etc.) under Configuration Information.

With the device alive on the network and licensed for use, you are ready to move on to adding devices and users and getting some results from your MARS.

## Assigning MARS User Accounts

MARS supports four classes of user: Admin, Security Analyst, Operator, and Notification Only. Members of each class have different sets of capabilities.

- **Admin** Users in this class have the capability to perform all configuration of the device itself and all other tasks of the other classes of users.

- **Security Analyst** A Security Analyst user can do anything at all, as far as normal operations of the MARS are concerned, but the analyst cannot change system-level settings. A Security Analyst cannot create other user accounts, or change the network settings of the MARS itself. Security Analysts can create Rules, Queries, and Reports, and add devices to the MARS, however.

- **Operator** Operator class users can run existing queries and reports and can open and close tickets in the MARS trouble ticketing system, but cannot perform any configuration activity to the device itself or create or edit Queries, Rules or Reports.

- **Notification Only** This class of user does not have the ability to perform any configuration of the MARS whatsoever, including building and running Queries, Rules, or Reports. These are typically managerial-level individuals who have a need to be informed under conditions that the MARS is capable of detecting.

Hopefully, during your planning exercise, you assigned roles to individuals in your organization. At this point, you can create the appropriate user accounts in the MARS for those individuals. The User Management tab can be found under either the Admin tab or the Management tab; they both take you to the same place (as shown in Figure 10-4).

## Adding Monitored Devices

Now is a good time to start feeding your MARS with the *Security Information* and *Events* that it will be *Managing*. MARS contains a list of supported devices as well as a mechanism for creating custom integrations (commonly referred to as *Custom Parsers,* but termed *User Defined Parser Templates* in version 6.0.4 of MARS). We will discuss Custom Parsers in the next chapter.

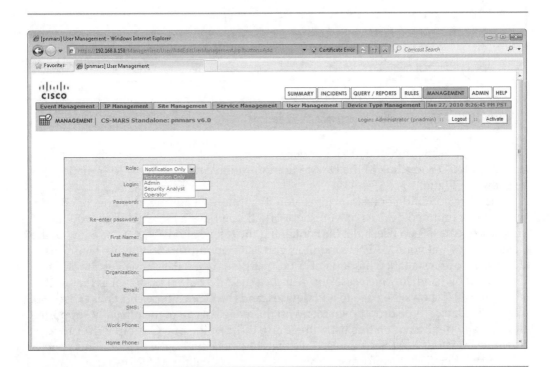

**Figure 10-4.**   User Management

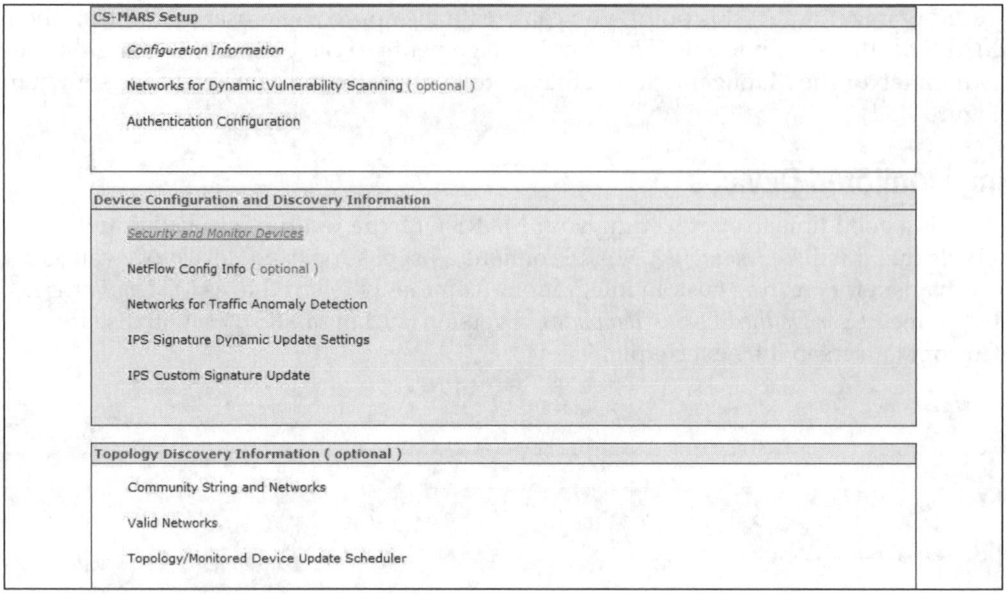

**Figure 10-5.** System Setup, adding monitored devices

Devices are added to the MARS under Admin | System Setup. Select the Security And Monitor Devices link in the Device Configuration And Discovery Information box, as shown in Figure 10-5.

The page you find yourself on gives you the options of adding, deleting, or editing any of the monitored devices on your network. If you have a large network, you may choose to create a Seed File: a flat file containing the information about all or many of the devices you want your MARS to monitor; you can find information on how to format that file in your installation literature. For our purposes, we will assume you are adding the devices by hand, in which case you will click the Add button as shown in Figure 10-6.

Figure 10-7 shows the page to add devices, and the Device Type chosen is "Cisco IOS 12.4". The Device Type drop-down menu on this page lists all of the officially supported devices; any device not on this list will require the creation of a Custom Parser to integrate into your MARS. As you select different device types, the fields on this page will change to reflect the information about that device that the MARS can use.

Here are some hints about the information you see on this screen:

■ **Access IP and Reporting IP**  If the IP address of the device that will be reflected in event information is different than the IP address that is used to manage the device, enter the management address in the Access IP field and the other in the Reporting IP field. MARS will use the Access IP to reach out to the device for various functions (like pulling down configuration information or pushing out mitigation).

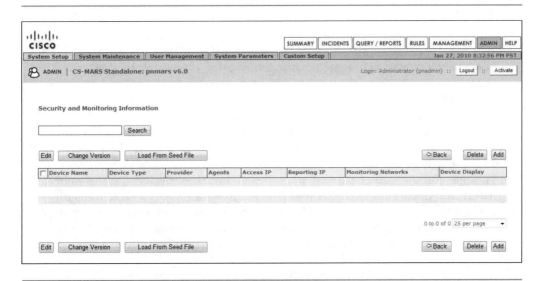

**Figure 10-6.**   Adding devices manually

- **Access Type**   The options in this field will change to reflect what MARS can use with the selected device. There may be one option—SNMP—or the options may include FTP, Telnet, and SSH.

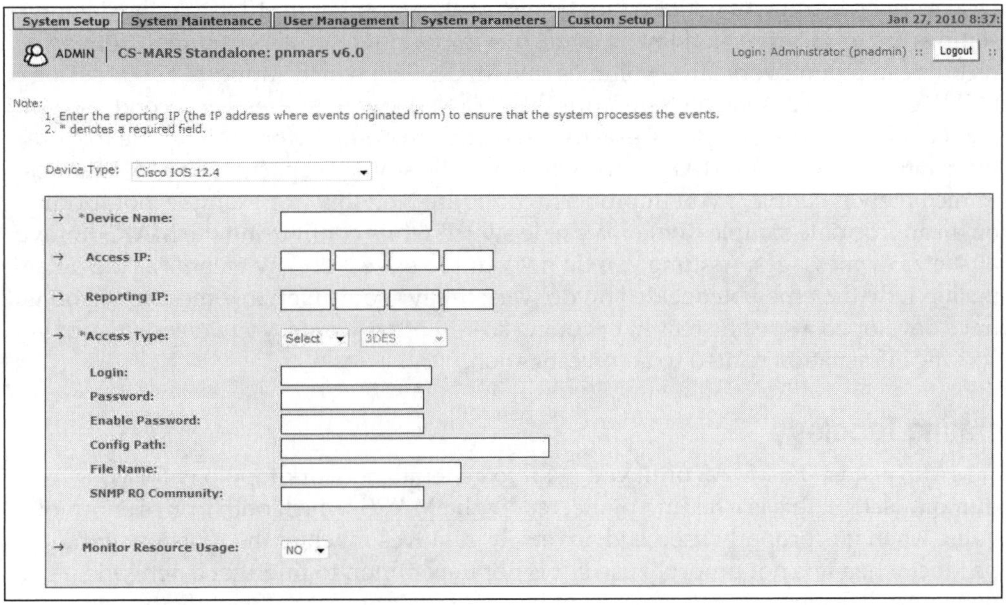

**Figure 10-7.**   Adding devices, detail

## Integrating Flow Data

In addition to consuming event information in the form of syslog and SNMP traps, MARS is capable of consuming NetFlow as well. *NetFlow* is the Cisco-proprietary standard for the type of aggregated traffic information often used by service providers to monitor connections and bill for data transfer. Other network vendors have proprietary or open standards for producing similar "flow data." If you are not currently producing NetFlow data from Cisco switches and routers on your network, we recommend you consider doing so. You will want to review the potential impact this will have on the devices themselves, which will produce the NetFlow data, as well as on the capacity of affected network segments. Enabling NetFlow on your routers and switches could require hardware upgrades to those devices (typically memory upgrades), and depending on the amount of NetFlow traffic you wish to transmit, it could impact network performance. NetFlow can be configured using a "sampling rate" that can dramatically limit the performance impact of your implementation, for example, and you should factor this and other considerations into your decision-making process.

Adding NetFlow data to your MARS can significantly increase the value you realize from your deployment, however. NetFlow messages, unlike syslog messages, contain aggregate information about a connection that could be typified as "this host transferred this much data to that host." This information is particularly useful in detecting traffic anomalies.

NetFlow is enabled on the Admin System Setup Page, as shown in Figure 10-5 by selecting the NetFlow Config Info (Optional) link in the Device Configuration And Discovery box. You will notice on that page, as shown in Figure 10-8, that the default settings are to *not* store NetFlow records. It is important to understand that NetFlow records can require very large volumes (the MARS 220, which supports 12,000 syslog/ SNMP events per second also supports *300,000* NetFlow messages per second), so you want to be very sure you know exactly what you are doing before you decide to store these messages on your MARS. Overwhelming the storage capacity of a MARS almost immediately is simple if you improperly configure NetFlow (for example, not turning on an appropriate sample rate) on a single switch while configuring the MARS to save all NetFlow messages. Assume you do not want to store NetFlow records as the default position. By the time you decide you do want to save some NetFlow messages, you will have developed a specific reason for doing so—in other words, you are looking for very specific information related to an investigation.

## Generating Topology

A MARS just isn't a MARS until you get it to generate network topology for you. To our knowledge, this is a feature pioneered by the MARS, which both brings enormous value when it is properly used and, inversely, removes much of the function of the product when it is not properly used. It is not uncommon to find that a network owner has installed a MARS device but has not configured it sufficiently to generate a topology map, so we would be remiss to understate the necessity of performing this task adequately.

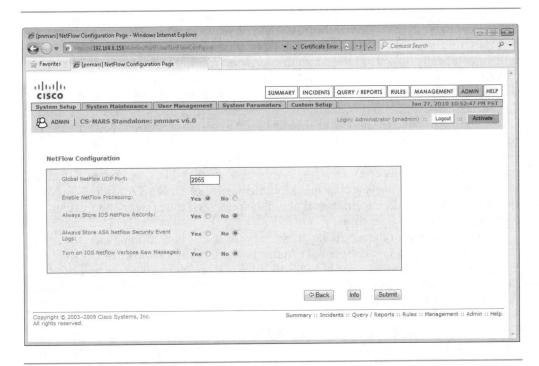

**Figure 10-8.**  NetFlow configuration

Recall the discussion of *sessionization* at the beginning of this chapter. MARS reassembles individual events *in the context of the network topology* to re-create the end-to-end session that the individual event was part of. Without configuring your MARS to generate a topology map of your network, it will not be able to sessionize events; in turn, it will not be able to match network traffic to many System Rules, and, in the end, it will not provide you the value you were seeking when you bought it.

Topology provides the additional benefit of telling you specifically how your network looks. The vast majority of network owners do not know for certain what their network map looks like. They have, perhaps, the diagrams that were initially drafted when planning the network or partial diagrams depicting plans for a section of the network. In reality, these plans were probably not enacted exactly as drawn, and since the initial implementation of the network, all sorts of random changes have been made for perfectly good individual reasons that (a) might not make so much sense if described all at once and (b) nobody ever bothered to document so no one has had to suffer through trying to explain them all at once. For these reasons, the ability for MARS to create a network topology map that is a literal representation of your network as it actually is not only ends up serving the purpose of enabling the MARS to do its job, but also quite frequently identifies networking issues (such as asymmetrical routing) that have bedeviled operations staff for extended periods of time.

To create a topology map in your MARS, provide the MARS access to the *connectivity devices* that make up the framework (topology) of your network—devices such as firewalls, routers, and switches. Once you have added these devices to the MARS, it will automatically download the configurations and routing tables from them. Your MARS will use this information to build the initial topology map, and it will update the map on an ongoing basis as event information and other sources provide more detail. The MARS can use SSL to communicate with these devices if they provide that support.

By adding monitored devices as described in the previous section, you will begin to gather information to create the topology. But the topology MARS can create does not simply consist of the devices that MARS receives event information from. As a monitored device sends event information about hosts that it has sent network traffic to, for example, these hosts will be added to the network topology. Additionally, MARS can be provided certain information that will help it crawl the network and gather topology information over time.

In the lower part of Figure 10-5, you will notice a box titled Topology Discovery Information (Optional). The three links in this box will allow you to enter SNMP discovery information that your MARS will use to fill out its topology awareness, to define the IP address ranges of all parts of your network so your MARS will recognize them as part of its domain, and to set schedules for active topology updating on the part of the MARS.

MARS also contains the open source tool Nessus, a vulnerability scanning tool. In addition, near the top of Figure 10-5 you will see a link titled Networks For Dynamic Vulnerability Scanning. The Nessus implementation in MARS is specifically set to a nondestructive scan level so it is relatively safe to use in production environments, but you will nonetheless want to perform the usual amount of diligence that you would employ when using Nessus before configuring your MARS to scan any part of your network (in other words, don't bring down the transaction database midday on a Wednesday by scanning too thoroughly). However, once you have gotten approval from all pertinent people, configuring MARS to actively scan your network will go a long way toward filling out the topology it creates both in scope and in detail.

Finally, MARS can pull vulnerability assessment data from certain major product vendors' solutions, specifically, in version 6.0.4 of MARS, Qualys, eEye REM 1.0, and McAfee Foundstone Vulnerability Assessment (VA) tools. If you are using any of these tools, it is highly recommended that you configure your MARS to pull this information in. To integrate these data sources, you use the same mechanism described previously to add a monitored device like a router or firewall. Three device types—QualysGuard ANY, and the two choices under SW Based Security Devices (Add SW Security Apps On New Host and Add SW Security Apps On Existing Host)—allow you to configure your MARS to gather this data on an ongoing basis. Configuration of Qualys is very straightforward, as shown in Figure 10-9; configuration for the other two common vulnerability assessment sources requires a bit more work, as shown in Figure 10-10.

Adding eEye and McAfee VA gives some insight into how to add other software security applications as well. Basic information is entered under the General tab,

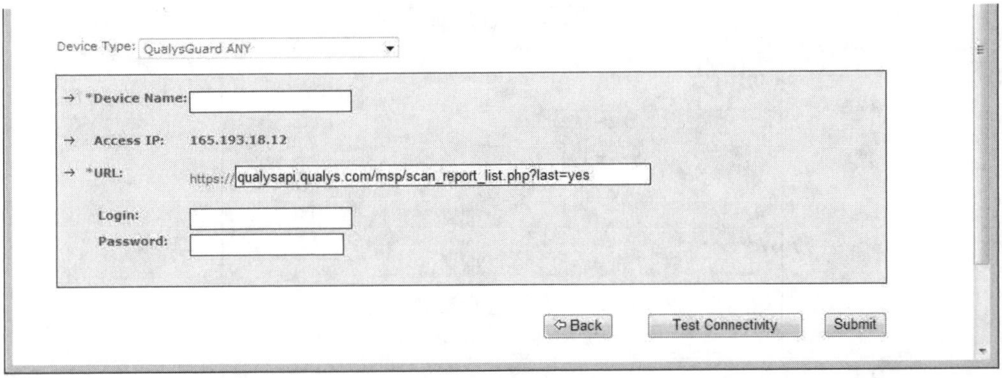

**Figure 10-9.**   Vulnerability assessment detail for Qualys

including the IP address of the device and the type of operating system running on the host. The Reporting Application tab allows you to select which of the two VA packages you are using, but also shows you the list of all of the software packages that MARS supports natively, as shown in Figure 10-11.

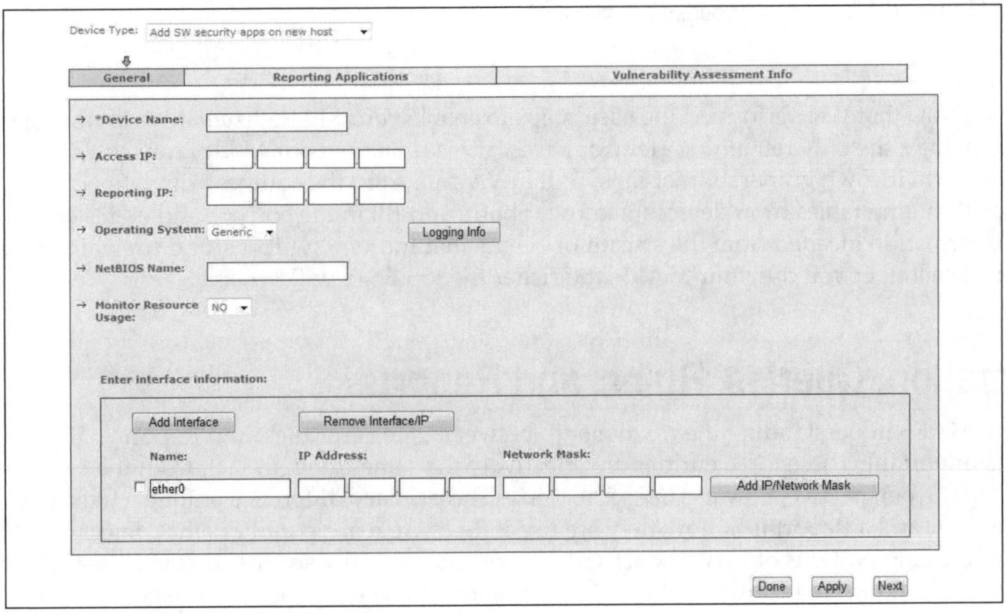

**Figure 10-10.**   Adding eEye or McAfee vulnerability assessment

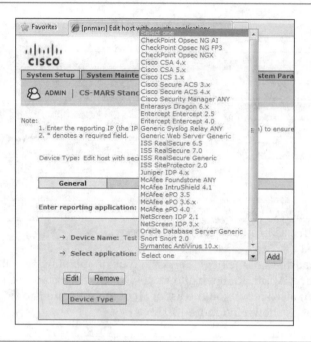

**Figure 10-11.** List of supported software applications

Now that you performed the basic steps to enable your MARS to create your network topology, the only remaining element necessary is time. As your MARS runs, it will perform its own vulnerability scans, pull in VA data from the sources you defined, pull routing tables from devices it knows about, and fill in the corners and edges with information gleaned from the stream of events that routers, switches, and firewalls send it. The longer you use your MARS, the richer the topology will become.

# Operation: Queries, Rules, and Reports

In MARS understanding the relationship between Queries, Rules, and Reports is important. These three entities are effectively the same thing. In fact, from the MARS' perspective, they are the same thing. The primary difference among a Query, a Rule, and a Report is in how they are used. *Rules* are real-time filters that detect interesting patterns of network activity. *Queries* are typically short and reactive—their specifications not recorded—whereas *Reports* tend to be longer and have specifications defined and recorded in the system.

## Queries

In a typical daily usage scenario, a MARS operator may find she wants to investigate some sort of behavior or event that she has noticed on the network. This could be due to some MARS incident that has occurred, or someone in the company has asked the MARS operator to check into something or the MARS operator has been alerted to something—such as a report of new type of attack or virus —and wants to see if there is evidence of it on her own network. At a time like this, MARS operators turn to the Query functionality.

When building a Query, the operator can specify as much or as little detail as desired. A common approach is to cast a wide net at first and then to narrow down based on the types of results discovered. Let's look at an example of a new type of attack that a security analyst has read about that uses port 32579, infects TriteWorks Triviality Server software running on a host, and then propagates itself using HTTP (port 80) to attack any systems running Gloatworts web server software.

The security analyst (Anita) first writes a simple one-line query using the MARS interface to look for any traffic that the MARS has seen running over port 32579. She clicks the Submit Inline button (as circled on the right in Figure 10-12) to run the query against traffic currently on the network. After a few minutes, she finds a single session from an external host to an internal server.

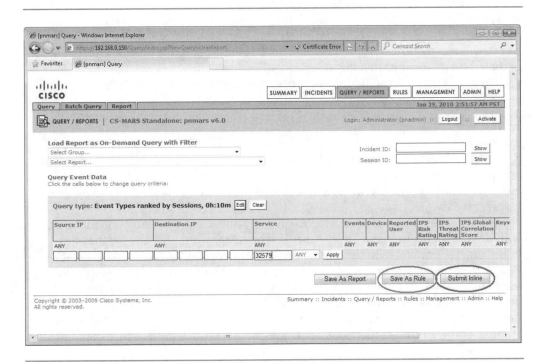

**Figure 10-12.**   Rule detail

Wanting to keep an eye on this threat, she saves her simple Query as a Rule by clicking on the Save As Rule button (shown circled on the left in Figure 10-12) and configures it to send her an email if any more sessions using this port appear on her network. A week later, she gets an email from the MARS with a link to an Incident that has been created because her Rule has been matched by network conditions. She clicks the link, investigates the Incident, and discovers that this time the attack has been targeted at a server running the potentially vulnerable TriteWorks software. Using the IP address of the attacking host and the target machine, she investigates further with the Query tool and finds that, following the initial attack, the two hosts had exchanged communications over port 80 after first attempting to connect over port 23. Finally, she queries the MARS to see what other traffic had originated from the—apparently compromised—target host following the initial attack, and she sees that this host is now probing the internal network over port 80 and 8080. It is safe to presume that the compromised host is actively searching the internal network for further hosts to compromise. Having confirmed the attack, Anita contacts the network operations staff authorized to make temporary changes to the perimeter firewall configuration and has them apply the blocking rule recommended by the MARS on the edge firewall. Anita works with network operations to resolve the incident, including using the MARS Query function to confirm that the firewall rule stopped the communication between the attacker and the internal host, and that the internal host stopped scanning the network once the attacker lost the control channel to it. Based on the post-engagement analysis of the attack, she creates two new Queries, one of which she saves as a Rule to alert network operations of a confirmed attack and another she saves as a Report, which will run monthly to provide management with a summary of the effectiveness of their defenses against this threat.

Thus goes the circle of life for a security operator using a MARS SIEM.

## System Rules

Rules in MARS come in two flavors: System Rules and User Inspection Rules. *System Rules* are built-in to the product and are supported by the vendor. *User Inspection Rules* are created by the organization that owns the particular MARS (that will be you). We'll talk a bit about the System Rules next and then take a look at building your own User Inspection Rules.

MARS System Rules are intended to give an "out-of-the-box" functionality that would serve most purposes. These Rules can be categorized logically (as they are in the Cisco documentation) into functional groups such as "System Access." Each Rule is meant to describe a set of conditions a facility owner would commonly want to be aware of on his network. For example, the System Access group contains Rules designed to detect password cracking/scanning/guessing attacks. The System Reconnaissance group contains Rules designed to detect scans of your network. As of the time of the writing of this book, there are 16 Rule groups in all, which contain a total

## A Note About Rules: SIEM Is Not Your Grandfather's IDS

Before going any further, we would like to clarify something about what SIEM rules are. It is not uncommon when discussing SIEM with those not familiar with the technology to be asked the question: "Isn't this the same as an Intrusion Detection System?" This is best answered by explaining the difference between an IDS *signature* and a SIEM *Rule*. An IDS sensor is a device that listens to traffic on a particular network segment and scans the data stream for bit patterns that match existing attack signatures. A SIEM is a device that resides at the logical level above IDS sensors and other devices that perform direct data handling or inspection. SIEMs take in the *output* of devices such as IDS sensors and combine it with the output of other systems to make determinations about the status of an attack. While at the IDS level, an attack must typically exactly match a very specific bit-pattern, at the SIEM level, it is usually not as important *how* something happens as *what* happens.

The MARS System Rule "Server Attack: SNMP - Success Likely" is a good example. The description of the rule given by MARS is as follows:

> *This correlation rule detects specific attacks on SNMP implementations on a host followed by suspicious activity on the targeted host. Suspicious activity may include the host scanning the network, creating excessive firewall deny traffic, a backdoor opening up at the server etc. The attack may be preceded by reconnaissance attempts targeted to that host. The attacks to RPC services include buffer overflows, remote command execution attempts using system privileges, denial of service attempts.*

This Rule would be matched if a scan was launched against a part of your network, including a specific host, *and* that host was then attacked by at least one of a set of exploits against SNMP *followed by* that host beginning to perform one of a set of anomalous types of behavior. In this scenario, an IDS sensor would simply report that it had seen an attack of a certain type pass by on a give network segment, which, while very useful, is only a very detailed account of what happened on a given network segment and does not, in itself, indicate that a vulnerable host was targeted or that it was compromised successfully. The MARS combines the "atomic" information from the IDS sensor with information from other sources on the network—including baselines of historic behavior of the attacked host—and uses this to match the higher level rule it contains.

of 144 built-in System Rules in MARS. It should be noted that it is Cisco's position that MARS does not need to have as many System Rules as other SIEM products to detect the same spectrum of threats, primarily because the topology awareness of the MARS allows multiple conditions to be detected by a single Rule.

## User Inspection Rules

As just described, User Inspection Rules often evolve from the normal operation of the MARS. Every organization's network is as unique as a fingerprint, and, therefore, some of the behavior patterns that will be of interest will be unique to a particular organization as well. User Inspection Rules can take virtually any form to describe a pattern of behavior.

When creating a User Inspection Rule, MARS walks the operator through a fairly intuitive step-by-step process. Each line in the new Rule specifies a particular condition that could occur on a network and is composed of the expected range of subconditions, such as *Source IP* and *Service Name* (aka Destination Port), as shown in Figure 10-13. The Rule Wizard takes you through the process of selecting the desired value for each condition. Each line can be logically associated with the following line using AND, OR, or FOLLOWED BY operators to describe complex conditions. After all conditions are specified, you can choose what action you want performed when the Rule conditions are met.

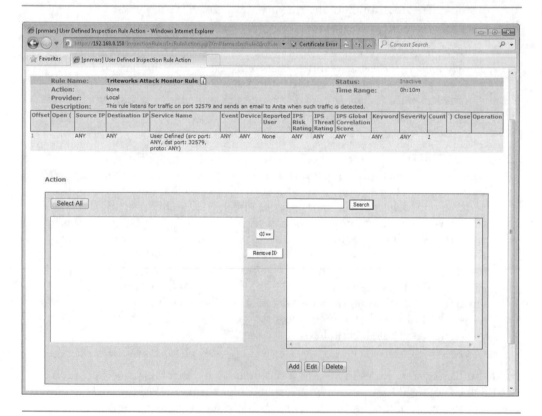

**Figure 10-13.** Creating a User Inspection Rule

System Rules can be duplicated to create User Inspection Rules that make them more specific to your own concerns and network (as shown circled in Figure 10-14), if you want to tune them more to your particular network or customize them to serve other purposes.

## Reports

As discussed previously, Queries can evolve into Rules or Reports to produce very specific sets of information you are interested in. MARS provides 144 built-in System Rules to provide a set of general reports to start with. Among these are sets of rules to provide high-level information such as which sources are creating the most traffic, which destinations are visited most, or what malware is most active on your network. Also included among the System Rules are rules designed to assist with regulatory compliance efforts.

Like Queries and Rules—because in MARS they are really all the same thing— Reports can be customized and evolved to match many of your reporting needs.

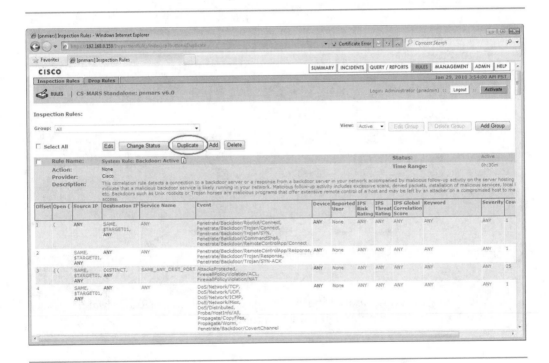

**Figure 10-14.** Copying Rules

## Mitigation

Reflecting on the original purpose of MARS—to provide security threat mitigation—one of the options you will have when certain Rules are met will be to apply a recommended command to cut off the control channel between an attacker and a compromised host on your network using a monitored router, switch, or firewall on your network. When this is an option, you will be able to select the appropriate device and command and "push" it to the device, as shown here.

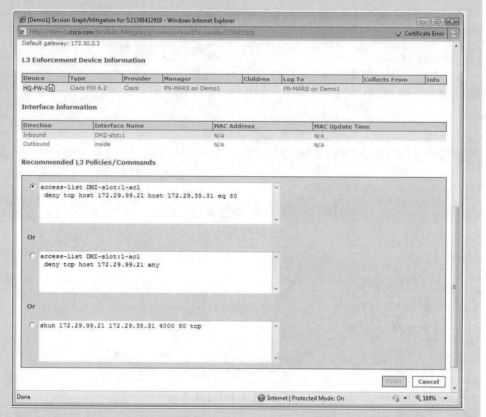

Alternately, you can choose to forward this command to the individual or group responsible for managing this device.

# Limitations

As of the writing of this chapter, Cisco Systems is not providing robust support for non-Cisco event sources. In effect, this means that any non-Cisco-brand devices or applications you want to integrate with your MARS may require you to leverage the Custom Parser feature in the product. This is a non-trivial exercise that should not be undertaken without fully considering the effort and complexities involved. In the following chapter, we will discuss Custom Parsers at some depth.

# Summary

MARS' capability to integrate topology awareness with information and event data remains a unique feature in the SIEM market. Limitations aside, MARS shows prospects of shaping the future direction of SIEM solutions and continues to be a product that should be evaluated by those whose network consists largely of Cisco equipment.

# CHAPTER 11 | Cisco MARS Advanced Techniques

W ith an understanding of the basic architecture and taxonomy in hand, it is time to dive deeper into the operation of your MARS. The operation of any SIEM is something that comes to you in stages, not unlike a great romance. Our goal is not to bring you to a "happily ever after" state with these brief chapters, but, rather, to introduce you two crazy kids and get you talking well enough that you can take it from there. With the introductions behind us, we'll start the conversation off and then you can carry it forward on your own.

In this chapter, we will go further in familiarizing you with the MARS user interface dashboards, take a look at the mechanism for integrating unsupported devices, and follow an operator through a typical incident investigation. This should give you enough of a running start to use your MARS daily and set you on the path to learning all the other arcane details not covered in these pages.

# Using the MARS Dashboard

As mentioned in the last chapter, MARS requires Internet Explorer 7 or greater and the Adobe SVG Viewer to display the user interface. Once you get all that together, using HTTPS log in to your MARS (for example, **https://yourmars.yourcompany.com**, replacing the *yourmars.yourcompany.com* with the correct URL or IP address of your MARS management interface), and you will see a screen that looks a lot like Figure 11-1. Since we have not yet taken you on a thorough tour of the MARS interface, let's get to know the layout of the MARS dashboard pages a little bit better.

The first row of buttons (Summary, Incidents, Query/Report, Rules, Management, Admin, and Help) will take you to major functionality areas. The second row of buttons will take you to subtopics under these major areas (in Figure 11-1 these are Dashboard, Network Status, and My Reports). You may enter one of these major areas (i.e., Admin), select a subtopic (i.e., User Management), and find that you're now in another major functional area (in this case, the Management major area would now be selected). You haven't clicked the wrong button; some subtopics simply relate to multiple areas of major functionality and are found in multiple locations.

**NOTE** You can see an example of this in the section "Building Your Own Custom Parsers": when clicking the User Defined Log Parser Templates link shown in Figure 11-22 under Admin, you will find yourself on the Management top-level page on the Device Type Management tab, as shown in Figure 11-27.

Two very important buttons, one of which you will find very useful if you understand it and very vexing if you do not, are on the right-hand side of the banner below the second row of buttons. The Logout button is self-explanatory, so we will

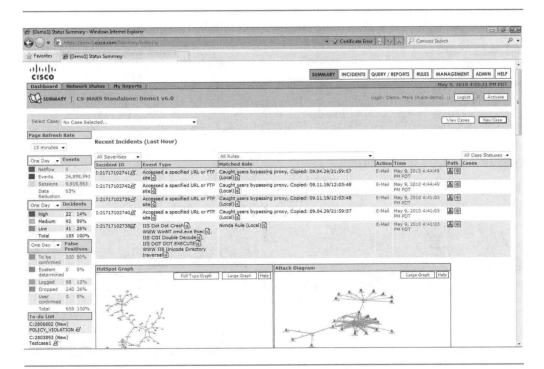

**Figure 11-1.** MARS Summary screen

focus on the Activate button instead. As you make changes in MARS, you will have to "activate" many of those changes. Without summarizing all of them at this point, suffice it to say, that if the Activate button is red, you have made some changes that have not been enacted fully, which probably explains why what you just did is not working. If the Activate button on your MARS screen is red, mostly likely you need to press it.

Below the banner with the Activate button on each page of the MARS user interface you'll find a row (shaded to match the color scheme of the parent page) providing case management functions. The Select Case drop-down lists the most recent unresolved cases; the View Cases button takes you directly to the Incidents page and the Cases subtopic. The New Case button will pop-up a window that allows you to create a new case to be tracked (Figure 11-2).

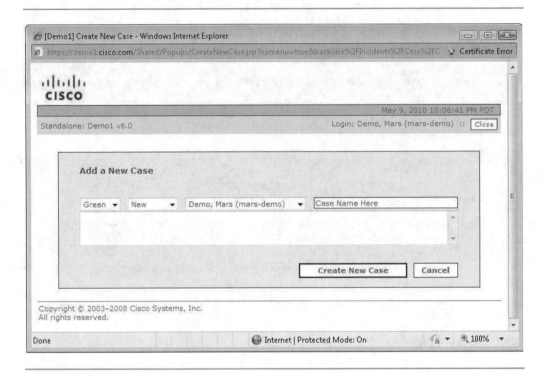

**Figure 11-2.**   Create New Case window

## Summary Page

The default configuration that comes with MARS provides a Summary page containing the information that an operator would want to find at a glance in most situations. This screen can be customized to a certain extent—you can configure your Summary page to include reports that you find particularly useful—but we will stick with the default settings for the purpose of this chapter.

The left pane of this default view allows you to set the automatic refresh for this page; displays the quantity of NetFlows, Events, and Sessions during the past 24 hours (remember, a Session is a collection of Events and/or Flows that represent a single end-to-end connection across your network); a count of Incidents by severity in the past day; a summary of False Positives of several classes, and a list of To Do's for the user who has logged in. Each of these timeframes can be reset to display this information for an interval of One Day, Two Days, a Week, a Month, or a Year.

The main pane of the Summary display shows the five most recent incidents recorded by your MARS. You can choose to display a specific severity (MARS speaks in color: red for High Severity, yellow for Medium, and green for Low). The default is to show the five most recent of any severity.

The rest of the page is occupied by a set of graphics that provide both a quick visual of the high-level state of the network as seen by MARS, as well as some specific tools that you will find very useful in identifying and investigating malicious activity. The two graphs displayed below Recent Incidents are quite valuable and take a certain amount of understanding to use properly, so we will go into more detail about each of them.

Figure 11-3 shows the HotSpot Graph. The HotSpot Graph summarizes the security of the network in the form of a topological representation where areas of the network that MARS deems to be of high concern are called out. As with all such graphs in MARS, you can zoom in to get more detail or click any icon to get information about the device or network represented.

The Hotspot Graph serves as an "at a glance" summary of the status of security on the network. Sitting at the console for the first time each day, you can get a feel for whether there are obvious concerns before you do anything else.

Figure 11-4 shows what you will find when you zoom in on the cluster of activity shown in the HotSpot graph by, in this case, clicking the cloud surrounded by red and brown dots. Clouds in these graphs represent network segments that are not fully discovered, and by clicking the "Gateway 47" cloud in the subsequent chart you will be given the opportunity to use SNMP to discover the gateway at the heart of the cluster of Incidents.

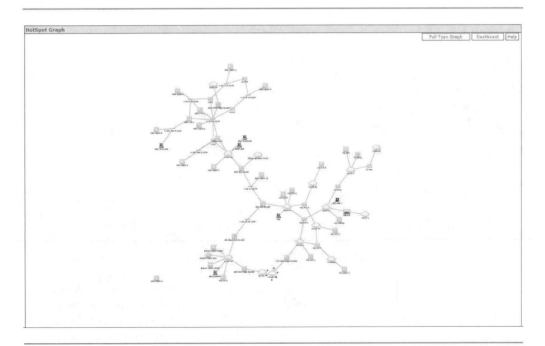

**Figure 11-3.**   HotSpot Graph

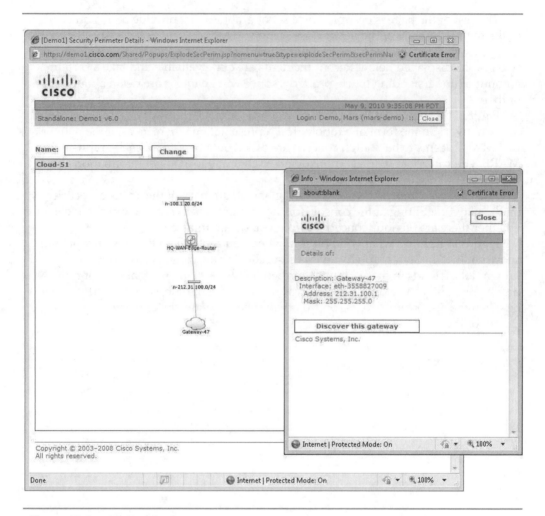

**Figure 11-4.**    HotSpot details

The Attack Diagram as shown in Figure 11-5 provides a view of the sessions involved in recent Incidents. This diagram comes in very handy as a next-step drill-down after reviewing the HotSpot Graph. Each of the hosts shown in the Attack Diagram has been involved in a recent Incident—either as a source (brown icons) or a destination (red icons) or both (purple icons, suspected compromised hosts). Mousing over the lines will highlight the paths of the incidents (they will turn red), helping you visualize the relationship between the attacker and target. The red numbers next to the lines tell you how many Sessions were generated between the given endpoints in recent Incidents.

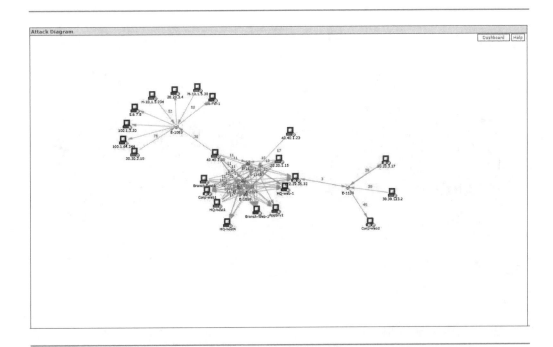

**Figure 11-5.**   Attack Diagram

The remaining four diagrams on the Summary page provide a graphical view of the traffic being monitored by your MARS. Figure 11-6 shows the volume of events and NetFlows being collected by the MARS (the demo system that Cisco provided did not have NetFlow implemented, so this graph shows only Received Events - Non-NetFlow). The Events And Sessions chart provides a graphical depiction of the data reduction gained by using topology information to create Sessions (as described in the previous chapter). In the example shown, you see how between 23,000 and 33,000 Events are reduced to between 6,000 and 9,000 Sessions.

The Top Destination Ports graph shows—not surprisingly—just that. As you see in Figure 11-7, each of the bands represents one of the top-ten most-used ports at a given time. This view is very useful, since worms and other types of attacks often cause an anomalous spike in traffic to a given port, which would be visible in many cases in this graph (MARS includes a default rule, "Sudden Increase of Traffic to a Port," that triggers in just such cases).

Figure 11-7 also shows the False Positive Events graph. In the case of our demo system, some serious tuning is needed, as evidenced by the average of four or more Unconfirmed False Positives being recorded every minute. One of the tasks of a MARS administrator is to identify these false positives and tune them out of the usable data set, which is touched on in the last section of this chapter (see "A Typical Day in the Life of a MARS Operator" and Figures 11-39 and 11-40 in particular).

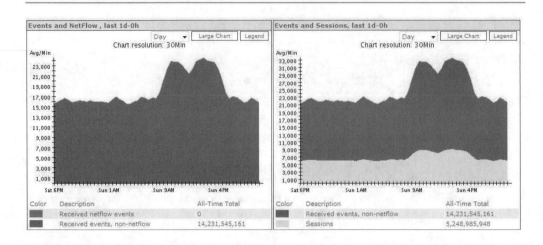

**Figure 11-6.** Events and NetFlow, and Events and Sessions graphs

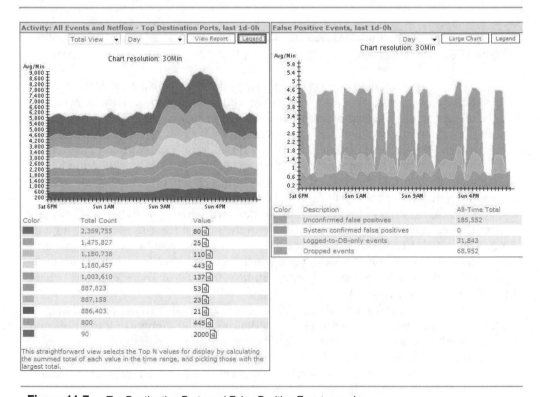

**Figure 11-7.** Top Destination Ports and False Positive Events graphs

# Incidents Page

All of the bad things happening on your network should result in a MARS Incident being created, so as a MARS operator, you can expect to spend a fair amount of time poking around in the Incidents major area. The subtopic tabs on this page are Incidents (not a typo, the major area and subtopic name are the same, as you can see in Figure 11-8); False Positives where you can tune out unwanted noise, and Cases, which is the MARS trouble-ticketing system.

As on the Summary page, you can choose to display incidents of a given severity (Red, Yellow, or Green). On this page, you can further sort incidents by the Rule (or Rule Group) they are associated with; incidents can also be associated with a given Case Status (All Case Statuses, All Open, New, Assigned, Resolved, or Closed). Any combination of these variables can be used to focus the list on your immediate area of interest (i.e., "Show me all Red Incidents involving Server Exploits that are currently Assigned to a MARS operator"). The screen will refresh with each selection made, but will remember your last selection so you can build that three-step logic.

This page also gives you the same time-windows that you saw on the Summary page (One Day, Two Days, a Week, a Month, or a Year).

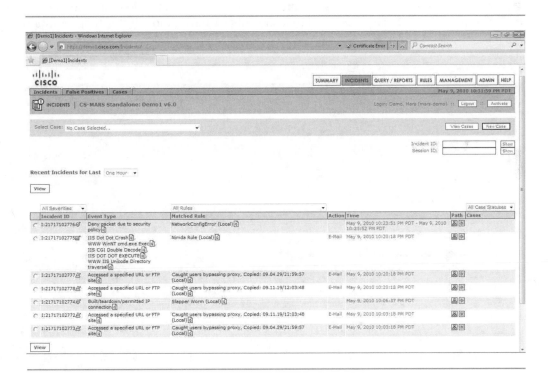

**Figure 11-8.**   Incidents page

## Query/Reports Page

As we discussed in the previous chapter, in MARS, Queries, Rules, and Reports are effectively the same things. Queries are usually ad-hoc logical structures; Rules are typically refined sets of logic that you want to be alerted on; and Reports are sets of logic that you wish to save and run periodically with the results being presented in report format. The fact that Cisco grouped Queries and Reports on the same tab is an indication of how similar these two really are.

On this page, you can see this logic coming together. As you can see in Figure 11-9, you are given the option to Load Report As On-Demand Query With Filter, which will take existing Reports and allow you to use them as active Queries. You can add information such as source or destination IP address or port, a specific Event or Event Type Group you are interested in, and then build a specific Query. You can then take the Query and select Save As Report, Save As Rule, or Submit Inline (the last option is synonymous with "run this query now").

In the example shown in Figure 11-10, you can see how the logic in a MARS Query is constructed. This Query shows the result of typical security analyst activity: a host on the internal network (10.1.2.37) is suspected of being compromised so the analyst asks the MARS to search first for any traffic from that specific IP address on port 597 (a port our fictional analyst has seen suspicious activity on) destined for any other host. This, by itself, won't tell her what she wants to know, so she has added the Operation FOLLOWED-BY and further specified that she only wants to know if this first condition

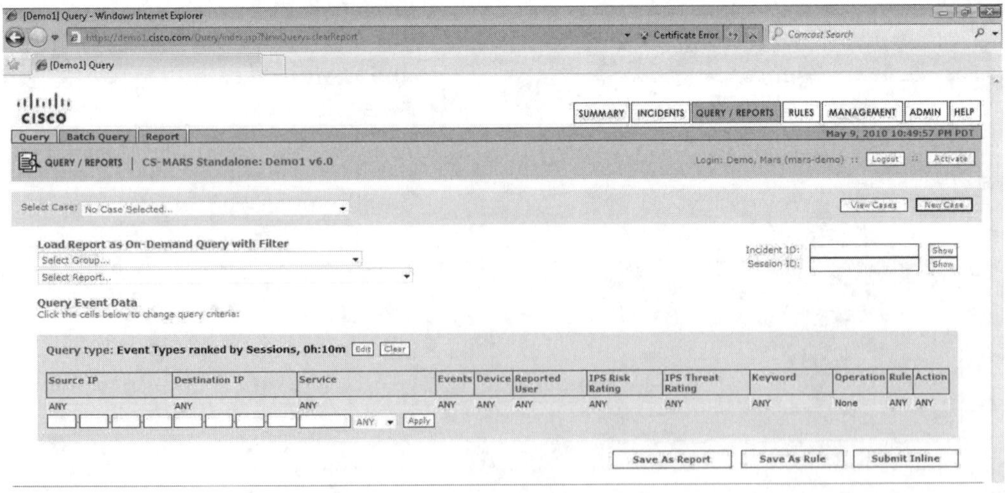

**Figure 11-9.** Query/Report page

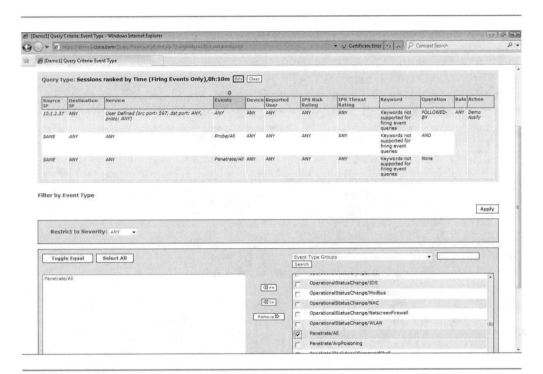

**Figure 11-10.**   Example Query

is proceeded by any traffic originating at the SAME host that has caused any Event in the "Probe/All" Event Type Group to be received by the MARS. Of course, a probe is just a probe, so our analyst has added an AND operator so her Query will only result in a match if this probe is also accompanied by an Event triggered by the SAME host that belongs to the "Penetrate/All" Event Type Group. If all these conditions are met, our analyst will have actionable evidence that the originally suspect host has been compromised and could justify quarantining that host until such time as it can be safely returned to duty.

## Rules Page

The Rules major function area includes only two subtopic tabs: Inspection Rules and Drop Rules, as illustrated in Figure 11-11. These mean, respectively, "I want to know when these conditions are met" and "I want to ignore these conditions." Drop Rules are a significant part of the tuning process; behavior that might cause concern on a different network may be normal operating procedure on yours, so you will want to create Drop Rules to keep from being distracted by alerts regarding that traffic.

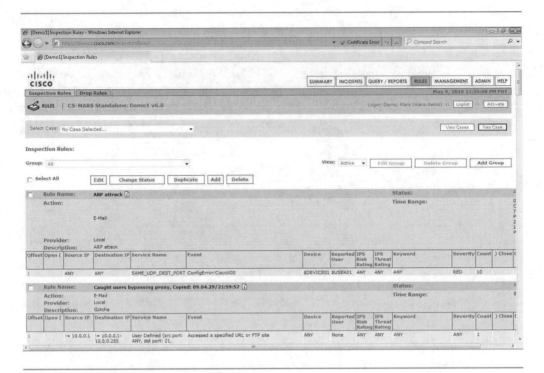

**Figure 11-11.** Rules page

On the Inspection Rules page, you will find all of the built-in ("System") Rules as well as any Rules you have created ("User Rules"). You can create or edit Rules on this page using the same logic employed for the Query/Report page (remember, MARS sees these as effectively the same things). When editing existing Rules, in most cases, we suggest using the Duplicate function to create a copy of the current rule and editing the copy of that Rule instead of the Rule itself. Figure 11-12 shows a Rule being edited. When you are satisfied that your new Rule is exactly what you want, then you can change the status for the old Rule to Inactive and make your new Rule active by selecting the new rule and changing its status to Active.

Don't forget to press the Activate button or your new rule will not function and the original rule will still be in effect. (Is the Activate button red? Then click it.)

When you view or edit an existing rule, you will see a Time Range value in the upper-right section of the rule display in the "0h:00m" format. Our example Rule has a time range of 30 minutes, meaning that all conditions must be met within that timeframe or the Rule will not fire. When you click on the "0h:30m," you are given the opportunity to change the timeframe, as shown in Figure 11-13.

One of the benefits of duplicating and modifying the System Rules is that you can follow the logic of the MARS developers and learn from their experience. Our example Rule is constructed to watch for backdoor services running on your network, look to

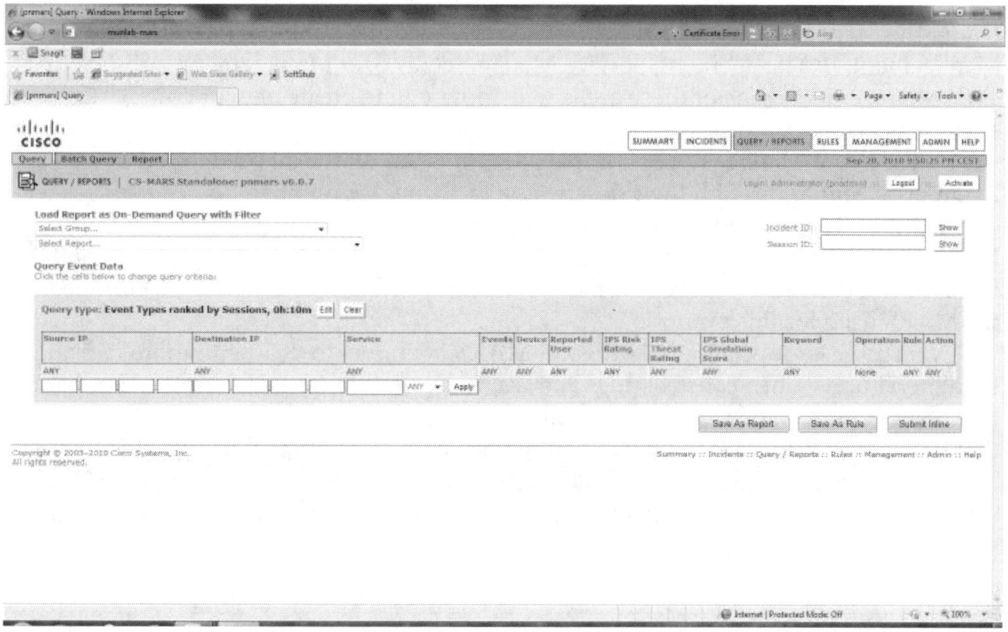

**Figure 11-12.** Example of a Rule being edited

match any attempt to install a backdoor, OR any activity that looks like a backdoor has been installed, FOLLOWED BY at least 25 Events involving the suspect internal host having traffic blocked by firewalls, OR any Event indicating the suspect internal host is actively attacking the network, OR any sign of a covert channel having been created to that internal host from another source, all within a 30 minute window. As attacks evolve, you may well find that you want to tune existing Rules (increasing the time range to catch lower-and-slower attacks of the same profile, for instance) to fit emergent scenarios.

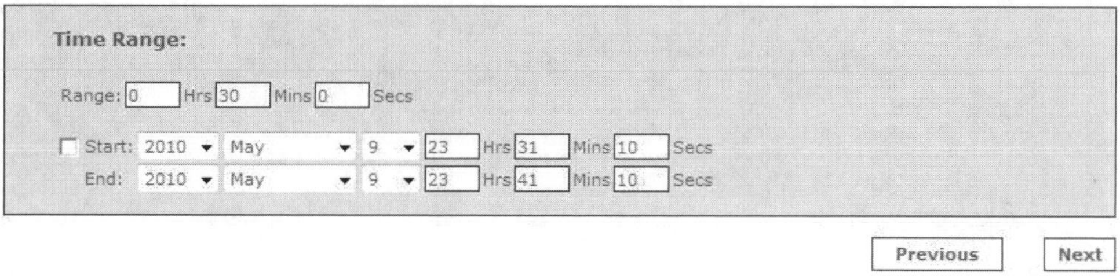

**Figure 11-13.** Setting Rule timeframe

## Management Page

Under the Management major function area you will find subtopic tabs for Event Management, IP Management, Service Management, User Management, and Device Type Management. Each of these areas will allow you to create new or edit existing entries in each area.

On the Event Management subtopic page, you can search all predefined Events and Event Types either through their description or their CVE number. You can edit, delete, or add Event Type Groups on this page, but Events themselves are either built into MARS at the factory or added by you using the custom parser that we will talk about later. As you can see in Figure 11-14, there are 29,207 Events or Event Type Groups in the MARS used for this example.

Event Type Groups allow MARS and MARS operators to deal with more logical than literal units when constructing Queries, Rules, and Reports. Figure 11-15 expands the Event Type "Sudden increase of traffic to a port" and illustrates the type of structure that you would want to use when creating your own Event Type Groups. This Event Type has been specified as has having a Red Severity and is a MARS-generated Event. It belongs to the Event Type Groups DOS/All and DOS/Network/Misc, each of which

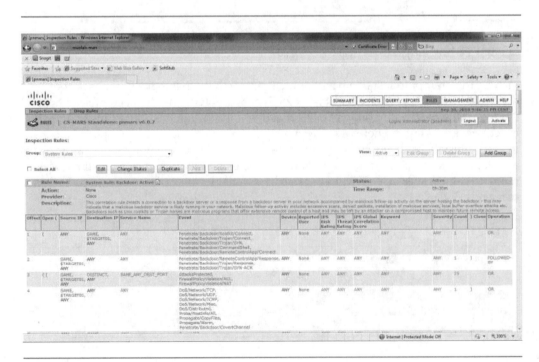

**Figure 11-14.**    Management page – Event Management view

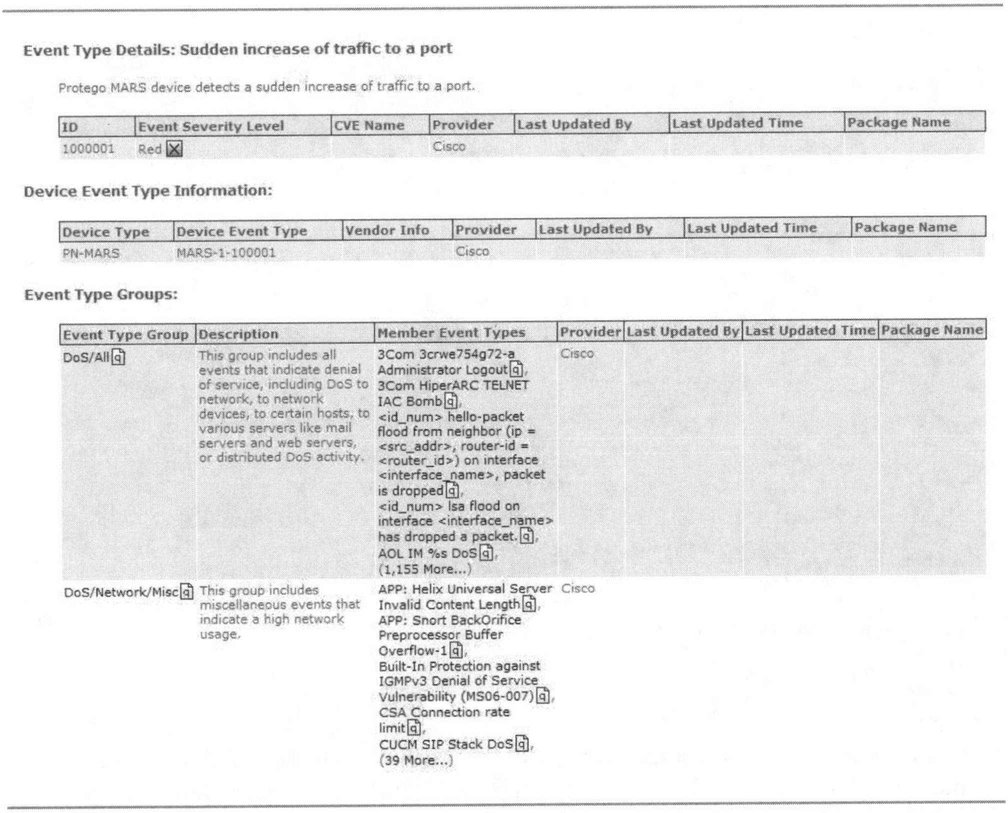

**Event Type Details: Sudden increase of traffic to a port**

Protego MARS device detects a sudden increase of traffic to a port.

| ID | Event Severity Level | CVE Name | Provider | Last Updated By | Last Updated Time | Package Name |
|---|---|---|---|---|---|---|
| 1000001 | Red ☒ | | Cisco | | | |

**Device Event Type Information:**

| Device Type | Device Event Type | Vendor Info | Provider | Last Updated By | Last Updated Time | Package Name |
|---|---|---|---|---|---|---|
| PN-MARS | MARS-1-100001 | | Cisco | | | |

**Event Type Groups:**

| Event Type Group | Description | Member Event Types | Provider | Last Updated By | Last Updated Time | Package Name |
|---|---|---|---|---|---|---|
| DoS/All🔍 | This group includes all events that indicate denial of service, including DoS to network, to network devices, to certain hosts, to various servers like mail servers and web servers, or distributed DoS activity. | 3Com 3crwe754g72-a Administrator Logout🔍, 3Com HiperARC TELNET IAC Bomb🔍, <id_num> hello-packet flood from neighbor (ip = <src_addr>, router-id = <router_id>) on interface <interface_name>, packet is dropped🔍, <id_num> lsa flood on interface <interface_name> has dropped a packet.🔍, AOL IM %s DoS🔍, (1,155 More...) | Cisco | | | |
| DoS/Network/Misc🔍 | This group includes miscellaneous events that indicate a high network usage. | APP: Helix Universal Server Invalid Content Length🔍, APP: Snort BackOrifice Preprocessor Buffer Overflow-1🔍, Built-In Protection against IGMPv3 Denial of Service Vulnerability (MS06-007)🔍, CSA Connection rate limit🔍, CUCM SIP Stack DoS🔍, (39 More...) | Cisco | | | |

**Figure 11-15.**    Event Type Group details

includes a variety of other Event Types that indicate the same or similar conditions. When creating Queries, Rules, and Reports you can use either the specific Event Type you want to see, but more often, you will most likely use the Event Type Group to catch any activity performing a similar function as part of an attack.

IP Management allows you to define specific IP addresses or collections/ranges of IP addresses as logical units. By clicking Add or selecting an existing object and choosing Edit you will be able to provide/edit a name, an IP address, and Netmask to define the logical unit. Figure 11-16 shows you what you will see on this page.

MARS defines services that might run on your network. Figure 11-17 shows the System Service for the popular network game Quake. As you can see from this example, you can define a service based on Protocol, Source Port/Range, and Destination Port/Range.

We discussed User Management in the previous chapter, and we will talk about Device Type Management in the section on "Adding Unsupported Devices to MARS."

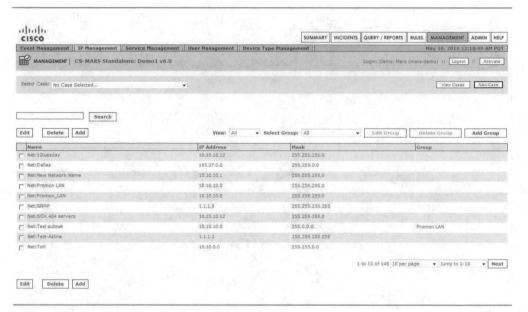

**Figure 11-16.** IP Management page

## Admin Page

Last but not least (by any stretch), we get to the Admin page. This major area tab includes subtopic tabs for System Setup, System Maintenance, User Management, System Parameters, and Custom Setup.

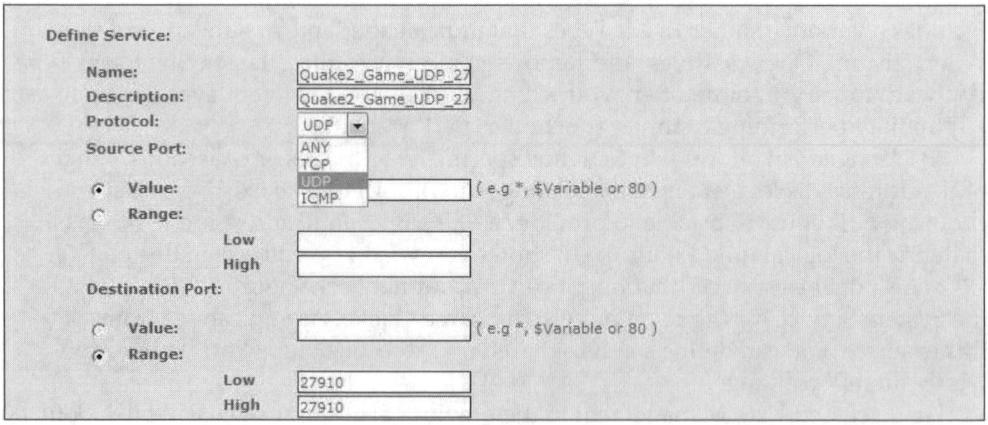

**Figure 11-17.** Service Management detail

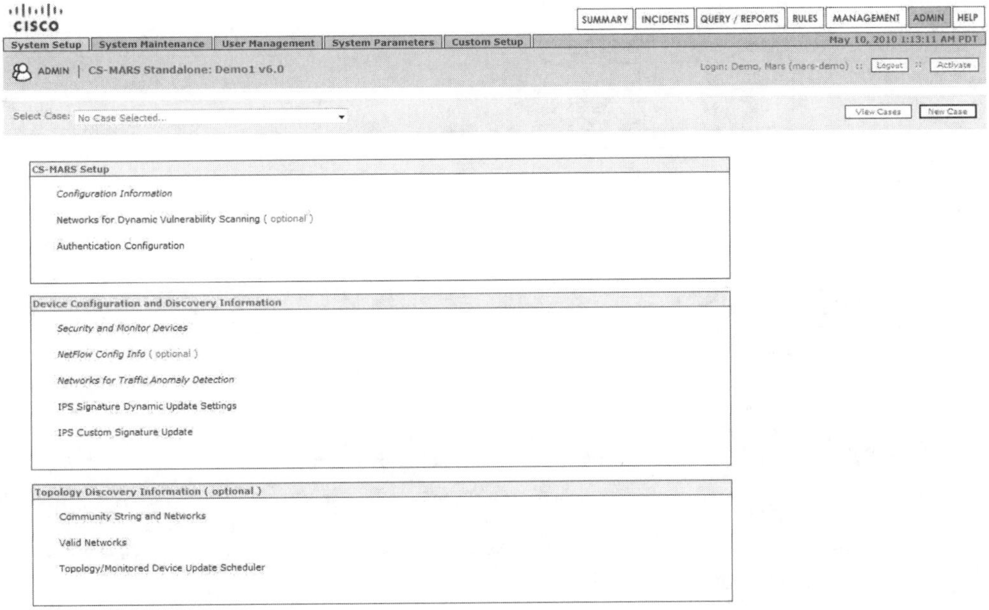

**Figure 11-18.**   Admin page – System Setup

The System Setup tab, shown in Figure 11-18, contains virtually all of the fields required to configure the MARS initially, including basic networking (Configuration Information), tying in RADIUS/TACACS authentication services (Authentication Configuration), adding in Event and Flow feeds from network devices and applications (Device Configuration and Discovery Information), and the SNMP Community Strings and Valid IP ranges for your networks.

The System Maintenance tab contains the locations for installing licenses and upgrades as well as certificates (so you don't get the red address bar and other warnings IE throws at us). Figure 11-19 shows this page. Logging by MARS is also managed on this page, allowing you to alter the MARS logging levels and investigate the MARS logs themselves in either formatted or raw views. The Data Archiving link on this page is where you connect your MARS to a NAS or other off-board data archiving solution for longer-term storage of the Events and other information that your MARS accumulates continuously.

The System Parameters page, shown in Figure 11-20, allows you to specify somewhat mundane information—such as proxy, SSL/SSH, and user timeout settings—as well as a few important settings. You will recall earlier in this chapter we stressed several times that any change will not be in effect until you press the Activate button? Under Activation Settings, you can set your MARS to press the Activate button automatically every 13, 30, 45, or 60 minutes (the default setting is NEVER).

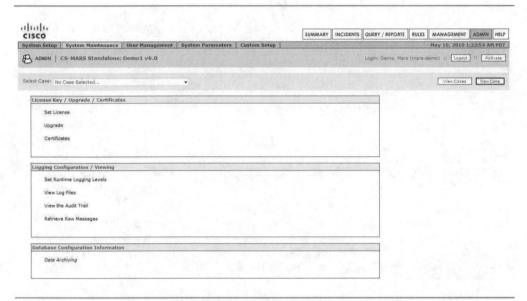

**Figure 11-19.**  Admin page – System Maintenance

Distributed Threat Mitigation Settings is a Cisco-specific function that coordinates the IPS signatures available on Cisco IOS routers. The MARS can act as an IPS signature police tactician, adding and removing signatures from Cisco IOS routers based on the activity of the given signature. MARS will regularly poll Cisco Connection Online

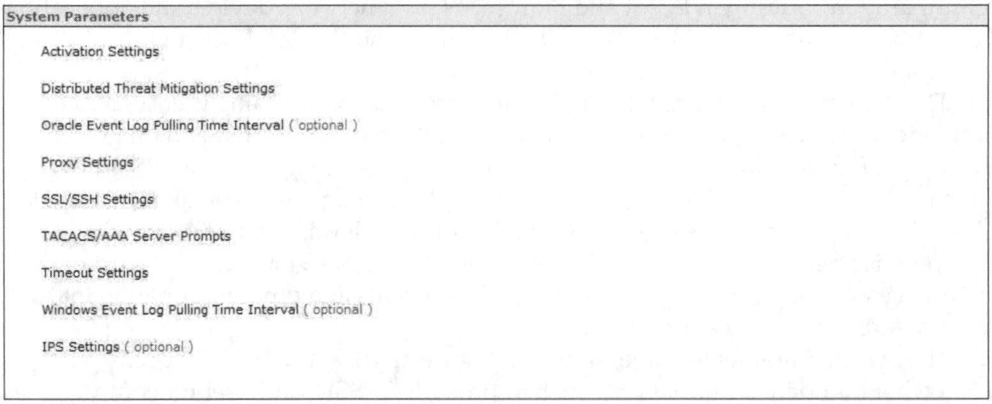

**Figure 11-20.**  Admin page – System Parameters

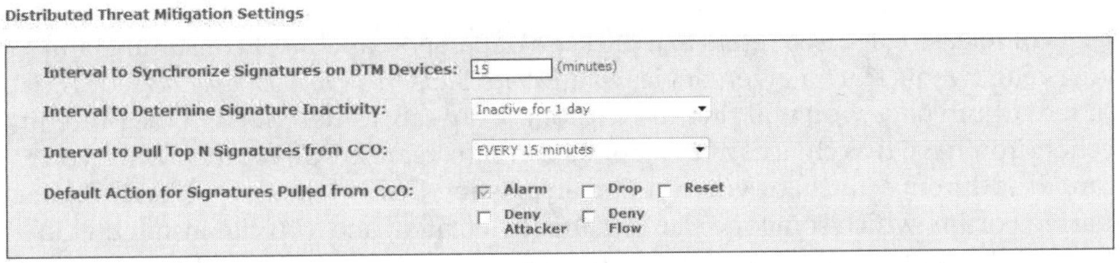

**Distributed Threat Mitigation Settings**

Interval to Synchronize Signatures on DTM Devices:  `15`  (minutes)

Interval to Determine Signature Inactivity:  `Inactive for 1 day ▼`

Interval to Pull Top N Signatures from CCO:  `EVERY 15 minutes ▼`

Default Action for Signatures Pulled from CCO:  ☑ Alarm  ☐ Drop  ☐ Reset  ☐ Deny Attacker  ☐ Deny Flow

**Figure 11-21.**   Admin page – Distributed Threat Mitigation

(CCO) (the public-facing website at cisco.com) for new IPS signatures and manage those on the routed infrastructure automatically. Figure 11-21 shows you what this page looks like.

Absolutely last but most definitively not least in the user interface is the Admin/ Custom Setup tab (shown in Figure 11-22). This is where you integrate MARS with unsupported devices. We will discuss this at some depth in the next section.

# Adding Unsupported Devices to MARS

The Achilles Heel of MARS is support for devices that are not supported out-of-the-box. As of the writing of this book, it seems unlikely that Cisco will be adding support for many new devices—and even fewer non-Cisco devices. Inasmuch as you wish to

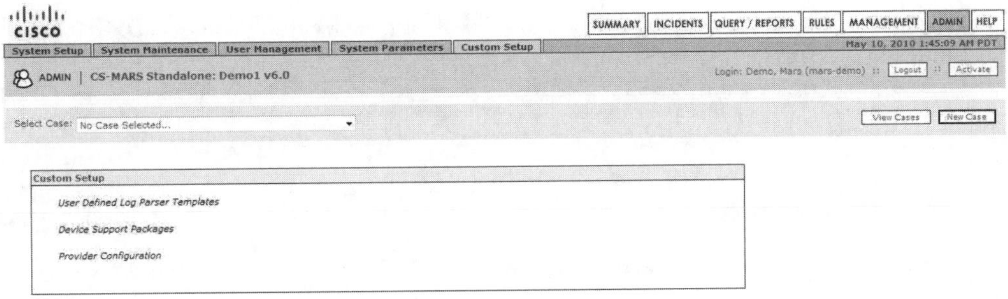

CISCO

SUMMARY | INCIDENTS | QUERY / REPORTS | RULES | MANAGEMENT | ADMIN | HELP

System Setup | System Maintenance | User Management | System Parameters | Custom Setup    May 10, 2010 1:45:09 AM PDT

ADMIN | CS-MARS Standalone: Demo1 v6.0    Login: Demo, Mars (mars-demo)  Logout  Activate

Select Case: No Case Selected...    View Cases    New Case

**Custom Setup**

User Defined Log Parser Templates

Device Support Packages

Provider Configuration

**Figure 11-22.**   Admin page – Custom Setup

feed other data sources into your MARS you will need to be familiar with the Custom Parser function that comes with the product.

As of release 6.0, Cisco refers to a package of parsers capable of consuming and processing Events from a given device as a *Device Support Framework package*, or *DSF*. On the Admin page, you will find the Custom Setup tab, as described in the preceding section. You have two choices at this point: you can create a DSF for the device you want to add from scratch, or you can find an existing DSF on the Cisco MARS Package Sharing Forum, which someone else has already created, and you can install that in your MARS. As of the writing of this book, there are only a small handful (less than five) DSFs available for download from the Cisco MARS Package Sharing Forum.

## Importing Device Support Packages

Assuming you can find an existing package—or that you have already created one for your own purposes and wish to import it into another MARS—you will choose the Device Support Packages option from the Custom Setup menu, as shown in Figure 11-23.

Selecting Import will take you to a page that allows you to browse your computer for the DSF package you wish to install (see Figure 11-24). On this page, you will also find a link to the Package Sharing Forum where you can search for a DSF or submit your own for other people's use. The DSFs on the Forum tend to be zipped files including a licensing statement text file as well as the DSF itself (another zipped file). Choose the DSF zip file and click Next. You will know immediately if you have a valid file; your MARS will attempt to interpret the file and will either accept it (Figure 11-25) or alert you that it is unable to read it.

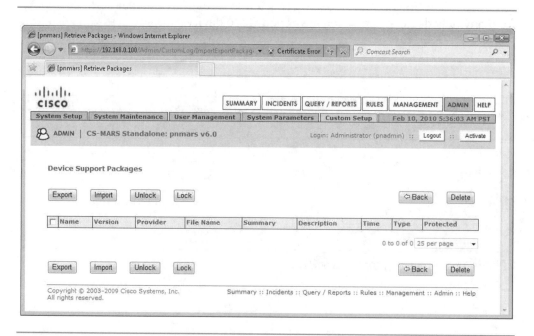

**Figure 11-23.**    Import/Export Device Support packages

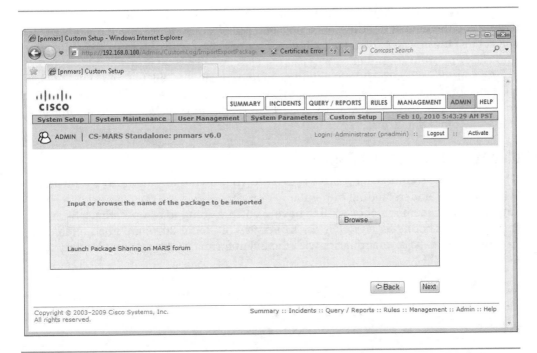

**Figure 11-24.** Import Device Support packages

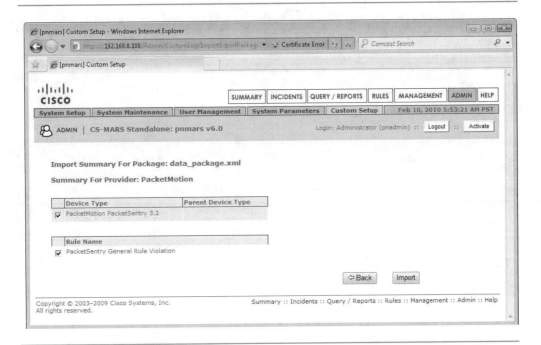

**Figure 11-25.** PacketMotion PacketSentry 3.2

As you can see in Figure 11-26, DSF files can also include Rules to be imported, saving you the time of building the associated Rule from scratch. Check the boxes to import just the device parser itself (Device Type) or also any Rules that are included, and click Import to continue.

As you see in Figure 11-26, you will need to Activate the DSF before using it. Click the Done button to finish the import, and click the red Activate button when you return to the next page. You are now ready to add this device to your MARS and begin using it like any other data source.

## Building Your Own Custom Parsers

The other, more common alternative is to build your own integration from scratch. This will require an understanding of regular expressions which are not covered here, but understanding them is a good skill to have if you are going to be operating a SIEM. Jeffery Friedl's book *Mastering Regular Expressions* (O'Reilly, 2006) is a good reference. You will need to have a familiarity with the Event format sent by the device you

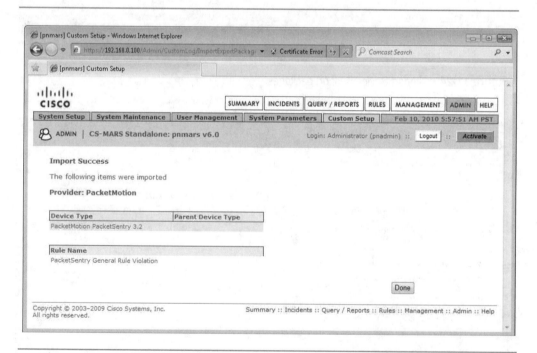

**Figure 11-26.**   Successful DSF import

want to add to your MARS as well. Some vendors provide very good documentation detailing the format for each type of log message, but an actual sample of the logs to be integrated can be used to determine the format as well. This process can be fairly long and complex, and, although we will not cover it completely in this chapter, we will discuss the concepts you need to understand to be able to work your way through the process.

To begin, select the User Defined Log Parser Templates link shown in Figure 11-22. You will find yourself on the Management top-level page on the Device Type Management subtopic tab, as shown in Figure 11-27.

On this page, you have the choice of either selecting Add (to create a new parser from scratch), or Derive From (to clone an existing parser and edit it to fit). You will also note that you can select Add Device Event Type from this page. We recommend that you attempt to map your new device to an existing device type; this allows your new device to use existing Rules, Queries, and Reports already in your MARS. A new device type may require you to edit existing Rules, Queries, and Reports to recognize your device or to create new Rules, Queries, and Reports that do. For the purpose of this illustration, we will choose Add to demonstrate how that works. Figure 11-28 shows that we are going to add our device as an Appliance. Selecting Appliance or Software will give you different options on the following screens.

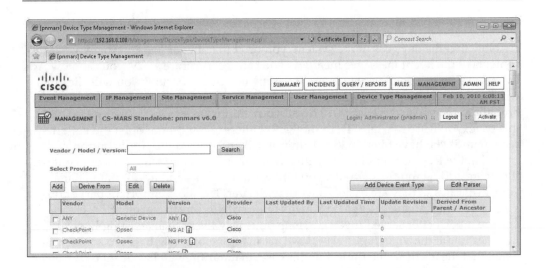

**Figure 11-27.** Device Type Management

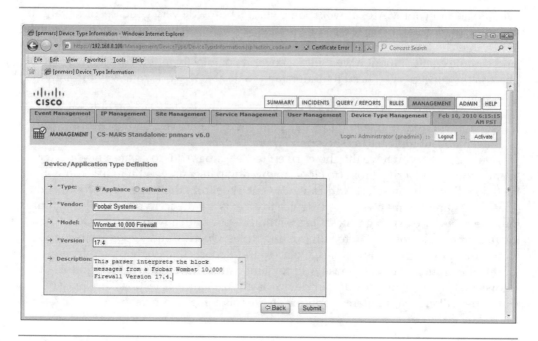

**Figure 11-28.** Adding a new device

Now that the device is in the system, you need to tell your MARS exactly what the contents of the Event messages mean. As you can see in Figure 11-29, you can now Add Events or Edit existing Events. Ignore the Activate button for now; you will click that when you are ready to bring your new parser online. Click the Add button and you are brought to the page where you will do all your editing, as shown in Figure 11-30. On this page, you'll see two tabs: Definition and Patterns. You cannot open the Patterns section until you have filled in the Definition tab and clicked the Apply button.

Fill in the Device Event ID box with a name that will make sense for your context. If you are adding multiple Events, you will want to use a standard format to name your Event IDs so they are easier to work with later. The most important part of this stage is the Map To Event Type box the fills most of this screen. As mentioned earlier, you are much better served if you can map your new Event to an existing Event Type. In the example shown in Figure 11-30, we are mapping our new Event to an existing Event that means the same thing—in this case, that our firewall has dropped a packet because, although it claims to be HTTP, it does not adhere to HTTP protocol rules. To save yourself the time of searching for the right Event Type to match to at this stage, you should have already looked through the existing supported devices and identified an appropriate Event Type to map to. Click the Apply button at the bottom of this screen, and you will now be able to edit the Patterns tab.

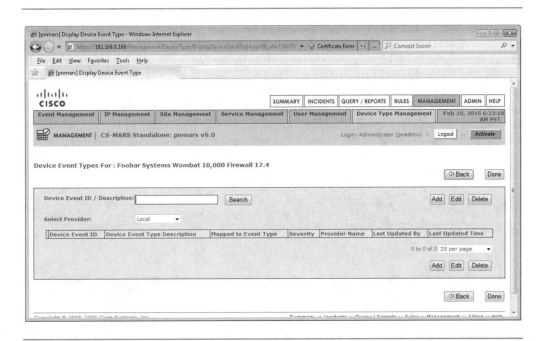

**Figure 11-29.** Add New Device, Appliance example

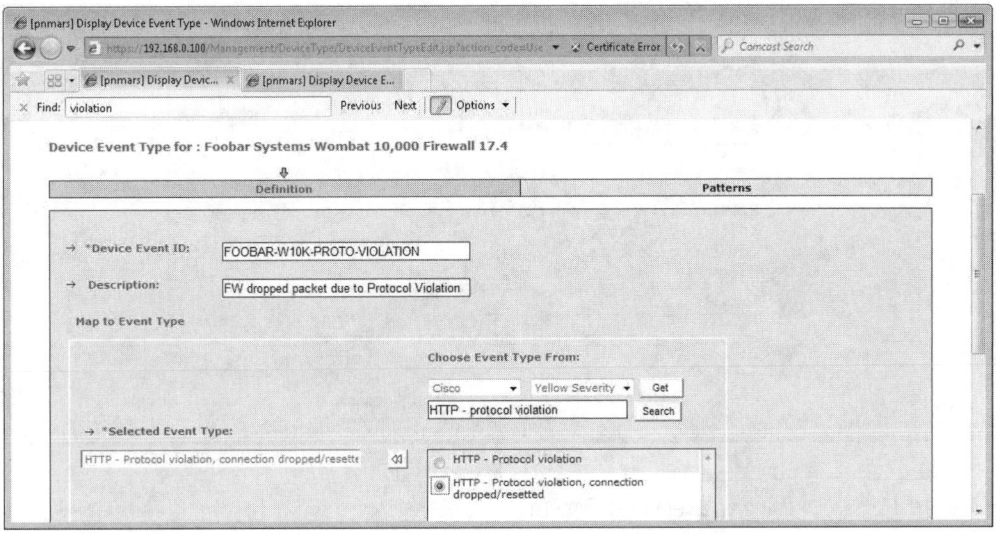

**Figure 11-30.** Custom Parser Event description

On the Patterns tab, you have the choice to Add, Edit, Delete, or Test a pattern. To begin, click the Add button and a window will pop up, as shown in Figure 11-31. On this screen, you will give the MARS the information it needs to find the first field in the Event messages it will be receiving from your new device.

Position is the order of the patterns as found in the Event message. In this example, the first part of our Event message begins with the text-string "Protocol" and is followed by a text-string that defines the protocol (i.e., TCP). The Key Pattern will match the text-string found in the message; you can consider this the beginning delimiter for the information this field will contain. The Parsed Field drop-down gives

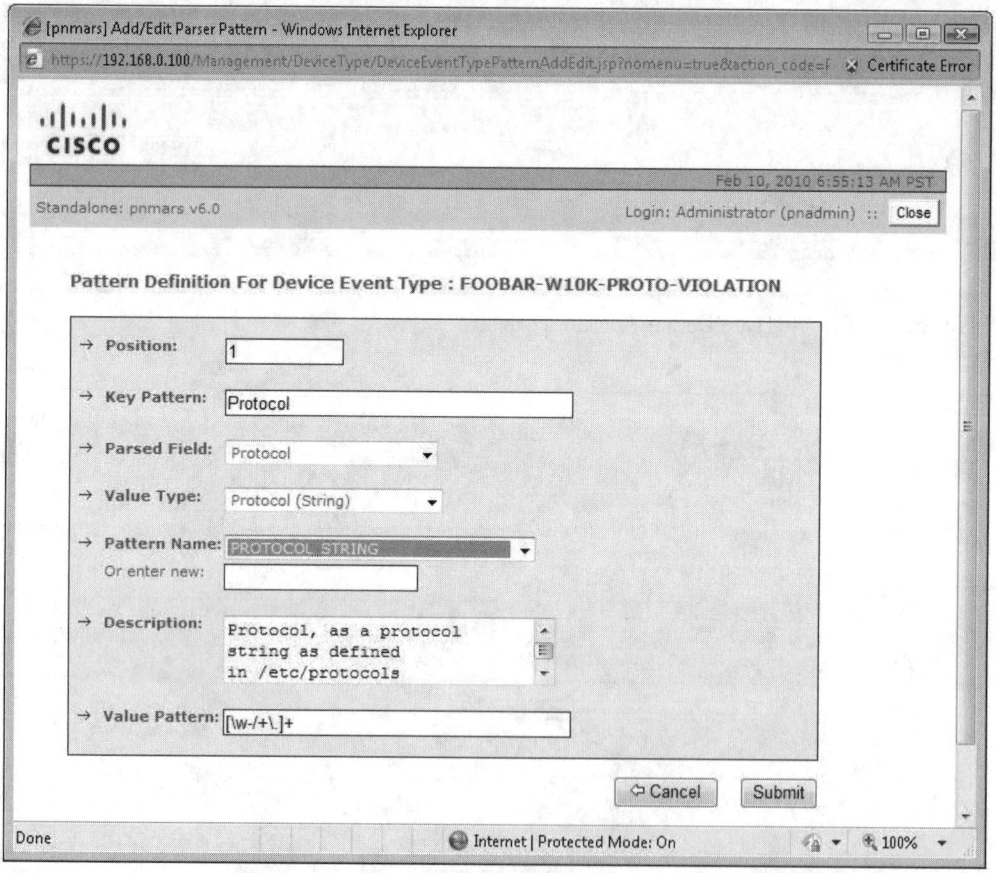

**Figure 11-31.** Adding an Event Field Pattern

you the list of field types that MARS can understand (i.e., Protocol, Source/Destination Address, User, and so forth). The Pattern Name box shows you existing patterns that MARS has already stored; you can select an existing pattern or create your own (which you can subsequently reuse). The information you enter under Description is strictly used to describe the pattern itself and is not interpreted by the MARS, and the Value Pattern is the regular expression that will capture the data in the given field. When you are satisfied that the field has been properly defined, click Submit.

It is a good idea to test each field before going on to add the next. You do not want to have to start over again. When you click the Test button, a window will pop up where you can paste your sample Event message and see if it is working. Figure 11-32 shows the results of our first test.

Repeat the process for the remaining fields in the Event message. When you have completed all fields, you will have a new parser for that Event message. Repeat the entire process until you have added all of the messages from the device you are adding. When you are fully satisfied, save this parser and click the red Activate button and your new device is ready to be used with your MARS.

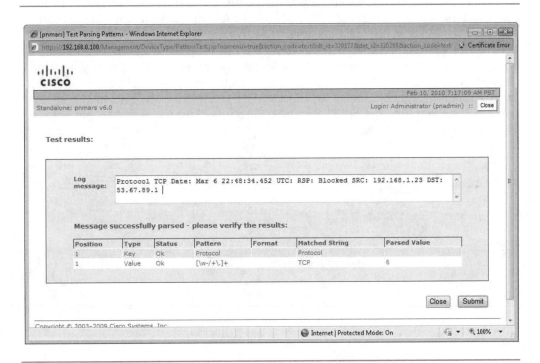

**Figure 11-32.** Testing Custom Parsers

# A Typical Day in the Life of a MARS Operator

Now that you're familiar with the interface and have all the necessary concepts in your head, your custom devices integrated with your MARS, and a full cup of coffee, you show up for work fresh and ready to start your day as a MARS operator. Before we leave you alone with your newfound love, we will spend one last moment together and walk you through a day that will become as familiar to you "As Time Goes By."

 **NOTE** Like all SIEMs, MARS will be more useful after having spent enough time on your network to build a broad picture. The first days after full implementation, you will see notable changes in the size of the topology discovered and the richness of the inventory and activity information provided by MARS. We will assume that—exhausted after the initial implementation—you took a well-deserved two-week vacation someplace warm, sandy, and stocked with cold drinks, and are now arriving back in the office.

Before you even get settled in your chair, your HotSpot Graph (Figure 11-33) shows you that all is not perfect in your world. A cluster of dots reveals that at least one area of the network is experiencing a less than perfect moment. You open the Attack Diagram (also shown in Figure 11-33) and spend a few moments looking at the most verbose offenders and their relationships to each other.

The HotSpot Graph shows a discovered view of the network and highlights the high-rated incidents in the diagram. You can quickly see if you have a problem on the network when you see lots of dots in a particular spot. When you drill down deeper into the diagram and click one of the links that led to the dots, you get a listing of the sessions, the source, the destination, and the name of the incident. You can see an example in Figure 11-34.

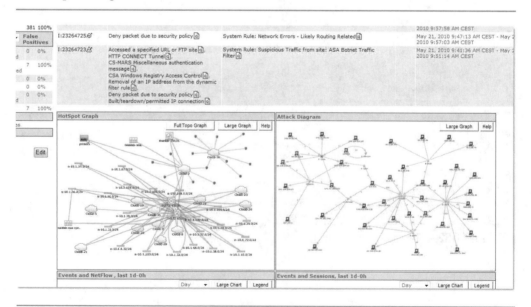

**Figure 11-33.**   HotSpot Graph and Attack Diagram

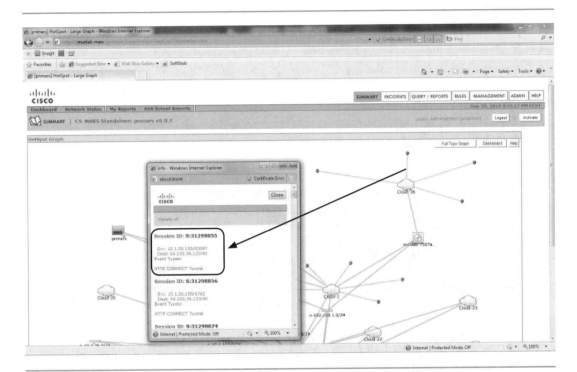

**Figure 11-34.**   HotSpot detail

You can now drill further down by clicking the Session itself, which brings you to a detailed description of the Events that make up this Session.

In this Session, you see the source IP address, including Network Address Translation. This is because MARS knows about the topology, so it can also show devices that are being NATed. To find out which DNS name corresponds to the IP, click the IP address itself, as shown in Figure 11-35, and you will see the results displayed in Figure 11-36.

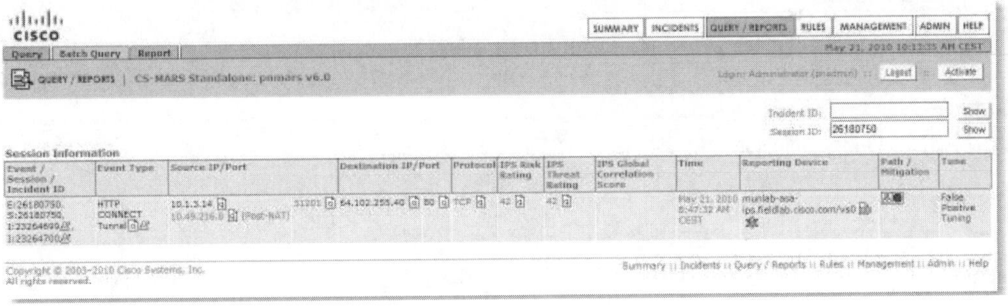

**Figure 11-35.**   Session detail

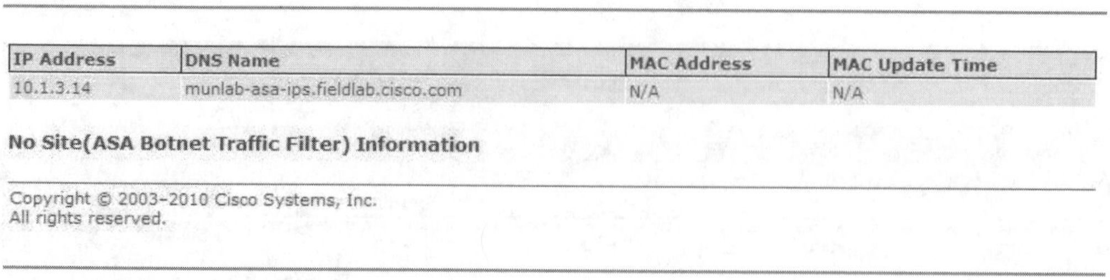

| IP Address | DNS Name | MAC Address | MAC Update Time |
|---|---|---|---|
| 10.1.3.14 | munlab-asa-ips.fieldlab.cisco.com | N/A | N/A |

**No Site(ASA Botnet Traffic Filter) Information**

**Figure 11-36.**    DNS resolution

In the Session table, you also see the Event Name, the Destination link, the port, and the device that generated this event. As it is an Event coming from an IPS Sensor, the Risk Rating and the Threat Rating are also included, showing you a value between 1 and 100 (100 being the most dangerous assigned threat).

We can drill down even further by running a Query to determine what else our source IP or destination IP has produced in a given timeframe. You do this by clicking the letter "q" beside the values. Let's click the letter "q" beside Destination, as shown in Figure 11-35. A new query, as you see in Figure 11-37, is constructed with the destination IP inserted. We then modify the timeframe to see what we want to see, such as all the Sessions with this destination IP.

After submitting the Query, we can see all the sessions with this specific destination in the last four hours and ten minutes, as shown in Figure 11-38.

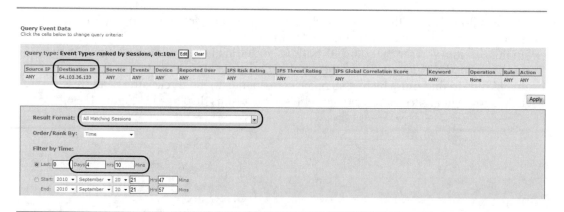

**Figure 11-37.**    Query definition

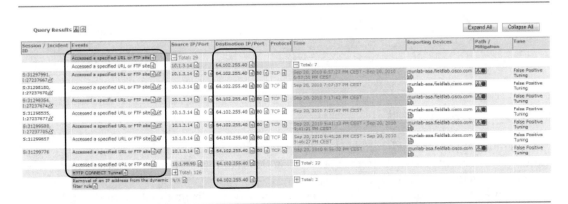

**Figure 11-38.** Query results

In these results, 10.1.3.14 has accessed this destination in the last four hours, but in addition to the HTTP CONNECT, we also see a message coming from the firewall, that it accessed a specific site URL, as seen in Figure 11-39.

Clicking the small icon under the Firewall brings up the raw message, telling us which site was accessed. In this case, it's the IronPort update site for the IPS module connecting via a HTTP CONNECT Tunnel, which means it is a proxy. This is OK, so we can tune it out as a false positive by clicking the False Positive Tuning button to the right of the session table, as shown in Figure 11-40.

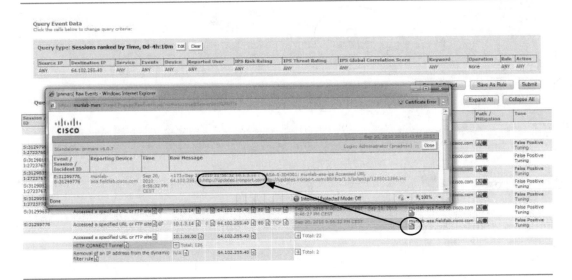

**Figure 11-39.** Raw Event detail

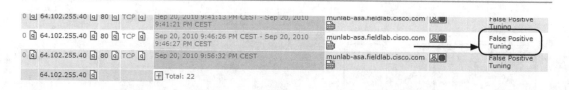

| | | | | | |
|---|---|---|---|---|---|
| 0 [q] 64.102.255.40 [q] 80 [q] TCP [q] | Sep 20, 2010 9:41:13 PM CEST - Sep 20, 2010 9:41:21 PM CEST | | munlab-asa.fieldlab.cisco.com | | False Positive Tuning |
| 0 [q] 64.102.255.40 [q] 80 [q] TCP [q] | Sep 20, 2010 9:46:26 PM CEST - Sep 20, 2010 9:46:27 PM CEST | | munlab-asa.fieldlab.cisco.com | | False Positive Tuning |
| 0 [q] 64.102.255.40 [q] 80 [q] TCP [q] | Sep 20, 2010 9:56:32 PM CEST | | munlab-asa.fieldlab.cisco.com | | False Positive Tuning |
| 64.102.255.40 [q] | [+] Total: 22 | | | | |

**Figure 11-40.**    False Positive Tuning

A similar approach can be done from the Attack Diagram. This diagram shows how different events correlate to the sources and destinations shown in Incidents and Events. Let us look at this host circled in Figure 11-41.

This host has produced three Events, as three links are attached to it. To find out the name of the Event, just click the small Event icon, and you will see a pop-up window, as shown in Figure 11-42.

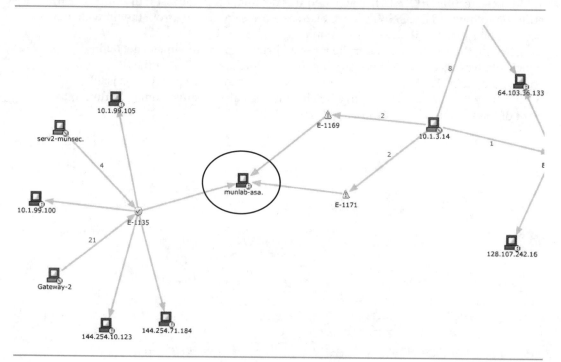

**Figure 11-41.**    Attack Diagram detail

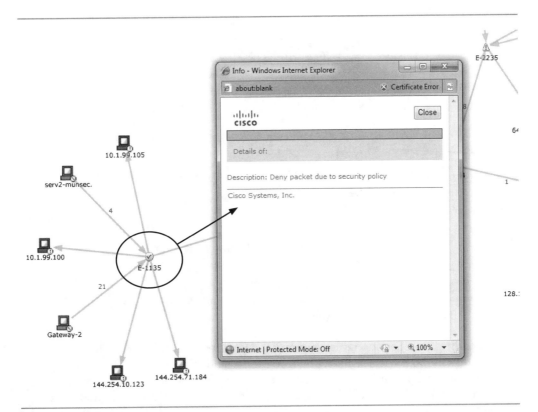

**Figure 11-42.**   Host detail on Attack Diagram

Something coming from this host has been causing a Deny somewhere. Now let us look a bit deeper into the information provided on the Attack Diagram and see what more we can learn about this misbehaving host. We see a small red number "4" beside the arrow leading from serv2-munsec to the Event; this means there have been four Denys in total caused by this host, which are related to an Incident. Click the link with the "4" to access the detail page shown in Figure 11-43.

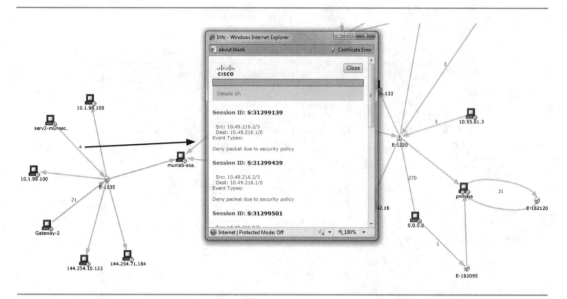

**Figure 11-43.** Sessions related to suspect host

This brings up a Session table, showing the four Sessions we want to investigate. Drilling down into those Sessions, and into the Session table, click the Path/Mitigation icon. This brings up a small topology, as seen in Figure 11-44, showing the related path through the network as MARS has determined it. We can clearly see that this packet was sent from our host and dropped at the ASA.

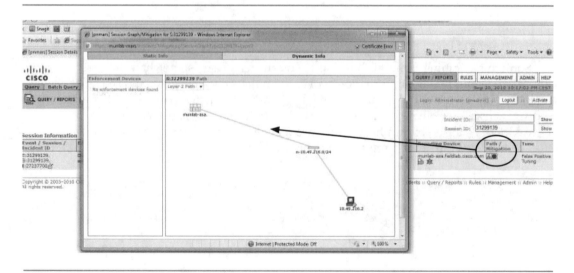

**Figure 11-44.** Session path detail

Now, once again, we can make the decision whether we need to tune the firewall or just continue to block this event.

The process we just described shows many of the basic activities you will find yourself involved in on a daily basis with your MARS. While many different paths will emerge as you identify, investigate, and resolve Incidents that your MARS presents to you, they will share a common pattern of identification, investigation, and resolution—similar to what we have just demonstrated.

# Limitations

The primary limitation to MARS is its support for Event sources. While it is possible to add any device that sends syslog or SNMP event messages, this process can be relatively cumbersome. In addition, devices added manually do not provide the performance of devices that are built into the system by the manufacturer (a good analogy is the difference in performance between a compiled program and an interpreted program or script).

# Summary

Although the future of MARS is unclear as of the writing of this book, it remains a useful tool in pure Cisco environments. As some of the features in MARS are outside the scope of expected SIEM behavior—such as the management of IPS signatures for Cisco IOS—it seems reasonable to assume that some of the functionality of MARS will live on in Cisco offerings regardless of what fate lies ahead for MARS as a standalone product.

# CHAPTER 12 | Q1 Labs QRadar Implementation

Q1 Labs entered the SIEM market in 2001 with a full-featured product line. They provide their technology in an appliance version (hardware and software) and in a software version that you can install on your own hardware. Their premier and keystone product is called QRadar SIEM. This all-in-one system includes everything you need to get your security information and event management services off the ground. The QRadar system helps to satisfy compliance requirements for event storage, traffic monitoring, and reporting, and includes the following functions to fulfill your organization's security requirements:

- Security event monitoring
- Network traffic monitoring
- Vulnerability scanner integration
- Asset inventory and profile generation
- Data analysis
- Data correlation
- Heuristic threat detection and prioritization
- Report generation

The QRadar SIEM 2100 Series Appliance is a modestly priced system for small- and medium-sized environments that do not foresee an increase in events per second (eps) or flows per second (fps) rates. Q1 Labs also provides a slightly more expensive system (QRadar SIEM 3100 Series Appliance) for the enterprise-level environment, which is immensely scalable for medium to large deployments. In the enterprise deployment, supplemental appliances can be strategically placed to provide monitoring, processing, and storage functions throughout the organization's network to create a hierarchical system that feeds into a central Management Console. This system scores high in several recent Gartner reports for Critical Capabilities and Use Cases for SIEM systems. The Q1 Labs QRadar SIEM system is one of the easiest to implement, is easily scaled, and also is capable of extensive fine tuning in a mature environment for minimized false positive alerts and refined flow and event analysis.

# QRadar Architecture Overview

The system begins with the QRadar SIEM Appliance. This system receives and stores event data from network endpoints, infrastructure, and security systems like syslog events and Windows Event Logs. The QRadar SIEM Appliance can also receive flow data from about half a dozen device manufacturers like Cisco's NetFlow and Juniper's J-flow. In addition, the system has one or more flow-monitoring ports that sniff traffic directly from the attached segment for packet storage, as well as complete and deep packet analysis (up to layer 7). The system also takes direct input from a variety of security systems and vulnerability scanners, like Nessus and QualysGuard. It parses these events, flows, and vulnerability scan reports, normalizes them, performs some initial classification and rule matching/filtering, stores them, and then begins the real work of a SIEM: data analysis and correlation.

Figure 12-1 maps out the Q1 Labs QRadar SIEM system flow.

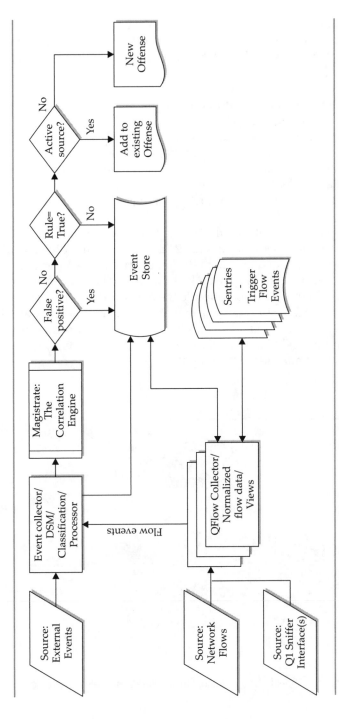

**Figure 12-1.** Q1 Labs QRadar SIEM system flow for small- to medium-scale organizations

Don't underestimate the importance of properly parsing and normalizing input from hundreds of different devices and scanners and interpreting packet and protocol information straight off the wire. This task is a huge one to get right, and QRadar does a good job of getting it right.

For small- to medium-sized organizations, the QRadar 2100 All-in-One SIEM system can be expanded to include additional QFlow Collector 1100 Series Appliances that provide flow monitoring in distributed locations (Figure 12-2).

For medium- to large-scale organizations, the QRadar 3100 Enterprise SIEM system can be expanded to include not only the additional QFlow Collector 1100 Series Appliances, but can also accommodate the dedicated Event Processor 1600 Series Appliances as well as the dedicated Flow Processor 1700 Series Appliances (Figure 12-3). These supplemental processing systems are typically deployed to process additional events at a central location or at disparate locations, reducing traffic to the main Management Console by normalizing the incoming events and flows. Each 1600 and 1700 Series Appliance provides an additional 2TB of storage, and directly attached storage appliances can be added to increase storage capacity even further.

Interestingly, if you are a do-it-yourself kind of guy or gal, these systems are all available as software only, where you provide the hardware and installation skills. However, the vast majority of Q1 Labs' customers seem to purchase the appliance and let the vendor provide and support the complete system, including hardware. If you chose to build your own QRadar system, follow the Q1 Labs recommendations on the hardware specification and consider beefing that up as much as your budget will allow.

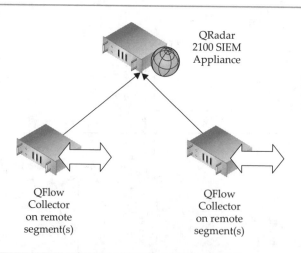

QRadar 2100 SIEM Appliance

QFlow Collector on remote segment(s)

QFlow Collector on remote segment(s)

**Figure 12-2.** QRadar 2100 All-in-One SEIM for small- to medium-scale organizations

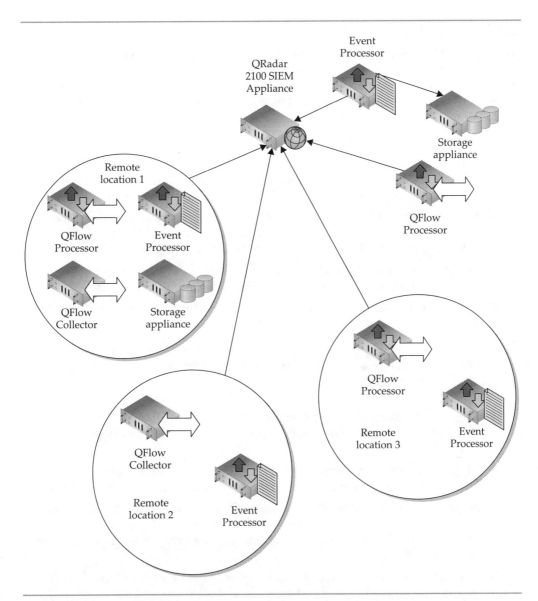

**Figure 12-3.**    QRadar 3100 Enterprise SIEM for medium- to large-scale organizations

These systems can also take advantage of iSCSI-attached storage systems. Depending on the size of your IT system and corporate or regulatory compliance requirements, this can be a very handy way to increase the storage capacity of the SIEM system.

# Q1 Labs Terms to Know

As expected, Q1 Labs has created names for many of their components, systems, services, and technologies that suit their needs and preferences and are based on how their system operates. You'll need to learn the Q1 Labs lingo to make it through the instruction manual and menu items. Following are some of the more commonly used Q1 Labs' terms that you should know when deploying the Q1 Labs QRadar SIEM system:

- **Adaptive Log Exporter (ALE)** QRadar agent for Windows systems to collect, parse, and export Windows event logs, including Microsoft IIS, Microsoft IAS, Microsoft Exchange using OWA or SMTP logs, and Trend Micro InterScan logs.

- **Building Block (BB)** A reusable filtering rule generally used within a more complex rule. For example, you can create a BB to select SMTP servers and then use it to exclude SMTP servers from a network sampling in another rule.

- **Device Support Module (DSM)** Used to parse incoming events from the device vendor's native format into the QRadar standardized format.

- **Flow** A collection of packets describing a communication between hosts that share some common properties.

 **NOTE** QRadar can aggregate, associate, and normalize flow data even when the flow data is supplied from different sources.

- **Log Source** Maps incoming event source format to a DSM for parsing enhancement or parsing override. There are two options: Predefined (faster) or Custom (slower).

- **Magistrate** Provides the core processing components for the SIEM. The Magistrate processes the event against the defined rules to create an offense.

- **Network Behavior Anomaly Detection (NBAD)** Network behavior anomaly detection is a solution for helping protect against zero-day attacks on the network. NBAD is the continuous monitoring of a network for unusual events or trends.

- **Offense** Perceived threat (sometimes referred to as an *incident* in other SIEM products).

- **Q1 Labs Event Identifier (QID)** Table of known, proprietary device events that assists in normalizing events to the QRadar Database format. The QID Map routes events into Category pipes, determines if an event should be forwarded to the Magistrate, and determines rate analysis. QID includes category, subcategory, severity, and credibility definitions.

- **QRadar Request Language (QRL)**   Definitions for flow data and network objects (Surveillance Views). Saved in Bookmarks.
- **Rules**   Series of tests that monitor events and flows for a pattern or matching condition to generate a response, typically an offense.
- **Sentries**   Monitors collections of views (flow filters) to generate events and alerts.
- **SuperFlow**   Flow-based compression with one record representing many flows of a similar pattern (stored as one flow but all data kept).
  - **Type A**   One-to-many—one source, many destinations = network scan
  - **Type B**   Many-to-one—many sources, one destination = DDoS
  - **Type C**   One-to-one and changing ports = host port scan
- **View**   Flow normalization, defines flow data filtering.

# Planning

Before attempting to install any SIEM and before you can expect to receive any good data from it, you must understand your environment, your objectives, and the impact the SIEM system will have on the IT system.

## Know Your Network

You must have a clear picture of your network architecture. Identify and document the following information regarding your network and the organization's IT assets. See Chapter 5, "The Anatomy of a SIEM":

- Locations.
- IP subnets.
- Infrastructure systems and services (network links, routers, managed switches, DNS, DHCP, NAT, and dial-in servers).
- Servers (application, database, terminal servers, web, SMTP, file, and print).
- Security systems (IDS, IPS, firewalls, vulnerability scanners, authentication servers, domain controllers, NAC, and VPN servers).
- Mission-critical processes and data (the crown jewels) and the potentially different security and compliance requirements for the various IT assets. Several different levels of security may be required for the different value categories or classifications of the IT assets.

For each of the preceding items, identify and document required ports and protocols and related traffic patterns (i.e., Where does this port/protocol traffic need to go? Where should this traffic not be going?). This will help you construct appropriate firewall rules to allow or block the traffic, as needed. This will also help you construct appropriate filtering and detection rules in the SIEM system to identify boundary violations.

# Plan Your QRadar SIEM Deployment

Before you decide which vendor's SIEM system to purchase, and which components to add to the purchase order, you should figure out how this system needs to integrate into your environment. You'll want to do some homework up front to help ensure a smooth acquisition and implementation process, minimizing the surprises.

1. For each system and service on your network, identify and document what flow and/or event information should be provided to the SIEM system, and identify and document how that data will be collected (pushed or pulled, syslog, snare, vendor agent, and so on) The definition of the collection method should also include various ports and protocols that will be used to commute the event and flow data to the SIEM system(s).

2. Considering the source's location and connectivity to the SIEM system(s), identify and document the estimated bandwidth and storage requirements for the flow and/or event data.

   Identify the number of events per minute per server by examining the event logs of the servers you wish to monitor with QRadar. Events vary in size by data source; for example, a Windows authentication event could be as large as 1KB but firewall events are often less then 150B. You can estimate the number of flows per minute by using the following formula: flows per minute (fpm) = (# of workstations * 10 fpm) + (# of servers * 150 fpm).

3. Talk to other groups responsible for systems that you wish to collect relevant network information from. Explain why collecting this information from their systems is important. You may choose to give the owners or administrators of those systems access to QRadar to allow them to search and report on that information.

4. You may discover the need to increase storage and the bandwidth between locations. You may offset some bandwidth requirements by adding flow or event processors at remote locations. These will collect and store data remotely while still allowing for centralized monitoring. You will also need to identify adjustments to firewall rules required to allow the network data from the source(s) to the SIEM system(s), as appropriate. The communications can also be compressed, encrypted, and tunneled.

5. Network connections among QRadar Appliances should typically be encrypted, especially when data is being passed on open networks. By default, the QRadar appliances use SSL encryption for their appliance-to-appliance communications. You should verify that this is functioning correctly.

6. Document all assumptions made, and limitations or restrictions imposed by current configuration, budget, or management. Be sure both you and management understand where on the network you might be missing sensors and/or feeds into the SIEM system. Develop and present plans to add these sensors and feeds to gain a vision of these blind spots on the network. If the QRadar system can't see an event, it can't respond or notify someone about the event.

7.  Based on the physical location, link bandwidth, SIEM system capabilities, and budget, develop the SIEM system hierarchy design. Identify specific device location, placement (Q1 Labs appliances are 1U and 2U rack-mount devices), clean and redundant AC power, event and flow data storage, connectivity and cooling requirements, physical security requirements for the SIEM system, etc.:

   ■ The QRadar 2100 SIEM Appliance (2U) for small and medium IT environments can handle 1,000 events per second (up to 750 event sources); up to 50,000 flows per second; and 50Mbps of flow data to the built-in QFlow Collector. The QRadar 2100 includes 2TB of onboard storage utilizing embedded RAID 10 for event and flow storage.

   Additional QFlow Collector Appliances (1000 series) (1U) can be added to increase capacity from 50Mbps up to 1Gbps of flow traffic, and they include embedded hardware RAID 10 for the system's OS. The QFlow Collector Appliance can be placed in remote locations to provide local collection of flow data. This appliance also provides dual-redundant power supplies. Additional Storage Appliances can add 2TB per unit.

   ■ The QRadar 3100 SIEM Appliance (2U) for medium and large IT environments can handle 5,000 events per second (up to 750 event sources); up to 200,000 flows per second; and 50Mbps of flow data to the built-in QFlow Collector. The QRadar 3100 includes 2TB of onboard storage utilizing embedded RAID 10 for the OS and for event and flow storage. This appliance also provides dual-redundant power supplies.

   Additional QFlow Collector Appliances (1000 series) (1U) can be added to increase capacity from 50Mbps up to 10Gbps of flow traffic, and they include embedded hardware RAID 10 for the system's OS.

   Additional Event Processor Appliances (1600 series) (2U) can add event capacity up to 10,000 events per second each. The QRadar 1600 series system includes 2TB of onboard storage utilizing embedded RAID 10 for the OS and for event and flow storage.

   Additional Flow Processors Appliances (1700 series) (2U) can be added to add flow capacity up to 1,000,000 flows per second each. The QRadar 1700 series system includes 2TB of RAID 10 for the OS and for event and flow storage.

   Additional directly attached Storage Appliances can be added to the 1600 and 1700 series appliances and can add an additional 2TB of onboard storage utilizing embedded RAID 10 for the OS and for event and flow storage per unit.

   The QFlow Collector, Event Processor, and Flow Processor Appliances can be placed in remote locations to provide local processing, storage, and collection of event and flow data.

   ■ Different QRadar models include different numbers on their 1Gbps network interfaces. Typically, one network interface (eth0) is assigned an IP address and is allocated to the Console and to the collection of pushed (to the

QRadar Appliance) flow and event data and pushed vulnerability scan data. Additional network interfaces (eth1, eth2, etc.) on the QRadar systems are typically not assigned an IP address and are used to monitor network traffic (sniff) directly off the segment that they are connected to. These QRadar network monitoring interfaces should connect to a spanning/mirror port or a network tap that feeds frames to the QRadar network interface at layer 2, the Data Link Layer, of the OSI model. Analysis of this input is performed up to layer 7, the Application Layer, of the OSI model.

8. Consider performing backups of the stored event and flow data. Many laws and regulations require maintaining these records for a number of years. If these records are demanded by a court, declaring that the archive was lost for any reason will be a compliance violation, and the organization may be subject to fines and other penalties.

9. Develop a plan for the security professionals who will need access to the configuration and data of these systems, and for the system administrators who will maintain the hardware and connectivity of these systems. (See "Managing Roles and Users" in the following section, "Initial Installation," for a guide to the roles available in the QRadar system.)

10. Verify that you have adequately designed for the prudent security of your valuable information assets and for compliance with all organizational policies and regulatory requirements.

# Initial Installation

Rack mount the QRadar system in a physically secure server room. While the QRadar device includes dual power supplies in case one fails, you should connect the AC power to an AC power source that includes an Uninterruptable Power Supply (UPS) in case the AC source fails. The storage database(s) within the QRadar can become corrupted if the system is not shut down cleanly. Be sure the system has adequate cooling and access to the desired network connections.

Although the QRadar is one of the simplest SIEM systems to get up and running, there are quite a few configuration parameters that should be confirmed, if not changed.

## Configuring the Underlying CentOS System

For local Console access, you can connect a monitor and keyboard to the QRadar Appliance. The QRadar system is based upon a CentOS v5.3 operating system. After you configure IP properties and assign interface roles, you can remotely connect to the underlying QRadar Appliance operating system by using ssh to get a remote command shell. Log in as **root** using the default password: **password**. You must enter the activation key provided with the QRadar Appliance. Choose one from the following basic system templates to establish default rules and sentry definitions:

- Enterprise
- University

Next, you must configure the system date, time, and network interface configuration settings. Finally, from the command line, you'll want to change the root password for the underlying CentOS operating system.

Once you have configured these basic settings at the command line, you will be able to use the Admin interface to perform SIEM administration as well as administration of the CentOS operating system.

## The QRadar Administrative Interface

The QRadar Administrative interface is the primary administrative tool. Connect to the QRadar interface using a browser addressed to **https://<*QRadar IP Address*>**. Because the system generates self-signed certificates, you may receive a certificate error warning. (This certificate can be replaced at a later time with a certificate from a trusted Certification Authority as described in the following chapter.) If you are certain that you're connected to the correct QRadar system, proceed to the website. Enter the username: **admin**, and the password you just created for root during the setup process.

You should be presented with the default view of the Dashboard. Notice the nine tabs and the Preferences and Help buttons beside the System Time, as shown in Figure 12-4.

Before the system is functional, you must configure several different areas of QRadar. These include:

- User Management
- System Configuration (thresholds, authentication, etc.)
- Deployment Configuration
- Flow and Event Source Configuration
- Vulnerability Assessment Configuration
- Offense Resolution Configuration
- Sentry and View Configuration
- License Management
- Backup and Restore Functions

**Figure 12-4.**    QRadar tabs

## QRadar Configuration Change Logging

All configuration changes are logged to a file named **/var/log/audit/audit.log**, and when it reaches 200MB, it gets archived as **/var/log/audit/audit.1.gz** with the number incrementing for each 200MB audit file.

## Managing Roles and Users

One of the first administrative configuration items to tackle will be to define user roles and create user accounts. Click the Admin tab to display the Admin interface. To display the User Management options, select System Configuration | User Management from the menu, as shown in Figure 12-5.

To manage user roles, click the User Roles icon. Now click Create Role.

The dialog shown in Figure 12-6 will appear. This dialog allows you to create a collection of access permissions to assign to a role. Build these roles, with their collection of access permissions, to map to your administration plan described previously. Click Next when the permissions are properly specified for the chosen role. These roles can be edited later if an adjustment is needed.

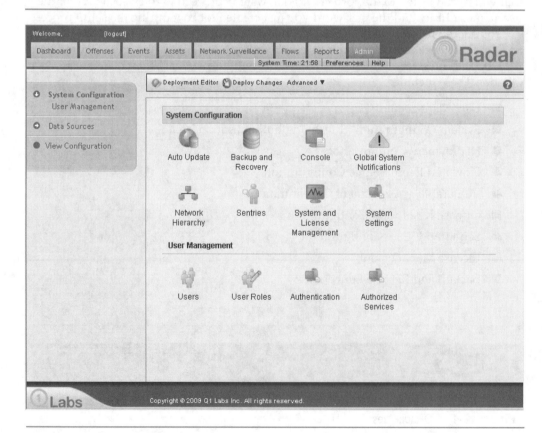

**Figure 12-5.** System Configuration

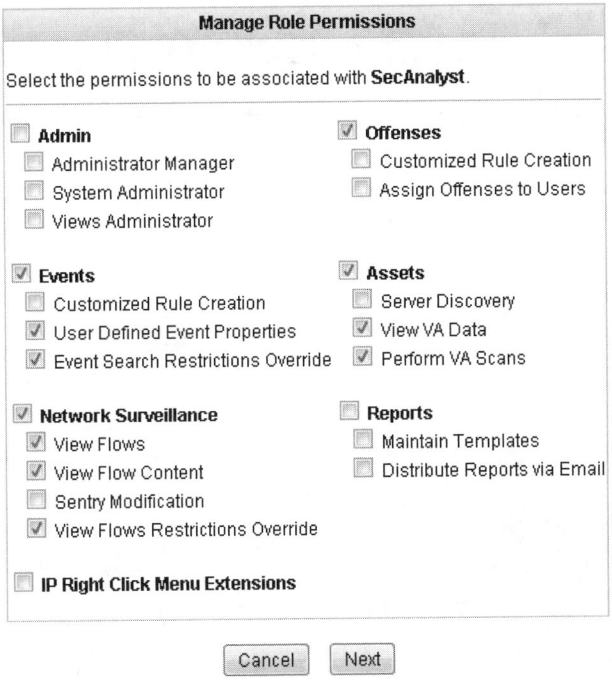

**Figure 12-6.**   Managing Role Permissions

The Add Devices to User Role dialog (Figure 12-7) will allow you to define which log sources (Devices) the members of the new user role are allowed to monitor. This list of devices will be assembled over time as the QRadar identifies nodes and after you create a network hierarchy, which is coming up in the following section.

Click Next to receive notification that you have successfully created the role. Click Return to view the list of User Roles, including the new role you just created.

Next, on the System Configuration panel in the Admin interface, click the Users icon. Now click Add. The User Details dialog, shown in Figure 12-8, appears.

Fill in the four fields and then select the desired role for the user from the Select Role drop-down list. Click Next. The resulting dialog will allow you to define which Network Objects members of the new role are allowed to monitor.

Q1 Labs provides a default network hierarchy (Network Objects) for starters, but this list of Network Objects (Figure 12-9) will be modified to reflect your network environment as you define your network hierarchy, coming up in the following section. Click Finish to create the user account.

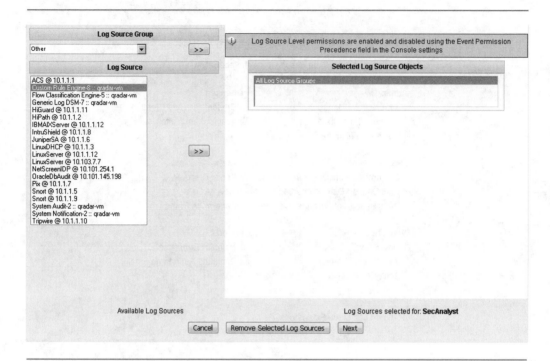

**Figure 12-7.**   Assigning devices to the User Role

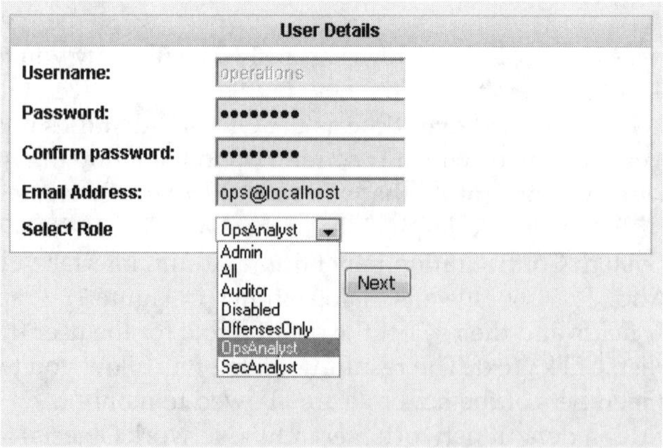

**Figure 12-8.**   Adding user accounts and assigning roles

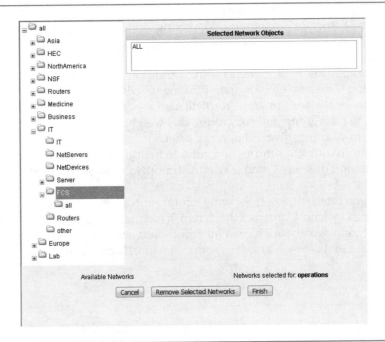

**Figure 12-9.**   Assigning Network Objects to the user

Click Finish to create the new user with the assigned role and permitted Network Objects. These user properties can be edited, and the user account can be disabled or deleted.

In the System Configuration panel on the Admin tab, select the Authentication icon. User authentication can be performed using the local QRadar system, RADIUS, or TACACS, or through LDAP and Kerberos connected to a directory service, like Windows Active Directory. To use an authentication system other than QRadar, the authentication system must be up and running with the desired user accounts, must be able to connect with the QRadar system, and the time on the authentication system must be synchronized with the time on the QRadar system.

## Defining Your Network Hierarchy

When defining your network hierarchy in QRadar, you generally want to group systems and users that perform similar duties on the network, ones that use the same applications and protocols. Place servers with unique functions alone to allow for rule tuning. Define large top-level groups first, and then create more specific subgroups.

For example, create an Eastern District top-level group. Then create subgroups within Eastern District for Accounting, Marketing, and Sales, because these different departments require different applications and require different network connectivity and protocols and can require different monitoring capabilities.

You will need to know IP subnets for the various groups. Group IP subnets together (*supernets*) using Classless Inter-Domain Routing (CIDR notation) whenever possible to improve processing performance. You will also assign a weight value, on a scale from 1 to 100, to each group and subgroup. This weight represents the network group's relative value to your organization as an IT asset.

You can assign different sentries and rules to monitor these groups and subgroups. You can also assign different QRadar administrators to manage these different groups and subgroups.

In the Admin interface, select System Configuration from the menu and select the Network Hierarchy icon. Construct the network hierarchy by clicking the Add button (Figure 12-10) for new network hierarchy groups and subgroups. This allows you to assign attributes to the new hierarchy group, shown in Figure 12-11.

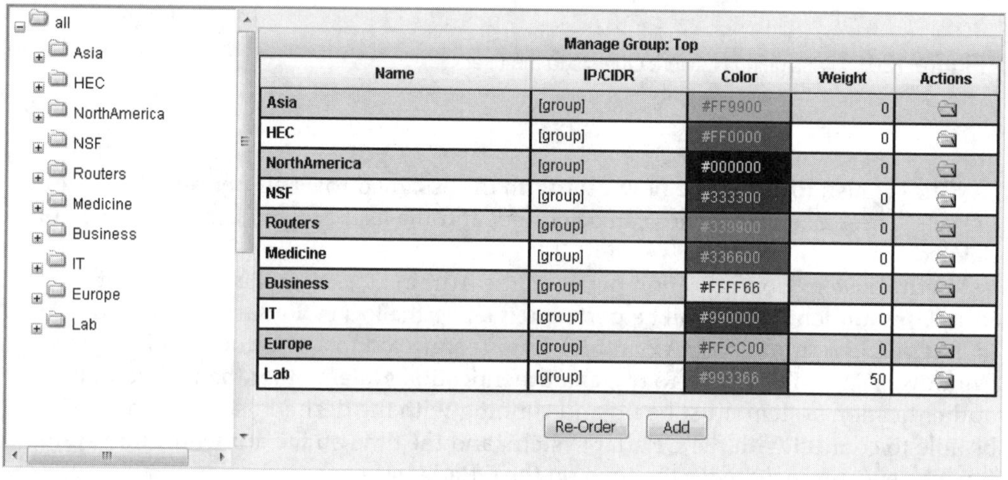

**Figure 12-10.** The network hierarchy

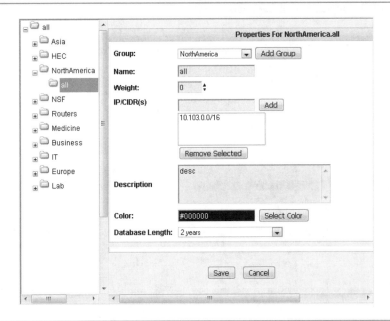

**Figure 12-11.** Configuring the network hierarchy

## System Configuration

To configure fundamental QRadar settings, in the System Configuration panel on the Admin tab, select the System Settings icon. Carefully review the settings configured on the QRadar System Settings interface (Figure 12-12). Adjust these settings to satisfy your specific QRadar configuration and compliance requirements. Settings like Log Retention Periods and Log Hashing (to validate the integrity of the log files) must meet or exceed all compliance requirements your organization may be subject to.

Another important system configuration location is the System Management interface, shown in Figure 12-13. On the System Configuration panel in the Admin tab, select the System and License Management icon to access the System and License Management interface.

If there are multiple QRadar devices in the environment, identify the QRadar Appliance you want to configure and select Manage System from the Actions menu on the System and License Management interface. This provides administrative access to

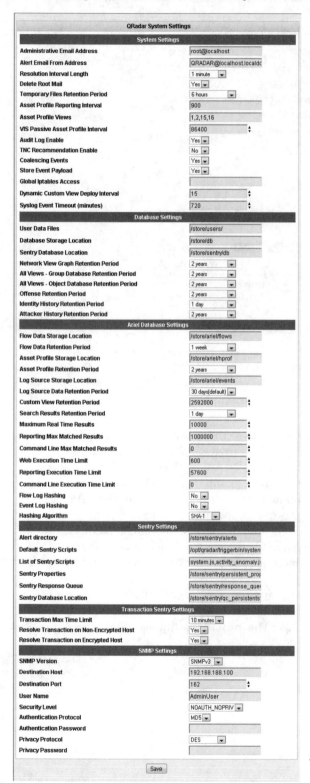

**Figure 12-12.** The System Settings interface

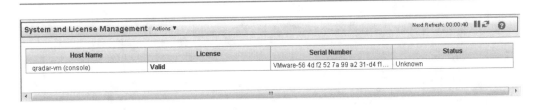

**Figure 12-13.**   The System and License Management interface

the underlying operating system on the QRadar Appliance. Log in to the web-based System Administration interface, shown in Figure 12-14, with the username: **root**, and the appropriate root password.

## Configuring Updates

The QRadar system can be configured to retrieve and install updates automatically from the Q1 Labs Qmmunity web site, so your system will have information on the latest threats, vulnerabilities, and geographic security activities and trends. These updates can be pushed to other QRadar systems as well or can be manually downloaded and installed. In addition, you can choose to replace existing security data with the updates, or if you have customized your system, you can merge these updates into your existing configuration information. Configuring specific updates within the QRadar system is covered in the next chapter.

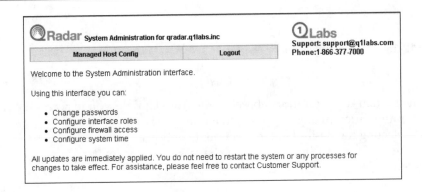

**Figure 12-14.**   The System Management interface

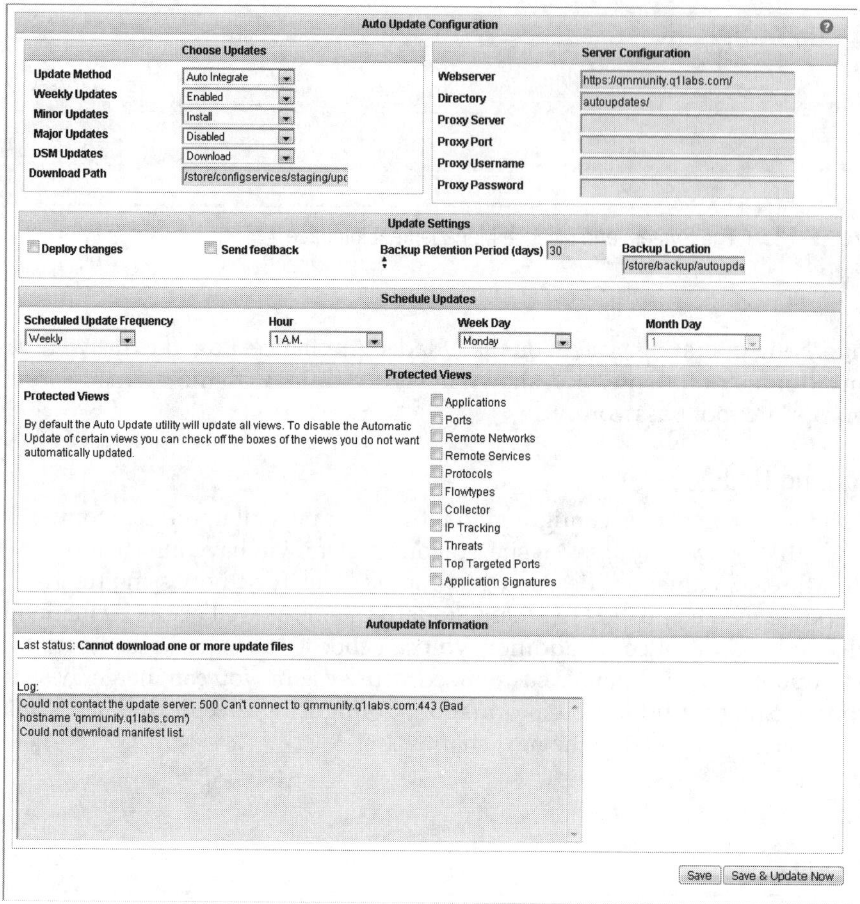

**Figure 12-15.** Configuring automatic updates

On the System Configuration tab, select the Auto Update icon to access the Auto Update Configuration dialog, as shown in Figure 12-15.

After selecting the desired automatic update options, click Save to have the update occur on the configured schedule, or select Save & Update Now to trigger the update immediately.

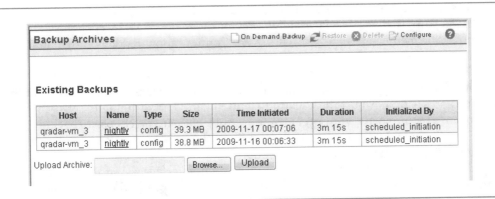

**Figure 12-16.** Initial Backup dialog

## Configuring Backup and Restore

On the System Configuration tab, select the Backup and Recovery icon to open the Backup Archives interface, as shown in Figure 12-16.

Backups can be triggered to run on demand by selecting the On Demand Backup button on the Backup Archives interface. You can add a name and description for your On Demand Backup, shown in Figure 12-17.

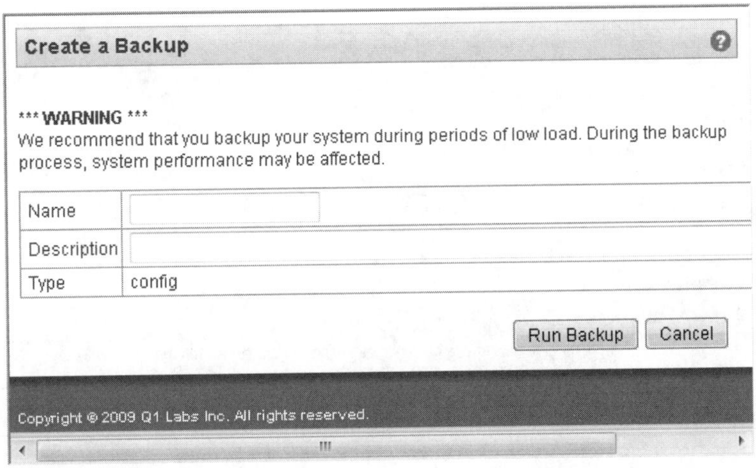

**Figure 12-17.** Creating a Backup on Demand

Scheduled backups can be configured to run daily at midnight or can be disabled. On the Backup Archives interface shown previously in Figure 12-16, click the Configure button on the menu bar. The Backup Recovery Configuration dialog is shown in Figure 12-18.

The default path to store the backup file is /store/backup on the local system. You may want to direct the backup to a network location to keep all backups centrally located and secured. Adjust the Backup Retention Period accordingly to satisfy any compliance requirements your organization is subject to. If you choose to backup configuration and data, you can use this configuration to select QRadar Appliances throughout the deployment to be backed up.

On the System Configuration panel in the Admin interface, select the Backup Recovery icon. Chose the Backup Archive you wish to restore, and then click Restore. Select the desired items to restore, as shown in Figure 12-19, and click Restore. The Restore process will only restore system configuration. Q1 Labs requests that you contact them if you need to restore archived data.

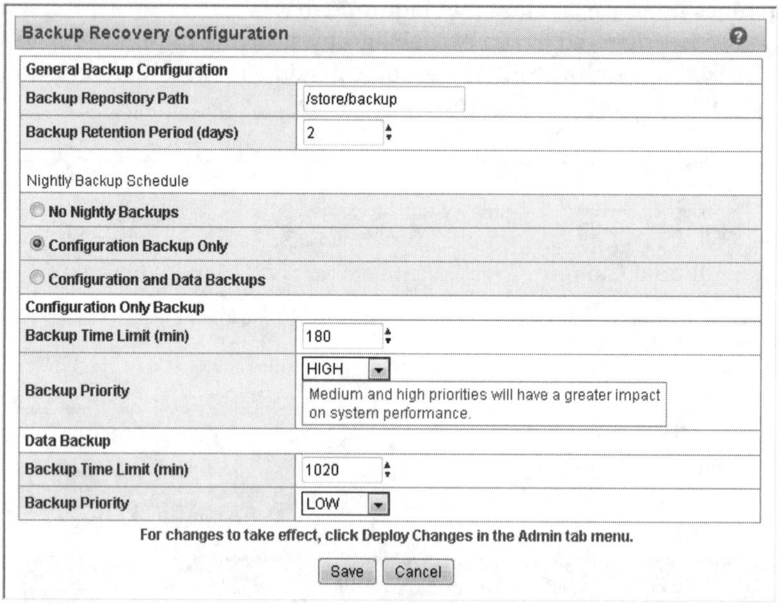

**Figure 12-18.**    Configuring backups

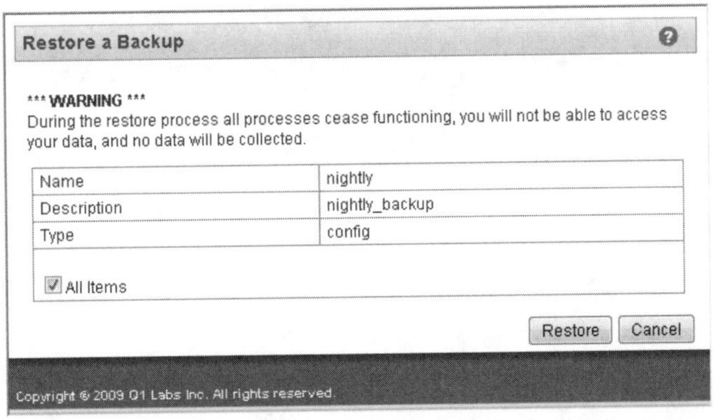

**Figure 12-19.** Configuring a Restore process

## Managing Assets

The QRadar system can learn about the assets on the network through QFlow data and through data from vulnerability scanners. Each identified asset includes an asset profile that details whatever is known about the asset, such as what ports are open and what services are installed on the node. You can actively scan for servers to build the asset inventory and profiles, and you can manually add assets to the inventory and edit their profile properties.

In the main QRadar interface, click the Assets tab on the main QRadar interface. From the Assets tab, shown in Figure 12-20, you can perform a selective search for desired assets, or you can select Show All assets.

Once the desired asset is located, you can right-click on the asset to display additional information about it, as shown in Figure 12-21. You can also edit the properties to include details that will help you and QRadar recognize the important attributes of a particular asset.

You can also configure QRadar to perform server discovery by selecting the type of server from a drop-down list (Figure 12-22), and selecting what network the server scan will be performed on.

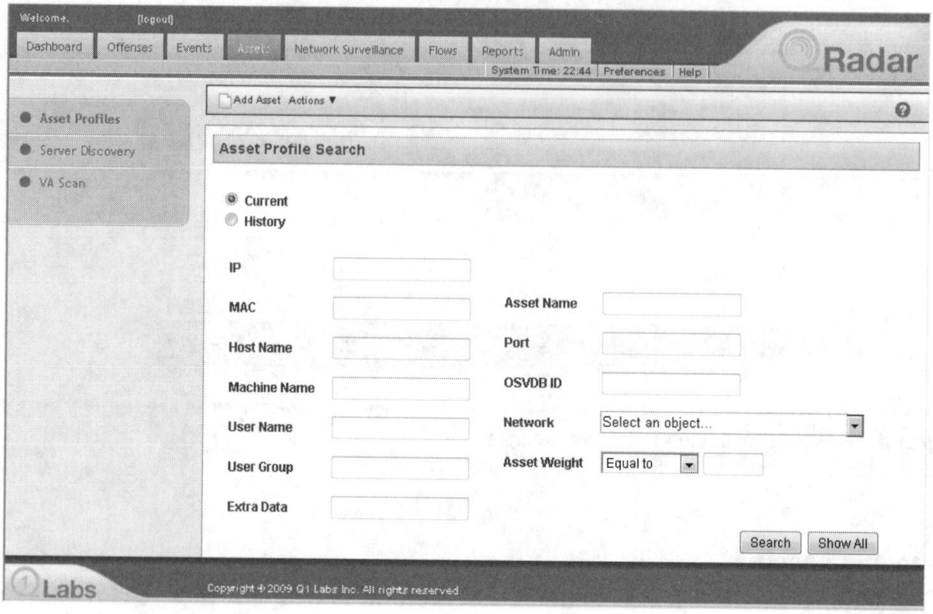

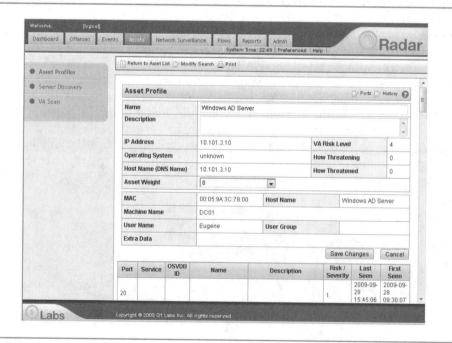

**Figure 12-20.**   Asset Manager

**Figure 12-21.**   Asset Profile

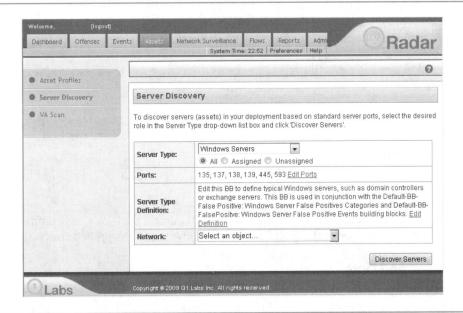

**Figure 12-22.**   Server Discovery

You should explore all icons and tabs on the main QRadar interface and on the Admin tab so you are aware of where specific configuration settings are located and what settings are available to be configured. The QRadar SIEM is a complex system. To extract the best possible information from it, you must understand how to fine-tune it to minimize false-positive alerts and to satisfy your organization's security needs. Using the False Positive Wizard is discussed in the next chapter.

# Getting Flow and Event Data into QRadar

Like all SIEM systems, one of the first and major tasks of getting any worthy information from your SIEM system is to get devices, systems, and scanners to feed their events and flow data to the correct SIEM collector.

At least one network interface on the QRadar Appliance should be configured with a valid IP address for the segment it is connected to. Other network interfaces on the QRadar Appliance will not be configured with an IP address and will be used to collect raw traffic (*frames*) off the network, typically through a spanned port or a network tap.

Some network nodes will be able to push flow and event data to the QRadar system. These include systems that are syslog and/or SNMP enabled or are enabled to send flow (NetFlow, JFlow, etc.) data to a remote device.

Some systems can be enabled for event exporting through the use of a third-party application, like Snare Agent for Windows from Intersect Alliance (http://www .intersectalliance.com/projects/SnareWindows/index.html), or WinAgents EventLog Translation Service from the WinAgents Software Group (http://www.winagents.com/ en/products/eventlog-syslog/index.php).

Other systems can take advantage of the Adaptive Log Exporter utility, developed by Q1 Labs, that installs on a Windows system and can be configured to collect and export logs to the QRadar Device Support Modules (DSMs) for proper parsing and further processing.

The following devices will need to be configured to export their data to the IP address of the QRadar management interface:

■ Flow sources such as routers and firewalls

■ Event sources—most network nodes, including routers, firewalls, and infrastructure systems

■ Vulnerability scanners

■ Servers and perhaps critical workstations

You will need to understand the transport mechanisms, protocols, and paths used by these export processes and adjust firewalls to allow the SIEM-related traffic through.

## Event Sources and Data

Virtually every node or endpoint on the network has the capability to perform logging. Even devices that are installed solely to submit data to the SIEM system will be logging the events related to the device itself, like logon attempts and configuration changes. Consider which devices you want to collect event data from for analysis and correlation with the QRadar system. Many devices may not be considered critical in your environment. You may, therefore, decide not to include their event data since it would consume additional bandwidth, storage, and processing power within the SIEM system. Just keep in mind that if you are not monitoring a system or device, you may be missing the vision on a compromised or misconfigured node on your network. It is generally advisable to include *everything* on the network in the SIEM analysis.

Network devices can push events to QRadar using RFC standard syslog services or through SNMP. QRadar can pull events from devices if the remote devices support any of the following log source protocols:

■ Syslog

■ Java Database Connector (JDBC)

■ OPSEC/LEA – Check Point Log Export API

■ Security Device Event Exchange (SDEE)—Cisco / SOAP based

■ Juniper Network Security Manager (NSM), modified syslog protocol

■ Simple Network Management Protocol (SNMP) v1, v2, and v3

The QRadar accepts standard syslog data on UDP port 514, and then uses the DSMs to identify the source device and properly parse each inbound event. If QRadar cannot identify the device or doesn't have a DSM for the device, you can construct a Universal DSM and define proper parsing and mapping into the QRadar format. This data is then normalized to reduce volume and eliminate redundancy. From there, the event data gets analyzed against defined rules and then stored. The analysis is largely based on a signature-base of known attacks, an anomaly detection engine for variations in behavior, and rules that can be customized for different networks with special concerns, such as compliance requirements and high value assets. These events are also used to identify assets and the IP subnets those assets are connected to. This helps to populate the QRadar Asset Inventory and Asset Profiles.

If the conditions in the rules are matched, the event is sent to the Magistrate that tracks all offenses. If the event is not related to an active offense, the Magistrate will declare a New Offense. If the event is related to an active offense, the Magistrate will add this event to the related existing offense.

## Flow Sources and Data

Flow data is usually generated by infrastructure devices like routers and firewalls. Many of the leading manufacturers of these types of devices include their own flow data technologies, like Q1 Labs' QFlow, Cisco Systems' NetFlow, Juniper Networks' J-Flow and Hewlett Packard's Sflow.

Flow data can be collected by QRadar in two different ways. Flow data can be fed by the network infrastructure devices to the QFlow Collector listening on the QRadar network interface with an IP address. Flow data can also be sniffed directly off the wire by directly connecting the QRadar network interface(s) without IP addressing to a spanned port or a network tap. The QRadar SIEM system understands 136 known protocols and adds to that list as new protocols are ratified or observed on the network.

This flow data gets normalized and then filtered in predefined or custom QRadar Views. Sentries monitor the Views and will trigger flow events that get fed to the QRadar Event Processor if the flow matches the flow behavioral profiles and anomaly detection parameters defined within the Sentry. From there, the flow event gets processed along with the other device events from event sources.

## Summary

Once you understand the various components of the Q1 Labs QRadar SIEM system, you must design the system architecture by estimating the log and flow loads at each physical location within your networking environment. You must take into consideration the available bandwidth on the links that connect these different locations with the Network Operation Center (NOC) or Security Operations Center (SOC), which will help you identify requirements and placement of the Flow and Event Processors and QFlow Collectors.

After that, you need to initialize the QRadar Appliance(s) on the network:

- Set administrative password(s).
- Configure the IP properties and interface roles for each system.
- Review and adjust, as desired, the appliance's system settings to comply with any internally defined or legislated security requirements.

■ Configure logging of the QRadar devices themselves.

■ Configure QRadar automatic updates.

■ Configure QRadar system backups.

Now you're ready for administrative provisioning:

■ Configure administrative user roles with permissions and assigned devices.

■ Add administrative users and assign roles.

■ Assign network objects to user roles.

■ Define a network hierarchy.

■ Define IT system assets and establish asset profiles.

Finally, you configure your IT systems to forward their logs to the appropriate QRadar collector.

Congratulations! With that done, you're up and running on the Q1 Labs QRadar SIEM system. Now get ready for some advanced tuning of your Q1 Labs QRadar SIEM system in the next chapter!

# CHAPTER 13

## Q1 Labs QRadar Advanced Techniques

Now that you have a good understanding of the architecture, processes, and capabilities of the QRadar system, it is time to explore the actions and capabilities that are available from within the QRadar console. The primary objective of any SIEM system is to provide automatic responses to predetermined conditions. In this chapter, you will learn how to tune the components that analyze the events and flows being received by the QRadar unit.

This chapter will describe the QRadar Dashboard and Event Viewer—what they are, what they do, and how they allow for quick analysis of incoming events and flows. You will learn about QRadar Views and their benefits, including a review of the Q1 Labs' precanned Views and how to create custom Views to organize flow data within the QRadar system. The chapter will continue with a description of the QRadar Sentries, including their benefits, the precanned Sentries, as well as how to create custom Sentries; custom Sentries can be used to filter the flow records to identify particular traffic patterns.

The next area of interest is the use of QRadar Rules—their components, the Rules Test Groups, Offense resolutions, stock Rules, and how to use the Custom Rules Wizard to create environmentally specific Rules. Custom Rules enable you to identify and respond to specific network events and offenses that may be unique to your network or business environment.

Additionally, you will learn the methodology for tuning the QRadar SIEM appliance, including updating Device Support Modules (DSMs) from Q1 Labs. DSMs are used to parse incoming events and provide mapping among the events coming in from disparate network devices within your network into the QRadar standardized format. Being able to understand the inbound events from the many different systems on your network, and then recording the accurately parsed data in a common format, is essential for analysis and for providing the above functionalities.

Finally, you will walk through the steps that, as a security professional/security analyst, you would undergo to process, recognize, and remediate a security incident within the QRadar system. The process starts after an event or flow has been received by the QRadar unit, which then filters this event and/or flow using objects known as Building Blocks (BB) and then passes that data into Views in order to build Sentries. These Sentries then generate internal events, which are sent to the Rules processing engine known as the Magistrate.

At this point, the Magistrate uses a weighting system, based on various configurable attributes, to determine if the network situation is hostile enough to produce an Offense. The Offense is the mechanism that alerts the security professional to begin analyzing the situation to mitigate any damage or losses to valuable information assets, and remediate the threat. Alerts can be configured to be sent to one or more email addresses.

After you have remediated the threat to your organization's network, in order to keep management up to date, you will use the QRadar system to develop reports to detail the specific actions that caused the hostile circumstances and the actions taken to ensure the situation has been rectified. In addition to keeping management informed, the report will show how well you have done your job.

# Using the QRadar Dashboard

The QRadar Dashboard is the first screen that appears when you log into the QRadar system. The Dashboard provides a quick visual on many aspects of the events and flows being received by the QRadar unit. The default views on the Dashboard detail different kinds of information and supply examples of how this information might assist in your analysis of the conditions within your environment. As you can see in Figure 13-1, a large amount of information is presented on the Dashboard.

**NOTE** The items available for viewing on the Dashboard are controlled by the Roles assigned to each user within the QRadar system.

Each of the default views contained on the QRadar Dashboard provide insight into the events and flows being received by the QRadar unit. Remember that each of these events and flow data summaries have been received by the QRadar system, typically through UDP port 514, and are then parsed by DSMs to convert the events and flows from various devices and systems into the QRadar format. After this normalization process, the data is then analyzed and stored in the database. The data is also displayed via these Dashboard monitors and views to provide easy visual clues to the security professional about active and new offenses. You can see the various attributes of the normalized events and flows on the Dashboard through drill-down type functions.

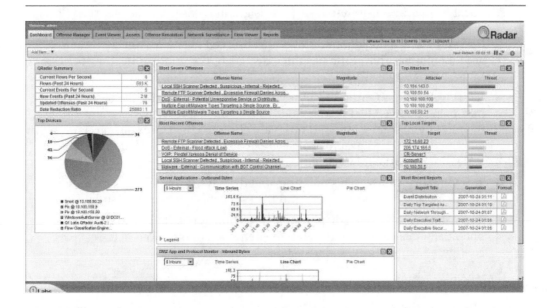

**Figure 13-1.**    QRadar Dashboard

## QRadar Dashboard Default Views

The Dashboard's default views can be added, removed, and arranged in any order to provide quick, visual displays for analysts. These displays can be customized for the organization's security posture, placing the areas of greatest concern in the most prominent positions. These views show the organization's current security status and current network usage. Notice the tabs along the top of the Dashboard and consider them in the context of this chapter, taking an incident from start to finish.

The following is a list of the default views that are available that can be included on the Dashboard display when you first log into the QRadar Dashboard:

- **QRadar Summary**   This view provides a list of basic QRadar counters. These counters include Current Flows Per Second, Flows (Past 24 Hours), Current Events Per Second, New Events (Past 24 Hours), Updated Offenses (Past 24 Hours), and the Data Reduction Ratio.

- **New Offenses Count Graph**   This graph shows the number of new Offenses that QRadar has defined from newly arrived events and flows, over a certain, configurable amount of time.

- **Most Severe Offenses**   This is a list of the active Offenses with the highest severity as determined by QRadar.

- **Most Recent Offenses**   This list displays the most recent Offenses captured by the QRadar system.

- **Local Networks – Inbound Bytes**   This graph is based on the observed flow data being received by QRadar from your defined local networks, and details the rate at which the inbound flows are observed over a certain configurable amount of time. This graph has three display options, including Time Series, Line Chart, and Pie Chart.

- **Local Networks – Outbound Bytes**   This graph is based on the observed flow data being received by QRadar from your defined local networks, and details the rate at which the outbound flows are observed over a certain configurable amount of time. This graph also has three display options, including Time Series, Line Chart, and Pie Chart.

- **Top Category Types**   This monitors and displays in a list format the number of Offenses by defined category and tracks the most active Offense categories.

- **Top Attackers**   This list displays the hosts that appear to be the sources of potentially malicious activity, with the definition of malicious activity being configured within the QRadar system.

## QRadar Views

QRadar Views are QRadar's method of organizing flow data for internal processing and for presentation in the various displays. Views are essentially filters applied to flow data and are based on Boolean logic. QRadar provides many default Views so you can quickly locate potentially malicious flow data. These Views are organized in a tree hierarchy for easy categorizing, creating, and editing.

## QRadar Default View Groups

The Views available within each of the following Global View types are known as *Unique View Groups* and contain groups that are used to satisfy some of QRadar's internal requirements and cannot be edited. These default read-only groups include:

- **InverseIsKnown**  Displays the server traffic when displayed in a Client View. When displaying the Server View, the client traffic is captured and displayed.

- **Other**  Presents traffic that does not match a property set or is not defined in the QRadar configuration.

- **Unknown**  Displays flow data that is unidentifiable by the QRadar system.

- **Nodetectattempt**  Presents flow data with no contents in the packet itself.

- **Known_to_client_or_server**  This view is similar to the InverseIsKnown View.

## QRadar Global Group Types

Global Views are for general traffic categorization. There are four general Global View types:

- **Ports View**  This view provides a display of the flow data organized by the network port information captured in the flow. The information that is garnered from the flow will be displayed whether it is TCP or UDP traffic. (QRadar does not differentiate between the two protocols; it will display both.) You have the ability to modify and create your own Ports Views to customize QRadar for your organization. The default Port Views available include

  - **GamePorts**  Displays traffic to and from known gaming ports.

  - **MailPorts**  Presents traffic associated with known email ports.

  - **TargetedPorts**  Displays the source and destination of traffic attempting to exploit commonly targeted ports.

  - **UnnamedPorts**  Presents traffic that does not have a specified port associated with it.

  - **WebPorts**  Displays traffic being received from known ports that are used for web communications.

  - **P2PPorts**  Displays the source and destination of traffic using known ports assigned to peer-to-peer (P2P) applications.

- **Applications View**  This view shows the applications associated with the flow data being received by QRadar. These applications are displayed using QRadar's Application ID headers for quick recognition and drill-down capabilities. The following are some of the default Applications View Groups available:

  - **Chat**  Displays traffic used by known Instant Messaging (IM) applications.

  - **DataTransfer**  Displays traffic including the source and destination that are utilizing known file and data transfer protocols, such as File Transfer

Protocol (FTP), Network File System (NFS), and Common Internet File System/Server Message Blocks (CIFS/SMB), among others.

- **DataWarehousing** Presents traffic including the source and destination that are utilizing known storage protocols, such as Internet Small Computer System Interface (iSCSI), Advanced Technology Attachment (ATA) over Ethernet (AoE), and Fiber Channel over IP (FCIP), among others.

- **Mail** Displays traffic including the source and destination utilizing email protocols such as Simple Mail Transfer Protocol (SMTP).

- **Misc** Displays traffic that is utilizing various miscellaneous protocols such as Dynamic Host Configuration Protocol (DHCP), Domain Name System (DNS), Remote Procedure Call (RPC), and Appletalk-IP, among others.

- **Remote Networks View** Displays the external or remote network ranges. QRadar does provide some Remote Network Groups that are updated by Q1 Labs. The following are some of the default Remote Network Views:

  - **Bogon** Displays traffic originating from an unassigned IP address (aka *Internet dark space,* or *darknet*).

  - **HostileNets** Classifies traffic originating from known hostile networks. This group contains a set of 20 CIDR ranges associated with known spam/botnet/phishing networks.

  - **Neighbors** Classifies traffic originating from remote networks being managed by the QRadar system and is empty by default.

  - **TrustedNetworks** As the name states, classifies traffic originating from trusted, nonhostile remote networks and is empty by default.

- **Remote Services View** This view organizes traffic by the typically undesirable service provided by a remote network. These views are displayed by IP address, not port. Some of the default views available are

  - **IRC_Servers** Displays the source and destination traffic of known IRC servers.

  - **Porn** Displays the source and destination traffic from known pornographic sites.

  - **Proxies** Displays the source and destination traffic from known open proxy servers.

  - **Reserved_IP_Ranges** Displays the source and destination of IANA-reserved IP address ranges.

  - **Spam** Displays the source and destination of traffic from known networks that produce and distribute spam.

  - **Spy_Adware** Displays source and destination of traffic from networks known to provide spyware or adware.

  - **Warez** Displays the source and destination of traffic from networks known for pirating software.

## Custom Views

While you can modify many of the default views and groups in your QRadar environment upon initial implementation, you can also create Custom Views. Custom Views are used to isolate and display unique and unusual traffic, or to organize traffic specified as "other" or "unknown" in a more specific manner. To configure these Custom Views, you must utilize the Custom View Equation Editor and use Boolean logic to define the criteria required to enable automatic, proactive analysis of your environment. These Custom Views can be used to produce detailed views that are aligned with your organization's security posture. Custom Views are organized into five default groups that include the Group, View, and Equation used for configuration. These Custom Views are defined by the initial template you choose upon installation and include

- IP Tracking Group
- Threats Group
- Attacker Target Analysis Group
- Target Analysis Group
- Policy Violation Group

To create these Custom Views, you will begin in the Administration Console. The Custom View tree structure used here looks very similar to the Global Views described earlier. Select the Admin tab located along the top of the QRadar Dashboard Console and select the View Configuration option on the left sidebar. Then select the Create New View option in order to begin creating your Custom View, as shown in Figure 13-2.

After you provide a name and a description for the Custom View Group, you will then begin to create your Custom View by selecting the Add Equation option. As you can see from Figure 13-3, you will assign or create a new Custom View Group, enter a name for the new Custom View, assign a weight or magnitude for this View within

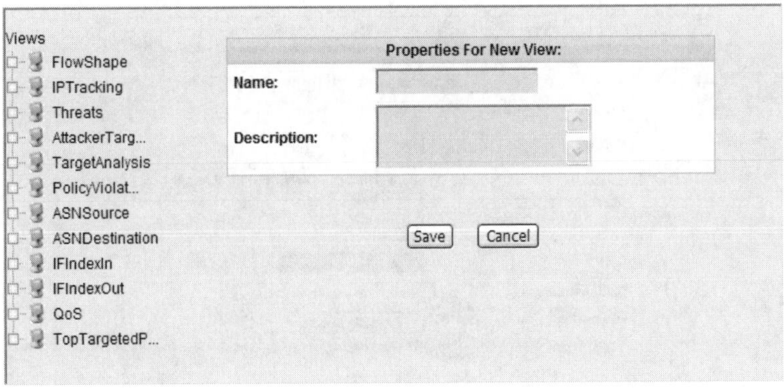

**Figure 13-2.** QRadar New Custom View Properties box

your network. You will enter a description of the View, a color for this View when it's displayed on your Dashboard , and then finally, the database length. You must define how long the data is to be held and available to be displayed. At this point, you will configure the additional View properties and begin building the Boolean logic using the Equation Editor, as shown in Figure 13-4.

## The Equation Editor

When building Custom Views, you must configure the Equation Editor. The Equation Editor allows you to build filter criteria for tests to be performed on the traffic being received, filtered, analyzed, and displayed by the QRadar system.

The Equation Editor uses standard algebraic logic to define the View statement that you will use while developing your Custom Views. The Equation Editor creates filters to use within your Custom View. Figure 13-4 shows the initial Equation Editor screen when building your Custom View.

As you can see from Figure 13-4, there are three areas to configure within the Equation Editor. The Objects section provides all of the available Source Categories defined from Global Views as well as other Custom Views. The Elements section includes specific parameters to define such as IP, port, or various flow types. Elements must be specifically configured to properly identify traffic on your network. These configurations include

- **Type**   This configuration determines the general type of traffic desired.
- **Name**   This is the name of the Element itself. This attribute is used when building equations.
- **Property**   This attribute defines the dimension of the Elements value and details the type of data present in the flow or event stream.
- **Value**   This is the actual data to be matched and displayed in the Custom View.

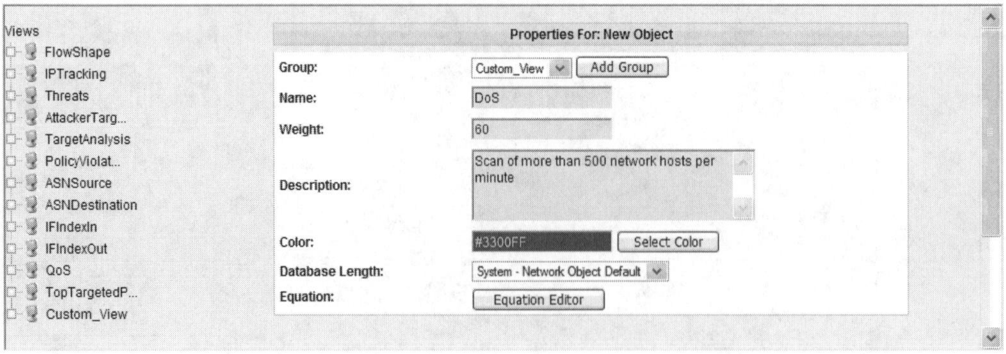

**Figure 13-3.**   QRadar New Custom View additional View Properties box

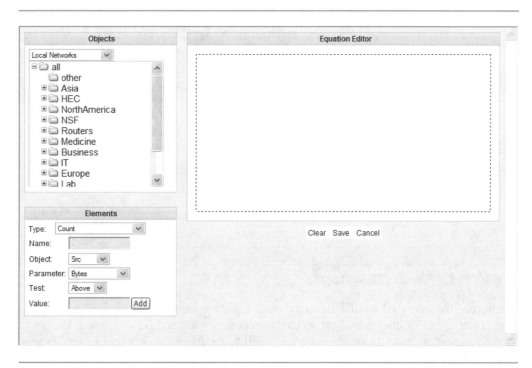

**Figure 13-4.**   QRadar Equation Editor

When building the equation for your Custom View, you will use both the Objects and Elements options. You can add the Custom View Object to the equation by double-clicking it. You then add your Elements to the equation by selecting the Add button on the Equation Editor. As you continue to build your equation, you will use Boolean logic to create the filter within the Custom View. The options for the Boolean logic calculations are AND, OR, and NOT operators, which provide the conditions for your View. Boolean functions are grouped by adding parentheses around the desired functions. In Boolean logic, the functions grouped by parentheses are calculated from the inner-most set of parentheses to the outermost set, just as in standard algebra.

## QRadar Equation Editor Examples

Figure 13-5 shows the details of a Custom View to identify UDP port scans on the network. It depicts multiple facets of what an analyst may want to identify, track, and potentially analyze. Typically, a security analyst who is looking for P2P applications watches for the UDP protocol, which is combined into a Superflow type. Once these flows have been recognized, the analyst then looks within those selected flows to see if the source of the flow is an application that is either not known by the QRadar system or not specified. While QRadar can assist in providing in-depth and detailed information regarding your network and the security of your organization in many situations, this scenario would warrant the building of a Custom View to provide a more thorough prognosis.

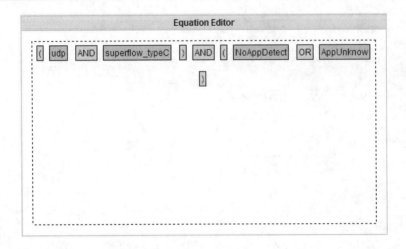

**Figure 13-5.** QRadar UDP port scan

In this instance, you would probably want to search for systems on your network that are using a P2P client application to download movies, music, and so on. Figure 13-6 shows what the appropriate equation would look like to enable this type of flow monitoring.

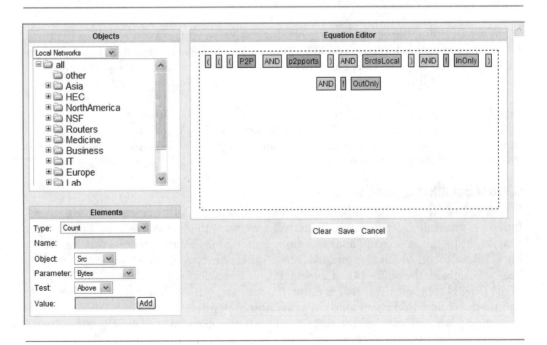

**Figure 13-6.** QRadar View to identify client P2P application usage

Figure 13-6 depicts an equation that would monitor and track any network user using a P2P client. The Elements are in blue; however, you will add a couple of Object definitions as well (shown in orange). As you can see, the equation is looking for the Object known as **P2P**, which includes all defined P2P applications known by the QRadar system. You also see the Object known as **p2pports**, which includes all known ports that are utilized by the P2P applications. Then, the equation finds any flows that match those conditions and are being generated by a device on the local network. This is done by AND-ing the **SrcIsLocal** (Source is local) Element. Next, the equation finds any flows that match the first three conditions and sees if those flows are not just inbound and outbound traffic. This requires that the flow be bidirectional between an entity outside of the local network and one on the local network and using one of the known P2P applications and known P2P ports. (The ! (also known as a *BANG*) in the equation symbolizes the Boolean NOT function.)

As you can see, default Views and Custom Views provide insight into what is happening on your network. However, using these advanced functions does impact the appliance's performance. This logic processing is CPU intensive. So, with that said, there are a few best practices that Q1 Labs recommends when using the Default and Custom View capabilities within the QRadar appliance:

- Disable any Views that do not provide visibility into your network. When you disable these Views, they will not be included in traffic filtering and will help to reduce the processing requirements for flow processing. As a first step, simply go through the list of available Views, and disable the ones that are not appropriate for your environment.

- Consolidate View Objects within the Equation Editor. Make your View Objects as general as possible to include all related targets (like P2P applications versus Kazaa). Doing this will decrease the input/output (I/O) to the RAM and onboard drives in the QRadar appliances.

*TIP* Be careful with this recommendation, however. Remember that the more consolidated your Objects are, the less granularity and detail the View will provide. Find the right balance between the necessary visibility and reduction in performance due to resource consumption.

- When building your View Object, allow no more than 200 hosts per View Object. When you include more than this amount, more processing time will be required for flow data to be received, analyzed, and displayed. The best way to provide the most information for analysis without burdening your QRadar appliance is to isolate particular networks, hosts, and services according to how critical they are to your organization. Then, when you have established their criticality, simply define Objects for each of these items.

# QRadar Sentries

As you read in the previous chapter, a *Sentry* is a logical filter that each flow record passes through as it is processed by the QRadar appliance. Sentries are used to identify particular traffic patterns and generate events on the identified traffic. The

Sentry-generated events are fed into the Event Processor for further analysis and correlation with other flows and events. Each inbound flow will pass through what is known as the Sentry list, where the flow patterns are matched to a defined Sentry or Sentries. When a match occurs, the appropriate Sentry will produce an event. As with Views, to improve processing performance, it is advisable to disable Sentries that are not applicable to your environment.

## QRadar Sentry Components

Sentries are made up of the following three components:

- **Logic Unit**   Includes specific algorithms used to test inbound flow and event objects within QRadar. The Logic Unit includes default variables, such as Bytes In, Bytes Out, or VNC Access from the Internet, and parameter evaluations for the Sentry being created. Logic Units perform basic logical filtering functions. They will determine if a violation has occurred and if an alert needs to be generated. Logic Units are typically not modified.

- **Package**   A collection of views linked together with Logic Units to construct a more complex filter. The View Objects used within a package are created from any defined View, with the exception of the main Network View. Packages can be applied to more than one Sentry so you can easily configure similar-type Sentries. All variables in the Package have priority over the Logic Unit variables.

- **Sentry**   A collection of Packages linked together to construct a more complex filter. Sentries can be applied to specific network locations to limit their monitoring scope. You can also specify additional restrictions, like protocol, source, and destination, upon the network location component Objects. The variables defined in the Sentry component have priority over both the Package and Logic Unit variables.

## QRadar Sentry Types

QRadar provides four distinct types of Sentries upon installation to meet your security requirements. The four types are

- **Security/Policy**   Monitors your deployment for security/policy violations, such as violations of usage-based policies, and can specify situations when application usage is allowed. If any traffic is detected that meets the Sentry criteria, an event is generated. The events that are generated from Security/Policy sentries are sent to the Event Processor, which correlates the Sentry event with the applicable asset profile data and with any related events received from the same, or other, network sources. The Sentry type allows you to select an auto learn option, in which the QRadar system learns system activity over a specifically configured timeframe. Once the timeframe has elapsed, the system will generate an alert when any Object that was not present during the learning time becomes active on your network. This type of Sentry does not use Logic Units as the Package contains the required matching logic.

- **Behavior** Monitors your environment for changes in behavior that occur regularly. The QRadar system ascertains how a particular Object ordinarily behaves over a certain period of time and records the number of hosts communicating over your network at different points during the day.

- **Anomaly** Monitors your environment for what is considered abnormal activity. The QRadar system detects the existence of new or unknown traffic being generated. This traffic is considered anomalous in that the traffic suddenly stops or the amount of time an Object is active changes beyond a defined threshold—say when a network Object that has been active 22 percent of the time suddenly drops to being active only 1 percent of the time.

- **Threshold** Monitors your environment for network activity that exceeds a configured threshold. QRadar monitors the relevant network Objects and identifies whenever a network flow threshold has been exceeded, like SFTP uploads that increase from a typical 0.3GB to 15GB today.

The Security/Policy Sentry will parse all incoming traffic for configured patterns as the traffic arrives in the QRadar system. This Sentry type is used to detect observed network threats to your environment. This is often referred to as a knowledge-based or signature-based monitor, as it identifies patterns that are predictable because either you or QRadar has seen it before. It knows the pattern or signature to look for.

The Behavior, Anomaly, and Threshold Sentries are known as Behavioral Sentries or Network Anomaly Sentries, in that the system does not parse the traffic as it arrives; it parses the traffic on user-defined time intervals. The values required to configure the different Sentry types will change based on the type of Sentry. You will use the New Sentry Wizard to walk through the steps of creating and configuring the Sentries, including selecting and/or creating Packages and Logic Units depending on your needs and selected Sentry design.

# QRadar Rules

QRadar defines a *Rule* as a collection of conditions that, when matched, trigger one or more consequent actions. You can configure Rules that allow QRadar to recognize and respond to specific event sequences or patterns. Rules allow you to detect specific events and forward notifications to either the Offense interface to generate a response to an external system such as syslog or SNMP or even email a user. A rule can also block the offensive activity to resolve the event (if the Resolution option is available). QRadar not only provides many stock Rules to provide this out-of-the-box functionality based on typical, known malicious patterns, but you can also create your own Rules using the Rules Wizard that will be discussed on the following pages.

Rules are a powerful analytical mechanism that can drive the analysis and remediation of malicious activity that may be passing through your environment. Based on the user's Role within the QRadar system and the network Objects assigned to that user, a user can create Rules for those areas of the network that he or she is responsible for. QRadar administrators or users with administrative privileges can configure Rules throughout the system. As with Views, you can and should disable QRadar Rules that will not be used within your environment. This will also aid in performance and system resource handling.

## QRadar Rule Types

QRadar provides two Rule types to enable you to analyze the events on your network proactively:

- **Event Rules**   Detects an event or a pattern of events that fit a specific profile. Event Rules can initiate a response when this pattern is found. These Rules are used to trigger an offense and perform specific actions in response to a single event or an assortment of events.

- **Offense Rule**   Monitors Offenses that meet a certain criteria. Offense Rules can initiate a response. This Rule is used to define unique responses to an Offense or sequence of Offences detected by the QRadar system.

## QRadar Rule Components

As you can see in Figure 13-7, there are three components you can employ when defining and creating QRadar Rules.

The following is a description of the components that a Rule may contain:

- **Functions**   You can use building blocks and other available Rules in order to create a multievent or multioffense function. You can also combine (OR) multiple Rules together using a function.

- **Building blocks**   A Rule without a defined response. A building block is used as a common condition within multiple Rules or to build intricate Rules or logic that you want to use in other Rules. Building blocks allow you to re-use specific Rule tests in other Rules.

- **Tests**   The specific property of an event or an Offense. Some examples include the source IP address, the destination port number, and the severity of an event.

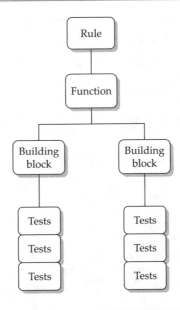

**Figure 13-7.** QRadar Rules components

## QRadar Custom Rules Wizard

Now that you are familiar with the various facets of a QRadar Rule, including the types
and possible components that it can contain, it is time to walk through the process of
creating a new QRadar Rule using the Custom Rule Wizard. The Custom Rule Wizard
divides the rule-creation process into four specific configuration items. Figure 13-8
shows the initial screen when you invoke the Custom Rule Wizard to create either
an Event Rule or an Offense Rule.

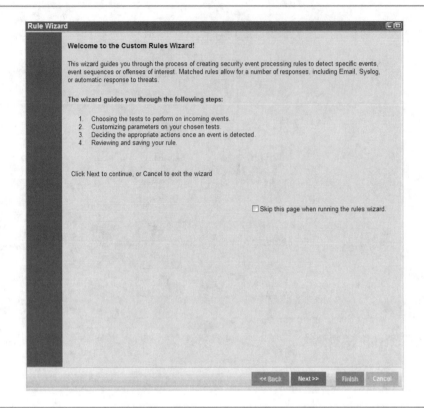

**Figure 13-8.** QRadar Custom Rule Wizard

The first step in defining your rule using the Custom Rule Wizard is to choose the tests to be performed on the incoming events. The tests are organized into groups according to their purpose within the system. In this step, the tests available will depend upon what type of Rule you would like to create. As an example, you can create a Rule that looks for events that have transpired after work hours. Figure 13-9 displays the Custom Rule Wizard with the appropriate configurations.

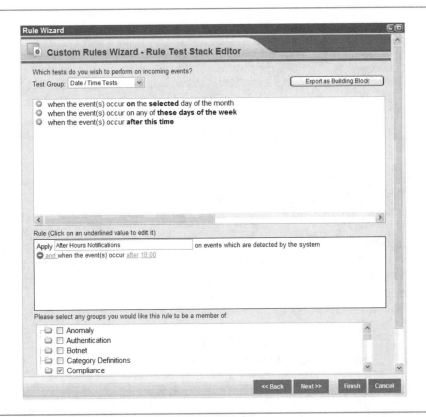

**Figure 13-9.**   QRadar Custom Rule Wizard Tests selection

As you can see, the Test Group Date Time has been chosen, and the option When The Events Occur After This Time has been selected. Then the time of 18:00 or 6:00 PM was specified. The rule has been named After Hours Notifications and this Rule has been specified as a member the Compliance Group.

The next step in creating your custom, After Hours Notifications Rule is to determine the Event Rule response along with various other actions that QRadar can perform. Figure 13-10 displays the actions that have been configured.

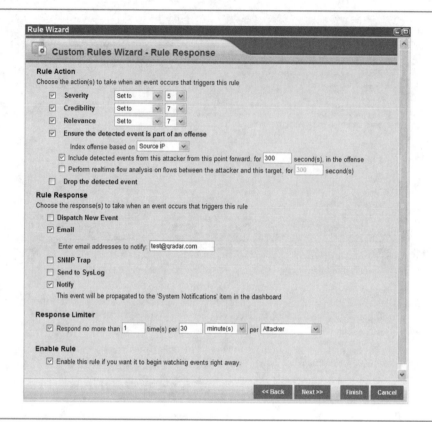

**Figure 13-10.** QRadar Custom Rule Wizard Rule Response selection

As you can see in Figure 13-10, appropriate priority measurements have been defined within the Actions area of the Wizard's input screen. Priority measurements are weighted between 0 and 10, and the QRadar system will automatically assign these configured values to the event/offense when the conditions of the event match the defined parameters of the Rule. In Figure 13-10, the sample Event Rule is configured with a severity level of 5, a credibility level of 7, and a relevance level of 7. When an event matches this Rule as configured, the QRadar system assigns these three values to the event for further processing. Through the use of customized Views and the tuning of Offenses, these values could be used to cause this event to pop up on a Dashboard View or to define this event as an Offense:

■ *Severity*, as the name implies, is how important you feel this event or identified flow is when the Rule's test conditions have been met. One way to determine this value is to ask, "How critical or valuable are the information assets that are being monitored by this particular Rule?"

- *Credibility* is a measure of how probable is it that the events and flows that meet the test conditions are actually an Offense within the environment.

- *Relevance* matches events to the organization's security policy or compliance requirements, as configured within the QRadar system, to evaluate whether the event is more or less significant in the context of your specific organizational concerns.

The next step in creating an Event Rule is to develop the Rule Response. You do this by selecting the option to Ensure The Detected Event Is Part Of An offense, whereby the Offense will be indexed according to the source IP. You will also specify how long you wish to track this source IP. In this example, once the test conditions have been met, the Event Rule settings have been configured to track the source IP system for a total of 300 seconds (5 minutes) after an initial login event occurs to see what actions are being performed.

In addition, once the test conditions have been met, the Event Rule settings have been configured to send an email and to propagate a notification to the Dashboard. Next, the Event Rule has been configured to limit the response of this Rule to no more than 1 time per 30 minutes per attacker. This limit reduces the number of redundant notifications for this Offense that you'll find in your inbox. Last but certainly not least, you must enable the Rule for it to be applied to event data. This checkbox allows you to build these complex Rules and only apply them when there is increased likelihood of their firing, such as when a high number of visitors are using the network in the conference room. You can disable the Rule to reduce processing demands on the QRadar system next week, when the conference room will be empty.

# The Offense Manager

As you learned in the previous chapter, a QRadar Offense typically includes multiple events from one host that matches a certain, user-defined criteria. Q1 Labs provides an interface that is separately licensed called the Offense Manager. The Offense Manager enables you to view all Offenses occurring within your QRadar environment. From the Offenses interface, you can investigate one or many QRadar Offenses to determine the source of a particular Offense within your organization's network. From within the Offenses interface, you have the ability to monitor and manage all identified Offenses as well.

Users with the appropriate QRadar privileges can assign Offenses to other users within the system. Upon initial viewing, the All Offenses window appears when you click the Offenses tab from within the Dashboard. When a user with the appropriate privileges assigns Offenses to you, they will appear in the My Offenses window. There are many ways in which you can view Offenses from within the Offenses interface. The following is a list of the available ways in which you can manage or view the Offenses caught by QRadar from within the system:

- **Viewing Offense By Category** Provides you with a view of all Offenses based on the high-level category that your organization has defined.

- **Managing Offenses By Attacker**  Allows you to view Offenses by attacker. All attackers within this view are listed with the highest magnitude first.
- **Managing Offenses By Targets**  Displays a list of local targets of the Offenses generated by the highest magnitude first.
- **Managing Offenses By Networks**  Displays a list of Offenses that are grouped by the network defined by your organization. All networks are listed with the highest magnitude first.

## Searching QRadar Offenses

Because many potential Offenses may take place in your enterprise that you will want to investigate using the Offense interface, QRadar provides a highly functional search engine. Figure 13-11 shows what the search parameters are that allow you to quickly begin your analysis of known Offenses within your environment.

As you can see, there are many ways in which you can search for Offenses within the QRadar system. With each of these search options, you can either find network Offenses based on a broad or restricted criteria. This capability makes it easy to find, investigate, and remediate the Offenses that the QRadar system has found lurking within your enterprise.

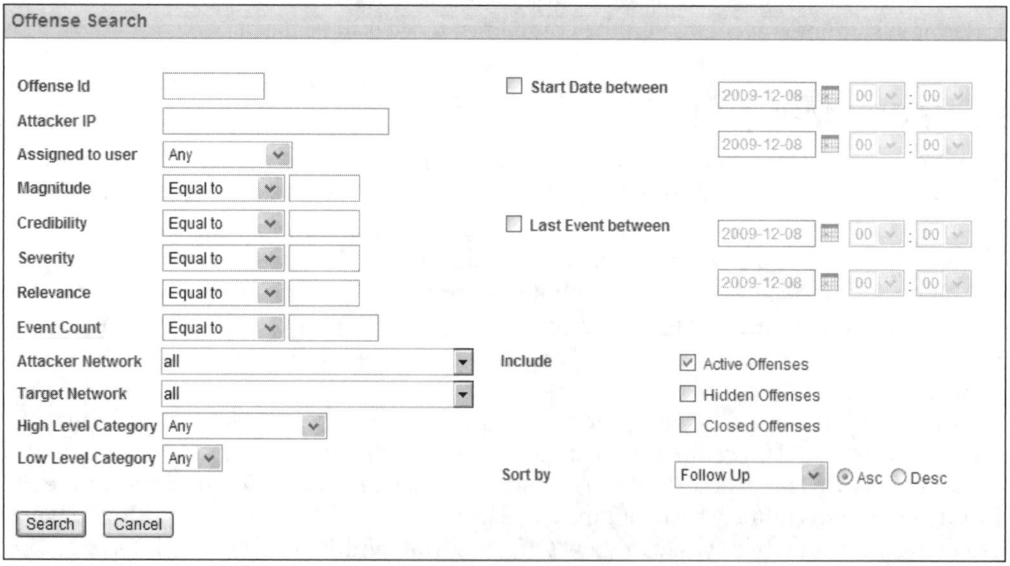

**Figure 13-11.**    QRadar Offense Search

# QRadar Tuning

QRadar provides immediate functionality right out of the box, with immediate views into the traffic being conducted on your network, benefiting the development and enforcement of your organization's security posture. Some QRadar features can also be tuned to provide substantial improvements and benefits. This section provides some tuning suggestions that will increase your system's performance and effectiveness. Please remember, however, that tuning of the QRadar system is an ongoing process, and should be conducted in a consistent and iterative manner to ensure that it meets your organization's standards. The goal is to bring into rapid focus the true-positive offensive event alerts and to minimize and eventually eliminate (oh yeah, dream on) false-positive offensive event alerts.

The tuning objectives relayed here will assist in suppressing false positives, avoid introducing false negatives, provide actionable data in the simplest format possible, and assist in adapting your security posture to new threats. These objectives are dependent on your organization's specific network environment and security posture.

## QRadar False Positive Wizard

In order to suppress false positives, you must first understand what a false positive is. In the security industry, a *false positive* is an event that triggers an Offense alert and/or response, but should not have. It's an event that meets enough tests and rules to trigger the system, but is not actually to a threat to your network environment. Think of false positives as being something like the boy who cried wolf. False-positive events are considered noise on the network and reducing their occurrence to very near zero is desirable.

An example of false-positive activity on some networks would be routine reconnaissance traffic (port scanning) of the network that is not followed by an attack. Depending on your environment, you may not be concerned with this type of traffic. In order to ensure that you are limiting the amount of false positives on your network, it is strongly recommended that you create a network hierarchy that defines what assets are important within your organization. Define uniquely desired and undesired traffic types for each section of the network. Performing this task will assist in drawing out the most relevant event or flow traffic possible, based upon the assets and the applications used within those networks. Since QRadar has the ability to listen to a network segment with one of its available NICs, you must direct as much network traffic as possible directly to the QRadar system, so it can sort, prioritize, and provide the insight required.

QRadar provides the False Positive Wizard to assist in preventing individual events from triggering Rules that may initiate an action or response for irrelevant traffic. You will create building blocks from event addresses and QID data that can be excluded from other rules. The Wizard will assist in detecting false positives that are created from simple events that are initiated by a single, suspected attacker and destined for a single target. If you require more complex exclusions, you will need to tune your QRadar Rules to ensure their precision and accuracy. In order to invoke the False Positive Wizard, you must select the Events tab from within the console. You will then select a false-positive event that should be excluded from any Rule to ensure that it will not be considered a relevant attack. The False Positive Wizard is shown in Figure 13-12.

As you can see from Figure 13-12, the selected event has a specific QID of 38750003 and the attacker is 172.16.30.76 with a target of 127.0.0.1. QRadar reads the details of the event and configures the wizard with the various parameters or details contained within it. You can then select which event detail assures you that this event is not a legitimate attack. After you have made these distinctions, you will configure the QRadar system to exclude this type of event from any rules that may be triggered by its presence.

To configure a QRadar Sentry to ignore certain Sentry-triggered events on a particular network, you will first have to determine which Sentry is creating the events. You can either disable the Sentry so you will not see these patterns within your QRadar system, or, if you have determined that you want to see these events, you can select the specific networks within the QRadar environment that should ignore the false-positive events and those that should not.

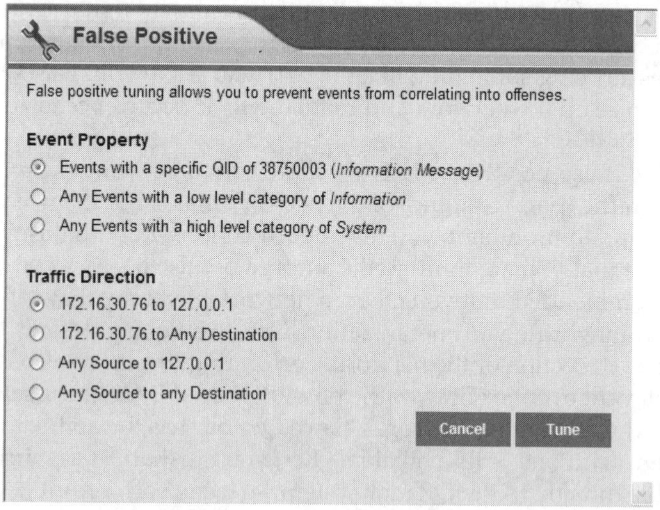

**False Positive**

False positive tuning allows you to prevent events from correlating into offenses.

**Event Property**
- ⦿ Events with a specific QID of 38750003 (*Information Message*)
- ○ Any Events with a low level category of *Information*
- ○ Any Events with a high level category of *System*

**Traffic Direction**
- ⦿ 172.16.30.76 to 127.0.0.1
- ○ 172.16.30.76 to Any Destination
- ○ Any Source to 127.0.0.1
- ○ Any Source to any Destination

[ Cancel ]  [ Tune ]

**Figure 13-12.**    QRadar False Positive Wizard

# QRadar DSMs and Custom DSMs

As you read previously, a QRadar Device Support Module (DSM) is the component that understands which type of device generated the received event, and then correctly parses the event data to align similar pieces of information accurately within the QRadar event database. The DSMs effectively integrate QRadar with the various types and manufacturers of the devices residing on your network. It is advisable that you deploy any Q1 Labs updates whenever they are available to ensure that you have the most current collection of DSMs.

## Manually Updating DSMs

Deploying major updates to your existing DSMs within the QRadar environment is easy. All you have to do is to log into the Q1 Labs Qmmunity web site to download the latest DSM software updates. These updates are provided in the RedHat Package Manager (RPM) format for easy distribution. After you have downloaded the new RPM, transfer it to the QRadar unit and then unpack it. Using the root credentials, log in to the QRadar console command-line interface (CLI) and install it using the following command:

```
rpm -Uvh <filename>
```

After the RPM file has been extracted to the appropriate area within the QRadar system, log in to the QRadar console as a user with administrative privileges, open the Administration console, and select the Deploy All Changes option to apply the new update(s) to the QRadar system.

## Automatically Updating DSMs

If you thought that was easy, QRadar also provides the ability to deploy minor changes to the DSMs automatically by scheduling downloads of these updates. Use the Automatic Updates option from within the Admin tab on the console. Simply select the update method and type. The automatic update options are presented in Figure 13-13.

As you can see from Figure 13-13, many options are available to assist in the management of your QRadar deployment. The only items covered in this chapter are the options for deploying changes to your DSMs. Under the Auto Update Configurations section, you will see the Choose Updates section. This area allows you to configure updates for the QRadar system. The configuration options are

- **Update Method**   Select the method you want to use for updating your system:
  - **Auto Integrate**   Integrates the new configuration files with your existing files to maintain the integrity of your information. This is the default setting.
  - **Auto Update**   Replaces your existing configuration files with the new configuration files.

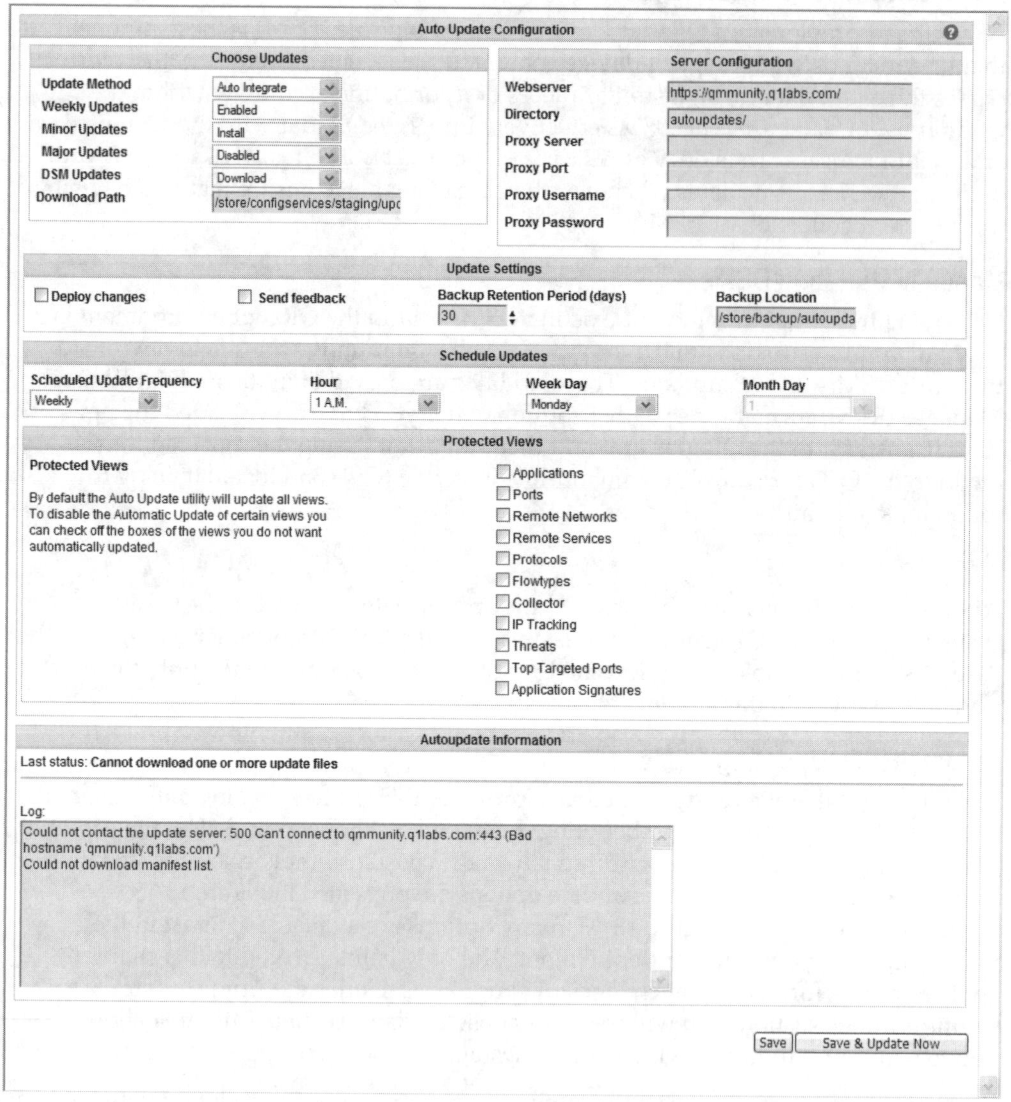

**Figure 13-13.** QRadar Automatic Updates

- **DSM Updates** Select the options for how to handle DSM updates:
  - **Disabled** Disables the option for your system to receive DSM updates.
  - **Download** Downloads the DSM updates to the designated download path location. This is the default setting.
- **Download Path** Specifies the directory path location to which you want to store DSM minor and major updates.

Continuing with the configuration of automatic updates, under the Update Settings section, the following configurations apply:

- ■ **Deploy Changes**   Deploy update changes automatically. If the checkbox is clear, a system notification appears in the Dashboard indicating that you must deploy changes. By default, the checkbox is clear.

- ■ **Send Feedback**   Send feedback to Q1 Labs regarding the update. Feedback is sent automatically using a web form if any errors occur with the update. By default, the checkbox is clear.

- ■ **Backup Retention Period (days)**   Specify the length of time, in days, that you want to store files that may be replaced during the update process. The files will be stored in the location specified in the Backup Location parameter.

- ■ **Backup Location**   Specify the location where you want to store backup files.

After you have decided how you will set up your automatic updates, now you must configure the scheduling parameters. These settings should be self-explanatory. After you have configured these automatic update options, you will then simply select Save And Update Now or simply Save. If you select Save And Update Now, the QRadar system will log into the Qmmunity site via an Internet connection and begin the process of updating your environment per these configured specifications.

## Customizing DSM Mappings

In the event that a QRadar DSM does not parse the raw events or normalized events from your network devices properly, you have the ability to customize this normalization process by mapping the attributes of the event received by the DSM to the QRadar format. In order for QRadar to normalize these incoming events, also known as a *log source*, QRadar automatically maps each event received from a DSM. Using the event-mapping tool, you can map a normalized or raw event to a High-Level and Low-Level Category or use QRadar's QID values. High-Level Categories include approximately 14 selected options such as System, Exploit, and Malware, for example. Low-Level Categories are context-sensitive and typically include 10 to 20 different parameters related to the High-Level Categories. This allows QRadar to map unknown device events to known QRadar events so they can be categorized and correlated appropriately within the QRadar system.

Using the Events tab from within the QRadar console, simply double-click an event that you would like to modify the mapping for. The attributes of that event will be displayed. You will then select the Map event icon at the top of the Events tab. The mapping tool is displayed in Figure 13-14.

Since the event that you have selected has not been normalized by the QRadar system, a QID will not be associated with it. The next step is to browse for events that are of the same type as the one you would like to alter the mapping for. This is done by browsing for either the category level, log source type, or the name of the event itself. After you have begun this search process, any events that match that criteria will be returned. Once these events are displayed, you will then associate this event type with an existing QRadar event by inputting the QID. Then all events that match this criteria

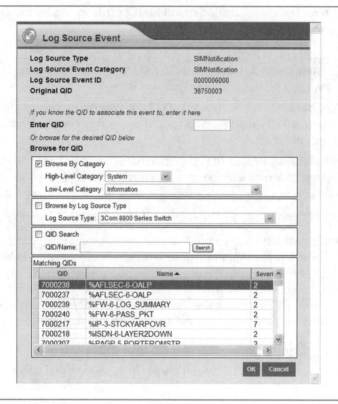

**Figure 13-14.** QRadar Event Mapping Tool

will be assigned the QRadar QID as they are received. This mapping allows QRadar to identify, parse, normalize, store, process, and correlate these new incoming events correctly and provides the utmost functionality for your environment.

## Replacing the QRadar SSL Certificates

QRadar uses Secure Socket Layer (SSL) to secure (encrypt) all communications between QRadar systems and between the Admin console and the QRadar system within your organization's network. QRadar provides a default SSL certificate for easy installation and implementation. However, this default certificate fails the certificate validation tests performed by your administrative systems that interface with the QRadar system, as it should, since the certificate was created by a Certification Authority (CA) that is not on your organization's CA trust list. If you accept the certificate validation error and move forward, the security mechanism for the SSL tunnel functions properly. The secure channel will be established. But you have now accepted the risk that you may possibly be connected to, and securely sharing information with, the wrong SSL server. In this case, the SSL server is the QRadar appliance. The SSL client is the administrator's web browser that is connecting to the QRadar appliance. To eliminate this (pesky) error and ensure the most secure environment for your organization, this SSL certificate should be replaced with a certificate from a trusted CA.

QRadar requires that you employ a Certificatation Authority (CA) to issue the trusted certificate for use within your QRadar environment, as you cannot replace the untrusted certificate with another untrusted certificate.

## Overview of SSL

Secure Sockets Layer (SSL) is the transaction security protocol used by web sites, web browsers, and other network components to provide an encrypted communications link between various devices throughout an enterprise. SSL has become an industry standard for secure network transmissions. To establish and use an SSL connection, the server component in a client/server process must be issued an SSL certificate by a CA. This certificate is used to strongly validate the identity of the server to the client (*server authentication*) and to establish the encrypted channel between the client and server. This SSL certificate is imported or accepted by the SSL server (the QRadar appliance) and stored in what is known as a *keystore* or a *certificate store*. When a client (the administrator's browser) attempts to connect to the SSL server, the SSL server sends a copy of the certificate to the client, as proof of the server's identity. In addition, the certificate carries an encryption key for the client to use to establish the secure SSL channel.

SSL certificates can be issued by

- **Private Certification Authorities (CA)**  Using publicly available software, which includes Open SSL or Microsoft's Certificate Services Manager, these CAs can issue SSL certificates. These certificates are not inherently trusted by browsers or network components because they are not issued by a recognized authority. These types of private certificate services are considered to be self-signed. Although they can be used for encrypting data, there is no third-party assurance regarding the identity of the server that is using the certificate. Untrusted certificates typically generates certificate errors when encountered by applications.

- **Public, trusted third-party CAs**  These CAs, like VeriSign, Entrust, or Thawte, use their trusted position to issue SSL certificates that are automatically trusted by most operating systems and applications.

Most browsers and operating systems include a preinstalled store of trusted Certification Authorities, known as the Trusted Root CA store. For the purpose of establishing SSL connections between QRadar components, and between the administrator's browser and the QRadar appliance, QRadar will trust any certificate that is issued, directly or indirectly, from a trusted CA that is in the Trusted Root CA store.

## Updating QRadar's UnTrusted Certificate

Following are the steps required to replace the default certificate with a certificate issued from a trusted CA to ensure proof-of-server identity (the correct QRadar appliance) and secure communications between QRadar components (the SSL tunnel).

**NOTE** SSL certificates issued from some vendors, such as VeriSign, typically will certify a private intermediate CA server. This intermediate CA server issues the replacement SSL certificate for the QRadar system. In addition to importing the new SSL certificate on the QRadar systems, you must also download and install the certificate from the intermediate CA during the configuration process. Certificates from trusted CAs can be acquired for a fee and expire after a predetermined period of time, typically one to two years. They will need to be renewed periodically.

The first step in this process is to obtain a certificate from a trusted Certificatation Authority. After you have received the trusted certificate, log in to your QRadar system using the root credentials.

**Using a Trusted Root CA**    If you did not use an intermediate CA, enter the following command from within the QRadar command-line interface (CLI) to begin the migration process:

```
/opt/qradar/bin/install_ssl_cert.sh -b
```

After entering this command, a series of messages and prompts will appear, at the end of which you will be prompted to enter the directory path for your private key file. After you have input the path to the private key file and pressed ENTER, you will be prompted to enter the directory path for your public key file. After you have input the path to the public key file and pressed ENTER, a series of messages and prompts appear detailing your current selections. You will then be prompted to continue and reconfigure the Apache system. At this particular prompt, simply input **Y** and press ENTER. You will see another series of messages that detail the status of the migration process. After you have received the successful status message, simply restart the host context process on all non-console systems in your deployment by entering this command:

```
service hostcontext restart
```

The certificates must be replaced on each QRadar appliance in the environment to completely eliminate the certificate errors and secure the environment.

**Using a Trusted Root and Intermediate CA**    If you use an intermediate CA, you must import a second certificate on the QRadar systems. Enter the following command from within the QRadar interface to begin the migration process:

```
/opt/qradar/bin/install_ssl_cert.sh -i
```

After entering this command, a series of messages and prompts will appear and then you will be prompted to enter the directory path for your private key file. After you have input the path to the private key file and pressed ENTER, you will be prompted to enter the directory path for your public key file. After you have input the path to the public key file and pressed ENTER, a prompt requesting that you enter the directory path for your intermediate key file is displayed. Simply provide the directory path to your intermediate certificate file and press ENTER. A series of messages and prompts will appear detailing your current selections. After the messages complete, you will be prompted to continue and reconfigure the Apache system. At this particular prompt, simply input **Y** and press ENTER to initiate another series of messages that detail the status of the migration process. After you have received the successful status message, simply restart the host context process on all non-console systems in your deployment by entering this command:

```
service hostcontext restart
```

As before, the certificates must be replaced on each QRadar appliance in the environment to eliminate certificate errors and secure the environment completely.

# Stepping Through the Process

Now that you have learned some of the advanced techniques as they pertain to content development and administration of the QRadar system, you are ready to step through a typical day in the life of a security analyst while using the QRadar product. Remember you can view events and flows from the various network devices that have and have not been correlated into Offenses from within the QRadar administrative console. This correlation process is a huge benefit for using any SIEM product, allowing you to develop content (Views, Sentries, DSMs, Rules, etc.) that will filter out the "noise" and provide you with all of the events or flows that are pertinent and are worthy of, or even require, some sort of investigation, analysis, and remediation. Throughout the rest of this chapter, you will go through the process involved in analyzing events that are being sent to your QRadar system, determining their validity, remediating the issue and then finishing with building the content to allow QRadar to monitor proactively for that event type and respond accordingly.

## Analyzing Events

To set the scene: You are an analyst for XYZ Corporation. Your job consists of monitoring the QRadar Dashboard for any malicious activity found within the corporation's network. Figure 13-15 depicts the custom dashboard that you have created to more efficiently view the events, flows, and Offenses of interest and concern within your network.

So you have grabbed your cup of coffee and entered your area within the Security Operations Center (SOC) ready to log into the QRadar console. You scan the top-left corner of the console to see if any new Offenses have been detected. The view says no activity was found during the past eight (8) hours. You then scan to the Top Rules Fired view, and observe an even distribution of rules. This means that no excessive number of rules have fired that would trigger massive amounts of actions and responses. Next,

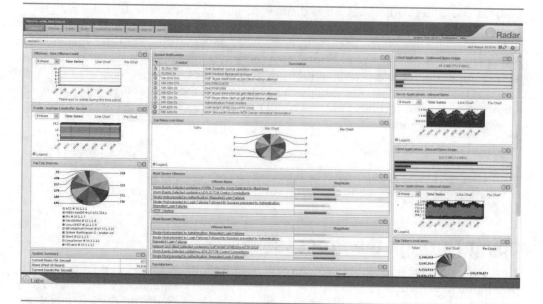

**Figure 13-15.**   QRadar Dashboard

you want to see the events being processed by the QRadar system. You first look at the Events – Average Events Per Second view. This view tells you the types and number of events that are being processed by the QRadar system over the past eight (8) hours. Figure 13-16 shows this view with the legend displayed.

As you can see in Figure 13-16, there are a number of Suspicious, Potential_Exploit, DoS, and Unknown activity events. This gets your attention. You wonder what's up.

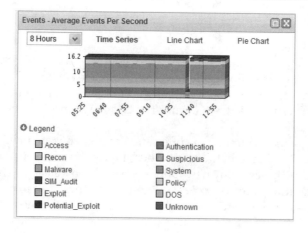

**Figure 13-16.**   QRadar Dashboard: Events – Average Events Per Second line chart

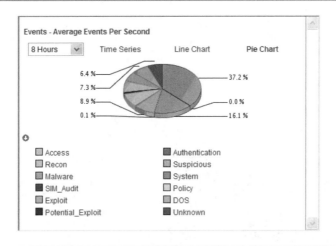

**Figure 13-17.**    QRadar Dashboard: Events – Average Events Per Second pie chart

One way to get a better picture of the percentage of events of these types is to switch the view from line chart to pie chart. You do this by selecting the Pie Chart option within the Average Events Per Second view and then see the graph shown in Figure 13-17.

Based upon the organization's security policy—your official playbook—the organization's threshold of tolerance for the event type of Suspicious is 5 percent. You are now "officially" concerned about the 7.3 percent of events that are classified as Suspicious. You must investigate these Suspicious events further to determine if there is a real threat, or if you are seeing some sort of false-positive alert and you need to tune the QRadar Rules to exclude these nonthreatening events. Meanwhile, your coffee has gotten quite cold.

The next step in the investigation is to switch to the Events screen, which will show all of the events streaming into the QRadar system. Simply click the Events tab in order to transition from the Dashboard to the Events interface. What you see are the events streaming "live" into the QRadar Inbound Events channel. These live events present what is happening in real-time within your environment. You see many events streaming in very quickly. You need to build a filter quickly in order to limit the stream to display only the events you are concerned with. Those are, of course, the events categorized as Suspicious.

You click on the Search icon to begin the process of building your filter for your current live channel. Please note that the filter is being applied to the current display of live events being seen on the Events interface. This filter will not replace any stored views, though you can save the filtered channel for future use. From the pull-down menu, select the New Event Search option. The resulting display, shown in Figure 13-18, shows you how to begin developing your filter in order to display only pertinent, relevant information so you can further your investigation.

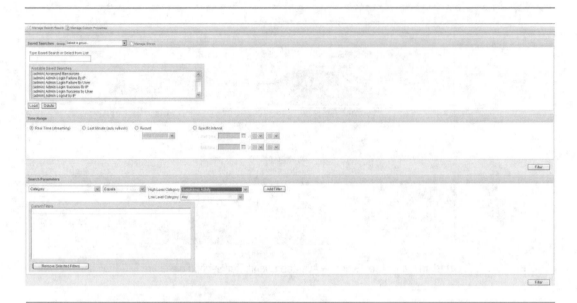

**Figure 13-18.**   Building a QRadar filter using Search for Category

To continue with your investigation, you perform the following actions. To determine what type of events are currently being reported as Suspicious in the live channel, you will keep the Time Range set to Real Time. Under the Search Parameters, from the first pull-down, select Category. Leave the condition of Equals because you want to find specific categories that match a specified value. From the pull-down menu for the High Level Category value, select the Suspicious Activity option. Leave the Low Level Category as Any, as you are mainly concerned with the High Level Category events pertaining to suspicious activity. Next, you select the Add Filter option to add it to the Current Filters parameters box. Then select the Filter option to apply the filter to the current screen.

This is where the power of the SIEM system begins to show itself. Because of the QRadar's capabilities to normalize the events streaming into the console quickly, you can limit views to just the important events related to the specific investigation—in real time! Figure 13-19 shows the results of applying this filter.

As you can see, QRadar is parsing many events that match the filter criteria. The column that should draw your attention first is the Magnitude column (the right-most column). As you read earlier, the magnitude of an event is QRadar's interpretation of the effects of this event as it pertains to the configuration of the environment. To further refine your vision of the most serious Suspicious events, you will build on this filter to view only the events that have a category of Suspicious Activity with a Magnitude of 6 or higher. You will select the Search option again, but this time you are going to select the Edit Search function. Figure 13-20 shows the search criteria after the Magnitude threshold adjustment.

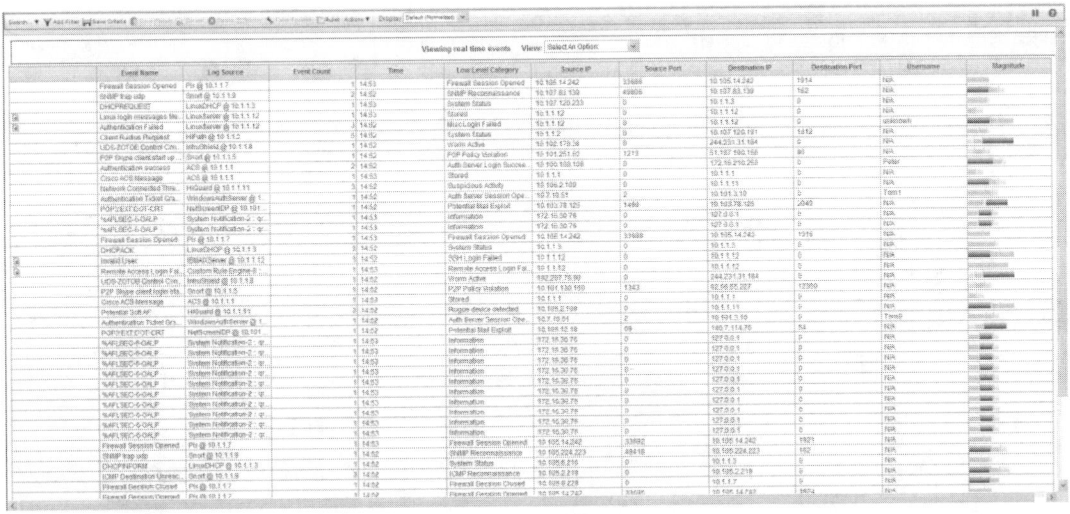

**Figure 13-19.**   Search Event Categories Results

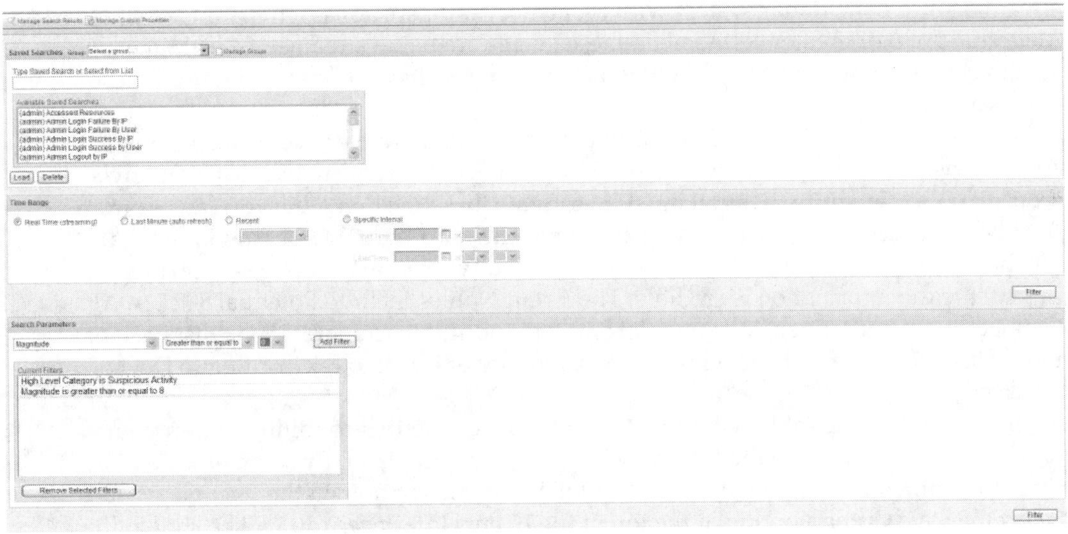

**Figure 13-20.**   Building a QRadar filter using Search for Category and Magnitude

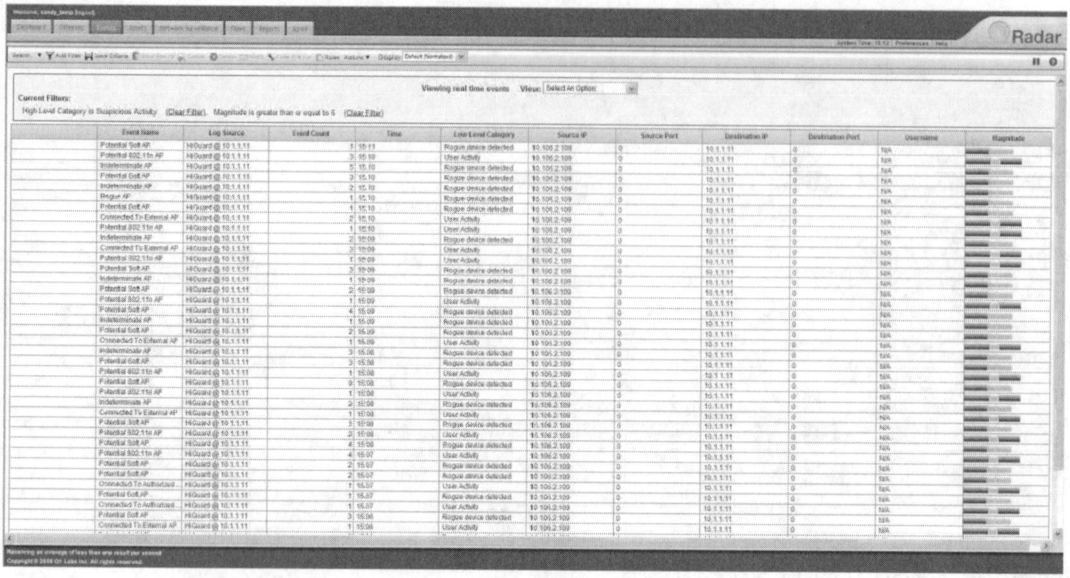

**Figure 13-21.** Search Event Categories and Magnitude results

After applying the new filter, Figure 13-21 shows the refined results of the events streaming into the QRadar system with a Category of Suspicious Activity and a Magnitude of 6 or greater. Remember, these events are being streamed in real time, so it may take a few moments for QRadar to return results as it has to wait until these events are captured.

As you can see in the Low Level Category column, there are several suspicious User Activity events, as well as Rogue Device Detected events on the network. Company security policies require that you must investigate these incidents. As you can see from the Log Source column, the reporting system is HiGuard @ 10.1.1.111. You know that HiGuard is a well-configured and well-maintained wireless IPS device, so you are pretty sure the information is credible. The Event Names include Potential 802.11n AP, Connected To Authorized AP, Potential Soft AP, and Indeterminate AP events. Each of these Suspicious events have a Low Level Category of User Activity or Rogue Device Detected.

Since you have spent time building the filters locating this condition within your network, you should save the filter so you can use it again later. By saving the Search filter content, you can access it using the Quick Searches option on the Events interface. Select the Save Criteria option at the top of the Events interface. You will be shown the dialog in Figure 13-22, which will allow you to save your current Search.

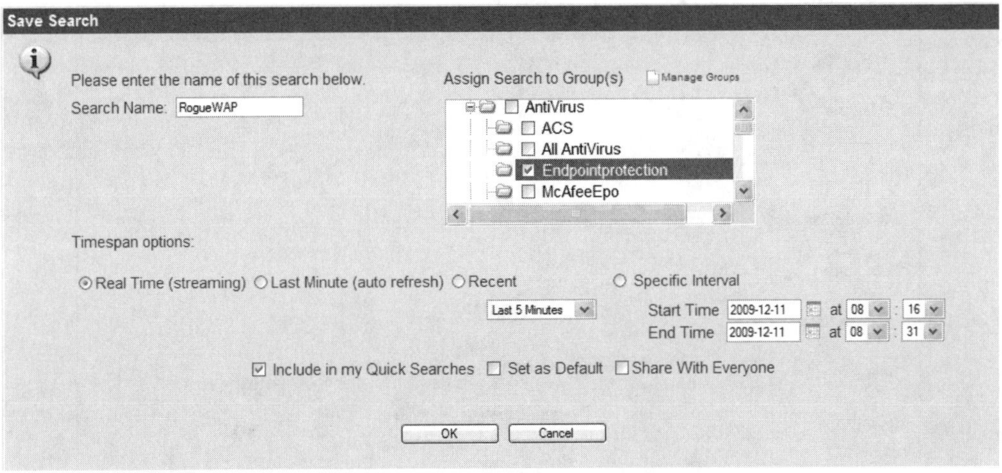

**Figure 13-22.** Save Search dialog box

As you can see in Figure 13-22, this Search has been named RogueWAP and placed in the Search Group called Endpointprotection. You now click OK and continue with the investigation.

As you watch the live events stream through the channel, you notice a bit of a pattern forming. It appears that when you see the Potential Soft AP and Indeterminate AP events, they are categorized as Rogue Device Detected; and when you see Potential 802.11n AP and the Connected To Authorized AP events, they are categorized as User Activity. This tells you that an AP is attempting to connect to the network and the AP is being authorized to connect by some type of user activity.

Next, you attempt to find out if the source IP attempting to connect and configure the rogue device is an asset defined within the QRadar Network Hierarchy. Note the IP address of the source machine, and then select the Assets tab at the top of the console. Figure 13-23 depicts the Asset Profile Search tab where you begin searching the QRadar Network Hierarchy for this source IP.

You then input the IP address of the source machine that, it seems, is attempting to connect this unauthorized access point to the network. You select Search, and to no avail, nothing comes up. It appears the system attempting to attach the access point to your network is not a member of your organization, though it does have a private IP that is compatible with your IP subnets. This leads you to conclude that, based on the events streaming into the QRadar system, a wireless access point is attempting to join your wireless infrastructure. Your HiGuard IPS is unable to identify the type of AP, so it reports the rogue device as an Indeterminate Access Point. It seems the rogue AP

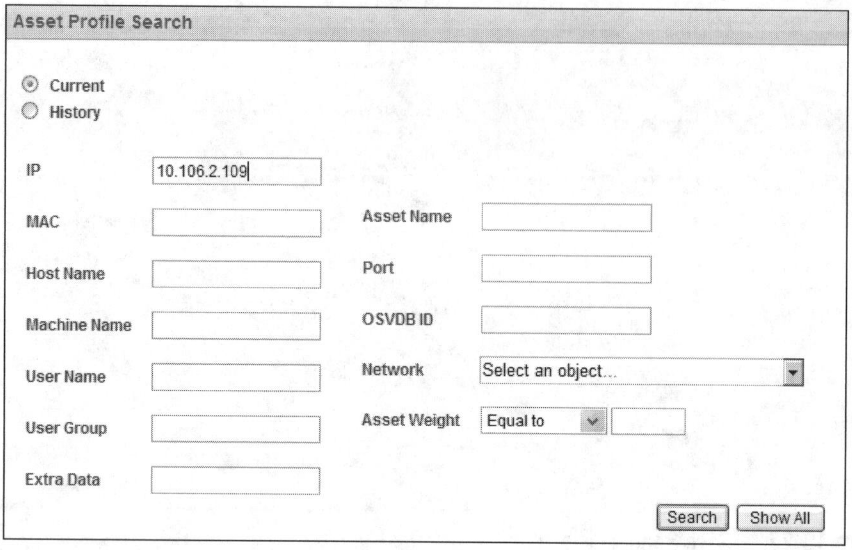

**Figure 13-23.**    Asset Profile Search tab

receives an internally assigned IP address from the DHCP server. It is, of course, against policy to connect this access point to the network.

Now the next item on the list of things to do is to contact the manager of the department where the HiGuard system is located and tell her that she must meet the IT administrator, who is on his way down, to determine where this rogue AP is and shut it down. Your company uses handheld wireless survey meters to locate wireless sources, like this rogue AP.

Good job! You have worked an incident from initial observation to conclusion by viewing events from the Dashboard. You have stopped a potential security risk to your environment. You aren't, however, done. Wouldn't it be easier to have the QRadar system draw these same conclusions on its own and programmatically notify the appropriate resources to mitigate the problem? And then utilize a configured tracking mechanism to see if this activity persists, and, furthermore, try to determine who is attempting to violate your organization's security policies? Of course! You will build a Rule and a report to show what has been happening on the network.

To configure this automated system, as you will recall from earlier sections of this chapter, you will select the Offenses tab. On the left-hand side, select the Rules option. From the Actions pull-down, select the New Event Rule to create a rule that captures these events, and generates the proper notifications to help to enforce the corporate policy against rogue devices on the network. Figure 13-24 shows the locations of the Offenses screen where you will build the New Event Rule.

The first step, presented in Figure 13-25, shows the Custom Rules Wizard Rule Test Stack Editor. As you can see, you have named the rule RogueAP, and assigned

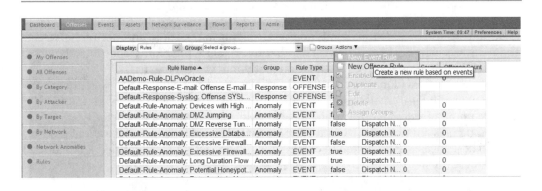

**Figure 13-24.** Building a New Event Rule

it to the Policy Rules Group. Next, you should select the test When The Event(s) Were Detected By One Or More Of *These Log Sources*. In this case, the log source is the HiGuard @ 10.1.1.11.

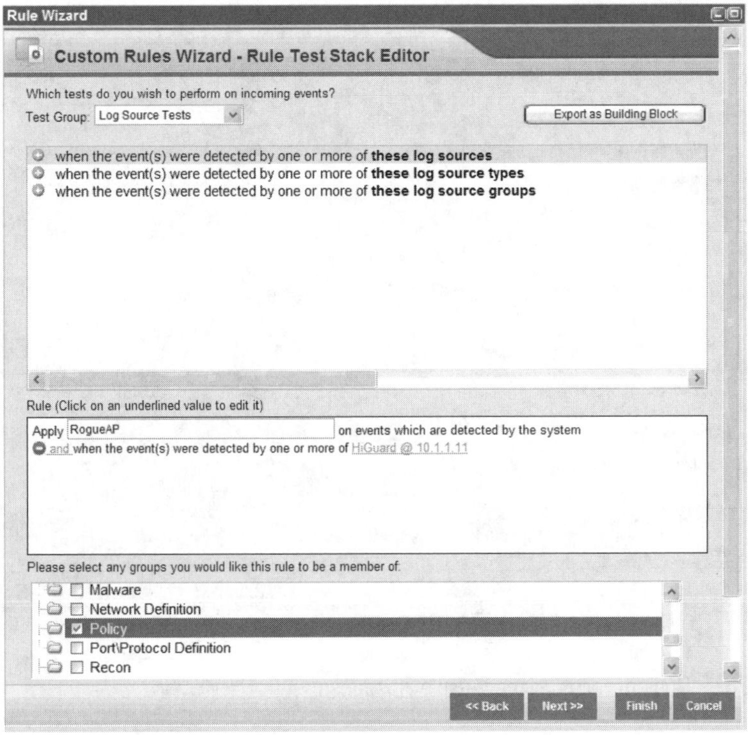

**Figure 13-25.** Custom Rules Wizard Rule Test Stack Editor

Click Next to continue building the new Rule to provide the proactive security processes. As you can see in Figure 13-26, you should configure the Rule to email the IT administrator, include the details about the events in question, and notify the SOC about any occurrences of this type of activity by enabling the Notify checkbox. Now you click Finish to save and close the Rule that you have just created.

This new Rule will monitor for this activity and, if fired, will add the event(s) as part of an Offense, email the IT administrator an alert, and add the event to the Dashboard as a System Notification. Now to determine if this type of activity is happening on your network, you can simply go to the Offenses interface and check it out. These measures are taken to ensure this type of activity is identified and stopped more efficiently in the future.

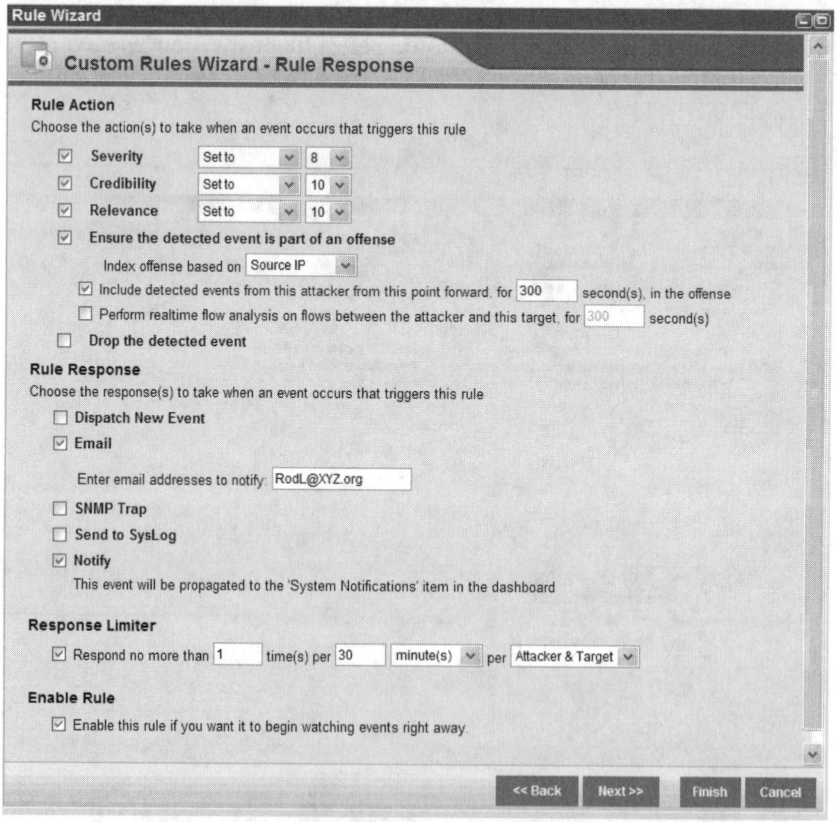

**Figure 13-26.**   Custom Rules Wizard – Rule Response

**TIP** Remember the steps that you have followed within this scenario can be applied not only to events, but also to flows as well. Instead of using the Events interface, you would use the Flows interface and perform many of the same functions described here.

Job well done! Now get back to work. There are new flows and events arriving every second.

# Summary

The QRadar system—with its many preconfigured components such as the Dashboard, default Views, Sentries, Device Support Modules (DSMs), Rules, and the Offense Manager—is perhaps the easiest SIEM system to get up and running. In addition, QRadar allows for fine-tuning, providing easy-to-use Wizards to construct your own custom content. This allows you to quickly and regularly knock down that unnecessarily time-consuming collection of false-positive events. QRadar is scalable to very large environments and is easy to navigate to focus rapidly on targets of interest. If your organization is scoping out the purchase of a new SIEM system, for the small business, medium business, the large enterprise, or just for a smaller division or branch of the organization, be sure they take a long and worthy look at the Q1 Labs QRadar system.

# CHAPTER 14 | ArcSight ESM v4.5 Implementation

A rcSight Inc., is a publicly traded corporation, founded in 2000, that specializes in security management products. ArcSight has several security products for a range of companies of different sizes, but their main products revolve around ArcSight's SEIM platform, the ArcSight ESM v4.5.

ArcSight's products are used in a wide range of corporate, government, and educational environments to detect security threats to these organizations and to demonstrate compliance with security regulatory standards to which these environments must adhere. By leveraging ArcSight v4.5 with your organization's security policy, you can actively monitor security across your network while maximizing your security team's time. The ArcSight v4.5 is not only designed to work as the focal point for your security team, bringing feeds from all of your devices into a centralized event repository, but it also has optional packages to demonstrate compliance with SOX, PCI, HIPAA, and several other security regulations.

## ArcSight Terminology and Concepts

ArcSight uses specific terms when describing its products and how they operate. The following is a list of terms and their definitions. Knowing these will make navigating the planning and installation process easier.

- **ArcSight ESM v4.5 Manager**   This piece acts as the CPU for ArcSight ESM v4.5. This application decrypts and decompresses events being sent from the ArcSight SmartConnectors, processes these logs based on predefined or user-defined rules, sends those logs to the database for storage, and queries the database looking for historical information.

- **ArcSight ESM v4.5 Database**   This is the Oracle Database 10g, which ArcSight ESM uses to store the events received from other devices, system configuration, and event rule sets. The current version of the database supported is Oracle 10.2.0.4.

- **ArcSight ESM v4.5 Partition Archiver**   The ArcSight ESM v4.5 Partition Archiver handles maintenance activity in the Oracle Database. The Partition Archiver will update database statistics at user-configurable intervals throughout the day, archive database partitions that have fallen out of your retention period window, and decompress and remount archived partitions when the ArcSight administrators reactivate partitions.

- **ArcSight ESM v4.5 Console**   The ArcSight ESM v4.5 Console is a Java application that runs on a variety of platforms and acts as your interface to the ArcSight ESM v4.5. Your organization's incident handlers will use this application to monitor your environment for security incidents and the engineers will use it to configure ArcSight ESM v4.5.

- **ArcSight SmartConnector**   An ArcSight SmartConnector is a piece of software that collects logs from a wide variety of devices, parses those logs into a format that the ArcSight ESM can work with, and sends the logs to the ArcSight Manager.

- **ArcSight ESM v4.5 Web** This web interface acts as a lightweight ArcSight console. It is designed to be populated with preconfigured dashboards and active channels that can be viewed through a web interface. This primarily allows for quick access to specific information for the security incident handlers or other members of your organization who require access.

- **Events per second (EPS)** This is the number of events generated per a single device or a group of devices per second. Normally it is used to calculate how many events are being sent to the ArcSight ESM v4.5 to determine if you are within the recommended processing range.

- **Common Event Format (CEF)** This format is the one in which ArcSight ESM v4.5 will parse logs generated by other devices.

- **Base event** A base event is an event generated from a device. An example of this would be a single Windows event from a Windows 2003 Server security event log or a log from a router/switch.

- **Correlated event** A correlated event is an event that is triggered off of logic in a rule or rules. The conditions of the rule use Boolean logic, which looks for certain base events that occur in a specific logical or defined order. An example of this would be a possible brute-force attack correlated event, which is triggered off of multiple failed login events each from the same source address, attempting to log in with the same user name.

- **Correlation event** A correlation event is the product of the conditions within the rule being met. This event goes through the correlation engine again to be compared to other content to provide further automated analysis of the network and the events being transmitted.

# Overview of ArcSight Products

Being a premier security product company, ArcSight has several products that can be scaled to most environments. Most of ArcSight's products are based on the same underlying technology as the ArcSight ESM v4.5 SEIM platform. The main ArcSight products will be expanded upon in the sections that follow. Some of these products can either be used as stand-alone products or as part of the total ArcSight ESM v4.5 deployment.

- ArcSight ESM v4.5
- ArcSight SmartConnectors
- ArcSight Express
- ArcSight Logger

# ArcSight ESM v4.5

The ArcSight ESM v4.5 is ArcSight's premier SEIM product and it is what most people are referring to when they discuss an ArcSight deployment. The current major version is ArcSight ESM version 4.5, which was released in 2009. ArcSight ESM v4.5 is an extremely adaptable system, able to handle security monitoring and aid in meeting any compliance requirements. ArcSight can be put to work in small organizations with minimal security staff or deployed in Managed Security Services Providers (MSSP), which provides 24/7 security monitoring for multiple clients.

ArcSight ESM v4.5 is available in two deployment options: as an appliance or as software to install on your own hardware. Each of these deployment methods has their own strengths and weaknesses that need to be taken into consideration when you decide how you want to deploy ArcSight ESM v4.5 to best meet your organization's needs. The first option for deployment is a 2U appliance, running the Oracle Enterprise Linux 4 64-bit version. This self-contained system has the ArcSight Manager and Oracle Database installed on the same appliance. This appliance allows you to rapidly deploy ArcSight ESM v4.5 in your environment. The second option— software—can be installed on your own hardware and OS.

## As an Appliance

As an appliance, ArcSight ESM v4.5 is relatively easy to get up and running in a short amount of time because you do not need to worry about the backend configuration of the Oracle Database or hardware. The appliance is designed to be a turnkey solution to get your ArcSight ESM v4.5 deployment up and running in a minimal amount of time. A long-term benefit of running ArcSight ESM v4.5 as an appliance is that you will not need to allocate personnel to administer patches for the appliance's underlying OS or perform other maintenance tasks.

One thing that you may want to consider when deploying ArcSight ESM v4.5 as an appliance is that it can be difficult to scale up as your environment grows because of the hardware limitations of the particular appliance model you are using. See Table 14-1 for detailed information on the ArcSight ESM appliance. Also the longevity of this system may be something you want to take into consideration. Since this is an appliance, the only way to upgrade the system is to replace an older appliance with a newer model.

## On Your Hardware

When installing ArcSight ESM v4.5 on your own hardware, you should understand that this option will require more of your organization's resources and time than deploying the ArcSight ESM v4.5 appliance. You will need to manage the storage requirements, backend Oracle Database, and patching of the system. You should have an intimate understanding of the Oracle Database being used and the OS that your ArcSight ESM v4.5 is installed on. This knowledge helps immensely when diagnosing problems or if you are ever in a position where you need to contact ArcSight for customer support.

What you lose in terms of deployment, installation, and management, however, you gain in the overall scalability of your ArcSight system. Because ArcSight ESM v4.5 is running on your own hardware, you can add more system resources when you

| | |
|---|---|
| Model | E7200 |
| Maximum EPS | 5000 EPS |
| Sustainable EPS | 3000 EPS |
| CPU | 2 * Intel Xeon E5504 Quad Core |
| RAM | 24GB |
| Storage | 6 * 600GB SAS drives (RAID 10) |
| Network interfaces | 4 * gigabit Ethernet |
| Power supply | Redundant |

**Table 14-1.**   ArcSight ESM Appliance E7200

determine they are needed. If your organization's log retention policy grows over time, you can add more storage space for archives. If you exceed the maximum EPS that your current system can manage, then you can migrate to new hardware relatively easily. This ability to grow ArcSight ESM v4.5 as needed adds to the system's longevity.

One of the first things you may want to take into account when deciding to run ArcSight ESM v4.5 on your own hardware is that unlike the ArcSight ESM v4.5 appliance, which is one 2U server, if you run ArcSight ESM v4.5 on your own hardware, you will need a minimum of two separate servers because ArcSight does not support running the ArcSight ESM v4.5 and its Oracle Database on the same server. Rack space, power requirements, OS licensing, and server costs should be taken into consideration when choosing to install ArcSight ESM v4.5 on your own hardware.

**Supported Hardware**   ArcSight ESM v4.5 can be installed on most current hardware platforms in use in today's enterprise environments. For Microsoft Windows or Linux systems, at minimum, it is recommended to have at least 2GB of RAM, 2GB of free hard-drive space, and a 32-bit or 64-bit architecture CPU for the ArcSight ESM v4.5 Manager server. With this configuration, your ArcSight ESM v4.5 deployment will be adequate for a small environment. As the number of log sources or the number of EPS increases, you will need to expand the hardware on your servers. More memory, faster processors, and more hard-drive space may be needed to accommodate growth.

The server that will run the Oracle database has minimum hardware requirements of 512MB of RAM, 2GB of free hard-drive space, and a 32-bit or 64-bit architecture CPU. These minimum hardware requirements are just for the Oracle Database 10g software and do not take into account the size of the actual database needed, the hard-drive space requirements for your offline log archives, or the number of events that your ArcSight ESM v4.5 system will be processing. These factors need to be taken into account when determining the hardware requirements for your ArcSight ESM v4.5 deployment. Hardware requirements for the ArcSight Manager and ArcSight Database servers are listed in Table 14-2.

|  | ArcSight ESM v4.5 Manager | ArcSight ESM v4.5 Database (Oracle 10g) |
|---|---|---|
| RAM | 2–4GB | 2–16GB |
| Free hard-drive space | 2GB | 2GB |
| CPU architecture | 32-bit or 64-bit | 32-bit or 64-bit |

**Table 14-2.** ArcSight ESM Minimum Hardware Requirements

**Supported Operating Systems**  The ArcSight ESM v4.5 Manager and Database are supported on Microsoft Windows Server 2003, RedHat Linux, IBM AIX, and Sun Solaris, listed in Table 14-3. On these platforms, ArcSight ESM v4.5 can be run on the 32-bit and 64-bit versions of the operating systems. You will gain a performance advantage from running ArcSight ESM v4.5 on 64-bit OSs, however, because a 64-bit OS allows for better memory management and the underlying OS will be able to take advantage of newer 64-bit CPUs.

All the ArcSight components can run on 64-bit operating systems, even though they are only 32-bit applications. The ArcSight ESM v4.5 Manager is the only component that has a native 64-bit version available for installation on Microsoft Windows Server 2003 or RedHat Linux. The version of the Oracle Database can be 32-bit or 64-bit, depending on the architecture it is being run on.

| Operating System | Manager (32-bit Application) | Manager (64-bit Application) | Database (32-bit Application) | Console (32-bit Application) | SmartConnector (32-bit Application) |
|---|---|---|---|---|---|
| Windows 2003 (32- or 64-bit) | X | X | X | X | X |
| RedHat Linux (32- or 64-bit) | X | X | X | X | X |
| IBM AIX 5L (64-bit) | X |  | X | X | X |
| Sun Solaris 9/10 (32- or 64-bit) | X |  | X | X | X |
| Mac OS X (32- or 64-bit) |  |  |  | X |  |

**Table 14-3.** ArcSight ESM Component Supported Operating Systems

# ArcSight SmartConnectors

The ArcSight SmartConnector is the application that brings the logs into ArcSight ESM v4.5. Preconfigured SmartConnectors are available that can bring in and properly parse logs for over 250 devices. These devices range from security-specific devices such enterprise-class IDSs to standard operating systems. Once the logs are collected from their devices, they are normalized to the ArcSight common event format (CEF). This allows the ArcSight ESM v4.5 Manager to process these logs more quickly, since the normalization is done at the connector. Much like the ArcSight ESM v4.5, you have two deployment options: an ArcSight SmartConnector appliance and as an application that can be installed on your own hardware.

## As a SmartConnector Appliance

With the ArcSight SmartConnector appliance, you can configure the connectors via a web-based management console. The ArcSight SmartConnector appliances currently come in three different models, as described in Table 14-4. The key differences among the models, besides the hardware specifications, are the recommended maximum EPS that the appliance can handle and the amount of space that is available for caching of events.

## As SmartConnector Software

This software can be loaded on any hardware or operating system that the ArcSight ESM v4.5 software can be installed on. With this installation package comes the ability to create a connector to process logs from any of the supported devices and beyond. What makes the SmartConnector application so versatile is what is known as a FlexConnector. A *FlexConnector* is a framework, developed by ArcSight, that allows users to create their own connectors for nonsupported devices. When developing a FlexConnector, you need to determine what types of logs you will be parsing. Are the logs in XML, csv, or flat file format, or are you connecting to a database? Then you will need to configure the connector to parse the logs. This flexibility allows you to adapt ArcSight to your environment even if you are using homegrown applications or nonsupported devices.

| Model | Maximum EPS | Cache Size |
|-------|-------------|------------|
| C1000 | 400 | 120GB |
| C3200 | 2,500 | 500GB |
| C5200 | 5,000 | 500GB (RAID 1) |

**Table 14-4.**  ArcSight Connector Appliances

## ArcSight Express

ArcSight Express is a specialized, scaled-down model of ArcSight ESM v4.5 designed to be a turnkey solution for small businesses with limited security staff on hand. It has been preconfigured with rules, reports, and dashboards that are specifically targeted at customers who want an automated system that can be deployed rapidly in order to aid in their environment's overall security and compliance. ArcSight Express comes in five appliance models, with the major differentiation among the models being the number of assets that can be managed, the number of devices that can feed logs into the system, and the maximum EPS managed by each appliance (see Table 14-5).

## ArcSight Logger

One of the biggest problems when dealing with any SEIM deployment or log management project in general is the sheer volume of logs that you will need to work with. ArcSight has come up with a solution to this problem in their ArcSight Logger appliance. What the ArcSight Logger does is it allows you to combine enterprise log management, operational log monitoring from infrastructure devices, and security

| Model | Maximum Network Devices | Maximum Desktops | Maximum EPS | Maximum Assets | Drive Space |
|---|---|---|---|---|---|
| L3200 | 50 | 100 | 500 | 5,000 | 8TB (RAID 1 w/ 2*1TB drives) |
| M7200-M | 50 | 100 | 500 | 5,000 | 1.6TB (RAID 10 w/ 6*600GB drives) |
| M7200-L | 100 | 250 | 1,000 | 10,000 | 1.6TB (RAID 10 w/ 6*600GB drives) |
| M7200-X | 250 | 500 | 2,500 | 25,000 | 1.6TB (RAID 10 w/ 6*600GB drives) |
| M7200-XL | 500 | 1,000 | 5,000 | 50,000 | 1.6TB (RAID 10 w/ 6*600GB drives) |

**Table 14-5.** ArcSight Express Configurations

monitoring into a single task. The ArcSight Logger allows for searching of all of these logs via field-based or unstructured queries. Searching through logs stored on this server can be equated to using a web search engine to comb the Internet for specific information. Once these logs are in the Logger appliance, you can split out the logs needed for security to the ArcSight ESM for security monitoring. This product is not necessarily a component of an ArcSight ESM v4.5 implementation, but adds a layer of log management that improves upon the ArcSight ESM v4.5.

# ArcSight ESM v4.5 Architecture Overview

Understanding how the data flows through the entire ArcSight process will help you better design your implementation. Figure 14-1 is an overview of how the ArcSight ESM v4.5 architecture communicates with all of its components.

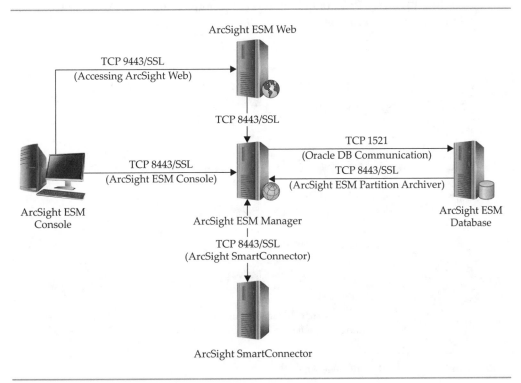

**Figure 14-1.** ArcSight ESM v4.5 architecture overview

The following is a typical scenario for logs coming from a device and how they are stored in the Oracle database:

1. *ArcSight SmartConnector receives logs.* The ArcSight SmartConnector can use either a push or pull method for obtaining the logs. Some logs, such as syslog, are pushed directly from the device to the ArcSight SmartConnector and all the SmartConnector does is listen for these logs to come in. Whereas with Windows Event logs, the ArcSight SmartConnector needs to be configured with server information and user login credentials in order to make a connection to the server to pull the logs. With the push method, the device pushes its logs to ArcSight, as shown in Figure 14-2, and with a pull method, ArcSight initiates the log retrieval process, as shown in Figure 14-3. The difference is which side initiates the communications.

2. *ArcSight SmartConnector processes logs.* No matter which format the logs use, the ArcSight SmartConnector will begin processing the logs into a format that the ArcSight ESM v4.5 can understand. This format is called the ArcSight Common Event Format (CEF).

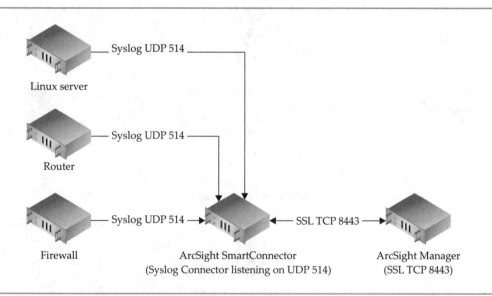

**Figure 14-2.**    ArcSight SmartConnector push

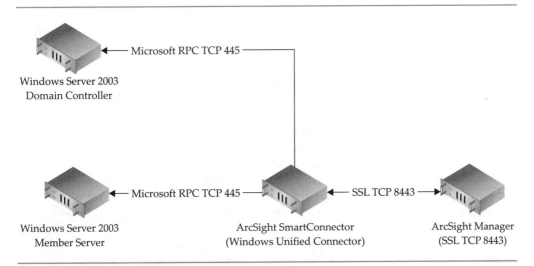

**Figure 14-3.** ArcSight SmartConnector pull

3. *ArcSight SmartConnector compresses and encrypts logs.* These logs are sent over SSL port 8443 to the ArcSight Manager. In order to secure transmission, the logs will be encrypted using a self-signed certificate generated from the ArcSight ESM v4.5 manager or a certificate generated from your CA. The logs are also compressed to reduce network utilization. These logs can be set to be transmitted real-time or set to be sent only at specific times. If ArcSight ESM v4.5 Manager is down or cannot keep up with the number of events, the connector will cache events. All communication between the ArcSight Manager and ArcSight SmartConnector is encrypted using the HTTPS protocol over TCP port 8443. This communication is bidirectional, meaning that either end of the ArcSight data flow stream can initiate the communication. This allows the Manager to push instructions to the connectors.

4. *ArcSight Manager receives logs.* The ArcSight Manager authenticates the incoming connection to ensure the connector sending traffic is allowed to send to this ArcSight ESM v4.5. The manager will then terminate the SSL connection from the connector, decrypt, and decompress the logs.

5. *ArcSight Manager processes logs.* The ArcSight Manager will begin processing the logs, applying rules to these logs, and combining events into a correlated event if the rule logic has been met.

6. *ArcSight Manager generates alerts.* Depending on how your rules are configured, ArcSight can send off alerts via email, or display these notifications within the console and web interface when certain events have occurred or event thresholds have been met.

7. *ArcSight Manager sends logs to ArcSight database.* The manager will communicate with the ArcSight Oracle Database instance on the database server to store the events in the database.

8. *Oracle Database stores events.* Once the Oracle Database has received the logs from the ArcSight Manager, it indexes the events for faster future retrieval.

As you can see, this process is fairly secure because it uses secure protocols for a majority of the data exchange. There are only two possible places in this communication process that may not be encrypted. When the ArcSight manager sends the events to the database using Oracle port TCP 1521, this traffic is never encrypted. The second place depends on which SmartConnector you have installed. If you are using syslog, for example, the logs are coming to the SmartConnector via UDP. By the very nature of this format, logs sent via this method will not be secure and there is no guaranteed delivery. Other SmartConnectors will be more secure, such as the Windows Unified Connector that uses Windows RPC to transfer the logs.

# Planning Your Deployment

Prior to purchasing the hardware or software, you will want plan what exactly it is you will be doing and how you will accomplish it. Benjamin Franklin once said, "An ounce of prevention is worth a pound of cure." This sums up your planning process. If you can determine all of your requirements and plan for as many possible setbacks as you can, then it will be that much easier as you progress with this project.

## Determine Goals

Prior to beginning an ArcSight ESM v4.5 deployment, there are several overall questions to answer, but one of the main questions that needs to be resolved prior to planning anything else is "What are the goals of this project?" Are you using ArcSight ESM v4.5 primarily to aid in incident response of security threats on your network? Are you planning on using ArcSight ESM v4.5 to assist in complying with regulatory requirements? Or some combination of the two? Or for something else? The size of these goals will determine the size of the equipment that you need to purchase. Also, if you are using ArcSight to monitor regulatory compliance, you may need to purchase auditors for these features. The scope of this project, as far as how many devices will be feeding into ArcSight ESM v4.5, will establish how much storage will be required. This is increasingly important depending on whether you are using ArcSight as an enterprise log-management solution.

## Manage Assets

In order to plan any proper deployment of ArcSight ESM v4.5, it is important to have a good understanding of the assets in your environment and your network topology. What type of devices will you be receiving logs from? How many of each of these devices will you be managing logs for? How many total devices? Which key devices need special attention? To sum up, what are you going to be looking at?

The number of events per second (EPS), meaning how many events a device will generate per second, along with how many assets you will be feeding into ArcSight ESM v4.5 determine what type of equipment ArcSight ESM v4.5 should be installed on. It would be prudent to get an estimate of how many EPS your proposed ArcSight ESM v4.5 deployment will be processing at a sustainable level and then take into account spikes in this activity.

By knowing what assets you have in your environment, you can determine your key assets. These devices could be storing highly sensitive information that is extremely important to your organization. Knowing this will ensure you put proper security measures in affect for those devices. You can categorize these assets and write specific rules that will alert you, in such a way that they stand out as important, that a severe security breach may have occurred.

One of the other important reasons to understand your network is because some of the rules in ArcSight ESM v4.5 are dependent on network asset information. For instance, some rules are based on virus propagation. If this virus was only able to infect Windows servers, if you saw similar traffic coming from a Linux server, you would know this is a false positive. The rule would look to see if the source address of this possible infection was a Windows server and would only trigger if it was categorized as such. This is one way in which knowing your environment can help eliminate false-positive events from taking up your incident handlers' time.

Is your environment a single LAN or do you have multiple sites? If you have multiple sites, what are the network connections like between them? What are their speeds and current utilization? Can you receive real-time events from devices or will you batch events to be sent when network activity is low, such as during off hours? This type of information will tell you not only where on your network to place ArcSight SmartConnectors, but also if the connectors will queue up events to be sent at specific times. Your operations team will probably appreciate it if you do not use all of the network pipe to push logs through during business hours.

## Determine ArcSight Hardware Requirements

Once you have a good understanding of your environment and what you need to monitor, you can determine hardware requirements for your ArcSight ESM v4.5. There are no hard-defined granular metrics for the hardware required for installing ArcSight ESM v4.5, but logic dictates that the more EPSs you will be processing, the more devices you will have reporting to your ArcSight Manager, and the more security incident handlers who will be using your ArcSight ESM v4.5, the more powerful the hardware you will require. It's best to use the ArcSight ESM v4.5 appliance hardware specifications, along with the EPS and assets management capabilities recommended, in order to begin determining your requirements

When installing ArcSight software onto your own servers, a key factor to take into account is that ArcSight software is written in the Java programming language and runs in a Java Virtual Machine (JVM) on these servers. The JVM runs the Java source code and acts as a self-contained sandbox in system memory. ArcSight ESM v4.5 is soft-coded to use certain resources on the server and will not exceed what system resources it has been allocated. This means you need to keep in mind the Java virtual memory heap size that the applications are configured to use. How much memory is allocated to the JVM memory heap really depends on each installation. You need to allocate enough memory so that *garbage collection,* the way in which a JVM recovers memory that is no longer being used, is not constantly going on. Garbage collection will initiate when your system runs out of usable memory and needs to recover it. The other side of garbage collection is that the size of the JVM can't be so large that garbage collection takes too long to complete.

You will also want to include at least a second network interface card (NIC) on each server, preferably gigabit Ethernet. These NICs will be used to connect the two servers together for database communication. The other NICs can also be used to split the management interface from the interfaces that the SmartConnectors use to send logs to the ArcSight ESM manager. This configuration allows you to manage the database server easily, but it does introduce some possible vulnerabilities into your setup. Since the network has direct access to the database server, it could be vulnerable to attack and possible compromise. If an attacker compromises your database server, he would be able to access and modify data stored in ArcSight.

Another possible and more secure setup would be to only have a single NIC in the database server and only have a crossover connection from the manager server to the database server. This limits the exposure of the database server from the local network. The difficulties with this configuration include having to log into the manager server and use that as an entry point into the database server. The real difficulty, however, is in applying patches to the OS, since you will need to copy patches to the database server manually. You could have a secondary NIC connected to the local LAN and have it shut off and only enable it to apply patches from a patch management system.

# Initial Installation

This section will be for the installation of the ArcSight ESM v4.5 software on your hardware, not the ArcSight ESM v4.5 appliance. Once you have obtained all of your hardware and software and your deployment plan has been set, you will begin the installation process. Here is a list of the steps that you will perform during the installation:

1. Rack mount and cable servers.
2. Install the OS and prepare servers for the ArcSight ESM v4.5 application.

3. Install the Oracle Database via ArcSight ESM v4.5 Database application on the database server.

4. Install ArcSight ESM v4.5 Manager on the manager server.

5. Install ArcSight ESM v4.5 Partition Archiver service on the database server.

6. Install and configure ArcSight SmartConnectors.

7. Install ArcSight ESM v4.5 Console.

## Mount and Cable Servers

More than likely the servers you will be using for the ArcSight ESM v4.5 Manager and Oracle Database are going to be rack-mountable. Since these servers are critical for security and compliance, it is recommended that you rack mount them in your data center or some other location that has adequate power, cooling, and network connectivity.

In order to ensure optimal communication between the server that runs the ArcSight ESM v4.5 Manager and the Oracle Database, you want to connect the second network interface on each of these servers directly to each other using a crossover cable. Using the crossover cable to communicate between the ArcSight ESM v4.5 Manager and the Oracle Database serves two purposes: The first purpose for the crossover cable is security. The communication between the ArcSight ESM v4.5 Manager and the Oracle Database is unencrypted using standard Oracle port TCP 1521. If this communication is sent through your network from the ArcSight Manager to the Oracle Database, then there is a possibility that this traffic could be intercepted or possibly tampered with. The second purpose of the crossover cable for database communications is for speed. Since you will not be going through routers or switches, you want the fastest possible speed between the ArcSight ESM v4.5 Manager and Oracle Database.

In order to ensure that the traffic is sent over the proper network interface, you will need to put private IP addresses on the crossover network interfaces that have both servers' network interfaces on the same subnet. Once you've done that, and you can properly ping each server from the other over the crossover link, you will need to add static DNS entries to each of these servers. You will need to do this because ArcSight ESM v4.5 uses DNS for resolution of the manager and database. Here are the locations of the hosts file, used for local static DNS entries on a Windows and Linux server, respectively.

Microsoft Windows:

```
C:\WINDOWS\system32\drivers\etc\hosts
```

Linux:

```
/etc/hosts
```

## Install and Configure Operating System

Since ArcSight ESM v4.5 can be run on multiple platforms, we will be focusing on the two most common installations: RedHat Linux and Microsoft.

### Linux

When installing ArcSight ESM v4.5 on a Linux server, you want to make sure you have installed a desktop environment, such as GNOME or KDE, on your server. This may go against what most Linux system admins would do when installing a new production server, but the ArcSight ESM on Linux systems uses a graphical installer package.

### Windows

ArcSight ESM v4.5 can be installed on Windows Server 2003 Standard or Enterprise edition with little to no special requirements. A default installation of Windows Server 2003 would be adequate to install and run ArcSight ESM.

## Install ArcSight ESM v4.5 Database Software and Oracle Database

The ArcSight ESM v4.5 Database installation application will perform a couple of different tasks that will install and configure your Oracle installation and prepare it for use with ArcSight ESM. Once you begin the installation process, the ArcSight installer application, shown in Figure 14-4, will guide you through the process. All the other pieces of ArcSight will use a similar installation method.

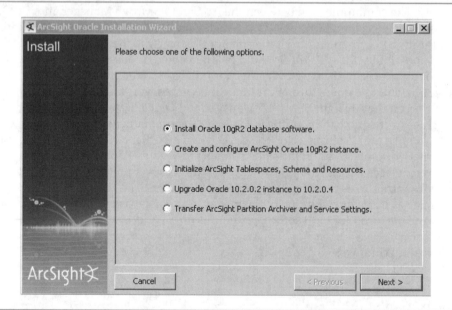

**Figure 14-4.** ArcSight Installation introduction

You will be prompted for an install location for the ArcSight software. On the database, this installation location is not for the Oracle Database application or the actual database files, but for the ArcSight ESM v4.5 Partition Archiver application, which will be configured later. You will be prompted if you want application shortcuts installed and then shown a summary of your installation options. After this, ArcSight will begin installing the Java Runtime Environment (JVM) and then begin the rest of the installation for the database.

## Install Oracle Database

The first piece of ArcSight ESM v4.5 that you will need to install is the Oracle Database. ArcSight ESM v4.5 requires Oracle Database version 10.2.0.4, as shown in Figure 10-5. This is the initial portion of the Oracle 10gR2 Database installation. You will need to have the embedded Oracle zip files from ArcSight in order to begin the installation. The ArcSight installer package will prompt for the location of these files (these files must remain compressed) and for the location of the Oracle home directory. You can change the default location during the install if needed.

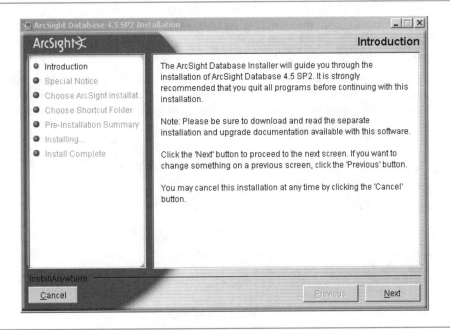

**Figure 14-5.** Database Installation Wizard

## Create and Configure ArcSight ESM v4.5 Database Instance

After the Oracle database software has been installed, you will be prompted to create and configure the Oracle ArcSight instance. The Oracle ArcSight instance is the actual database that will hold all the information for ArcSight.

- **ArcSight SID and database template to use** This is the starting point for your ArcSight installation. When you chose a template (the choices are detailed in Table 14-6), the ArcSight Database installation application will prepopulate some of the required fields based off of specifications in the template. These can be changed from the defaults during the installation.

- **Allowed TNS clients** You need to specify either the hostname or IP addresses that are able to make connections to this database instance. This is a built-in security feature of the Oracle 10g database.

- **Location of Oracle Home directory** The user can change this.

- **Redo logs** Decide if you will automatically be saving Redo logs and, if so, in what location.

- **Oracle SYS account and Oracle SYSTEM account** Oracle has specific restrictions on the complexity of the passwords used. Passwords must be between 6 and 32 characters, consist of only letters, numbers, or the special characters ( _ , # , $ ). The password must also start with a letter. These password requirements apply to all Oracle passwords used.

- **Oracle Enterprise Manager** Oracle DBSNMP and Oracle SYSMAN. This portion only needs to be completed if you plan on using the Oracle Enterprise Manager. This tool is used to manage the Oracle Database, but is optional.

|  | Small | Medium | Standard | Large |
|---|---|---|---|---|
| Total memory (GB) | .5 | 1 | 2 | 4 |
| Number of CPUs | 1 | 1 | 2 | 2 |
| Redo logs (GB) | 3×.25 | 3×1 | 3×2 | 3×3 |

**Table 14-6.** ArcSight Database Templates

## Initialize ArcSight Tablespaces, Schemas, and Resources

You will be prompted to specify usernames and passwords for two new Oracle user accounts. These special accounts will be used within the ArcSight application. The two user accounts to be created are:

- **ArcSight Database User**   This account is used by the ArcSight ESM v4.5 Manager to access the Oracle Database. By default, the username is arcsight, but it can be changed.

- **System User**   This is a failsafe account that can be used to unlock any ArcSight resources. By default, the username is systemuser, but it, too, can be changed.

The next step in the installation process will be to allocate space to your Oracle database. You will be prompted for the size and number of data files to be allocated for the ArcSight Database tablespaces listed next. It is recommended to use a smaller number of larger-sized data files instead of a larger number of smaller-sized data files. Perform these calculations prior to proceeding based on your hard-disk space size and how many events you plan on processing per day. If this is misconfigured, you could cause your server to run out of space and will have to perform a cleanup before you can move on with the installation. It is better to go too small and add on in the future than to go too big when setting up the database data files.

- **ARC_SYSTEM_DATA tablespace**   Objects in ArcSight ESM, such as information regarding your assets, zones, networks, or categories, are stored in this tablespace. The default size, which is determined by the database template you chose to use, should be adequate for most environments.

- **ARC_SYSTEM_INDEX tablespace**   This is an index of the ARC_SYSTEM_DATA tablespace and the default size, which is determined by the database template you chose to use, should be adequate for most environments.

- **ARC_EVENT_DATA tablespace**   This tablespace is where all the events are stored for your active partition days. The more events generated per day and the number of days that will be active, the larger this tablespace will need to be in order to accommodate all the data. Plan for a very high amount of read-write operations to be performed on this tablespace, so it should be placed on a drive or array of drives that can maintain a high rate of read-write operations.

- **ARC_EVENT_INDEX tablespace**   This tablespace is the index of the events that ArcSight ESM processes. This tablespace will grow rapidly, and it is recommended that this tablespace should be two to three times the size of the ARC_EVENT_DATA tablespace. Though the recommendation is that the ARC_EVENT_INDEX be significantly larger than the other tablespaces, ArcSight can function properly at any size as long as the ARC_EVENT_INDEX tablespace is greater than or equal to the ARC_EVENT_DATA tablespace.

- **ARC_UNDO tablespace**   Instead of using Oracle's default UNDO tablespace, ArcSight will create its own and sets the Oracle default tablespace to inactive. The default size, which is determined by the database template you chose to use, should be adequate for most environments.

- **ARC_TEMP tablespace**   This is a temporary tablespace specifically for the ArcSight database. It is used primarily for sorting data. The default size, which is determined by the database template you chose to use, should be adequate for most environments.

## Install ArcSight ESM v4.5 Manager

The installation of the ArcSight ESM v4.5 is fairly straightforward in comparison to the Oracle Database installation. Once again, you will see the familiar ArcSight installer package, which will prompt for the location where you want to install the ArcSight application and then begin the installation process. You will need the following information to complete the installation process:

- **FIPS 140-2 mode**   Running ArcSight ESM in this mode ensures that it will comply with FIPS 140-2. Running your servers in this mode is not recommended, unless you are a federal agency required to conform to FIPS and you have an in-depth understanding of this standard.

- **Define Manager information**   You will need to define the Manager information, including the Manager's full FQDN and the port that the ArcSight Manager software will be listening on for connections.

- **License file**   Point to the file containing your license. ArcSight will provide this information.

- **Java memory heap size**   As mentioned earlier, this is the amount of memory that Java will allocate for use by the ArcSight ESM v4.5 application.

- **Key Pair**   ArcSight requires SSL encryption to function. You will be prompted for information to generate a self-signed key pair, signed CA, or Demo. Depending upon your selection, you will be prompted for the appropriate SSL information. Use of the demo certificate is not recommended, since it is only provided by ArcSight for testing and demonstration purposes.

- **Database information**   Set location and credentials for authentication to the Oracle Database.

- **User authentication method**   Indicate whether you are going to use the built-in user database, Windows AD, LDAP, RADIUS, or Custom JAAS plug-in for user authentication.

- **Administrator account**   Set up the admin account for the ArcSight ESM v4.5.

- **Define ArcSight packages**   These are the preconfigured packages designed by ArcSight. They include packages to handle antivirus, configuration changes, intrusion detection devices, network monitoring, and the ArcSight Express.

- **SMTP options**   ArcSight can be configured to send out email alerts, and we recommend you configure this option. ArcSight does offer the option to use an external or internal email server to relay these messages. You can also configure ArcSight to accept incoming emails to acknowledge alerts it has generated.

- **ArcSight Web**   If you have chosen to install the ArcSight Web application, you will be prompted for the URL and port that you will be using.

- **Automated asset creation**   By enabling this, the ArcSight SmartConnector will be allowed to generate and categorize assets it discovers. If a SmartConnector discovers an IP address or hostname in a log that it does not have a record of, the SmartConnector will create an asset and begin generating more information as the SmartConnector discovers it.

## Java Certificates

If you chose to use a self-signed key pair, during the installation of the ArcSight ESM v4.5 Manager, you will be prompted for information that will be used to generate this self-signed key pair. You will need to provide location and organizational information that will be included in the key pair. Like all Java applications, this key will be stored in the CACERTS file, which is located in the JRE directory of the Managers installation directory.

```
%ArcSight Manager%\jre\lib\security\cacerts
```

You will need this key-pair order to secure communications between the different ArcSight components. In order to export this key pair into a certificate file, you will need to use the KeyTool GUI application built into ArcSight ESM v4.5, by running the following command:

```
%ArcSight Manager%\bin\arcsight.bat keytoolgui
```

This command will bring up the KeyTool GUI application. Open the CACERTS file, which is located at

```
%ArcSightManager%\jre\lib\security
```

The default password for a Java CACERTS file is changeit and that is exactly what you should do! Change the password for this file right away. Once the password is changed, you will want to export the certificates that you will need, as shown in Figure 14-6.

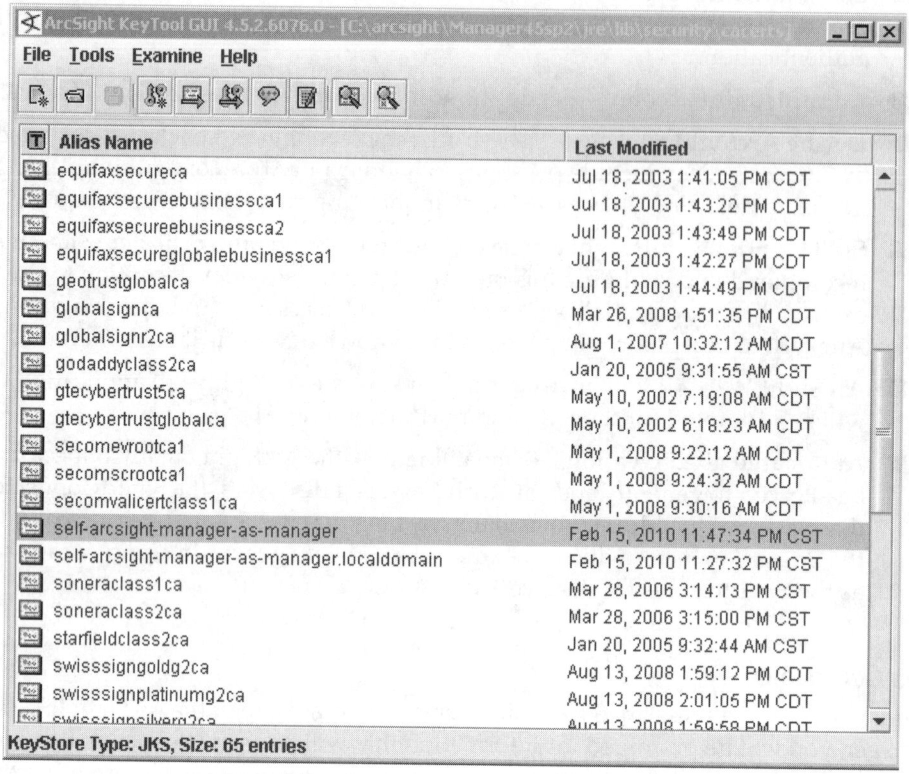

**Figure 14-6.**   KeyTool GUI application

You will need to locate the self-signed certificate for ArcSight ESM v4.5 management server. The ArcSight SmartConnectors, ArcSight Console, and ArcSight ESM will use this certificate to encrypt communications between each component. Export this certificate out and save it in a secure location. You will need it when installing any new ArcSight SmartConnectors.

## Configure ArcSight Partition Archiver

When the ArcSight ESM v4.5 Manager and Database applications have been installed, you will need to return to the server with the installed database in order to configure the ArcSight Partition Archiver. Log in to the database server and run the following command from the bin directory where the ArcSight database software is installed:

```
%ArcSight Database%\bin\arcsight.bat database pc
```

The configuration application for the Partition Archiver will launch. It is a step-through installation program, like the other ArcSight ESM v4.5 installations, but you will need to answer some questions. The following are some of the configuration decisions that you will need make prior to installing the Partition Archiver:

- What are the retention requirements for your organization?

- How many days of events should be kept in the live database? These events are stored in the ARC_SYSTEM_DATA tablespace and are assessable immediately though the ArcSight Console.

- How many days of events should you have as reserve? This acts as a safety net in case there is ever an issue with archiving older partitions. The Partition Archiver will create partitions and allocate space for a specific number of days ahead that will be used if it cannot archive prior partitions.

- Where will you be storing archived partitions? The number of logs and the time you need to retain them determines the size of this storage space.

 **NOTE** When archived partitions are brought back online through the ArcSight ESM v4.5 Console, these data files are uncompressed and mounted into the database in the archive directory. This should be taken into account when determining where your archive directory will be, since you will need enough free space to bring however many archived partitions back online as you see fit.

- How many days should be archived? This is based on your organization's retention requirements.

- To whom should alert emails be sent and what is the severity level of notifications?

- How many days should the compression waiting period be?

- Should the Partition Archiver be run as a service?

Once the Partition Archiver service is installed and configured, it will show up in the ArcSight Console under the Connectors listing. The Partition Archiver does not affect the way events are stored in the database or manipulate any of the data. It is used only to perform maintenance tasks on the database. If the Partition Archiver is down, the ArcSight ESM v4.5 Manager will still continue to push events into the database and events that are stored previously in the database will be available. If the Partition Archiver is offline, database statistics will not be updated and old partitions will not be archived from the live database or deleted from the archive directory. If you have properly allocated an adequate reserve period for your database, a short interruption in service should not be a cause for alarm, but if this outage lasts longer than your reserve period or it was set improperly, your database can very quickly run out of space.

## Install ArcSight SmartConnector

Like the rest of the ArcSight software, the ArcSight SmartConnector comes as an installable package and is relatively straightforward—up to a point. To begin the installation of each SmartConnector, you need to know a few things. You will be prompted to provide this information during the installation process:

■ The ArcSight ESM v4.5 Manager hostname and the port the connector will be communicating with

■ A login to that Manager that has either admin rights or SmartConnector installer rights

■ The appropriate certificate for this Manager using the KeyTool GUI application to the CACERTS file

■ The location where you want to install the SmartConnector software

■ The SmartConnector you want to install

Since the SmartConnector application contains all of the prebuilt connectors within ArcSight, as shown in Figure 14-7, at a point in the installation process, the application will branch off into very specific requirements once you have selected the connector.

As an example, we will set up a syslog connector for your ArcSight ESM v4.5. After you choose syslog from the list, you are prompted for the port to listen on for syslog traffic and which source IP addresses will be allowed access. By default, the port is UDP 514 and any source IP address. Then you assign the SmartConnector a name that will define it in the ArcSight Console. You can set this to run as a service or

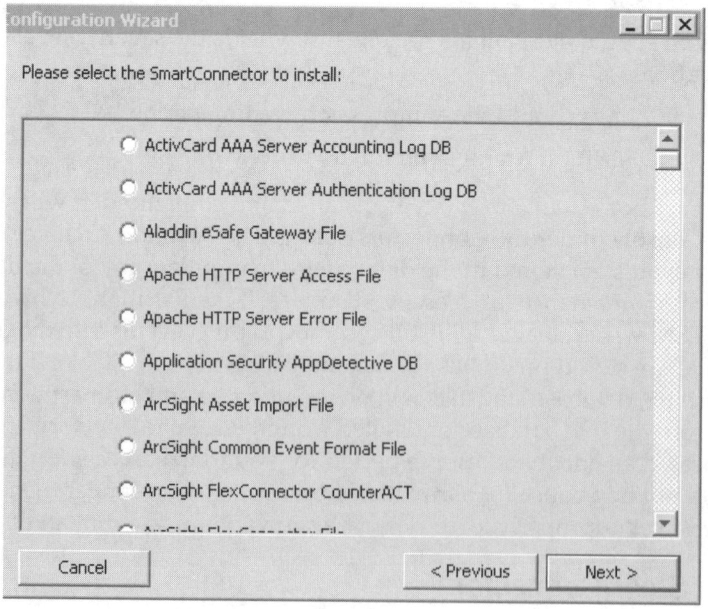

**Figure 14-7.**   SmartConnector Configuration Wizard

as a standalone application that you will start manually. Once this is done, the SmartConnector is ready to begin receiving logs from any device able to send via syslog.

## Install ArcSight Console

Now you can get into the ArcSight ESM v4.5 and begin to see what is going on. First, you need to install the ArcSight ESM v4.5 Console on your workstation, however. The installation process for the ArcSight ESM v4.5 Console is the same as for the rest of the ArcSight software. You will be prompted for an installation location and whether to install shortcuts for the Console. Once you've done this, the ArcSight ESM v4.5 Console is ready for use.

When you launch the ArcSight ESM v4.5 Console application, you will be prompted with the login screen, shown in Figure 14-8, which will require login credentials and the name of the ArcSight ESM v4.5 Manager server you wish to connect to. The ArcSight ESM v4.5 Console can connect to multiple servers and will store previously associated managers.

You will need the admin credentials that you created when installing the Oracle Database to make the initial connection to the ArcSight ESM v4.5 Manager. Like the SmartConnectors, the Console requires the certificate in order to connect, but unlike the SmartConnectors, the Console will prompt the user to accept the certificate. This certificate is then stored in the CACERTS file for this console.

The ArcSight ESM v4.5 Console, shown in Figure 14-9, is your main interface into viewing the events that are being stored in the database and managing ArcSight ESM v4.5.

**Figure 14-8.**    ArcSight Console Login window

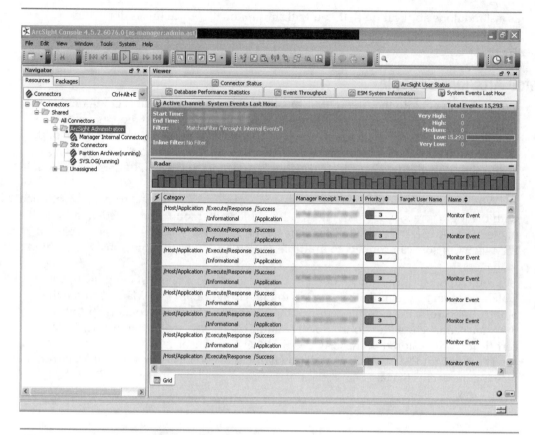

**Figure 14-9.**    ArcSight ESM v4.5 Console

# Summary

At this point, ArcSight ESM v4.5 is operational and taking in feeds from devices, processing events, and generating alerts. Your ArcSight ESM v4.5 is working off only default information that was preinstalled with your installation. From this point on, it's up to you to configure ArcSight for your needs and your environment. In the next chapter, we will go into more advanced ArcSight subjects.

# CHAPTER 15

ArcSight ESM v4.5 Advanced Techniques

Once your ArcSight ESM instance is up and running the sheer volume of information coming in and what you can do with it can be pretty overwhelming. You can employ ArcSight as an operational asset to help you better handle visualization of network logs; at the same time, there are also many things you will need to do to ensure that ArcSight keeps running smoothly. Each of these tasks can be grouped into either an operational or maintenance task.

# Operations: Dealing with Data

Using ArcSight to investigate possible security incidents, monitoring system logs of the various devices on your network for potential issues, and storing logs for compliance are operational tasks: this is the actual day-to-day operations of the SIEM. Using ArcSight you can take the information that you have to add value to your operations.

One of the first things you will want to do is make sense of all this incoming information. ArcSight was designed for this task and can do it very well; however, ArcSight is only as smart as you tell it to be. Although ArcSight contains built-in logic that will make some sense of this information right out of the box, you will need to write filters and rules for your specific environment. Separating useful information from irrelevant information is going to be an ongoing task in ArcSight.

## Filters

Filters are the basis for most everything that you will do in ArcSight. A *filter* is a collection of logic that is designed to pick out very specific data from all the different feeds coming into ArcSight. Think of it as a water filter for information: you pass dirty unusable information through it and out comes the usable information that you want. The filter can be as simple as looking for a specific source IP address, which, in ArcSight ESM v4.5, is also referred to as the *attacker,* or as complex as looking for multiple source IP addresses, destination IP addresses, and ports, along with user information to search for very specific traffic on your network.

Filters are the building blocks that you will use to create rules, active channels, and reports. It is best practice to develop individual filters that only look for specific things so you can reuse the filters later on. By creating reusable content in ArcSight, you limit the chance of making a mistake. If you find yourself constantly writing the same filter in different rules, you will save time in the long run by reusing filters, and you can then share these filters with other members of your team who use ArcSight. Reusable content allows you to make a single change to the parent filter that will be reflected in all the other content that uses this filter.

The filter shown in Figure 15-1 is designed to pick out anonymous FTP traffic. The *Attacker Address* is the source IP address of the connection. The *Target User Name* is the user account that the FTP connection will be using for authentication on the destination. And the *Target Port* of 21 is for the FTP destination connection port.

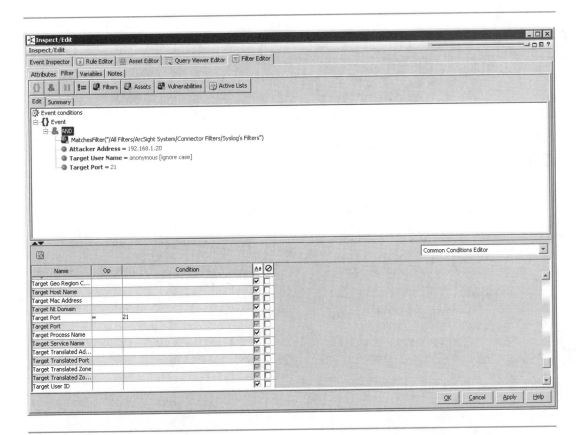

**Figure 15-1.** Anonymous FTP filter

Another filter is being used in this filter so this filter will require all this information to come in via the syslog connector.

## Rules

A rule can be built off of filters or off of logic developed within the rule itself, by defining actions to take in response to triggers. You can use an individual filter or chain several filters together using Boolean logic to look for specific events. Going back to the filter shown from Figure 15-1, it has been modified in Figure 15-2 to show how a rule would be built using multiple filters to trigger off of anonymous FTP activity.

### Aggregation

You might not want to have a rule trigger off of every single instance of the condition being met. You can set the aggregation to trigger this rule after only a specific number

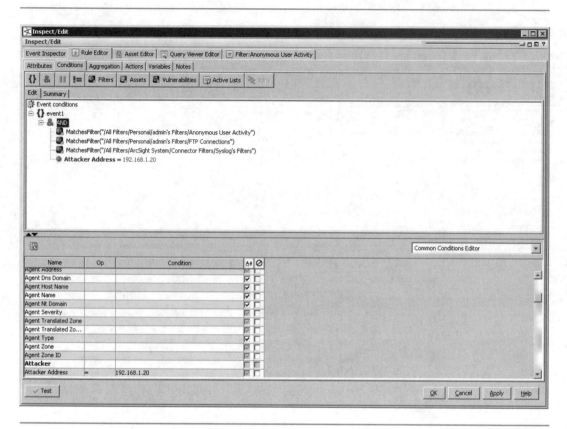

**Figure 15-2.**    Anonymous FTP rule using multiple filters

of conditional matches in a specific time frame have occurred, in which certain fields are either unique or identical. For instance, in a TCP port scan of a device, you can set the rule to look at events originating from a specific attacker to a specific target where the target ports are all unique. The aggregation triggers can be any of the following:

- Number of conditional matches in a specific amount of time
- Aggregate only when specific fields are unique (for any field in ArcSight)
- Aggregate only when specific fields are identical (for any field in ArcSight)

## Action

Before determining what action will be taken when a rule is triggered, you need to decide when these actions will occur. ArcSight has built-in intervals you can use to trigger the actions. You will not need to trigger off of each specific interval and you can set specific actions to happen at each criteria that is listed here. These criteria allow you to ensure that you are not being flooded with information from a rule that is triggering numerous times.

- **On First Event**   This is what you want ArcSight to do on the first instance of the conditions of the rule being met.

- **On Subsequent Events**   After the first set of conditions are met, don't do anything. But if those same conditions are met after a specific time has elapsed, do something.

- **On Every Event**   You can have an action occur every time the condition is met.

- **On First Threshold**   You can set thresholds that need to be met before triggering an action. A threshold can be used if you know that this event will happen many times and you want to stop your system from being overloaded with information. This setting now includes the Aggregate tab, the number and time specified, along with identical and unique fields. The nonthreshold settings are primarily used simply with conditions.

- **On Subsequent Thresholds**   Much like the subsequent events, On Subsequent Thresholds allows you can to set an action to happen on subsequent threshold triggers.

- **On Every Threshold**   Do you want to be notified on every threshold trigger? Much like the other threshold criteria, this one requires setting the aggregation numbers.

- **On Time Unit**   This sets the action to happen after a specific number of minutes and works similarly to thresholds.

Once you have determined when actions should be taken, you need to decide what those actions are. The following are some of the actions that can be taken per each of the rule triggers listed here:

- **Send Notifications**   Either an email or an SMS will be sent to a group, notifying them that the rule has triggered. You can also require those notified to acknowledge the rule trigger.

- **Execute Command**   Use this to set up an active response within ArcSight or other external systems. Examples are to trigger a scan of a specific address or to shut down a port on a switch.

- **Create a Case or Add to Existing Case**   You can select a rule to create a case in the internal ArcSight ticketing system or to add to a case that has already been created.

- **Add or Remove from Active List**   Specific information from an event can be added to an Active List, providing the Active List is configured to store that information.

- **Add or Remove from Session List**   Specific information from an event can be added to an Session List, providing the Session List is configured to store that information.

These particular actions give you a wide range of response options when a rule is triggered and also allow you to designate levels of importance for events.

### Rule Tuning

Tuning your ArcSight ESM installation is part art and part science. You will need to have a good understanding of what exactly it is you are looking for in order to weed out false positives and also ensure that you are not being too specific and thus creating false negatives. Proper network modeling can greatly aid in rule tuning by ensuring that you have as much information as possible about your source or destination so you can use that information to create effective rules.

## Lists

ArcSight has a method of monitoring assets called lists. A *list* is a temporary location in memory used to hold information that can be used in other correlation or monitoring activities. Information is added to a list based on rules that are triggered when looking for specific criteria matches. You may have lists of suspicious IP addresses, VPN activity, or other types of specific values. These lists can be used to watch particular assets and can raise an internal alarm in the system that a problem may be occurring. If ArcSight sees a source IP address performing reconnaissance probes against your network, for instance, this can be a predecessor to other attacks on your network. You can set ArcSight to add this source IP address to a watch list of suspicious IP addresses. ArcSight lets you use two different types of lists:

- **Active Lists**   You can add specific information to this type of list automatically via rules or manually. Each list has a specific time to live (TTL) for its assets. The TTL is the amount of time the assets will remain on the list. The assets on an Active List are constantly being reevaluated and the TTL is reset on each event that triggers an addition to an Active List type. If a TTL is set to 0, then the information will never be removed from the Active List.

- **Session Lists**   A Session list differs from an Active List in a couple of ways. One, Session Lists are designed to be used for specific time periods, not just as placeholders for field information, in which the information can expire and be taken off the list. Session Lists are also used to monitor session activity.

## Trending

Trending is a very powerful tool that can be used in ArcSight to look for changes in activity over time. You can use trending to gather information for specific events over time. For example, perhaps you want to monitor how many events are received by an ArcSight SmartConnector per hour over a very long time period. Trends can be used to speed up queries, since you are not querying all events in the timeframe that you need data from. By using trending you only need to query the trends that you have already generated. In this way, you are breaking up the processing load for a query or report over time.

## Active Channels

Active Channels are going to be an invaluable tool when investigating incidents and performing real-time monitoring of your environment. Active Channels allow you to see the results of a filter over a specific time period. When viewing an Active Channel, such as shown in Figure 15-3, you can choose to view the data from a selected period of time or in near real time.

When creating a new Active Channel, you will need to navigate to the Active Channel drop-down and then right-click Active Channels, or select shared Active Channels and then New Active Channel. When creating a new Active Channel, specific information is required:

- **Channel name**   A unique name to designate the Active Channel.

- **Start and end time to monitor**   What period of time do you want to monitor?

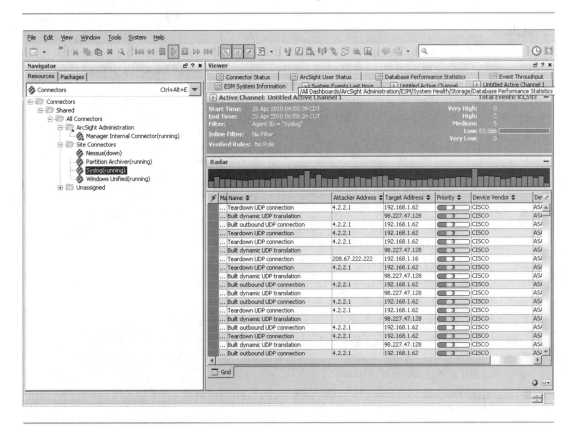

**Figure 15-3.**   Active Channels

- **Timestamp to use** You can either use the end time from the actual device that generated the logs or from the ArcSight Manager that received the event.

- **Evaluate on attach or continuously evaluate** This option lets you set the Active Channel to either display only the specific time period you designate or show a near real-time scrolling of events. If you select Continuously Evaluate, you will need to set the end time as **$Now**.

- **Filter to be used** The filter to be used can either be one that you have already created or one you create specifically for this Active Channel. When you click Define, a filter editor box will pop up.

- **Fields to use** This lets you define what fields you want to display in the Active Channel. You can reconfigure this by right-clicking at the top of the events in the Active Channel and either customizing the columns or selecting another field set. A *field set* is a grouping of columns that you define to display information.

## Investigate

Once you have an Active Channel running and you are examining the results, you may see something that you would like to investigate further. You can easily dig deeper into the Active Channel by right-clicking on any field in the ArcSight Console and selecting Investigate. Investigate gives you the following options as to what you will want to look at and how you will want to display the information:

- **Create Channel** This option creates a new channel to examine either a specific condition or everything *except* that specific condition. For example, if you are looking at an attacker IP address, and you want to see all events using this specific attacker IP address, you would use this setting to look for them.

- **Add** Add opens a new channel that includes all of the original conditions plus the new condition or not, which, using the example above, would be a specific attacker IP address. This new channel will be a subset of the original channel and will not change the original channel in any way.

- **Add Condition** This option adds the properties of whatever field you are on to the currently open Conditions Editor.

- **Show Exploited Vulnerability** This option lists potentially exploitable vulnerabilities based on the information within the event you have selected.

- **Show Targeted Asset** This shows you any information that ArcSight has gathered about the target asset.

- **Session Events** A new view within the channel appears, showing all events that have the same session information (attacker, target, and port) as the event selected.

- **Attacker Target Traffic**   A new view within the channel appears, showing any traffic going to or coming from the same address as the event selected.

- **Event Context Channel**   A new view within the channel appears, showing the details of events that occurred within a specified time before and after the selected event. This option is very helpful when trying to determine the series of events that led up to the event you are investigating and to see if anything happened after the event occurred as well.

These options allow you to improve already created filters to aid in specifically targeting just the information that you are searching for.

ArcSight also allows you to use an Active Channel as a diagnostic tool. You can select a specific rule (or rules) and apply it to the events within your current Active Channel. You can then verify the validity and correctness of rule conditions as well as determine if the thresholds/conditions have been met previously. This way you can test to see if the rule actually triggers off of events that you are monitoring, which is especially important before migrating a rule to production so your testing does not interfere with the others using ArcSight.

## Notifications

To set up a notification, you will need to create a functional group to receive these notifications. This is usually a group within your organization, such as the CERT Team built into ArcSight. Then you will need to determine escalation levels, which can be equated to the tier system that you may use in your environment. This allows you to design your rules to escalate alerts through the tiers of your organization.

Once you have created your group and determined the escalation levels within that group, you need to add a new destination. You have four options for notifications available within ArcSight, but the notification method may require external services to be in place.

- **Console**   Allows you to send a console message to a group in the ArcSight Console.

- **Email**   By using an external email server or the internal email server built into ArcSight, you can send an email out to a user or group.

- **Pager**   This notification will send an SMS message to a cell phone or pager and will only work if you have the systems in place within your organization to send out text messages to your users.

- **Cell Phone**   This is not a widely used notification method, but you can set the notification to send an email message specifically to a cell phone.

You do have a wide variety of notification options available within ArcSight itself, and these options should be enough to meet most of your notification needs.

# Cases

Cases are a built-in internal ticketing, remediation, and collaboration system. Cases allow you to mark a single event or multiple events and add them to a case for further investigation. Once the events are assigned to a specific case, you can add other information pertaining to the events in question or a specific incident and what steps you have taken to investigate further. Cases are a useful tool when working with different tier levels in your organization. A level 1 incident handler can create a case for an investigation and then send the case, along with any notes and event details, up to the next level. These cases can also be used to retain historical information about events in your environment. One thing to note is that events that fall out of the retention period set for your system will be removed from a case.

# Exporting Information

When you find useful information in ArcSight, you may want to export it. ArcSight provides ways to export this information relatively easily. You can configure ArcSight to export to a ticketing system in your environment or to generate reports. ArcSight currently has a system in place to export events to the Remedy ticketing system. for all other external ticketing systems, you will need to build a flexconnector to export the information. A *flexconnector* is an ArcSight SmartConnector that allows you to customize it to parse logs not supported by ArcSight.

## Field Sets

A *field set* is a collection of the fields that you want to export. A field set can be thought of as a spreadsheet, where you specify which columns you wish to view. Field sets are primarily used when viewing or exporting information from an Active Channel. When exporting events from an Active List using the fields set within the list, the output will be in a CSV file format. By default, ArcSight uses a field set that provides you with most of the information within your Active Channel, but you can edit this at any time.

## Reports

Like most things in ArcSight, if you can figure out the logic needed to pull out events from your system, you can generate a report from it. A report is designed to give you information by using trends or queries against the database, or information about anything held within an Active or Session List.

To create a query, you will need to have the following information:

- **Name**   A unique and specific name for this query
- **Query On**   You can query off of
  - Events
  - Cases
  - Notifications
  - Assets

- Trends
- Active Lists
- Session Lists
- **Start and End Times**   Set the beginning and end time for this query.
- **Timestamp to Use**   You can use the manager receipt time or end-time timestamp from the device logs.
- **Row Limit**   The maximum number of rows to be displayed in this query.
- **Fields**   This option allows you to designate which fields you will be querying on and the order in which they will be processed. You can also apply functions to the fields, such as a count of unique events.
- **Condition**   You can apply a prebuilt filter to this query or create a new one.

Once you have created the query or trend, you will need to define the report. When creating the report, you need to designate the template you want to use to format the report. ArcSight has a wide variety of prebuilt templates or you can create your own. After that, you need to assign a query, trend, Active List, or Session List to be used as input for your report. Finally, you can set parameters for the report, such as what output file format to use, page size, the user to run it as, and who should receive the report.

# Managing Assets and Networks

When deciding to implement the ArcSight ESM v4.5 in your organization to provide real-time monitoring, historic analysis, and the automated response necessary to manage the risks associated with doing business today, your primary configuration consideration is to define your ArcSight ESM network model. The ArcSight ESM network model is comprised of three objects: the event schema, asset modeling information, and network modeling information. Each of these items works in conjunction to facilitate the building of detailed correlation criteria as well as determine the priority of the events being processed by the ArcSight ESM Manager.

The event schema is the result of the ArcSight normalization process, which takes the format of events from different devices on your network and "normalizes" them into a common format that is displayed within the ArcSight ESM Console. Over 400 data fields are divided into 17 groups that make up the ArcSight event schema. This schema provides the infrastructure that drives event aggregation and correlation.

## The ArcSight SmartConnector

Some of the main fields within the event schema are the categorization fields. These fields consist of information automatically supplied by the ArcSight SmartConnector:

- **Category Object**   Defines the entity being targeted by the event.
- **Category Behavior**   What is being done to the object as determined by ArcSight ESM and the device vendor.

- **Category Outcome**   The result of the behavior on the object; the only options are success, failure, or attempt.

- **Category Technique**   The nature of the behavior represented on the object as determined by the ArcSight ESM and the device vendor.

- **Category Device Group**   Indicates if the event is of one type or another based on the device(s) connected to the ArcSight SmartConnector. This device group can be something like a firewall, IDS, IPS, etc.

- **Category Significance**   Indicates the security risk based on various data points within your network, such as information from the device and the asset model.

- **Category Tuple Description**   Is the prose description of the event category, assembled from the category components listed previously. Basically, this tells you in layperson's terms what this event is, where it originated, and where it might be going.

Normalization provides significant value when building content with the ArcSight ESM, in that you can build a filter that specifies you want to monitor traffic blocked by the firewalls within your organization. If you were to use the Category Device Group designation within your filter conditions, you will not have to alter this filter's conditions if you were to swap out your firewall with one from another vendor, as ArcSight will still see these events as coming from the Category Device Group of firewalls, making this filter's conditions vendor neutral. If you specify that you want to view events from your perimeter firewalls within this filter, you could simply add the Asset Category (defined in the next section) for the perimeter and only monitor perimeter firewall events.

## The ArcSight Asset Model

The ArcSight Asset Model is where you define the various assets within your organization that you would like to monitor. In order to receive the maximum benefits from ArcSight ESM, you should attempt to provide the following information about your assets. Always configure your most critical assets within ArcSight ESM first in order to facilitate the most accurate information about those assets. The following is a list of the ArcSight Asset Model's attributes:

- **Vulnerabilities**   This is defined as any hardware, firmware, or software state that leaves an asset open for potential exploitation. ArcSight ESM offers many ways in which to retrieve vulnerability information about your assets. In order to provide this vulnerability information, one option is to run a vulnerability scan of your network and import that information either manually or automatically using an ArcSight SmartConnector into the ArcSight ESM Manager. The other option is to use a subscription service known as iDefense in order to connect to the iDefense database to maintain your vulnerability information within the ArcSight ESM.

- **Location** This configuration is optional but can provide many details about the origin and the end point of an event and can be defined when the location of your asset is geographically different from the mapping database that ArcSight ESM uses.

- **Asset Categories** Describes the properties of an asset when evaluating threats or behaviors associated with an event. Although this option must be set and maintained manually, it provides information such as asset identity, ownership, and criticality, which can be used when building content like filters, rules, data monitors, and reports for correlating the events associated with this asset.

## The ArcSight Network Model

The ArcSight Network Model is where you define how the groupings of the assets you are monitoring are depicted within your organization. To receive the maximum benefits from ArcSight ESM, you should provide the following information about your network and the assets it contains. Each of the attributes of the Network Model are central to creating ArcSight ESM resources, in that you can create a rule that monitors specific traffic from any asset group, range, zone, network, or customer and have the flexibility to add or remove assets from those areas and not have to update the resource itself. The following is a list of the ArcSight Network Model's attributes:

- **Asset** An *asset* is defined as any network endpoint with an IP address, MAC address, host name, or external ID. When configuring your assets within the Network Model, be sure you understand that every visible interface is considered a separate asset; for instance, multiple IP addresses on a single piece of hardware are considered alternate devices within the asset. While ArcSight ESM automatically creates assets to model the network nodes that host ArcSight components (Database, Consoles, Manager, Connectors), you should define every important asset on your network first. This information, in conjunction with the asset modeling information (vulnerabilities, location, and asset categorization), are major factors when building content within ArcSight ESM. You can also configure Asset Groups, which are logical groupings of assets, and asset ranges, which define a group of assets within the same IP range. Asset ranges are helpful when you don't want to define every asset within an IP range, such as DHCP clients.

- **Zones** Can represent any part of the network and are identified by a congruous block of IP addresses. Zones usually represent a functional group within the network or a subnet, and every asset or asset range must be associated with a zone. In addition, a network using subnets or containing one or more private networks requires zones so ArcSight ESM can resolve the IP addresses of assets.

- **Networks** A logical collection of zones. if you have two or more NAT subnets that use the same private address space, you will define a network. Networks must be associated to a zone. The assets within that zone will then automatically be associated to that network.

■ **Customers** Are used mainly to support Managed Security Support Providers (MSSPs) but are useful to clearly identifying and separating event traffic from multiple cost centers or business units. When configuring customers, you will assign multiple customers to one SmartConnector when the associated networks are using the same private IP address ranges.

As you can see, there are many elements to consider prior to implementing your ArcSight ESM. By clearly defining these items, however, you can build effective and efficient content that is valuable to your organization. Individual resources can be reused to supply information about the network traffic within your organization. Leveraging the Network Model and the categorization fields can provide for vendor neutral conditions and reporting capabilities down to the individual asset or for all of the assets within your zone or network. The possibilities are endless and can only be realized if you take the time needed to define your critical assets initially within the Network Model.

# Management and Troubleshooting

Using ArcSight for its intended purpose as a SEIM is only one of the things you will need to do. Maintaining and troubleshooting issues will be another task that will take up some of your time. If set up and configured properly, ArcSight can be a very stable platform, requiring very little user interaction on the backend, but even if it is stable, you will need to perform routine maintenance and system monitoring to ensure that it is operating as well as it can.

## Log and Configuration Files

ArcSight is designed to handle a multitude of logs from a variety of devices, and, in so doing, ArcSight itself generates a lot of logs. Oddly enough, ArcSight doesn't actually bring all the information from these logs into itself and process them, as it does with other devices. These logs are all stored in text files on the different ArcSight servers being used. The logs can be easily read by most people or parsed and searched using standard text-processing tools. Even though they are all stored in text files, not all of the logs are formatted the same way. You may need to keep that in mind when writing parsers for these files.

Each server will generate its own logs. Some of these logs may be similar among the different components, but they are each specific to that component. You need to have a good understanding of each of these logs— the information they contain and their format. By understanding this now, troubleshooting issues later will be much faster and you may be able to stop potential issues prior to their becoming more serious.

### ArcSight Database Server

The server where the Oracle Database is installed holds logs pertaining to the Oracle Database and the ArcSight Partition Archiver.

| Log Location | Log | Description |
|---|---|---|
| %ARCSIGHTDB%\logs | agent.log | This is the partition archiver log that shows when errors occur with partition archiving and reactiviation. If you are receiving errors when trying to reactivate a partition, this will be one of the first places to look. |
| | agent.out.wrapper.log | Information regarding the startup and shutdown of the ArcSight Partition Archiver will be listed in this log. |
| %ORACLEHOME%\admin\arcsight\bdump | alert_arcsight.log | Contains alerts generated by the database itself, regarding the state of database instances and any errors within the database. |
| %ORACLEHOME%\network\log | listener.log | Contains information regarding the Oracle listener service, its state, and any errors generated by the listener service. |

## ArcSight Manager Server

The ArcSight Manager is where you will find the logs pertaining to ArcSight ESM as a whole. These logs give you information about the health of the ArcSight ESM and how it is utilizing its resources. By default, these logs will roll over and will store the current log and the previous nine older log files. The size of each log is user-configurable, but is 10MB for most logs.

| Log Location | Log | Description |
|---|---|---|
| Log Location: %ARCSIGHTMANAGER%\logs\default | partitionarchiver.log | Information related to the Partition Archiver service. This log file can be used in conjunction with the agent log file on the database server when troubleshooting problems with archiving partitions. The Partition Archiver is a connector that utilizes a similar framework as the other connectors. |

| Log Location | Log | Description |
| --- | --- | --- |
| Log Location:<br>%ARCSIGHTMANAGER%\<br>logs\default *(cont.)* | partitioncompressor.log | Contains information about any errors during partition compression. |
| | partitionmanager.log | Contains information about errors during partition creation. |
| | partitionstatusupdator.log | The statistics for the partitions are updated, by default, six times per day. This log gives you information about and any errors related to this process. |
| | server.log | This primary log is where you will look when determining the overall health of the ArcSight Manager. It contains information details regarding any JVM errors or exceptions generated by the ArcSight Manager. You will also see internal details for the Manager. |
| | server.report.log | Information on all the reports generated by ArcSight and the status of currently running queries. If you have an issue with generating a report, this log is the one you would want to check. |
| | server.std.log | If you have performance issues and you are thinking about expanding JVM memory allocation, look through these logs. Information concerning the JVM and command-line output from the Manager is stored here. This log is where you will look if you are having issues with your ArcSight deployment. |
| | server.status.log | Contains overall information about Active Lists, ArcSight users, and SmartConnectors. This log also contains information about Java Managed Beans (MBeans). |

## ArcSight SmartConnectors

Like the ArcSight Manager and Database, the ArcSight SmartConnectors generate logs that you will want to monitor to determine the system's health.

| Log Location | Log | Description |
| --- | --- | --- |
| %ARCSIGHTSMARTCONNECTOR%\current\logs | agent.log | Contains overall information about how the SmartConnector is processing incoming logs. |
| | agent.out.wrapper.log | Contains information concerning the JVM that the SmartConnector is running in. This log also contains environmental information. |

## ArcSight Web

The ArcSight Web runs on its own web server and will generate logs for it as well.

| Log Location | Log | Description |
| --- | --- | --- |
| %ArcSightWeb%\logs\default | server.status.log | Gives you information regarding the overall health of the web server and any current open sessions. |
| | webserver.log | If an issue is occurring with the web server contacting the ArcSight Manager, this log will give you information that you can use for troubleshooting. |
| | webserver.std.log | Contains any errors generated by the web server and memory utilization. This contains the command-line output for the web manager, including start/stop messages, thread dumps, exceptions, and memory status. |

| Log Location | Log | Description |
|---|---|---|
| %ArcSightWeb%\logs\default *(cont.)* | webserver.pulse.log | Holds detailed information on the communication between the web server and manager. |
| | webwizard.log | Contains information on the installation of the web manager. |

## ArcSight Console

The ArcSight console, which is loaded on your workstation, has four log files.

| Log Location | Log | Description |
|---|---|---|
| %ARCSIGHTCONSOLE%\ current\logs | console.log | Contains general information concerning the ArcSight ESM console. This log will tell you if there are any login issues or exceptions thrown by the console. Primarily used for troubleshooting connectivity issues between the ArcSight Console and ArcSight Manager. |
| | sendlogs.log | The console has a built-in utility for packaging and sending logs from your system to ArcSight support. This log holds information regarding that process. |
| | consolewizard.log | This log contains information about the installation of the console. Any errors or issues that occur during the installation process will be recorded here. |
| | velocity.log | Contains any issues concerning the velocity templates being used. |

## Logfu

Logfu is a utility developed by ArcSight to visually graph information contained in the various logs ArcSight generates. Logfu can give you a visual representation of different statistics from ArcSight components, such as JVM utilization or EPS. You can run Logfu on the Manager or SmartConnectors. Logfu will generate an HTML report, which it will label logfu.html and store in a folder labeled Logfu-*date-time*, along with the logs you are analyzing. The logs that Logfu will analyze are the server.std.log, the server.log, and the server.status.log.

Logfu needs to be run in the directory containing the logs that you want to analyze, so you will need to either copy the logs to the bin directory or add the path to the bin directory so you can run the commands anywhere on your system. The command to run Logfu is **%ArcSightManager%\bin\arcsight.bat logfu** *–switch.* Following are the switches that you can use when running Logfu.

Optional parameters are used to specify the time period of the log that will be analyzed:

- **-bln <base log file name>**   Allows you to specify a custom log file to analyze.
- **-f <start date and time>**   The start time to begin analyzing logs. The format required is *mm/dd/yyyy hh:mm:ss.*
- **-l <for the last time frame>**   This parameter will only analyze logs for a specific amount of time prior to the starting point. An example would be to only analyze logs for the last 12 hours. The format required is the time frame in digits and then the designator, for example, 12h, 60s, or 365d.
- **-mempercent <%>**   How much memory you want to allocate to Logfu to plot the graph.
- **-t <end date and time>**   An end date and time for analysis. The format required is *mm/dd/yyyy hh:mm:ss.*

Options specify which log will be analyzed:

- **-a**   Performs analysis of agent logs.
- **-c**   Performs analysis of console logs.
- **-h**   Displays help information.
- **-i**   Displays only information regarding the files, no analysis of log files will be done.
- **-m**   Performs analysis of manager logs.
- **-noex**   Do not process exceptions.
- **-noplot**   Do not plot information to graph.

The information that can be graphed from these logs includes JVM memory utilization, JVM garbage collection, and EPS statistics on the ArcSight SmartConnectors and ArcSight Manager. Once you create these graphs, you can save them as graphic files for inclusion in reports.

## Database

The ArcSight Database server primarily does two things. It holds the two Oracle Databases in the ArcSight instance, the first being the database that holds the ArcSight resources and the second being the database that stores the events. The server also contains the Partition Archiver that manages partition and archiving functions. You will want to monitor both of these parts on a regular basis to ensure they are functioning properly.

**DBCHECK**

ArcSight has several built-in systems to perform checks against itself and its components. The main check used against the Oracle Database is the DBCHECK. DBCHECK will run an analysis against your database looking for specific issues that may cause problems with your operations. To run this check, log in to the ArcSight Database server and enter the following command:

```
%ArcSightDB%\bin\arcsight dbcheck
```

This script will generate a report, in HTML format, with multiple files and an index.html file to start with, on the status of your database. DBCHECK is used prior to performing any type of patching or system upgrades to ArcSight ESM primarily. Running it from time to time to look for any inconsistencies in the database that you may not see during everyday operations is also a good idea.

## Partitions

The Oracle Database used by ArcSight to store all of the logs is not really a turnkey solution. You can't just set it up and never look at it again. The database will require monitoring to ensure that everything is operating correctly.

**GetPartitionInfo40.sql**    If you need to a good overall view of your database and partitions, you can run a built-in SQL query called *GetPartitionInfo40.sql*. You will need to acquire this script from ArcSight technical support, since only an old version, GetPartitionInfo .sql, is included with the default install of ArcSight and is not used with ArcSight ESM versions 4.0 and higher. In order to run this script, follow these steps:

1. Log into the ArcSight Database server.
2. Navigate to %ArcSightDB%\utilities\database\oracle\common\sql.
3. Execute the command **sqlplus.exe**.
4. Log in using the Oracle account that you set up for ArcSight to communicate with the Oracle Database.
5. Once at the Oracle command prompt, type **@GetPartitionInfo40.sql**.
6. The SQL scripts will run and prompt for which partitions to report on. The wildcard for all partitions is %.
7. When the script has completed running, it will exit from the Oracle prompt.

The log will be stored in this directory as partitioninfo.log. You will want to rename this file so you can save it for your historical records, since the next time you run GetPartitionInfo40.sql, the script will overwrite any previous results that are still named as the default partitioninfo.log.

The following is some of the information that you can gather from the report generated by this script:

- Information about the version of Oracle you are running
- The Oracle Database instance being used by ArcSight
- The database configuration
- The tablespaces that are mounted in the database
- The partition retention information and history of changes made to this configuration
- The partition scheduled task configuration and history of changes made to this configuration
- Information on the partition archiving and compression to include success and failures
- How many events were processed per partition

This information can be used to troubleshoot issues related to your partition archiving and compression process. This is also the first thing that ArcSight customer support will ask if you were to contact them with a possible database issue.

**Changing Partition Retention Settings**    As time goes by and you either lose or gain storage space, you may need to change the partition retention period that you have set within ArcSight. The command to complete this task is as follows:

```
%ArcSightDB%\bin\arcsightdatabase pc
```

This will bring up a wizard that will make a connection to the database using your ArcSight ESM credentials and give you the following options to change. When dealing with partitions, remember that each partition is a 24-hour period, from 12:00:00 AM to 11:59:59 PM. This time period is hard set in the system and is not user-changeable.

- **Online Retention Period**    The number of days that will be active in the Oracle database and available for you to work with immediately.
- **Online Reserve Period**    The amount of buffer space, in days, that you build into the database to allow for issues with partition archiving. These partitions are created in advance and will take events from the max overflow partition if there are any date/time issues with a device sending events to the Manager.
- **Offline Archive Period**    The number of days that will be kept in a compressed archived format in the archive directory.

Keep in mind that changing the archive retention period is *not* a retroactive process. If you change the retention period to a shorter amount of time, only archive partitions created after this change was made will be affected. Any previous archived partitions will not take this change and will continue with the configuration that was in place when that archived partition was created. Also, if you have the partition retention period set to a lesser time frame and then change it to a longer period of time, the older archived partitions will still use the original shorter time frame.

**Half-Baked Partitions**  A *half-baked partition* is one where there is a discrepancy with the status of an ArcSight partition between the ArcSight ESM and the Oracle Database. The most common scenario is when the Oracle Database keeps an archived partition mounted and the ArcSight Manager lists the partition as archived. To repair this, you will need to fix these discrepancies and have the partition dismounted from the Oracle Database and archived within ArcSight. Here are the steps and commands to repair a half-baked partition:

1. Stop the ArcSight Manager Service.

2. Log in to the Oracle Database using your ArcSight credentials.

3. Run the following commands, where **XXXXXXXX** is the date of the partition you need to fix:

```
SQL> UPDATE arc_partition SET ACTIVE='NO', ARCHIVED='YES',
ARCHIVE_STATUS='SUCCESS' WHERE ID IN (SELECT ID FROM arc_resources WHERE
NAME IN ('XXXXXXXX'));

SQL> COMMIT;

SQL> UPDATE arc_partition_shadow SET ACTIVE='NO', ARCHIVED='YES',
ARCHIVE_STATUS='SUCCESS' WHERE ID IN (SELECT ID FROM arc_resources WHERE
NAME IN ('XXXXXXXX'));

SQL> COMMIT ;
```

4. You need to change both the **arc_partition tablespace** and the **arc_partition_shadow** tablespace to have the partition labeled as archived.

5. Once this is done, restart the ArcSight Manager and run another GetPartitioninfo. sql to see if the ArcSight Manager and Oracle Database are now in sync.

# System Patching and Upgrades

Patches and upgrades come with the territory of working in the IT world these days. Patching and performing system upgrades on your system will provide fixes to security vulnerabilities, aid in application stability, and possibly add application enhancements.

## OS Patching

From time to time, you will need to apply patches to the underlying OS that ArcSight is running on. In order to patch the underlying OS, it's best to err on the side of caution since you may not know exactly what behind-the-scenes changes are incorporated into the patch. Best practice is to test all OS patches on a QA machine to ensure that there is no interaction between ArcSight and the new patch. If you do not have a test environment, you will want to do a lot of research on the patches to better understand if the patches will affect ArcSight before loading the patch on your production system.

If a reboot is required to patch the underlying server OS, you need to be very careful about a couple of things to avoid causing some issues with the ArcSight ESM. Also keep in mind that the ArcSight SmartConnectors are queuing up events while your servers are rebooting and you may have an increased load on the servers when the ArcSight Manager and Database servers come back online, depending on how long the ArcSight Manager and Database server were offline.

The first thing you will want to be aware of is that you should not bring down ArcSight ESM during its standard database management times. These maintenance times were set up during the initial installation. By default, the times are 01:00, 03:00, 06:00, 10:00, 15:00, and 21:00. It is recommended to wait at least one hour after any of these times before shutting down any of the ArcSight services. If you are unsure when the designated maintenance times are, you can check in the GetPartitionInfo.sql results. These statistics updates are not essential to the operation of ArcSight, but are used for monitoring. If one of the statistic updates is missed or does not complete in the appropriate amount of time, the statistics will be updated on the next scheduled run.

The second possible issue you may come across is the order in which you bring down the different ArcSight components. It is recommended to start and stop the system as a whole in a specific order, otherwise you may run into issues with your instance of the Oracle Database. The order in which you will want to bring down ArcSight is listed here:

1. Stop the ArcSight ESM Partition Archiver service.

2. Stop the ArcSight ESM Web service.

3. Stop the ArcSight ESM Manager service.

4. Stop the Oracle ArcSight instance.

5. Stop the Oracle ArcSight Listener. Stopping this service is not explicitly required, but it is recommended.

When bringing the system back online, if the services are not set to autostart, you just need to bring the services back online in the reverse order from that listed above. One thing to keep in mind when restarting all the services is that the ArcSight Manager may take some time to fully launch. On a Windows Server, the ArcSight Manager service may appear to be hung up or you may receive an error stating that the service took too long to start. You will want to tail the server.std.log file located in the %ArcSightManager%\logs\default folder and monitor the progress of the ArcSight Manager coming back online. Depending on your ArcSight configuration, the ArcSight Manager service is loading and processing a significant amount of information and may take longer than Windows has allocated to the process.

## ArcSight ESM Patching and Upgrading

There will come a time when you will need to apply patches and other upgrades to your ArcSight instance. For the most part, the upgrade process for ArcSight is pretty straightforward, and as long as you follow the instructions provided with the upgrade, you shouldn't really have an issue.

**ArcSight SmartConnectors**    ArcSight performs most of its upgrades by installing a complete new version of the software and then copying over the old configuration files and logs to the new instance. An example of how ArcSight handles upgrades would be the ArcSight SmartConnector upgrade process. When you upgrade the SmartConnectors, ArcSight will rename the old SmartConnector folder from CURRENT to the version number of that particular SmartConnector installation. These upgrades can only be run from the Manager one at a time.

This allows you the advantage of easy rollback if a new version causes any issues. In the Console, all you will need to do is right-click the connector and select Send Command | Upgrade | Rollback Upgrade. You will then be prompted for which version to roll back to. This functionality of being able to roll back connectors on the fly aids in maintaining a high level of availability and uptime for ArcSight, but this feature can also use up system resources over time. Since ArcSight will not delete old versions of the connectors from your server, if you do not go in and manually clean out the old versions from time to time, you may begin running out of drive space on the server.

**ArcSight ESM**    Similar to the process ArcSight performs for upgrades to connectors, a service pack upgrade really isn't an upgrade, but rather a completely new install. The installation process will just copy over your configuration and data from the previous install point and use these in the new installation. During the upgrade process, you will be asked for a location for the installation. It is recommended to use a different install location than your previous instance so you have the option to roll back to a previous ArcSight component version.

When performing an upgrade to your ArcSight ESM deployment, the most important thing to remember is to perform a full backup of ArcSight, including the Manager and Database application along with the Oracle Database prior to any type of patching or upgrade.

**CAUTION**  It needs to be stated again—that's how important backups are: *always perform a full backup prior to installing any upgrades whatsoever.*

ArcSight breaks the upgrade into steps. It begins the upgrade process by performing a test of the first portion that it will upgrade, and if the test is successful, it performs the first step. After that step is completed, ArcSight performs another test prior to performing the next upgrade step. This pattern will repeat until the upgrade has been completed. At any point during this process, if one of the tests fails, there really is only one backout procedure and that is to restore from a backup. You can limit the possibility of needing to restore from a backup if an upgrade fails by performing all the tests and preliminary steps listed in the documentation provided with each ArcSight patch, service pack, or version upgrade.

### Oracle Database Patching

It is recommended to only patch the Oracle Database with patches that are approved by ArcSight. This is so ArcSight can ensure that their application performs properly with the Oracle Database. Since ArcSight and Oracle are so tightly integrated in the ArcSight ESM platform, it is extremely important to have these two pieces of software operating together smoothly. ArcSight v4.5 will only run on Oracle 10.0.2.0.4 and not on the Oracle 11g platform.

# Tips and Tricks

The following sections discuss some concepts to try and keep in mind when configuring and running your ArcSight ESM deployment. Some of them are just common sense, but hopefully, they will save you some headaches down the road.

### Assets

Maintain good lines of communication with other members of your organization. You want to know ahead of time if something new is going to be added to your environment so you can analyze if the logs are going to be needed and prepare ArcSight for the new asset.

### ArcSight Manager

Make sure the JVM heap is large enough so the garbage collection is not running constantly, but not so large that the JVM garbage collection takes a long time to run. This information can be found in the server.std.log or by running Logfu. You can make changes to the JVM heap size at any time, but you will need to stop the ArcSight Manager first.

### ArcSight Database

Here are some tips and tricks for working with the ArcSight Database:

- If you're not an experienced Oracle DBA, don't mess around with the inner workings of the ArcSight database. Even if you are an experienced Oracle DBA, it's best not to mess around with the database without first consulting ArcSight support.

- ArcSight has a built-in notification system that will email out system alerts to user-defined email addresses. It is recommended that you configure this during the ArcSight ESM v4.5 installation. With this notification system in place, you will be alerted to system issues.

■ Make sure there are no errors with the partition archiving process. This single process, if left unmonitored, can bring your entire ArcSight deployment to a halt. If the Partition Archiver is not archiving partitions properly, then your database will begin to utilize more and more space until you run out.

■ Along with the Partition Archiver, you're going to want to keep an eye on the database size daily. You don't want the fact that you are running out of database room to sneak up on you. You will want to know well in advance if there are any issues that need to be addressed. Plus, if you have significant spikes in database utilization, it could be a sign that there are other issues that you need to address.

■ When reactivating partitions, keep in mind that the partitions reactivate in the same directory as the partition archives. You will need to ensure that you have enough free space on that drive to accommodate the unarchived partitions you want to reactivate.

## ArcSight Console

Here are some tips and tricks for running the ArcSight Console:

■ Each instance of the ArcSight Console connected to the ArcSight Manager uses up system resources on the ArcSight Manager. What you do on the ArcSight Console can impact the performance of the ArcSight ESM v4.5 Manager, thus reducing its capabilities. How many people will be using ArcSight at the same time, what they will be doing with it, and what type of queries they will be running should be taken into account when planning the hardware that ArcSight will be running on.

■ Active Lists and Session Lists consume RAM on the ArcSight Manager. When developing content that uses Active Lists, remember to have the entries expire within a reasonable amount of time. When using Session Lists, you will need to manually clear out the entries that are stored in the Session List, since these lists do not have expiration times.

## ArcSight SmartConnectors

Here are some tips and tricks for working with the ArcSight SmartConnectors:

■ Make sure the cache size is large enough to accommodate long periods with the system offline. If you have a hardware or software outage on your ArcSight Manager server and it is down for ten days, the manager will not be processing new events and the connectors will cache incoming logs. If you have allocated enough cache for each connector, then, when the ArcSight Manager comes back online, you will not have lost any information, and the

ArcSight SmartConnectors will begin sending in all the cached logs. If you have not set the cache size to a reasonable amount for your environment, you have the possibility of losing data. When the Manager comes back online, the SmartConnectors will begin sending the logs in a 70 percent to 30 percent ratio, with 70 percent being new incoming real-time logs and the 30 percent being cached logs. The SmartConnector will continue doing this until the cache is empty.

■ Turning on Preserve Raw Event in the ArcSight SmartConnector configuration is a good step for determining parsing issues, but only leave it on for the minimum amount of time required. Preserving raw events can take up significant space in your database.

# Summary

As you can see, there are many things you can do with ArcSight and this is just the tip of the iceberg. Use this information as a stepping stone to developing a useful and efficient ArcSight deployment for your organization. Take your time, plan the deployment thoroughly and properly, and if you are unsure about what you are doing, don't be afraid to consult with other ArcSight users out there.

# APPENDIX | The Ways and Means of the Security Analyst

Now that you have read the entire book, you see the power that the SIEM system can provide to your organization. Your next questions might be these:

- How does an interested IT professional or security professional develop his or her skills, experience, and resume to qualify for a position as a SIEM security analyst?
- What type of vision is required of a SIEM security professional/analyst to identify, qualify, and remediate security incidents quickly?

Read on. This appendix attempts to answer these well-targeted, upwardly mobile, and constructive questions.

# What Is a Security Analyst?

The effective security analyst combines a rich and diverse collection of personal and professional attributes. These attributes begin with a solid foundation of technical knowledge and skills, which includes formal technical training and certification. Add to that seasoning through experience. Then add a dash of refined daily habits and personality traits that include an inquisitive nature, persistence, and diligence. Security professionals are held to, and often hold themselves to, a higher standard of ethics.

## Recommended Professional Background

Contrary to popular belief, not everyone can be successful as a security analyst. Many individual facets should be considered before you embark on the adventures of becoming or continuing a career as a security analyst. The following is a description of the specific skills that are often recommended, and in some cases required, to be an effective security analyst within the security operations center for an organization.

Some of the recommended professional experiences and skills would include a solid understanding of information technology, and relatively large time spent in being in the IT industry. Although the IT industry comprises many different disciplines, a security analyst should have real-world experience as a network administrator, network engineer, or system administrator within the private sector, government agencies, or the military.

Background experiences in the private sector versus government IT experience have their pros and cons. If you've worked for the government, the value of information obtained is often immeasurable. Because much of the information the government holds and protects could lead to the loss of human life if lost or exposed, it can be difficult to ascertain the true value of the information, though it would be very high. And it warrants nothing but the absolute finest protection available, whatever the cost. For that reason, government IT professionals often receive whatever tools, software, and hardware they need to help them protect valuable information assets. This lets the IT professional see and use a wide array of technologies, but it also does them a disservice when they transfer into the private sector, where resources are more limited.

In the private sector, where the life of the business depends on profitability, the IT professional is constrained with rigid cost justification for each and every tool requested. Limited resources means that a more practical and counter-balanced approach is required in making technology decisions.

Although the following descriptions of the various disciplines within the IT industry are relatively clear and distinct, note that all of the tasks and requirements of these positions are subject to the desires, definitions, and resource capabilities of the organization itself. In reality, the line between the various positions defined here are somewhat blurred. In a smaller organization, an IT professional may be required to wear many hats, and one person may be assigned responsibilities from all three levels described next. An IT professional working in a large and well-developed organization will typically be assigned tasks limited to a narrow scope.

## System Administrator

A system administrator is an individual who installs, supports, and maintains the various computing systems, including end user computers, peripherals, and servers within the organization. In some cases, the system administrator is charged to plan for, and respond to, service outages and other network complications. The system administrator is often responsible for supporting the end users, ensuring their daily functionality.

## Network Administrator

Typically, a network administrator is an individual who maintains the overall health of the corporate network, deploying and configuring individual servers and infrastructure devices for specific functions, as required and specified by management. The network administrator is often responsible for providing the maintenance and monitoring of the network and ensuring that connectivity using the corporation's LAN/WAN infrastructure is available and capable of achieving the required business objectives. The network administrator has a very hands-on job that requires detailed knowledge of many different systems and configuration parameters. IT system availability is the primary objective of the network administrator.

## Network Engineer

A network engineer is typically involved in developing the architecture of the overall IT system. It is typically an individual who designs, coordinates implementation, and troubleshoots systemic network issues, to provide availability and security of the organization's communications. The network engineer is typically responsible for the selection of specific products and technologies to satisfy the functional requirements, while justifying the costs of each selection. This person is typically not involved with end user support or daily maintenance of specific systems.

## Commonalities

Even though each of these positions requires some sort of clarity and distinction in its duties, all have some tasks in common. Anyone working within any of these disciplines within the IT industry will have experience in various networking devices and technologies. These devices and technologies include routers, switches, firewalls, malware protection and patching, IDS/IPS technologies, VPN and WAN technologies, operating systems including Windows and Linux, and system and protocol vulnerabilities. A good security analyst will understand these technologies, as well as others, and will know how they work together to provide an infrastructure that provides confidentiality, integrity, and availability of the resources for the network users who require them.

Another commonality is the required familiarity of the protocols used with regard to the communications among these devices. The most common protocol used is TCP/IP. As you are probably aware, TCP/IP is the set of communications protocols used for the Internet and other comparable networks. Its name is based on the two protocols contained within it: the Transmission Control Protocol (TCP), which operates at Layer four of the Open Systems Interconnection (OSI) model, and the Internet Protocol (IP) which operates at Layer three of the OSI model.

Of course, another facet of the skill set of a security analyst is a comprehension of corporate policy, to be combined with legal and regulatory compliance requirements. These types of requirements can come in the form of organizational security policies, such as remote user connectivity, hardware use, and software use policies. These requirements can also be mandated by the government, such as SOX, FISMA, and HIPAA, based upon the industry in which your organization is involved. A good analyst will understand which security and regulatory requirements their organization must adhere to so that they are able to help assure compliance.

# Security Analyst's Areas of Study

Having a firm grasp of operating systems (such as Windows, Linux, and UNIX), business applications (such as email systems, database applications, and CRM applications), networking infrastructure systems and services (such as DNS, DHCP, routers, switches, and firewalls), networking protocols (such as TCP/IP, UDP, and ICMP), organizational security policies, and regulatory requirements is important. An analyst may have additional areas of expertise as well.

This lengthy list of knowledge, skills, and experience is enough to get you in the door, however. But to excel as a security professional or security analyst, you may want to dive deeper into other specific areas of study, or specializations. Some of the specialties include IT/cyber laws and regulations, hacker skills, developer/programming skills, and skills in digital forensic analysis. No matter what role you play within the security operations center (SOC) environment, you'll probably be required to understand attacker methodologies to uncover various activities within the network before they become a legitimate attack. You may also be required to have some coding skills in different types of programming languages that can allow for quicker identification, reaction, and remediation of the possible attacks within your network.

A knowledge of IT/cyber laws and regulations can provide insight into what is happening in the world of cyber-legislation and how these laws can affect your organization, from the standpoint of the prosecution of attackers as well as the areas of potential liability and increased exposure to lawsuits after a violation. Many different cases have been documented and brought through various legal systems throughout the world. Some such cases include illegal distribution of copyrighted materials, web site defacing, theft of PII, extortion attempts (hire my security consulting company or I'll release the sensitive data I was able to steal from your company), and many more. As a security analyst, knowing what laws protect and affect your organization can assist you in ensuring that your organization adheres to the regulations imposed on it by the various government agencies. Having an understanding of these laws, and especially the ramifications of not adhering to them, provides a security analyst with the ammunition to employ various protective processes and procedures that are required by the laws imposed. This knowledge may also provide the analyst the insights and justifications to convince management to employ appropriate protective processes and systems.

Digital forensics is a branch of forensic science pertaining to any evidence of wrongdoing found in computers and digital storage media for various purposes. The goal of digital forensics is to explain the current state of a computer system, a storage medium, an electronic document, or even packets moving across a network.

An organization may require an analyst who possesses digital forensics skills for many reasons, including the following:

- When required for legal proceedings, to analyze computer systems, media, and communications belonging to defendants or litigants

- To recover an organization's or user's data in the event of a hardware or software failure or accidental deletion

- To analyze a computer system after a compromising event to determine how the attacker gained access to the system and what actions the attacker performed

- To gather evidence to use against an employee that an organization suspects of wrongdoings

- To perform analysis of backups from lost or stolen systems to identify what data is now exposed

While these items will assist in making a security analyst a true asset to any organization, other common skills should also be attained at some point in time during the analyst's career. A security analyst must be known for his or her ability to detect attack signatures and methods accurately, precisely pinpoint the point of entry, and whether it is an internal user or an external force accessing specific IT resources. Specifically, you should have a firm understanding of attacker methodologies. This knowledge provides you with the familiarity of the various types of attacks to which your organization may be subjected. Every security professional should understand the basics of attacks, such as a replay attacks, man in the middle attacks, buffer overflows, and DoS and DDoS attacks, to name a few. After all, how can you successfully uncover one of these attacks if you are not aware of the telltale signs and footprints of these exploits? If you cannot recognize the behavior of a virus or worm in your network, how can you determine how to stop it from doing its damage?

Another skill set that is highly recommended is the ability to develop and understand at least some forms of code. This does not mean that you need to build an application to provide for SIEM-like functionality. It does mean that you should be able to, at a minimum, write and interpret scripts. If you know how to create .BAT or .CMD files, this skill can assist you in incident recovery actions in a more efficient, effective, and automated manner. Knowledge of various types of programming languages can also assist in reverse-engineering contaminants and malware in your network. As an example, imagine you identify malware within your IT system that is in the form of a self-propagating, zero-day worm. In this case, your IDS and antivirus applications probably will not have the specific signature to assist in recognizing and abbreviating this attack. Your ability to decipher the malicious code can assist you in dissecting the various components of the worm to see what actions it performs, when those actions will be performed, and, hopefully, how to stop and eradicate the malware.

### Task and Project Management

A security analyst must be able to take a task or project from inception (detection of a potential security incident) to completion (the IT system returns to a "Normal" state). As a security analyst, you will also have to multitask when it comes to the various and vast amounts of events that are being forwarded from the multitude of devices into the organization's SOC. When the events/incidents/violations are handed off to you from a security operator, you will be required to verify them as true-positive security concerns based on your knowledge and experience. You must then analyze and assess the situation to mitigate the damages by limiting the scope of the incident and eradicating the malicious content and activity (stabilize the patient and stop the bleeding). Next, you must remediate the vulnerabilities that lead to the exploit to disallow the identified attack vectors or ensure that these violations can be automatically dealt with in the future.

## Typical Mindset of a Security Analyst

As stated, not everyone wants to be, can be, or should be a security analyst. Although you may possess the skills discussed so far, particular psychological attributes are worth consideration if you want to become, or continue your career as, a security analyst.

### Impeccable Ethics

A security analyst must be totally trusted by their peers, supervisors, and the organization's managers. A security analyst is responsible for accessing and analyzing what could be highly confidential data whose confidentiality is critical to the success of an organization. A security analyst may also have access to various hardware/software devices that either store or transmit that confidential data. The security professional/analyst often has access to confidential and critical systems and information that would otherwise not be made available to the security analyst for business need. Couple this access with knowledge of various attack tools and methodologies, a security analyst is in the position to introduce worms, viruses, root kits, and backdoors, and he or she has the ability to ensure that these attack vectors are not seen or monitored. Not only is a security analyst in the position to obfuscate the events being monitored, but if an attack were to occur, a security analyst would be the first line of defense against this activity.

In summary, the security professional

- has access to the most sensitive data.
- has tools to create unseen backdoors for future access.
- has access and often control of the monitoring systems that might detect the violation, and can therefore remain undetected.
- would be the primary investigator if suspicious activity is noticed by others.
- could terminate the activities to eliminate the trail, or steer the investigation far away from the real trail.
- could falsify information and evidence to deflect any further investigations and remain undetected.

### Attitude and Personality Traits

No matter the environment or the organization, because of differing mindsets and job objectives, production often views security as a hindrance to the business and the objectives set forth by the organization's leaders. Production workers seek to ensure availability at all cost. Security's position is that if it isn't secure, pull its plug.

Anyone in the security industry realizes that the notion of security being nothing but a hindrance is inaccurate, however. A security professional is facilitating transactions and production's capabilities to ensure that they are more secure and reliable. However, when security practices are employed on the production floor, it appears to the individuals affected that these new processes are making their job more difficult, and therefore these practices are viewed as an obstruction to their jobs.

Nevertheless, the response and reaction of the security analyst must be nonabrasive. Although the security analyst's intent is to assist the organization in matters of security, it is not always seen as assistance. Sometimes, the security analyst will have to "call out" an individual for not following approved security practices, which can add tension and appear to validate their claims of being contrary. A security analyst must not get flustered or stressed out easily, must maintain a calm persona, and should not feel as though he or she is being attacked by anyone within the organization.

# Role of a Security Analyst Within an Organization

Although you're now familiar with the various recommendations regarding what traits you should possess as a security analyst, when you are entering the realm of security within an organization, you may start this adventure as a member of the security operator role, typically the entry level for security operations. If you are beginning your adventures in the security industry in the role of a security operator, you should consider the following suggestions that may assist you in a quick ascent through the ranks of the security industry, and within your organization's SOC.

## Ascending the Security Professions Ladder

You must understand the technologies that provide the communications, storage, security, and availability within your organization's information technology infrastructure. Having a firm understanding of these components and systems, their function, and how to administer, maintain, and support them gives you a huge advantage as an up-and-coming security professional.

Following is a list of some of the devices and technologies with which you should be familiar:

- The OSI model (no IT education is complete without understanding this model)
- TCP/IP
- Encryption (SSL, PKI, ciphers)
- Intrusion detection systems/intrusion protection systems, including NIDS, HIDS, NIPS, and HIPS
- Antivirus and antispyware software
- Firewalls
- Routers
- Switches
- VLANs
- VPN technologies for WAN and LAN purposes, such as SSH, IPSec, and PPTP
- Authentication technologies, including Kerberos, digital certificates, token devices, and AAA protocols such as RADIUS, TACACS, TACACS+, and Diameter
- Wireless devices
- DNS
- DHCP

Many other technologies are incorporated into networks, not only for application and production support, but for security purposes as well.

A true asset to any organization knows the organization and its business and security objectives. One way that you can stand out among your peers is to know your organization's security policies, procedures, and the SOC hierarchy. This vision will allow you to assist in overseeing that other individuals are adhering to those processes and procedures. Your enforcement of company policy not only helps your organization to maintain its security posture, but it is also often recognized appreciatively by your supervisors, which can help your career.

Management needs and expects core personnel to come up with solutions to problems. To be recognized as a core employee, you should adopt the mentality expressed an old adage: "Don't present management with a problem; present management with a solution." Approaching your management with nothing but problems doesn't help in correcting these problems but may get you labeled as a complainer. No one likes a complainer! In knowing the organization's security policies and procedures, and monitoring the various events within the SOC, you will be in a positive position to provide solutions to the problems facing the SOC on a daily basis. An important aspect of being a security analyst, or an aspiring security analyst, is to rely on the organization's policies and procedures to help guide you to creative solutions.

Using all of your knowledge on attack methodologies, network and security devices, and organizational policies, you can and should provide solutions, not just objections. Remember that knowing the organization's hierarchy is especially important here. It would be inappropriate to share your solutions with your boss's boss. Remember the chain of command within your organization. If you were to skip your direct supervisor and propose your solution to the SOC manager, or the CISO, these actions can actually be seen in a negative light. Your direct manager is responsible for ensuring that everyone within his or her area of concern is performing as expected. You do not want to blindside your direct supervisor when a manager suggests a solution you have provided elsewhere, even if your solution is very effective.

## Restrictions and Responsibilities of a Security Analyst

Typically, some inherent restrictions are forced upon a security professional. These restrictions will often impede the implementation of your recommended solutions, or require that you pursue your proposed adjustments through predefined channels. Even though you may have created and provided a solid, effective resolution to a security issue, you may not be authorized to implement your solution into the standard practices of your organization.

When you are proposing a solution, remember to adhere to the organization's hierarchy. Your immediate supervisor probably has greater vision on the current political climate within the organization. Knowing where, when, and how to introduce a new concept will increase the chances of implementation and success with the deployment of your well-tuned suggestion. In addition, recognize that your boss got to be your boss probably because he or she, too, has had some worthy experience and has provided some worthy suggestions in the past. Look to him or her as an ally, possibly even being able to provide enhancements and fine-tuning to your proposed solution. Typically, working in concert with your manager will help get your solution implemented. It will bring visibility to your creativity and passion for your current role within the organization and the security of the organization. It will show that you are a team player in a team-oriented industry. This can only help you while you gain experience and knowledge as a part of your pursuit of greater opportunities.

To maintain balance within the security structure of an organization, and following the concept of separation of duties to avoid granting any one individual too much authority, members of security operations will not usually have any administrative permissions or authority on the IT assets that are being monitored. The assets in question include firewalls, routers, servers, data resources, and directory services servers, to name a few, even though these assets, along with so many others, are forwarding their events into your organization's SOC for monitoring. A natural boundary exists between the personnel in IT and the personnel in security. Although they should, and technically do, complement each other, in typical organizations, these two departments are separate and distinct, and often don't work well together. While experience says that the difficulty typically lies on the IT side of the fence, the disparity still affects everyone involved in ensuring the availability and protection of the valuable information assets of the organization.

One technique you can use to help relieve tension between the two job functions is to implement formal change management procedures within the organization. The change management process identifies to all involved, including IT personnel, that the changes being introduced are being reviewed, recognized, and authorized by management as required changes.

Another technique to help develop cooperation is to provide early warning and alerts (if using a SIEM or SIEM-like technology) to the IT staff a server is down, a firewall configuration changes, or a wireless device attempts to connect to the organization's network. Although this will assist in gaining cooperation between the IT department and the security department, it will not and should not provide any security professional within the organization the ability to administer IT systems themselves. What it will do is begin establishing a cooperative relationship between departments that can allow for the implementation of specific projects.

Although you may not have direct authority to administer the IT devices within your organization, you may be tasked with administering specific security devices used to monitor those IT systems. These devices include SIEM applications and components, IDS/IPS, and various proxy technologies. As an aspiring or current security analyst, you should understand the various security and networking devices used and needed within your organization's network. Knowing what a SIEM can do for your SOC and how to configure the content (such as filters, parsers, device categories, and rules) to enable a proactive analysis of the events being forwarded into your SOC gives your peers and managers immeasurable confidence in your skills. If you are not familiar with the capabilities of a SIEM system, you're on the right track in reading this book. The knowledge gained by the time spent understanding the topics discussed here can certainly assist you in your journey toward becoming a security analyst.

# Suggested Certifications for a Security Analyst

Many different bodies of knowledge—such as security and networking devices, attacker methodologies, specializations, and competencies—typically accompany a security analyst in his or her career. Following are some of the specific technology certifications, not only in the security industry, but in the IT industry as well, that will enhance your security analyst resume. There is no such thing as knowing too much.

The more exposure and knowledge you obtain about the various technologies used within IT systems and the protection of those systems, the more likely you will be promoted and ascend the corporate ladder to whatever your desired IT or security professional destination might be.

In addition to this list, many worthy training opportunities are available in the industry that do not include a formal certification. As a true professional in the industry, you should continuously be searching out and partaking of relevant conferences, webinars, specific vendor/product training opportunities, whitepapers, current events/news, periodicals, and other sources of information. In this day and age, with "e-everything" just a mouse click away, the list of accessible and cost-effective supplemental training materials is endless. Immerse yourself in the latest events, developments, technology, trends, and culture of your chosen industry. You are the professional, after all—right?

## General Security Certifications

Following are some security- and network-related certifications that you should consider acquiring. These certifications validate your studies and your ambition to the prospective hiring company, and as a result, your resume might float to the top of the stack.

### Security+

This entry-level security certification is provided by CompTIA and is a vendor-neutral certification that requires the candidate to show competency in general system security, network infrastructure, access control, and organizational security.

**Prerequisites** Candidates should have at least two years of networking experience, with an emphasis on security. Candidates should also possess the CompTIA Network+ certification.

**Exam Specifics** The questions on the exam are based on five domains:

- General security concepts
- Communications security
- Infrastructure security
- Basics of cryptography
- Operational/organizational security

The exam comprises 100 questions. The time allowed for the exam is 90 minutes. Passing score is a 750 on a scale of 100 to 900.

### CISSP

This vendor-neutral certification is provided by ISC2 (Information Systems Security Certification Consortium, Inc.). According to ISC2, the CISSP was the first certification in the field of information security accredited by the ANSI Standard 17024:2003.

**Prerequisites**   Candidates must have at least 5 years of information technology security experience, which includes a minimum of 2 years within any two of the following ten domains:

- Access control
- Application development security
- Business continuity and disaster recovery planning
- Cryptography
- Information security governance and risk management
- Legal, regulations, investigations, and compliance
- Operations security
- Physical (environmental) security
- Security architecture and design
- Telecommunications and network security

**Exam specifics**   The 250 multiple-choice questions are based on topics from the ten domains. The candidate must often choose the best of the multiple correct answers or the best of the selection of all wrong answers. This is a difficult exam. The time allowed for the exam is 6 hours. Passing score is a 700.

Even if the candidate is to pass the exam, the candidate will not receive certification at that time. Two other tasks must be performed to complete the CISSP certification process:

- The candidate must submit and execute a properly completed Endorsement Form and must provide multiple sources of employment to verify the candidate's experience. The candidate must also successfully pass an audit, if selected, concerning his or her declarations regarding professional experience displayed on the Endorsement Form.
- An existing CISSP, in good standing with ISC2, is required to endorse the candidate as well.

## CISA (Certified Information Systems Auditor)

This certification is provided by ISACA and is acknowledged worldwide as a criterion of achievement among IS audit, control, and security professionals alike.

**Prerequisites**   This test requires that the candidate have a minimum of 5 years of professional IS auditing, control or security work experience based on the following six job practice areas:

- IS audit process
- IT governance

- Systems and infrastructure lifecycle management
- IT service delivery and support
- Protection of information assets
- Business continuity and disaster recovery

The candidate may request substitutions and waivers of the obligatory experience.

**Exam Specifics**   The 200 multiple-choice questions on the exam are based on the six job practice areas. The exam is offered only in June and December each year.

## CISM (Certified Information Security Manager)

This certification is provided by ISACA and was developed specifically for experienced information security managers and those who possess pertinent information security management responsibilities. Likely candidates for the CISM certification are people who manage, design, oversee, and/or evaluate an organization's information security infrastructure.

**Prerequisites**   Candidates should have a minimum of 5 years of information security work experience, with a minimum of 3 years of information security management work experience in three or more of the following job practice areas:

- Information security governance
- Information risk management
- Information security program development
- Information security program management
- Incident management and response

**Exam Specifics**   The 200 multiple-choice questions on the exam are based on the five job practice areas. Candidates have 4 hours in which to complete the exam, which is offered only in June and December each year.

## QSA (Qualified Security Assessor)

This certification is provided by the Payment Card Industry (PCI) Security Standards Council and developed for individuals who are employed by QSA-certified companies that perform evaluations of any organization that processes credit cards against the 12 high-level Payment Card Industry Data Security Standard (PCI DSS) control objectives.

**Prerequisites**   The QSA prerequisite process includes three potential parts: the qualification of the security company itself, the qualification of the company's employee(s) who will be performing and/or managing the on-site PCI DSS Assessments, and, optionally, the qualification of Principle and Associate QSAs where needed to support global market needs.

Prior to participating in any of the PCI SSC training workshops to become eligible for the QSA designation, the candidate must meet the following requirements:

- PCI SSC strongly prefers all candidates be full-time employees of a Validated QSA company. Some exceptions are made for contractors; however, the QSA company may have to meet additional requirement for the approval of a contractor QSA.

- QSA applicants must meet either of the following minimum requirements: a CISSP, CISA, or CISM Certification, or 5 years of IT security experience. Each candidate must submit a resume reflecting these requirements.

- All QSA program candidates must sign and accept the PCI SSC QSA Employee Certification form and submit it at the time of attending training.

**Exam Specifics**   The QSA certified or candidate company must first submit the required documentation, including certifications, business license, insurance certificates, and the registration fee. All individuals who will be involved in assessing security for the company's clients must undergo and pass the Council's QSA training course and receive official certification. Individual fees apply. A Council representative will schedule training for the prospective QSA's employees, and the company will be notified whether they pass or fail the test at the end of the course. (Quoted from the pcistandards.org web site.) The exam is 60 multiple choice questions and the candidate is allocated up to 3 hours to complete the exam. The passing score is 75 percent.

## GISF (Information Security Fundamentals)

This entry-level security certification provided by GIAC was developed for individuals who need an overview of risk management and defense in depth techniques.

**Prerequisites**   Although there are no specific prerequisites for any GIAC certifications, if candidates need help in mastering the objectives for this certification, the GIAC web site provides links to various resources.

**Exam Specifics**   The time allowed for the exam is 4 hours. The exam has 150 questions, and a 70 percent minimum passing score is required.

## GSEC (Security Essentials Certification)

This certification is provided by GIAC and was developed to ensure that the candidates can demonstrate that they are qualified and can demonstrate an understanding of information security beyond simple terminology and concepts.

**Prerequisites**   Although specific prerequisites are required for any GIAC certifications, if candidates need help in mastering the objectives for this certification, the GIAC web site provides links to various resources.

**Exam Specifics**   The length of exam is 5 hours. The exam has 180 questions, and a 70 percent minimum passing score is required.

## GCED (Certified Enterprise Defender)

Provided by GIAC, the GCED builds on the security skills accumulated by any candidate who had taken the GSEC, as this certification assesses more advanced, technical skills that are needed to defend the enterprise environment and protect an organization as a whole.

**Prerequisites**   Although there are no specific prerequisites for any GIAC certifications, if candidates need help in mastering the objectives for this certification, the GIAC web site offers links to various resources.

**Exam Specifics**   The time allowed for the exam is 4 hours. The exam has 150 questions, and a 68.7 percent minimum passing score is required.

## GCIA (Certified Intrusion Analysis)

Provided by GIAC, this certification was developed to ensure that individuals responsible for network and host monitoring, traffic analysis, and intrusion detection have the knowledge and abilities to configure and monitor intrusion detection systems, and to read, interpret, and analyze network traffic and related log files.

**Prerequisites**   There are no specific prerequisites for any GIAC certifications. If candidates need help in mastering the objectives for this certification, the GIAC web site offers links to various resources.

**Exam Specifics**   The time allowed for the exam is 4 hours. The exam has 150 questions, and a 67.3 percent minimum passing score is required.

## GCFA (Certified Forensics Analyst)

Provided by GIAC, the GCFA was developed to ensure that individuals responsible for forensic investigation/analysis, advanced incident handling, or formal incident investigation have the knowledge and abilities to handle advanced incident handling situations, carry out formal incident investigations, and perform forensic investigation of networks and hosts.

**Prerequisites**   No specific prerequisites are required for any GIAC certifications. If candidates need help in mastering the objectives for this certification, the GIAC web site offers links to various resources.

**Exam Specifics**   The time allowed for the exam is 4 hours. The exam has 150 questions, and a 69.3 percent minimum passing score is required.

## CEH (Certified Ethical Hacker)

Provided by EC-Council, the CEH was developed to assist a skilled professional in understanding how to look for weaknesses and vulnerabilities in target systems using the same knowledge and tools used by malicious hackers.

**Prerequisites**   To successfully pass the CEH exam, the candidate must either have 2 years of network security experience and/or sit the CEH training workshop.

**Exam Specifics**   The time allowed for the exam is 4 hours. The exam has 150 questions, and a 70 percent minimum passing score is required.

### ECSA/LPT (EC-Council Certified Security Analyst and Licensed Penetration Tester)

The ECSA/LPT certification is provided by EC-Council and was developed to expand on the knowledge learned from the Certified Ethical Hacker (CEH) certification to show how to analyze an environment using penetration testing methods and techniques. The LPT component of the certification includes the concepts of successfully negotiating the initial penetration testing agreement, complete with client and consultant protections, to executing the professional penetration test, to completing and presenting to management the final penetration testing findings report with remediation recommendations.

**Prerequisites**   The candidate must either have 2 years of network security experience and/or sit the ECSA/LPT training workshop. It is also recommended that the candidate pass the CEH exam, because the topics taught during the CEH training provide a foundational knowledge for the ECSA/LPT.

**Exam Specifics**   The length of ECSA/LPT exam is 2 hours. The exam has 50 questions, and a 70 percent minimum passing score is required.

### CCE (Certified Cost Engineer)

Provided by AACE, the CCE was developed to recognize individuals who meet a demanding set of earned value management criteria by a rigorous examination, experience, education, and ethical qualifications.

**Prerequisites**   The candidate must have 8 years of professional experience in the industry of cost engineering. AACE allows 4 years of that 8-year requirement be obtained by receiving a degree from a university in various industries.

**Exam Specifics**   The time allowed for the exam is 7 hours, and a 70 percent minimum passing score is required.

## Vendor-Specific Security Certifications

This section describes the vendor-specific security certifications that may benefit the security analyst.

### MCSE (Microsoft Certified Systems Engineer)

This certification is provided by Microsoft and was developed to prove the candidate's ability to design, implement, and administer infrastructures for business solutions based on Microsoft 2000 Windows Server and other Windows Server platforms.

**Prerequisites**   The candidate must have 1 to 2 years of experience in designing, installing, configuring, and troubleshooting network systems.

**Exam Specifics**   To obtain the MCSE designation on Windows Server 2003 certification, the candidate must pass seven exams in any order (see Microsoft's web site for specifics):

- Four exams on networking systems
- One exam on client operating systems
- One exam on design
- One elective exam

## CCENT (Cisco Certified Entry Networking Technician)

The CCENT is provided by Cisco and was developed to confirm the candidate's ability to install, operate, and troubleshoot a small enterprise branch network, including basic network security. The exam will prove the competence and skills required for entry-level network support positions.

**Prerequisites**   No specific prerequisites are required for the CCENT certification. If candidates need help in mastering the objectives for this certification, the Cisco web site offers links to various resources.

**Exam Specifics**   The time allowed for the exam is 90 minutes. The exam includes 40 to 50 questions, and the passing score is determined by a statistical analysis based on the amount and difficulty of the questions presented.

## CCNA with Security Designation (Cisco Certified Network Associate)

The certification is provided by Cisco and was developed to confirm the candidate's ability to develop a security infrastructure, recognize threats and vulnerabilities to networks, and mitigate security threats.

**Prerequisites**   Any valid CCNA certification qualifies a candidate for the exam.

**Exam Specifics**   The time allowed for the exam is 90 minutes. The exam includes 55 to 65 questions, and the passing score is determined by a statistical analysis based on the amount and difficulty of the questions presented.

## CCSP (Cisco Certified Security Professional)

The CCSP is provided by Cisco and was developed to confirm the candidate's ability to secure Cisco networks, including the knowledge required to secure and manage network infrastructures to protect efficiency, mitigate threats, and reduce costs associated with security infrastructure management.

**Prerequisites**   A valid CCNA Security or CCNA + SND, or any CCIE certification, is required for the candidate to take the CCSP.

**Exam Specifics**   Three exams are required—one elective and one of three Cisco-specific exams are required to obtain the CCSP designation. The time allowed for the exam is up to 90 minutes. The exam has from 55 to 75 questions, and the passing score is determined by a statistical analysis based on the amount and difficulty of the questions presented.

## SIEM Security Certifications

On top of the preceding background certifications, if you hope to specialize in the SIEM systems, there is nothing better than learning the specifics of a particular system than by attending formal vendor training and then being certified on that system.

### ACSA (ArcSight Certified Security Analyst)

The ACSA is provided by ArcSight and was developed to introduce ArcSight ESM concepts, terminology, and introductory content development skills.

**Prerequisites**    Although no specific prerequisites exist for the ACSA certification, if a candidate needs help in mastering the objectives for this certification, the ArcSight web site offers links to various resources.

**Exam Specifics**    The time allowed for the exam is 1 hour. The exam has 25 questions, and a 70 percent minimum passing score is required.

### Building Use Cases

This exam is provided by ArcSight and was developed assist the candidate in determining business objectives and developing ArcSight ESM content specifically toward those business objectives.

**Prerequisites**    To be successful in passing the Building Use Case exam, the candidate should have taken and passed the ACSA and should have 6 months of ArcSight ESM authoring experience.

**Exam Specifics**    The time allowed for the exam is 1 hour. The exam has 25 questions, and a 70 percent minimum passing score is required.

### Customized Training

This exam is provided by Q1 Labs' Training Services and assists in addressing specific educational requirements that leverage your Q1 deployment to introduce real-world examples that use your organization's data.

**Prerequisites**    No specific prerequisites exist for the Q1 custom training. If candidates need help in mastering the objectives for this certification, the Q1 Labs web site offers links to various resources.

# Suggested Security Analyst Resources

One of the best ways to find resources that pertain to the tasks, duties, and processes that a security analyst will endure is to simply perform a web search. Many web sites provide information on new threats and assist in developing communities for individuals who have like intentions, such as security analysts.

The following organizations provide many services and resources that a security analyst will find both interesting and nearly a requirement. This is only a sample of the many valuable and useful security-related resources available. To maintain your organization's security posture, you, as the security analyst, must stay on top of new threats, trends, and various knowledge bases as they pertain to mitigation and laws that may apply to your organization.

- ANSI (American National Standards Institute)
- CERT Coordination Center
- CIS (Center for Internet Security)
- CompTIA (The Computing Technology Industry Association)
- CSIA (Cyber Security Industry Alliance)
- GIAC (Global Information Assurance Certification)
- ISACA (Information Systems Audit and Control Association)
- ISC2 (International Information Systems Security Certification Consortium)
- ISA (Internet Security Alliance)
- IEEE (Institute of Electrical and Electronics Engineers)
- SANS Institute
- SRI International (Stanford Research Institute)

# Classic Security Analyst Case Studies

As a security analyst, you will be responsible for monitoring the multitude of events from numerous and diverse IT systems throughout your network that are being fed into and processed by your SIEM system. From the parsing, filtering, categorization, prioritization, correlation, and rule construction configured as "content" within your SIEM system, you must quickly and accurately determine the possibility, or, in fact, actuality of an attack taking place.

One of the key takeaways from these case studies is for you to recognize and understand the various attributes of an attack, like its fingerprint, to be sure the attack isn't happening elsewhere on the network. Understanding what an intruder or attacker is doing is half of the battle. You may not have all the tools you need to gain a 360-degree view of the event flow within your network. You will likely be able to capture only bits and pieces and will have to infer the hacker's intentions. Get comfortable with the fact that after noticing something suspicious, your first assumptions and theories will probably be wrong. You will typically begin by increasing your visibility on the suspected target area, like turning on the lights to get a better view of the action. As you begin to develop theories on what is happening, you will begin verifying your theories, or proving them wrong, only to have those new findings steer you toward new theories to be verified.

As you begin to zero-in on the truth of the event, you will assess the current losses and the rate of loss to calibrate the scope and scale of your initial response to the severity of the attack. As losses increase, the severity of your response will probably grow logarithmically. If losses are low, you may let the bad guy run for a while, hoping to learn more about who he is, what tools and techniques he is using, what his target is, and perhaps even gathering evidence for potential prosecution. You would do this only if you were certain your network were experiencing negligible losses, and you were certain that you weren't focused on the attacker's distraction event, while he is elsewhere, stealing the keys to the kingdom behind your back.

If you realize that the attack is inflicting moderate to substantial losses, your response may be quite a bit more severe, even to the point of shutting down ports, servers, Internet connections, and perhaps even the IT systems throughout entire facilities.

The following five steps are typically performed when you're determining and responding to any type of attack within the network:

1. *Determine a recognizable characteristic of the attack.* Determine the attack vector that the malicious activity is attempting to utilize. What are some of the commonalities of the attack: ports, protocols, payload, and so on? A term you may hear used to define this fingerprint of the attack is *extract metric*, which is a measure of some data element (such as the attacked port number) you are able to extract from the massive volume of events hitting the system by means of rules, filtering, correlation, and so on. An extract metric identifies how often you are recognizing the attacker's earmark.

2. *Focus on the malicious activity.* Use the tools that are at your disposal to filter out the normal, non-attack–related traffic to draw out the attack profile.

3. *Take proactive measures.* Build the required content within the tools to notify or alert security analysts automatically of this type of attacker activity. Do this to detect whether the scope of the attack is growing. More alerts firing means the attack is growing.

4. *Record activity.* Build the reporting functionality to measure the success of the newly implemented monitoring and alerting measures to simplify the interpretation of the relevant attack data. This is often not accomplished until after incident response has achieved a satisfactory level of success.

5. *Review countermeasures.* Be sure to review the countermeasures in place to ensure that they are still effective, as various mutations of worms, viruses, and attack vectors can surface. This is an iterative process and should be reviewed at certain defined intervals.

In the following sections, you will be presented with three security analyst case studies and the various items that should be monitored to detect these attacks within your organization's network. The three cases cover how to understand and identify the following:

■ The Conficker worm infection

■ A SQL injection attack

■ A zero-day attack

## Understanding and Recognizing the Conficker Worm

The Conficker worm (a.k.a. Downup, Downadup, and Kido) is a computer worm that was created to target Microsoft Windows operating systems. Conficker was first detected in November 2008, wherein Microsoft released an advisory of this worm's malicious capabilities along with a security bulletin describing how to patch vulnerable systems. The Conficker uses flaws in the Windows NetBIOS/Server service to connect computers into a virtual computer that can be remotely controlled by the malware authors.

One of the most difficult aspects of the Conficker worm is that many variants have been released since its inception and introduction. These variants allow the worm to spread more rapidly by using removable media. These variants are often able to defend themselves against corrective actions by disabling antivirus programs. They also often use a built-in dictionary attack to gain permission to write to the local system and infect the host further.

Taking the preceding five steps into consideration, determine how you can successfully detect, remediate, and build the logic necessary to ensure that your organization does not fall prey to this type of malicious activity.

When you extract the metrics involved as they pertain to the Conficker worm, you find that a unique signature of the worm is the initiation of a multitude of SMB sessions on TCP port 445 of an infected host attempting to communicate to another target host on the network. The subtle challenge with drawing out this attacker metric is that many legitimate network components use SMB session on TCP port 445, so this type of activity occurs daily. The solution to isolating the malicious activity from the normal activity is to establish baselines of normal traffic levels and set thresholds of tolerance on this TCP port 445 traffic. Determining normal activity from abnormal activity is the first step of effectively monitoring for the malicious activities from Conficker.

Another metric found within the Conficker worm is the activity associated with establishing sessions to certain "known bad" web sites. Conficker then upgrades itself to a different variant. Another metric that can be identified as an earmark of Conficker is that it plants an infecting AutoRun function on all connected removable media to aid in further penetration and distribution of itself. Variants may also block DNS lookups, disable AutoUpdates, disable SafeMode, and disable antivirus (AV) and antispyware (AS) processes.

To identify Conficker's malicious activity within your network, you can use the SIEM system and other tools that are at your disposal to capture and highlight the system events and other indications that are elements of this attack profile. The increased confidence of a true-positive attack incident is based upon the increase in the combination of these metrics being precisely extracted and brought into focus from the mass of mostly normal events occurring within your IT system. You will be looking for "abnormal" or excessively high levels of communications between a single host and other hosts within the network using SMB sessions over TCP/445. Add to that the initiating host, a potential newly infected host, attempting to contact specific, known URLs, and the unusual activities regarding the several identified services. All of these items together are indications of potential Conficker infestations.

An event that you might watch for would be an IDS/IPS of notification of the heightened levels of NetBIOS SMB activity when a host is infected with a component of the Conficker and is attempting to spread through the network, exploiting the vulnerability in the target system's server service. The event logs of Windows systems will include an entry if the AutoRun feature has been enabled. This feature is commonly turned off after becoming recognized as a common and successful attack vector. An analyst can begin to monitor whether any alterations to running DNS, AutoUpdate, AV, or AS processes thereafter begin. And lastly, NetBIOS traffic, being primarily a LAN-based protocol versus a protocol used on the Internet, is typically not allowed to pass through exterior firewalls. If you see a sudden spike in dropped NetBIOS packets from those exterior firewalls, it may be an indication of the presence of the malicious Conficker worm.

After you have determined the metrics for the Conficker malware activities and you've used some of the information provided by various network devices such as your IDS/IPS and firewalls, you can begin to build the content necessary to detect these activities proactively and notify an analyst to begin the process of remediation.

At this point, the discussion turns to tuning your SIEM application to provide for proactive monitoring of the events being forwarded by the various networking and security devices to your SOC environment.

Using ArcSight ESM as the example SIEM system, the following content can be created to monitor these activities proactively within your organization's network and provide alerting, reporting, and real-time displays of Conficker activity within your network.

Please note that the process presented here is one available option. There are many different ways to create content on the SIEM system to provide the required results and to analyze, track, report, and alert. The following types of ArcSight resources to be created can provide these functions:

- **Filters**   These resources provide filtering logic using Boolean conditions to filter out, or in, specific event criteria. For this exercise, the filter that will be created is Conficker Infection Found. This filter will show the events that are created (correlated events) when the conditions within the rule have been met.

- **Active channels**   These resources provide the capabilities to view, in real time or historically, the various events within your ArcSight ESM environment. For this exercise, the active channel that will be created will display Conficker activity as analyzed by ArcSight through the correlation engine (rules). This active channel will use the Conficker Infection Found filter to display known Conficker activity in real time.

- **Active lists**   These resources are a temporary holding area that can have entries added automatically using rules, or manually, to be correlated by other resources. For this exercise, the active lists that are going to be created are HTTP (will hold the IP addresses of the known systems that Conficker contacts using HTTP), Infected Systems (will hold the IP addresses, zones, host names, and NT domain of infected systems). These active lists will be used by the Rules.

- **Rules**   These resources allow you to monitor proactively the events being forwarded into the ArcSight ESM system. The correlation engine facilitates the ability to correlate events between disparate devices and infer meaning to them, to send a notification of the desired activities for analyst remediation. For this exercise, the rule to be created will be named Found Conficker. This rule will use the HTTP active list to watch any activity from any internal asset to any IP address contained within the HTTP list, which are known addresses that Conficker uses. The rule will then write that asset's information to the Infected Systems active list for tracking, monitoring, and reporting. After it writes to the Infected System active list, a notification will be sent to the security analyst to inform him or her of this activity, including all of the asset information of the infected system.

Figure A-1 shows the relationships among the resources.

This Infected System Report allows you to measure the success of the newly implemented ArcSight resources to ensure that the Conficker worm is being detected. This report uses the entries captured within the Infected System Active List. As noted, this active list provides the target IP, host name, zone, and NT domain of the asset that has been infected with the Conficker worm.

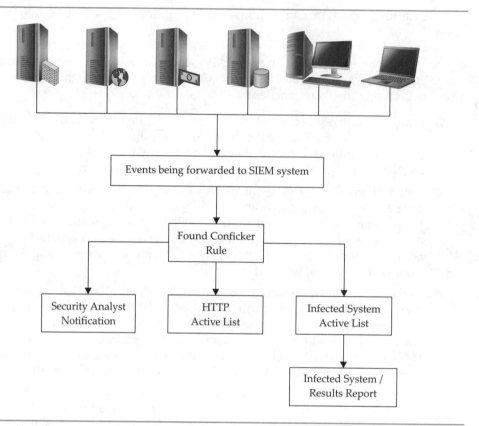

**Figure A-1.** Conficker resource relationships

As a security analyst responsible for creating content within the organization's SIEM application, you must review the countermeasures that you have created to ensure that they are still effective. Remember that monitoring and fine-tuning is an iterative process and should be repeated at certain defined intervals to verify the effectiveness of detection.

## Understanding and Recognizing a SQL Injection Attack

A SQL injection is a code injection technique that exploits a security vulnerability occurring in the database connectivity of an application that connects to a SQL database. The vulnerability is present when user input into the application is not properly qualified or filtered.

Most SQL injection attacks occur when, instead of entering the type of data into a user input field that the application is expecting, the attacker directly inserts executable code into user input field. That inappropriate input, the SQL injection attack code, is then merged with SQL commands and is executed by the SQL server, which then performs a specific and unexpected action. Often, the attacker is provided console access to the SQL server with the level of privilege on the SQL server associated with the credentials that executed the application. Now working on the SQL server, the attacker will entrench; create additional back doors; cover her tracks; explore and pillage the information and data on the SQL server; try to escalate her privilege; perhaps download her collection of dirty tools, her root kit, to effectively "root" the server; and use the SQL server as her attacker system to penetrate deeper into the IT system. Lovely.

A less direct SQL injection attacker inserts malicious code into string fields that are destined for storage in a table or as metadata within the SQL database. When the stored strings are later combined into a dynamic SQL command, the malicious code is executed and the damaging action takes place, with similar attacker access and actions to follow.

**NOTE** SQL injection attacks are approximately 100 percent preventable. Every user input field can be filtered to allow only the type of data that the field is intended to receive and to reject all other types of input. If the field is intended to hold phone numbers or ZIP codes, you can disallow all alpha characters. If the field is intended for the two-character state code, you can truncate all input characters beyond the second character, and disallow numbers. This is referred to as "qualifying the user input data." The qualifying rules often get much more sophisticated than these basic examples, but they can be written and included in the application's code and could prevent approximately 100 percent of all SQL injection attacks.

In this case study, the scenario is this: You work for a life insurance company and you have developed an Internet-based web site so customers can view and update their policies. This web site includes web-based forms, where users can input personally identifiable information (PII) (the stuff bad guys use to steal identities), including username, password, first name, last name, email address, Social Security number, home address, home city, home state, home ZIP code, life insurance policy number, and date of life insurance issuance. As you can see, a lot of information is captured on this form that could be used by a hacker for malicious purposes.

One way to identify a SQL injection attack is to monitor for the events that often occur during the exploratory phase of the SQL injection attack. Within this phase of the attack, the attacker is attempting to uncover information about the system and the database. Targets include data such as table names, data types and acceptable lengths, user login information, host operating system, as well as information about local accounts hosted in the database. When the attacker attempts to discover your database structures, she will send SQL commands through the unqualified user input fields, to be parsed by the SQL database. These SQL commands are designed to provoke various error messages that provide pieces of information about the database structure. By inputting data types and formats that the application isn't expecting, the server responds, by default, with error messages that contain sensitive information, such as column and table names, and the data types expected in each of the columns. (These error messages can be identified and tracked by the SIEM system.) With the right information from these provoked error messages in hand, the attacker can input a SQL command to create a new, highly privileged user directly in the SQL database. This attack bypasses any security restrictions and monitoring on user account creation, since this account was written directly to the SQL database and not created through the administrative interface in the database management system. Using the new, highly privileged user account, the attacker pillages all the information she desires from the database. Afterwards, she can drop the user account and make sure her tracks on the system have been covered.

The various malicious activities that can be performed while the attacker has access include the following:

- *Use the built-in, extended stored procedures.* These are compiled Dynamic Link Libraries (DLLs) that are built into SQL Server to perform various functions such as running programs, sending email, and interacting with the registry.

- *Run queries on linked servers.* A mechanism within SQL Server allows SQL servers to be linked to allow a command on one database server to access and manipulate data on another.

- *Upload and execute custom extended stored procedures.* Malicious extended stored procedure DLLs can be uploaded to the database server, or any server to which the database server has access, in a multitude of ways. After the DLL is uploaded, it can be executed using command line interface (CLI) commands. To cover her tracks, after the malicious activity has been accomplished, the attacker can then remove the DLL.

As a security analyst, you must determine how you can accurately extract metrics to define the attack vectors used while an attacker is attempting to perform a SQL injection, by successfully building the logic within the SIEM system necessary to detect precisely and alert on this SQL injection attack. To spot this type of SQL injection attack, you must ensure that the system that is providing the SQL Server services to your network has the proper level of logging enabled, and that these logs are being forwarded to your SIEM system. This includes the OS and the SQL Server application logs. Realize that error messages are common within any production environment. Users will often incorrectly input usernames and passwords. You must configure an appropriate threshold of tolerance to determine at which point this activity will be deemed malicious and the SIEM system will begin to escalate this activity throughout the workflow.

Using the ArcSight ESM as the example SIEM system, the following content (which may also be called SIEM system resources) can be created to monitor these SQL injection activities proactively and provide alerting, reporting, and real-time displays of potential SQL injection activity within your network. Note that the process presented here is only one available option, and many different methods can be used to create resources to produce the required results. Typically, additional functionality is provided within SIEM systems to analyze, track, report, and alert even further.

The following various types of ArcSight content will be created for this SQL injection exercise:

- **Filters**   The filter that will be created is SQL Errors. This filter will show the events that are created when SQL errors are encountered. The errors to be detected by this filter will not be internal SQL errors, but user-generated errors.

- **Active channels**   The active channel that will be created will display potential SQL injection activity (generated errors) and the activities performed after such an error. This active channel will use the SQL Errors filter to display these SQL errors and activities on the SQL system(s) after the detected errors, in real time.

- **Active lists**   The active lists that are going to be created are Possible SQL Injection (holds the target IP address, target zone, target NT domain, and attacker IP address) and SQL Injection Attack Occurred (holds target IP address, target zone, target NT domain, target username, attacker IP address, and attacker username). These active lists will be used by the rules.

- **Rules**   The rules to be created will be named Possible SQL Injection and SQL Injection Attack Occurring. The Possible SQL Injection rule will monitor all the SQL error messages being forwarded to the SIEM, and if more than three errors are generated (the threshold of tolerance) by the same attacker IP address within 1 minute, the rule will write the attacker and target information to the Possible SQL Injection active list and send a notification to a security analyst for investigation. The SQL Injection Attack Occurring rule will monitor all the SQL error messages, and if an error is generated from the same attacker IP address already located in the Possible SQL Injection active list (which means that at least four errors have been generated from the same target IP from the same attacker IP) within 1 minute, the rule will write the attacker and target information to the SQL Injection Attack Occurred active list. The SQL Injection Attack Occurring rule will also be configured to send a notification to a security analyst for alerting purposes and possibly for further remediation.

As you can see in Figure A-2, the next step is the introduction of the SQL Injection Entry/Results Report.

This SQL Injection Entry/Results Report allows you to measure the success of the newly implemented ArcSight resources to ensure that the various means to initiate a SQL injection attack are being detected. This report uses the entries captured within the Possible SQL Injection active list and the SQL Injection Attack Occurred active list. With both of these active lists in the same report, you will be able to see how many possible SQL injection events became actual attacks. If you have a case management system available, you can feed this data into it to create a produced and reusable process to track and manage this type of malicious activity within your organization's network.

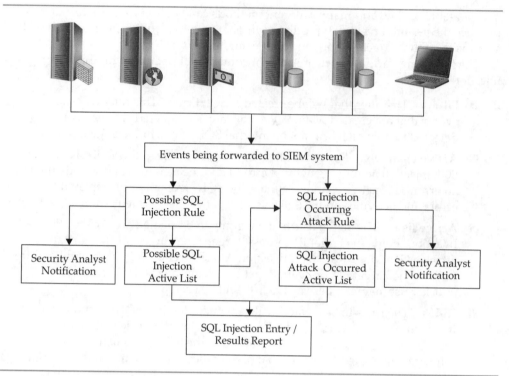

**Figure A-2.** ArcSight ESM SQL injection relationships

It is not uncommon for a security analyst to be responsible for creating content within the organization's SIEM application. It may also be your duty to review the countermeasures that you have implemented to ensure that they remain effective over time. Remember that the creation and continued use of SIEM system content is an iterative process and should be reviewed and possibly refined at specific, defined intervals.

## Understanding and Recognizing a Zero-Day Attack

Bad guys are relentless in their pursuit of new ways to exploit systems. When a bad guy develops a successful exploit for a new weakness or vulnerability in an operating system, application, or system basic input/output system (BIOS) that can be exploited, he is sitting on a gold mine. The bad guy has an undetectable free run to attack and compromise IT systems. He can penetrate and pillage, and then penetrate deeper and pillage more. Since this attack and vulnerability have not yet been seen or identified by the public, there is no known patch or fix to eliminate the vulnerability, nor is there an antivirus or IDS/IPS signature to recognize, alert, and control the attack. When an attacker first uses his new exploit on public targets, also called "in the wild," for the first 24 hours, the attacker is running a zero-day attack (since the public awareness of the attack isn't yet a day old). The attack window is the period of time from when a vulnerability first gets exploited "in the wild," and while the system vendor develops and supplies the corrective patch, and until consumers begin to apply the corrective patch en masse. During this time, your IT system is most vulnerable.

In this scenario, you are the security analyst for a large, multinational corporation. You are responsible for the monitoring, detection, and remediation of the many different types of potential attacks concerning the possible exploits and vulnerabilities present within your organization's network. Although you are not responsible for updating the organization's system's OS or application patches, you are responsible for protecting the confidentiality, integrity, and availability of the corporation's data while in transit and at rest.

To extract metrics accurately to define the zero-day attack vectors while your system or network is within the attack window, your first and most important step is to understand what normal operational behavior is for your IT systems. When you understand what constitutes typical activity, you'll find it easier to recognize abnormal activity. Since there is no known signature for this zero-day attack, you can only recognize it for its aberrant actions and behaviors. While some IDS/IPS systems include behavior-based detectors, most systems are strictly signature-based detectors that rely on known attack signatures. IDS/IPS systems that perform only signature analysis will not help you with a zero-day attack. Behavior-based systems track specified network parameters, such as FTP downloaded bytes per hour or SQL queries per minute. Many systems actually learn trends to adjust automatically over time to accommodate changes, such as a natural and gradual increase in VPN traffic as the outside sales force grows.

After the normal behavior for your environment is established, you can set thresholds to identify acceptable levels of deviation from what is normal. If the threshold is set too wide, it will delay the alert of an actual attack. The organization will experience higher losses, and the attacker will have more time to entrench and cover his tracks. If the threshold is set too narrow, you will be overwhelmed with false-positive alerts, keeping you forever in a fire-drill mode and providing cover for the actual, more rare, attack. The goal is to strike the proper balance between these two ends of the spectrum.

The SIEM system is an excellent tool for monitoring and developing baselines of normal behavior, as well as for developing content to alert you when a threshold is reached. By focusing the SIEM on infrastructure systems, such as routers, firewalls, and critical servers, that can report statistics of behavior, you will be focusing on the systems that provide the proper metrics to detect zero-day attacks.

The actual abnormal behavior you are looking for can come in many different forms. You will need to review your environment carefully and identify your most sensitive systems to determine what and where to configure your behavior-based monitoring and detecting. While the following list of common targets to monitor is a good start, it is by no means conclusive. After understanding and incorporating this list of metrics into your SIEM content, you will need to brainstorm about the special concerns and security requirements to fine-tune the list for your world. To provide early detection of a zero-day attack, identify normal use baselines and thresholds for the following metrics:

- **Sudden or unexpected increase in network traffic**   All types of traffic, because you never know what mechanism the zero-day attack will use to upload additional malware, or to extract large amounts of your most valuable data.

- **Sudden or unexpected increase in typical protocols**   In addition to watching all traffic as a whole, you must watch for individual protocol abnormalities. Although one type of common traffic may drop, a single type may spike because of malicious activities.

- **The presence and detection of unexpected protocols**   If, for example, IRC has been disallowed on the network, if and when it shows up, you should know about it immediately and rapidly pursue its removal (even if it is not associated with a zero-day attack).

- **The absence of monitoring data into the SOC**   If an attacker can get his foot in the door, he will want to probe around and explore. He certainly doesn't want you to see him, so a common "next step" for the attacker is to disable logging or the transmission of the logs to the SOC. When the logs stop arriving at the SOC, you should quickly find out why and get them going again.

- **Unexpected system configuration changes**   The attacker will want to create additional back doors for himself or will introduce additional system vulnerabilities, so that if one or more of his entry ways are detected or eliminated through routine patching, he has other ways to get back in. Track the system configuration mechanisms for your most critical IT assets. These configuration changes may take the form of new services starting or changes to personal firewall rules.

- **Failure of patch installation, or antivirus or IDS/IPD signature updates**   The successful zero-day attack will be useful only until the attack window closes. That window will close when you install the vendor's patch to mitigate the vulnerability, or the AV/IDS/IPS vendor releases updates that include the signature of the attacker's malware or exploit. If the attacker can break the patching/updating system, he can extend his ill-conceived access to and use of your systems.

- **Sudden increase in authentication errors**   As the bad guy moves around to pillage your valuable resources, he will often be challenged for credentials, such as when accessing a network share. Until he can acquire legitimate and authorized credentials, he will trigger authentication errors.

- **Sudden increase in Access Denied errors**   Even though the attacker may acquire legitimate credentials, he likely will not know the limits of the authorization. As he attempts to pillage resources where he has no privileges, the failed access will trigger Access Denied errors.

Build correlated rules to recognize when multiple thresholds have been breached. Multiple threshold breaches significantly increase the likelihood of a true-positive attack.

While many types of zero-day attacks can be perpetuated through your organization's environment, following these steps can assist in uncovering this type of activity. However, as a security analyst, it is your duty to review the countermeasures you have created regularly to ensure that they remain effective over time. As always, remember that this is an iterative process and should be reviewed at defined intervals.

# Index